BIRTH RI

This multi-disciplinary collection of essays from the Cambridge Socio-Legal Group is concerned with the varying circumstances, manner, timing and experiences of birth. It contains essays from a wide range of disciplines including law, medicine, anthropology, history, and sociology, examining birth from the perspectives of mother, doctor, midwife and father. Questions considered in the book include: who has power during the birthing process? How has the experience of birth changed over time? Should birth mark a significant change in the legal status of the foetus? What is the proper role of birth registration? What role, if any, do fathers have in the birthing process? What legal rights should the woman have to refuse treatment during the birthing process? What is the significance of changes of the age at which women give birth? This stimulating collection of papers provides new insights into one of life's most momentous moments.

Birth Rites and Rights

Edited by

FATEMEH EBTEHAJ
JONATHAN HERRING
MARTIN H JOHNSON
AND
MARTIN RICHARDS

On behalf of the Cambridge Socio-Legal Group

·HART·
PUBLISHING

OXFORD AND PORTLAND, OREGON
2011

Hart Publishing, 16C Worcester Place, OX1 2JW
Telephone: +44 (0)1865 517530 Fax: +44 (0)1865 510710
E-mail: mail@hartpub.co.uk
Website: http://www.hartpub.co.uk

Published in North America (US and Canada) by
Hart Publishing
c/o International Specialized Book Services
920 NE 58th Avenue, Suite 300
Portland, OR 97213-3786
USA
Tel: +1 503 287 3093 or toll-free: (1) 800 944 6190
Fax: +1 503 280 8832
E-mail: orders@isbs.com
Website: www.isbs.com

British Library Cataloguing in Publication Data
Data Available

ISBN: 978-1-84946-188-7

Typeset by Criteria International
Printed and bound in Great Britain by
Page Bros (Norwich) Ltd

Acknowledgements

This book is the ninth in a series by the Cambridge Sociolegal Group and is a product of a three day workshop held in Cambridge in March 2010.

We are grateful to the Wellcome Trust and the Modern Law Review for grants to support the workshop, and we thank the Centre for Family Research for hosting the event, especially Susan Golombok who was most helpful, and Christ's College, Cambridge, and its staff.

We would like to acknowledge the contributors for their participation in this stimulating project, the discussants for their insightful comments, and Frances Murton for her careful sub-editing of the whole manuscript.

The Editors
Cambridge
September 2010

Contents

Notes on Contributors

Hossam Abdalla is Clinical Director of the UK's largest IVF unit, the Lister Fertility Clinic, which he founded in 1988. He is recognised as one of the leading experts in the field of assisted conception and has been a member of the Human Fertilisation and Embryology Authority since 2004. For 6 years prior to that he was on the executive committee board of the British Fertility Society. He has published widely in scientific and medical journals and has a keen interest in ethical and legal aspects of assisted conception.

Salim Al-Gailani is a Research Associate in the history of the reproductive sciences at the Department of History and Philosophy of Science, University of Cambridge. He recently completed a PhD thesis on the early history of antenatal care in Britain.

Helen Austerberry is a Research Officer at the Social Science Research Unit, Institute of Education. She is currently part of a team conducting a comparative study of the experiences of first-time mothers in the 1970s and the early years of the 21st century, *Women's experiences of childbirth: continuities and discontinuities in social and medical aspects of first childbirth*. She has worked on a national evaluation of a support programme for pregnant teenagers and teenage mothers (*Sure Start Plus*), a trial of forms of postnatal support for new mothers living in disadvantaged areas (*The Social Support and Family Health Study*) and an evaluation of a local Sure Start breastfeeding peer support programme.

Françoise Barbira Freedman is an affiliated lecturer in Social Anthropology at the University of Cambridge. She has a long term involvement in interdisciplinary maternal and child health research projects with Amazonian Forest People both as a researcher and as a supervisor, including two clinical trials on medicinal plants. As the founder of the Birthlight Trust, she has developed practical applications for childbirth education on the basis of her experience of pregnancy and early motherhood in Amazonia. She has co-authored two books on cultural change and health with Axel Kroeger (WHO) and her Birthlight books have been disseminated worldwide through foreign editions.

Susan Bewley has been Consultant Obstetrician at Guy's & St Thomas' NHS Foundation Trust since 1994 and Honorary Senior Lecturer at Kings College London. She trained in maternal-fetal medicine, and has led innovative service developments, researched severe maternal morbidity and written extensively about high-risk and complex obstetric practice. She co-edited and contributed to three RCOG Expert Study Groups (on *Ethics in Obstetrics & Gynaecology*, *Violence against Women*, 1997 and *Reproductive Ageing*, 2009), an OUP textbook (*Training in Obstetrics & Gynaecology: the essential curriculum*, 2009) and more recently *Abuse of the Doctor-patient Relationship*, 2010.

Peter Braude is Head of the Department of Women's Health at King's College London, and consultant gynaecologist at Guy's and St Thomas' NHS Foundation Trust Assisted Conception Unit. He directs the Centre for Preimplantation Genetic Diagnosis at Guy's, which is the most active and successful of the HFEA licensed PGD programmes in the UK. He is a former member of the Human Fertilisation and Embryology Authority and chair of the Scientific Advisory Committee for the Royal College of Obstetricians and Gynaecologists. He currently sits on the DH Advisory Committee on the Safety of Blood Tissues and Organs.

Richard Collier is Professor of Law at Newcastle University, UK. He has published widely in the area of law and gender and his books include *Men, Law and Gender: Essays on the 'Man' of Law* (Routledge, 2010), *Fragmenting Fatherhood: A Socio-Legal Study* (with Sally Sheldon, Hart, 2008), *Masculinities, Crime and Criminology: Men, Corporeality and the Criminal(ised) Body* (Sage, 1998), *Masculinity, Law and the Family* (Routledge, 1995) and *Fathers' Rights Activism and Law Reform in Comparative Perspective* (edited with Sally Sheldon, Hart, 2007). He is presently researching the book *Family Men: Fatherhood, Law and Gender from the Late Nineteenth Century to the Present* and is conducting a project on male lawyers, masculinities and work-life balance in the legal profession. Richard is an editorial board member of Social and Legal Studies: An International Journal.

Irenee Daly is a psychology PhD student in The Centre for Family Research at the University of Cambridge. Her academic interests are in gender, reproductive technologies and how the media communicate to the public advances in science and technologies, especially reproductive technologies. Her doctoral research concerns women's understanding and knowledge of age-related fertility decline.

Shelley Day Sclater was formerly a lawyer, an academic psychologist and Professor of Psychosocial Studies at University of East London. She now works as a freelance writer and researcher. She was a founder member of the Cambridge Socio-Legal Group and co-editor of their early publications. She has published extensively in the area of socio-legal studies, has written course materials for the Open University and is now doing what she always wanted to do - writing fiction. One of her short stories has recently won a prize, see http://www.litandphil.org.uk/html_pages/LP_home.html.

Fatemeh Ebtehaj is an associate member of the Centre for Family Research, University of Cambridge. Her research focuses mainly on Iranian migrants and exiles, with a particular interest in issues related to gender, self and identity, narrative and discourse analysis. Her current research highlights the impact of migration on ageing and on the care of the elderly. She has been a contributor to, and co-editor of, the Cambridge Socio-Legal Group's *Kinship Matters* (Hart, 2006), *Death Rites and Rights* (Hart, 2007), and *Regulating Autonomy: Sex, Reproduction and Family* (Hart 2009).

Tarek El-Toukhy is a Consultant in Reproductive Medicine and Surgery and Pre-implantation Genetic Diagnosis (PGD) at the Assisted Conception Unit at Guy's and St. Thomas' Hospital in London and Assistant Professor of Obstetrics and Gynaecology at Cairo University. His clinical and research interests are in the fields of recurrent in-vitro fertilisation failure, pre-implantation genetic diagnosis and minimal access reproductive surgery. He has published over 70 original articles, reviews and opinion papers. He is a scientific editor for BJOG International and peer-reviews for a number of medical journals including the BMJ.

Lin Foo is an Academic Foundation Doctor with the Bartholomews and The London Hospital NHS Trust, currently working in the field of women's health. She qualified from Southampton Medical School with a BM in clinical medicine and surgery, and a 1st Class BSc (*Hons*) in Genetics. She has been appointed Sexual and Reproductive Health Fellow for the Royal Society of Medicine. Lin has a keen interest in maternal medicine, and is involved in research on gestational diabetes at the Institute of Cell and Molecular Science, London.

Alison Forhead is a University Lecturer in the Department of Physiology, Development and Neuroscience at the University of Cambridge. Her research interests are in mammalian endocrinology and the hormonal control of growth and development in the fetus. She has published over 80 papers in scientific journals.

Abigail Fowden holds a personal chair in the Department of Physiology, Development and Neuroscience at the University of Cambridge and is a Professorial Fellow at Girton College. Her research interests are in the control of intrauterine development with particular emphasis on the role of hormones in these processes. She has published over 200 original papers and scholarly reviews and is regularly invited to present lectures at national and international conferences. She was awarded an ScD degree in 2001 and the Joan Mott Prize of the Physiological Society for her research in 2008.

Jonathan Herring is a Fellow of Law at Exeter College, Oxford University and a Lecturer in Law at the Faculty of Law, Oxford University. He is the author of many leading textbooks including *Family Law* (4th ed, Pearson, 2009); *Criminal Law* (3rd ed, OUP, 2010); *Criminal Law* (6th ed, Macmillan, 2009); and *Medical Law and Ethics* (3rd ed, OUP, 2010). He has also written a monograph on older people and the law: *Older People in Law and Society* (OUP, 2009).

Emily Jackson is a Professor of Law at the London School of Economics. She is also Deputy Chair of the Human Fertilisation and Embryology Authority, and a member of the BMA Medical Ethics Committee and the Ethics Committees of the Royal College of Physicians and the Royal College of Pathologists. Her research interests are in the field of medical law and ethics, in particular reproductive and end of life issues, and more recently the regulation of the pharmaceutical industry. She is the author of *Regulating Reproduction* (Hart, 2001) and *Medical Law* (2ⁿᵈ edition, Oxford UP, 2010).

Martin H Johnson is Professor of Reproductive Sciences in the Anatomy School at the University of Cambridge UK. He was a member of the Human Fertilisation and Embryology Authority (1993–1999) and specialist scientific advisor to the Joint Lords and Commons Committee scrutinising the Draft Human Embryos and Tissue Bill (2007). In 2004 he was elected a scientific Fellow of the Royal College of Obstetricians and Gynaecologists. He is author of *Essential Reproduction* (seventh edition, Blackwell Science due 2012), co-editor of *Sexuality Repositioned* (2004), and *Death Rites and Rights* (2007), and has published over 250 papers on reproductive science, ethics, law, history and medical education.

Tamara Kayali recently completed a PhD thesis at the Centre for Family Research at the University of Cambridge. Her thesis is titled *The Real Me: Control, Responsibility and the Self in Depression*. She has supervised courses in the Social Context of Health and Illness and the Ethics of Medicine at Cambridge and has recently been appointed as Research Officer at Rethink in London. She has also worked in pharmaceutical policy at the Australian Department of Health and Ageing, and as a freelance science journalist.

Mavis Kirkham is Emeritus Professor of Midwifery at Sheffield Hallam University and holds honorary professorial positions at the University of Huddersfield and the University of Technology Sydney. She has worked continuously as a midwife researcher and a clinical midwife for nearly forty years. Her books include *Informed Choice in Maternity Care,* (Palgrave 2004*), Birth Centres: a social model of maternity care* (Elsevier 2003), *The Midwife/Mother Relationship* (Palgrave, 2ⁿᵈ edition 2010) and *Exploring the Dirty Side of Women's Health* (Routledge 2007). Her clinical work is now mainly concerned with home births.

Julie McCandless is a Lecturer in Law at the London School of Economics and Political Science. She teaches in the fields of medical and family law. Julie was previously a lecturer at Oxford Brookes University and was recently awarded her doctorate by Keele University, where she was a member of the AHRC Centre for Research on Law, Gender and Sexuality (CLGS). Her research interests encompass the regulation of gender and the family, and she has a particular interest in issues pertaining to human reproduction and parenthood. Her doctoral research was a gender-informed analysis of parenthood law in the context of assisted reproduction. She is currently pursuing research on birth registration.

Frances Murton is an associate member of the Centre for Family Research, University of Cambridge and has worked on a number of studies on the psychosocial aspects of new genetic and reproductive technologies including the experiences of parents receiving a diagnosis of foetal abnormality. She was formerly a social worker specialising in work with children and families. She has assisted the editors of earlier publications from the Cambridge Socio-legal Group.

Ann Oakley is Professor of Sociology and Social Policy at the Institute of Education, University of London, where she founded both the Social Science Research Unit and the EPPI-Centre. She has worked in social research for 45 years and has undertaken many projects concerned with the health and welfare of women, children and families. Her book publications range from *Sex, Gender and Society* (1972), *The Sociology of Housework* (1974), *Becoming a Mother* (1979) and *Women Confined: Towards a Sociology of Childbirth* (1980) to, more recently, *Gender on Planet Earth* (2002), *The Ann Oakley Reader: Gender, Women and Social Science* (2005) and *Fracture: Adventures of a Broken Body* (2007).

Martin Richards is Emeritus Professor of Family Research at the Centre for Family Research, University of Cambridge. His research concerns psychosocial and bioethical aspects of genetic and reproductive technologies. He has been a member of the Human Fertilisation and Embryology Law and Ethics Committee and Biobank UK Ethics and Governance Council. Recent publications include *Which children can we choose?* in an earlier Cambridge Socio -Legal Group collection: *Regulating Autonomy: Sex, Reproduction and Family*, (Hart, 2009); *Reading the runes of my genome: an exploration of retail genetics*, New Genetics and Society, 2010; *Blackwell Companion to the Sociology of Families* (edited with J. Scott and J.K. Treas) (Blackwell, 2003 and 2012).

Mary Sawtell is currently a Research Officer at the Social Science Research Unit, Institute of Education. Previously she practiced as a health visitor in both the UK and Africa. She is currently a member of a research team conducting a comparative study of the experiences of first-time mothers in the 1970s and the early years of the 21st century, *Women's experiences of childbirth: continuities and discontinuities in social and medical aspects of first childbirth*. She has also conducted a study of homeless mothers and mothers to be, worked on a national evaluation of a support programme for pregnant teenagers and teenage mothers (*Sure Start Plus*) and on a trial of forms of postnatal support for new mothers living in disadvantaged areas (*The Social Support and Family Health Study*).

Rosamund Scott is Professor of Medical Law and Ethics in the Centre of Medical Law and Ethics, School of Law, King's College London. She has a background in philosophy and law and her research interests are largely in the field of reproductive ethics and law. Her publications include *Rights, Duties and* *the Body: Law and Ethics of the Maternal-Fetal Conflict* (2002) and *Choosing Possible Lives: Law and Ethics of Prenatal and Preimplantation Genetic Diagnosis,* (2007, AHRC part-funded). In addition, she has been and remains involved in a number of collaborative research projects, such as a major new interdisciplinary initiative - LABTEC - The London and Brighton Translational Ethics Centre (Wellcome Trust, 2009-14). She is a member of a number of committees and boards, including the Editorial Board of the *Journal of Medical Ethics*, the Editorial Advisory Board of *Clinical Ethics* and the RCOG Ethics Committee. She is also a barrister.

Sally Sheldon is a Professor of Law at the University of Kent. She has published widely in the area of medical law, including a book on the regulation of abortion, *Beyond Control: Medical Power and Abortion Law* (1997), and a co-edited collection of essays on *Feminist Perspectives on Health Care Law* (1998). More recently, she has co-authored a socio-legal study of fatherhood: *Fragmenting Fatherhood* (2008) and co-edited *Fathers' Rights Activism and Law Reform* (2007), both with Richard Collier of Newcastle Law School. Her recent work centres on the amendments introduced by the Human Fertilisation and Embryology Act (2008). Sally is an editor of the journals, *Social & Legal Studies* and *Feminist Legal Studies* and a Trustee of the British Pregnancy Advisory Service.

Vicki Strange is a senior research officer at the Social Science Research Unit at the Institute of Education, London. She currently co-directs '*Women's experiences of childbirth: continuities and discontinuities in social and medical aspects of first childbirth*' – a comparative study of the experiences of first-time mothers in the 1970s and the early years of the 21ˢᵗ century. Her previous work has mostly focused on women and young people's health. Recent co-authored publications include *A pilot whole-school intervention to improve school ethos and reduce substance use* (Bonell et al., 2010 in Health Education) and *Process evaluation of the Intervention with Microfinance for AIDS and Gender Equity (IMAGE) in rural South Africa*(Hargreaves et al, 2009 in 'Health Education Research).

Meg Wiggins is a Senior Research Officer at the Social Science Research Unit, Institute of Education, University of London. She currently co-directs '*Women's experiences of childbirth: continuities and discontinuities in social and medical aspects of first childbirth*' – a comparative study of the experiences of first-time mothers in the 1970s and the early years of the 21ˢᵗ century. She has carried out a number of studies of maternity services concentrating primarily on women's experiences of information use and support provided.   Previous work has included the co-ordination of the Social Support and Family Health Study, a randomised control trial of postnatal support for new mothers living in disadvantaged inner city areas. She has also led three large-scale national evaluations of UK Government initiatives relating to the health of young people: the Sure Start Plus initiative; the Young People's Development Programme, and the Teenage Health Demonstration Sites.

Francis Woodman is a lecturer in the History of Art and Architecture at the University of Cambridge, Institute of Continuing Education. He is author of several works including *The Architectural History of Canterbury Cathedral*, (RKP, 1981) and *Kings' College Chapel*, (RKP, 1986). He was a previous contributor to this series, with *Purgatory: The Beginning and the End*, in *Death Rites and Rights* (Hart 2007). His interest in medieval women, their lives and patronage stems back to the mid 70s when he published *The Hollands and Canterbury Cathedral* (Canterbury Cathedral Chronicles, 70, 1976), one of the earliest such studies on medieval women, their marriages, kinship and financial independence. His latest study, *Women Behaving Badly*, will appear in the British Archaeological Association Transactions of the Newcastle Conference, 2010 (forthcoming).

Introduction: Birth Writes

MARTIN RICHARDS

T HIS MULTI-DISCIPLINARY collection of essays is concerned with the varying circumstances, manner, timing and experiences of birth and the practices and social institutions for its conduct.

We often speak of birth as a beginning. But, of course, not so for babies for whom birth is the transition from the uterine world to an outside social world. We may date a beginning from the baby – making of the parents, or perhaps when an egg attracts a sperm and the process of biological development of the embryo is initiated. In the world of collaborative reproduction a new life may begin when a technician penetrates a captive egg with a needle and injects a single immature sperm.

With the coming of ultrasound scans, parents, and others, have begun to know their babies a little better before their birth. The announcement of the good news to friends and family may well take the form of an emailed scan image taken before the mother is even aware of her baby's movements. Ultrasound images have made the appearance of the unborn familiar. Some fetuses move further into the social world and may acquire their own pages on Facebook long before their birth. But while a fetus may become a named and gendered person in the eyes of parents and others before birth, legal personhood is only acquired at the moment of birth.

In biological and social terms the timing of birth is a movable feast. Conventionally, the gestational age of a baby is measured from the first day of the last menstrual period of the mother, approximately fourteen days before fertilisation actually occurs, and is thus 'premature' in the new era of assisted reproduction, where conception can be precisely timed. In western medicine, the age of a fetus is now generally established independently of the mother's account, from fetal measurements after an ultrasound scan carried out at about twelve weeks. A delivery between 38–42 weeks is generally considered the normal range. Births at later gestational ages are now rare as these are generally avoided through obstetric induction of labour. Preterm birth, however, remains largely unpreventable and is a continuing public health issue because of the significant risks to children born too immature and/or too small. With specialised neonatal care about half the children born at 24 weeks will survive but a significant number of these will face immediate and long term medical and social problems.

While birth may be simply a step on life's journey, its timing has a considerable and lasting social significance throughout our lives. We celebrate birthdays and use them as markers for all sorts of status changes. Occasionally, a birth happening one side or other of midnight can significantly influence life chances – as some fiction writers have plotted. Increasingly, our birth date has become a common personal identifier. During the day I began writing this introduction I was twice asked for my date of birth – when making an appointment to see my GP and when applying for a visa for a forthcoming holiday.

We can observe persisting temporal patterns in birth times – fewer births at weekends and, somewhat ironically given the reason for the celebration, the day of the year with fewest births is Christmas Day. This is because for the majority of births, at least in the industrialised world, it is doctors, not mothers or their babies, who determine the time of birth. And that is an important issue which is discussed later in the book in the context of mothers' experience and choices in childbirth (Chapters 1 and 2).

But while it is increasingly common obstetric practice to bring forward the time of a birth through a Caesarean section or induction of labour, there is little that can be done to avoid a preterm birth. Indeed, despite its social significance of the time of birth, we have only a limited understanding of the normal physiological processes in women and their babies which initiate labour – paradoxically knowing much more about sheep and goats which have been the subject of much experimental investigation.

As well as decisions about when a particular pregnancy will end, there are choices about when in a lifetime we want to have children. The most striking current features of our reproductive demography is the rising mean age of mothers at their first birth which now for the first time ever is over thirty (see Chapters 13 and 14). This is a trend that may be seen across Europe and elsewhere. In the UK, at least, the postponement of child bearing is strongly associated with level of education. There is a two year gap between the mean age at first birth for those with and without higher education qualifications. But the average figures hide growing social divisions. While those with further education postpone births, those at the other end of the educational scale continue to have their children early and have larger completed families. The other significant demographic link is with immigration; those arriving most recently have larger families, usually following the patterns of the cultures from which they come. But typically, succeeding generations come to follow the general UK patterns. The recent rise in the birth rate in the UK is significantly associated with immigration.

Fertility (technically, fecundity), in the sense of the capacity to conceive, begins to fall for women from their mid twenties and does so precipitously from their mid thirties. Thus, postponing childbearing to the thirties will mean that more women will have difficulties in getting pregnant and in sustaining a pregnancy to term. As the mean age at first birth has risen, increasing numbers of women have turned to the fertility clinics (Chapter 13) for assistance with conception. However, the success rate of IVF also declines with age. For example, figures from the Human Fertilisation and Embryology Authority show that in 2007 an IVF cycle successfully produced a baby for 32% of women under 35 receiving treatment but only 12% of those aged 40–42. So some will be beaten by their biological clock, and a growing number of women who postpone child bearing will remain childless despite their assisted and unassisted attempts at conception.

Earlier I wrote of birth as a moveable feast, but though birth may take place over a wide range of gestational ages, as I mentioned, preterm birth is not without its hazards for children. Alison Forhead and Abigail Fowden (Chapter 7) discuss an important treatment for premature babies to assist their breathing and its complications. Being born too soon may cut short developmental processes that prepare babies for life outside the womb. A baby's lungs, for example, must develop to the point where they can clear themselves of fluid so that with the beginning of breathing they can begin to absorb oxygen from the air. If this doesn't happen adequately, breathing, even with the assistance of a respirator, may be impaired and lack of oxygen in the blood can cause further problems for the baby. Prevention of preterm birth would be a great step forward. And at least part of it is preventable – the iatrogenic prematurity that arises from collaborative reproduction in the fertility clinic. As Peter Braude and Tarek El-Toukhy (Chapter 14) describe, IVF, as currently practiced, produces a much increased incidence of twins (and occasionally triplets). Multiple birth babies are much more likely to be preterm (and low birth weight[1]) and children born prematurely run an increased risk of a number of medical, social and educational problems.

Alongside the legal change in status from fetus to child at birth, the State has had a role in the registration of births. Civil registration began in 1837. This served both the State's demographic and bureaucratic interest in the population, as well as being a proof of an individual's status. Recording the fact of a birth and the mother's and child's names has never been particularly problematic – at least until the development of gestational surrogacy. But with surrogacy, as in the more usual situation, tradition has prevailed and a woman becomes a mother (in UK law and some other jurisdictions) through the act of birth, regardless of whether the commissioning couple provided the egg or the embryo. Thus, legally, a further step is required to transfer rights and duties to commissioning parents. But what about fathers? For married parents there is no difficulty in birth registration as the presumption has always been that a

---

[1] Being born early and of low birth weight are often of course associated but each carries its particular risks for the health of the child. But being born too soon is generally most significant because it may mean being born before all systems of the body are sufficiently mature to adequately equip a baby for extra utero life.

husband is also the father. What of children born to unmarried mothers? With rising numbers of children born to cohabiting couples, it became possible for a father to accompany a mother and register a birth with both their names. Recent British legislation (the Welfare Reform Act, 2009), however, will require unmarried mothers to register the name of a baby's father (except in a few situations to be set out in regulations) and this raises new questions about the purposes of birth registration. Has registration become a new means of aiding the collection of child maintenance costs, or perhaps a boost to child welfare by encouraging their father's engagement in their lives, as some have suggested? Here, as elsewhere in matters of father-child relationships, a new argument has emerged: that a child's genetic identity is involved and that a child needs to know – has a right to know? – who their father is. The 'genetic identity' claim is an interesting one, as it seems it has only come into play since the advent of DNA paternity testing: perhaps a case of can do, should do. Prior to the advent of DNA fingerprinting in the 1980s, it was only possible to rule out potential fathers, either because they were not in the right place at the right time ('over the seven seas', for example) or more recently through blood group tests. But now (except in the case of so-called identical twin fathers) comparisons of DNA samples from a child and putative father can establish paternity with a very high degree of accuracy.

The book is divided into four sections. The first deals with the experiences and rites of birth. Historical change is the theme for the sociological perspective of Ann Oakley and her colleagues (Chapter 1) while Françoise Barbira Freedman's chapter (2) is an anthropologist's account of the rites of birthing. The first of these chapters involves a return visit to a large London hospital comparing a group of mothers delivering in 1975/6 with some in 2007. One of the most striking differences was that in the first study only one of fifty five mothers had a Caesarean section, while in the second more recent sample this was the mode of delivery for almost half the fifty eight mothers. But the experiences in the recent group were polarised between those having Caesarean sections or an instrumental delivery with epidurals and a small number who had a 'natural' birth in the midwife-led birthing centre within the hospital. These mothers gave birth vaginally without induction, epidurals or other interventions. Given these striking changes in the conduct of birth, it is perhaps appropriate that Susan Bewley and Lin Foo (Chapter 3) ask whether doctors are still improving childbirth, while Mavis Kirkham examines the relationship of mothers and their midwives in Chapter 4.

Section 2, which turns to the status and consequences of birth, begins with Jonathan Herring's examination of the legal and moral significance of birth (Chapter 5). What about conflicts between the interests of mother and fetus? In certain situations a mother can have an abortion and terminate a pregnancy. But what about occasions when a mother – perhaps on religious grounds – refuses a treatment which might benefit the fetus? Should we try to enforce a maternal prenatal duty of care for the fetus? While a fetus may be seen to lack legal personhood, do we consider that its moral status may grow gradually through pregnancy? Rosamund Scott navigates a careful path through these fraught and controversial issues in Chapter 6. In Chapter 7 Alison Forhead and Abigail Fowden look at a dilemma in the treatment of preterm babies and they examine the evidence for the use of a drug which helps to mature the lungs of preterm babies and seems undoubtedly a benefit in the short term. But there are worrying signs of longer term problems. How should we proceed?

Today, a father is much more likely to be present at the birth than was the case a generation ago – is this a sign of a new fatherhood? Richard Collier (Chapter 8) shows how the idea of the father as uninvolved or tangential in relation to birth has been challenged by social and legal developments around parenting.

The third section concerning the aftermath of birth, begins with Rebecca Probert's chapter (9) which is concerned with birth inside and outside marriage as an indicator of legal parenthood and entitlement. She reviews the religious rite of baptism and the legal rule of registration and how the recording of information about legal parenthood has changed over time. She notes the interesting historical continuity that in 2008 six percent of children were registered without a father's name, a not very different figure from the six percent of births outside marriage in 1868, most of which were registered. We have already raised the question of the purpose of birth registration. Julie McCandless (Chapter 10) examines some of the issues raised by the most recent legislation in the area and the role that registrars have in policing the rather different provision that exist for registration of a birth that follows treatment in a fertility clinic, as compared with situations where others have made their own arrangements for collaborate reproduction.

Then we turn to history with Frank Woodman's chapter about royal inheritance in the middle ages (Chapter 11) and Shelley Day-Sclater (Chapter 12) on the emergence of puerperal insanity as a discrete category of mental disease. Both are examples of the long shadows that may be cast by birth over the lives of others.

The final section of the book focuses on the timing of birth. Irenee Daly (Chapter 13) concentrates on that section of the population who are increasingly postponing having their babies until their thirties. Do they fit the stereotype of women too engaged in their career to contemplate having a family at the age when their own mother had them? The trend for those with professional qualifications to postpone births is very widespread so clearly general social factors are at work here. Some leave it too late and their sub-fertility leads them to the fertility clinic. And Peter Braude and Tarek El-Toukhy (Chapter 14) take up the story from the perspective of the clinic. The use of assisted reproductive technologies will help some to have babies but the same biological clock keeps ticking inside and outside the clinic. Success rates for IVF fall as women get older as we have already noted. This chapter also considers the epidemic of multiple births that has been produced by the fertility clinics and the strategies for better practice that could reduce this.

The Human Fertility and Embryology Authority – the UK regulatory body for the fertility industry – publishes tables of clinic success rates which can be used by women in deciding where to go to seek fertility treatment. However, Emily Jackson and Hossam Abdulla (Chapter 15) are sceptical about whether the publication of these so-called 'success rates' are, in practice, helpful in enabling patients to make informed choices about their treatment. Worse, they suggest the league tables may be damaging in that in the commercial world of fertility treatment they provide incentives for practices that may be less than ideal patient care.

Part 1:

Experiences and Rites of Birth

1

Becoming a Mother: Continuities and Discontinuities over Three Decades

ANN OAKLEY, MEG WIGGINS, VICKI STRANGE, MARY SAWTELL
AND HELEN AUSTERBERRY

I. INTRODUCTION

GIVING BIRTH FOR the first time is part of a broader socio-cultural transition, that from non-mother to mother. The experiences of women in pregnancy and childbirth are part of a complex of factors influencing the shape and outcome of that transition. Maternity care policies and practices, themselves subject to historical and cultural change, operate in a context of continuities and discontinuities in women's lives. This chapter offers one perspective on the transition to motherhood through the particular lens of two research projects using a similar methodology but separated by three decades. The aims of the chapter are, using data from these two studies, to look at some of the ways in which women's experiences of pregnancy and childbirth in the UK have changed or remained constant since the 1970s. Our goals in conducting a 'repeat' study were to look at the impact on women's experiences of the substantial policy and practice changes in the management of childbirth that have occurred since the 1970s. An important context for these changes is shifts in women's position and in family life. We were particularly interested in how influential or otherwise experiences of the maternity care system itself are in shaping how women feel about becoming mothers today as compared with in the past.

NOTE ON THE CHALLENGES OF REPEAT STUDIES

The definition of a 'repeat' or 'restudy' is: '…a deliberate intent to repeat insofar as possible a previous research study using the same research design and methods to investigate similar theoretical concerns usually with the goal of better understanding social change' (Davies and Charles, 2002, p. 1). Researchers in the social sciences have not paid much attention to replication research, in part perhaps because of a funding bias against knowledge accumulation (Klein et al., 2000). Uncritical replication of exactly the same methods is usually not a feature of such studies (Neuliep, 1991). For example, particular research or interview questions often need to be reworked to reflect changes in language or the framing of issues; practices of measuring such dimensions as social class and ethnicity also develop and these cannot be ignored in new studies. The important constant is the theoretical and conceptual framework which is common to both original and repeat studies. With respect to the two studies discussed in this chapter, the framework is one which locates women's transition to motherhood in the context of studies of life transitions generally, but particularises the contribution of social and health care factors to the outcome of this transition, defined as how women feel about their experiences of pregnancy, childbirth, and early motherhood.

II. BACKGROUND: THE TWO STUDIES

The original study was carried out by one of us (AO) in 1974–9. A sample of women having their babies in a West London hospital in 1975–6 was interviewed twice in pregnancy and twice in the early postnatal months. The aims of the project were to gather first-hand accounts of the process of the transition to motherhood at a time when research of this kind was scarce; and to examine links between social and health care factors, on the one hand, and the 'outcome' of the transition to motherhood, on the other. The main publications from the project were two books: *Becoming a Mother* (Oakley, 1979a), later republished as *From Here to Maternity* (Oakley, 1981, 1986), which used mainly qualitative interview data; and *Women Confined* (Oakley, 1980), a more analytic approach to the data, which presented a theoretical model of childbirth as a life transition. Other publications from the project included an extended literature review looking at the conceptualisation of women as mothers in psychology, sociology and medicine (Oakley 1979b); a focussed paper on medical and social factors in postpartum depression (Oakley & Chamberlain, 1981); and reflections on the 'advice' literature then available for first-time mothers (Oakley, 1982).

The second study, which is still ongoing, has been designed to replicate as far as possible the methods and intentions of the first study. However, unlike the original study, it is a team effort, led by Vicki Strange and Meg Wiggins, with all the authors of this chapter contributing. The study began in 2007 and will finish in 2011. The sample of women has been recruited from the same hospital using similar methods as in the original study, and, as before, two pregnancy and two post-natal interviews have been carried out. But because the relationship between motherhood and employment has changed significantly since the

1970s, this second study is being extended to allow for a fifth interview when the babies are 18 months old.

The first study (S1) recruited 66 women, of whom 55 continued with their pregnancies and were interviewed four times. The second study (S2) recruited 71 women, of whom 58 contributed data at all four interview points. Table 1 shows the demographic profile of the two samples.

Table 1: Demographic Profiles of Women in S1 and S2

	S1[N=55]	S2 [N=58]
Average age	26 yrs	31 yrs
Partner status: – Married & living together – Living with partner (not married) – Has partner, but not living together – Single (no partner)	87% (48) 13% (7) 0 0	50% (29) 34% (20) 10% (6) 5% (3)
'Country of origin': Britain [S1]; 'inside UK' [S2] Elsewhere: Ireland/N.America [S1]; 'outside UK'[S2]	84% (46) 16% (9)	50% (29) 40% (29)
Ethnicity: – White British – White other [mainly other European] – Mixed – Asian/Asian British – Black/Black British – Chinese/other	100% White British/other	43% (25) 29% (17) 4% (2) 9% (5) 12% (7) 4% (2)
Social Class: * – I Professional occupations – II Managerial and technical – IIIN skilled – non manual – IIIM skilled– manual – IV partly skilled – V unskilled – Unclassified *(students)*	4% (2) 27% (15) 62% (34) 0% (0) 7% (4) 0% (0) 0% (0)	7% (4) 52% (30) 19% (11) 5% (3) 5% (3) 2% (1) 10% (6)

* Social class of study women (using the conversion between Social class and NS-SEC operational categories)

The picture in Table 1 reflects population changes since the 1970s and also the different criteria used to select the two samples. S1 recruited only married or cohabiting women born in Britain, Ireland or the USA; S2 included single women and same sex partnerships and women conversant in English irrespective of country of birth. Table 1 shows that the women in S2 are more culturally diverse and more likely to be single than those in S1; they are also older – 31 years compared with 26 years. The S2 women's occupational profiles indicate a somewhat more middle class sample – 59% of S2 women are social class I or II, compared with 31% of S1 women. These differences in the populations of women taking part in the two studies reflect broad social changes since the 1970s; they are also germane to some of the findings we discuss below.

Both samples of women were recruited directly from hospital booking clinics, and interviewed as soon after this as possible (S1: 26 weeks before the birth, S2: 24 weeks before), and then as close as was feasible to one month before birth and six weeks and five months after birth. All the interviews were transcribed and the qualitative and quantitative data analysed using various standard techniques.

Many types and levels of comparison can be made between the findings of the two studies. In this chapter we limit ourselves to a brief discussion of five themes: confirmation of pregnancy and choice of maternity care; expectations about childbirth and patterns of birth 'management'; postnatal care; social support; and information resources.

III. BECOMING A PREGNANT PATIENT

The 'medicalization' of reproduction and the absence of choice for childbearing women as to place and type of care were issues highlighted in 1970s debates about maternity care (see eg Arms, 1975; Cartwright, 1979; Zander & Chamberlain, 1984). Since then much has changed. The presence of a 'consumer' voice in health care is now accepted as legitimate (King's Fund Centre, 1993; Expert Maternity Group, 1993). The latest UK policy statement promises choice with respect to place and type of antenatal, intranatal and postnatal care, continuity of care, and a strategy 'that will put women and their partners at the centre of their local maternity service provision' (Department of Health, 2007, p. 7). This is a very different rhetoric from the 'doctor knows best' tone of the policy statements that underpinned the development of the maternity services in the 1970s and before.

In S1, all the women visited their GPs in early pregnancy to have their pregnancy confirmed and arrange their maternity care. Although some GPs provided antenatal care in their surgeries, most referred women to hospital. Many women either knew or suspected they were pregnant before visiting the doctor, but pregnancy tests could not be purchased over the pharmacy counter, and this first visit to the GP was therefore important, though not always successful, as an official medical confirmation:

(S1 – 'DJ', 23 years, Jewellery assembler, married)
I told her (GP) my symptoms – that I wasn't feeling up to scratch. She asked me if I'd missed my periods and I said yes. She said it is possible that you could be pregnant. She looked through my records and said I'd been regular since I'd started so I was probably pregnant: come back in two months time…I was, not upset, but dubious

> I suppose that she didn't examine me or anything. She just took it for granted. But it still didn't ease my mind. I wanted to know myself. I wanted to tell my husband. He knew that I might be, but he said to go and find out: we didn't want to build our hopes up. But all I could say was 'probably' when I came back.

In S1 a minority of women – 38% – were examined at this first consultation. Just 16% received any advice about pregnancy. No GP suggested the possibility of a home birth, though 9% of the women said they had considered this as a possible option. Most women – 58% – were simply told that they would have their baby in a particular hospital; 61% were given no choice (or information about the options) as to who (GP, hospital, local authority clinic), would do their antenatal care.

In contrast, almost all the women in S2 confirmed their pregnancy themselves with over-the-counter pregnancy tests. These are able accurately to confirm a pregnancy at four weeks compared to the test used in the 1970s which required women to be around eight weeks pregnant. Consequently women in S2 began their new 'pregnant' identities earlier, often before they were aware of any pregnancy symptoms. Earlier confirmation meant that women in S2 were more likely to be aware of early miscarriages and anxiety about this dominated many women's accounts of the first trimester. As it was for women in the 1970s study, the main function of the visit to the GP was to obtain a referral to the hospital which would provide most of their care. Also as in S1, these consultations were commonly very short, and it was rare for women to be given guidance by their GPs to as to specific sources of information. No S2 women reported that their GP discussed options with regard to the types of care available or where they might deliver their baby (eg home birth, birthing centres). A few women were clear before meeting with the GP that they wanted to go to the study hospital for their antenatal care, and a few, who did not live near the hospital, went to great lengths to get a referral. But, most commonly, the GPs listed a few local hospitals and then highlighted the study hospital as a good option because it was local, most women in this area went there, or they knew of satisfied patients. None of the women reported being given any factual information by their GPs that might help them make an informed choice about which hospital they should 'choose', though in some cases they did access this themselves via the internet:

> (S2, 'GM', 33 years, Marketing executive, married)
> I think there was a (study hospital) website, or an NHS website that you could access all the hospitals through and I remember I'd read about certain areas and then I read about (study hospital) and a number of other hospitals. But I mainly, apart from just the information that was out there that had been put out by the hospital itself, there was also like a lot of mother sort of chat groups, online groups, that had loads of information up.

Interestingly, and despite the universal use of home pregnancy tests, there was a very similar emphasis among many of the women in the two studies on the need for some kind of official confirmation of the pregnancy:

(S2, 'SH', 31 years, Staff development consultant, married)
I went to the GP, I took a urine sample with me thinking I was being really clever and good and then she didn't need it 'cause they don't do tests there. She said... your home pregnancy test is as reliable as anything they would do, so she didn't actually confirm the pregnancy to me, which was kind of like... 'cause you kind of want someone else to say, 'yes, you're pregnant'.

In S1, it was as though women could not believe their own experiences of being pregnant. In S2, strikingly, the evidence of sometimes multiple self-conducted pregnancy tests was not regarded as sufficient medical proof that women had embarked on their new careers as pregnant women.

A major difference between the two studies concerned the use of ultrasound scans. In the 1970s, ultrasound imaging of pregnancy was still relatively new, and the main function of a routine scan at about 11 weeks of pregnancy was for pregnancy dating. Around a third of S1 women did not have an ultrasound scan at all. Some reported having 'endless' ultrasounds, when there was medical uncertainty around dates. Today, scans are a normal part of pregnancy. They have assumed a key role as a means of screening for birth defects, and in the study hospital two routine NHS scans are offered – one at around 11 weeks (for dating and nuchal fold screening) and the second at about 22 weeks (the so-called 'anomaly' scan). All the S2 women had at least one NHS scan (range 1–7). Another key change since the 1970s was in the use of private scans. In S1 one woman had a private scan while in S2 a third of the women (n=20) had paid for at least one private scan (range 0–2). The highest total number of scans for any one woman was nine (this woman had IVF, amniocentesis, and there were concerns about the baby's growth). In some cases, private scans were used instead of NHS scans, and were sometimes recommended by a clinician for convenience or speed (there was very little flexibility around appointment dates for NHS scans). Some women who had already had one private scan chose to have another of these instead of an NHS scan because they were impressed by the perceived superior quality of the experience (clearer image, more time, more information from staff). In other cases, private scans were used in addition to NHS scans at the instigation of the women for particular reasons, for example, to provide reassurance before and after a long trip abroad, or to get '3D' and '4D' images to keep as a record.

Women were often anxious prior to a scan, and some were critical of the quality of care provided; however, in general, scans were viewed as a very positive experience:

(S2, 'CB', 28 years, PhD student, married)
We had like five pictures because she kept taking nice shots as she was going which was really nice, so that was a really good experience. We were kind of on a bit of a high when we left there and then knowing the sex we were texting and calling people.

In particular, the first routine scan provided reassurance, despite positive pregnancy tests and GP appointments, that women really were pregnant. Often they did not 'go public' about the pregnancy until they had seen the fetus on the screen:

> (S2, 'NH', 37 years, Human resources manager, married)
> It was quite a magical thing, I mean like the first scan I was just in floods of tears because...I hadn't believed that I was actually pregnant with a real baby... You know I could have sat and watched it for hours really.

The opportunity to visualise the fetus at an early stage of pregnancy impresses upon women the fact that they are bearing a child rather than simply pregnant; in this sense it has the capacity to alter women's relationships with their unborn children and their views of themselves as mothers (Dykes and Stjernqvist, 2001). Information about the fetal body affects maternal perceptions and feelings, as it does also, perhaps even more notably, in the case of fathers-to-be (Barbour, 1990). A clear difference between the two studies was in the perception of possible disadvantages of scanning. In S1, not only was there considerable dispute between women and maternity care staff about the need for, and accuracy of, ultrasound in pregnancy dating, but there was concern among some women that ultrasound might damage the baby. Although scanning technology has changed greatly in the last 30 years, in S2 only a few women questioned the value of the information an individual scan provided, and just one woman expressed concern that ultrasound might damage the baby (as one partner also did – see quote below). There was a strong sense among the S2 women that more is always better despite continuing medical debates about the health effects of ultrasound (Independent Advisory Group, 2010). This decline over time in concern among women about the possible disadvantages of ultrasound has been noted in a systematic review of 74 primary studies (Garcia et al., 2002).

Acceptance of ultrasound both as diagnostic tool and as 'entertainment' (Furness, 1990) extended even to those women who otherwise wished to avoid medical intervention:

> (S2, 'SY', 23 years, Dancer, living with partner)
> It was nice, really, really nice. If I [could] I would go for another scan I think. Yeah, it's a beautiful thing, seeing what [the baby] is doing.

> (S2, 'ML', 32 years, business analyst, living with partner)
> I think [my partner] does too much research on the internet or maybe he just questions things, good for him I suppose, but he was concerned about the length of the time that I was being scanned ...[I'm] sure it will be fine, and they did say it would be fine, but he was just a little bit concerned.

IV. BIRTH: EXPECTATIONS AND REALITY

At S1, women's expectations of giving birth were informed by ideas of 'nature', 'instinct' and medical 'experts' knowing best. Women did not expect a high degree of control over what happened to them in giving birth, though many expressed a desire for this:

> (S1, JM, 28 years, Rebate officer, married)
> I suppose there are a couple of things which still worry me a bit. The first one is having a shave and the enema which I find extremely distasteful. And the other thing is this business about being cut and stitched which I don't particularly fancy...I dreamt I was sort of sitting on this chair giving birth and the baby sort of got stuck in the perineum ... and the doctor came along and cut it and it came out so quickly that I had to catch it but it didn't hurt at all. Is that wishful thinking?

At both time periods, the study hospital was regarded by medical professionals as a centre of excellence in terms of medical care. Many women considered the hospital to have a good reputation. The need for expert medical guidance continues to be a feature of contemporary childbirth, though discourses of 'medical' and 'natural' childbirth (Cosslett, 1994; Miller, 2007) are considerably intertwined, as the following quote illustrates:

> (S2 'JR', 37 years, Novelist/business manager, living with partner)
> I'm doing all this hypno-birthing stuff, I'm listening to positive stuff all the time... It's mostly re-framing everything so instead of contractions it isn't sort of pain... it's sensations, so it's just trying to re-programme your expectation around it and that you're in control and that your body and your baby know what to do and then you just use visualisation to control the contractions and imagine blowing up balloons... visualising the cervix opening and it getting softer and jelly-like...It's a lot about breath control. My friend did it and didn't even take a paracetamol, but who knows. I'd be quite partial to some gas and air so we'll see. We're very much hoping to go to the birth centre but obviously that's very dependent on circumstances and, because I'm over 35, if I'm just 40 weeks and 2 days or something late, they want to induce.
> **How do you feel about that?**
> Not good... I thought I'd have my fourteen days but apparently not, because of my age.
> **So what will you do, will you go with their... ?**
> I don't know, I would go in for the appointment and discuss it really I guess, I will put this baby's health first... you know, if they're saying it's dangerous then we'll do it... for sure.

The predominant desire expressed by women in S2 was of having a 'natural' birth, by which they meant birth in a hospital environment but with a minimum of medical intervention. The degree to which women anticipated medical intervention varied, from a belief that everything would go smoothly (nature would prevail), to a fear of the situation spiralling rapidly into a medical emergency.

The most common medical interventions in S1 were instrumental delivery (48%) and epidural analgesia (79%), with only two women having a Caesarean section. In S2 the most common were Caesarean section (43%) and epidurals (72%), with a fall in the number having instrumental deliveries (21%). This increase in the Caesarean section rate between the two studies reflects national trends: in England and Wales the rate rose from 5.8% in 1975 to 22.7% in 2003–4 (Macfarlane et al., 2000; Government Statistics Service, 2005). Similar percentages of women in the two studies (21% and 25%) experienced induced labours. In S2, birth experiences had polarised into two different extremes: those for whom it is a midwife-led 'natural' experience; and those for whom it is an entirely surgical experience.

Of the 58 women in S2, eleven gave birth vaginally without induced labours, epidurals, or other intervention. Most of these women gave birth in the midwife-led birthing centre within the hospital, but separate from the traditional delivery suite. Epidural pain relief was not available in this unit, but birthing pools and other forms of 'alternative' pain relief were encouraged. The option of this birth centre was a departure from the first study:

(S2, 'AP', 24 years, Student, married)
What were the best aspects of labour from your point of view?
Probably falling asleep in the[birthing pool]... it was really very relaxing and having my partner there and music playing and low lighting and knowing I'd meet my baby. (...) I was really happy [to be able to get in the birth centre] and I was trying to stick to my birth plan which I managed to do and was quite happy about.

Seven women had elective Caesarean sections and 18 had emergency ones. Four women who had elective Caesareans did so following recommendations by medical staff because their babies were breech. The vaginal delivery of babies presenting as breech that was 'allowed' at the time of the first study, was not an option for women in the second. Two women had had other health problems (gynaecological surgery when younger, retinal surgery) and had been told by doctors in the past that they would be unable to deliver a baby vaginally. When doctors told these women at 36 weeks pregnant that they disagreed with this view and did not think an elective Caesarean section was necessary, the women did not feel confident or comfortable in going ahead with a vaginal delivery. Another woman chose a Caesarean section because she was very frightened of the pain and possible damage to herself from vaginal birth:

(S2, 'HT', 36 years, Nurse, married)
[My husband] is an anaesthetist and he kept asking me what was I planning (....) so I kind of said well, you know, I don't know. I've never had a normal delivery. I've never had an operation (....). I know that I don't want to have instruments and I don't want to have any pain, I was very happy to have an epidural and that increases the likelihood of prolonged labour and instrumental delivery and I didn't want episiotomies or ripping and he was basically saying to me, 'look if you end up having a very long labour then you'll end up having a C-section anyway'.

There was very little discussion of the relative risks of Caesarean section and vaginal delivery. The main reasons for women having emergency Caesarean sections were long labours ('failure to progress') and/or babies being distressed. In-between the two extremes of natural/midwife-led and surgical birth, there were 10 women who gave birth vaginally in the more medicalised delivery suite, despite induced labours and/or epidural pain relief.

In the 1970s, the women frequently described their experience of labour using the term 'shock'. This related primarily to the unexpected nature of the pain, feelings of lack of control, and the invasiveness of medical intervention:

> (S1, 'EF', 28 years, Publisher's assistant, married)
> It woke me from a deep sleep – such a sudden strong pain... The way I woke up shocked me, I was suffering from shock after it.

In S2 a significant number of women still used the language of trauma to describe their labour experiences:

> (S2, 'EP', 32 years, Marketing executive, married)
> I came out of [labour] and said I felt traumatised from it...when we got home...I actually couldn't close my eyes, I was like 'oh my god that was majorly traumatic'. I think a combination of being left for a few hours and am I doing the right thing, having a bit of a moment of beating myself up about should I have an epidural and then the pure concept of pushing her out (laughs) and pulling her out and then being stitched up... even on the ward, when the pain really kicks in after the epidural wears off, you try and run to the loo and you realise you're not going to make it, all of that, all of this stuff that's going on with your body I think is the trauma really. Just utterly hit by a truck, in every way possible.

Women who had experienced long labours were exhausted and for some (eg those who had 'failed' forceps, ventouse, epidurals, and/or babies in distress), the birth experience was both physically and emotionally traumatising. A comparison of women's experiences of childbirth over the period from 1987 to 2000 by Green and colleagues (2003) shows that first-time mothers were considerably more anxious in 2000 and more likely to describe themselves as 'frightened' and 'overwhelmed' in labour than their counterparts in 1987.

Despite discourses around shock, and the high degree of emergency medical intervention, most women in S2 described the experience as one in which they felt they had exercised a degree of control – 46% said they had good control. This was a change from S1, where 69% said they had not felt in control of themselves or what went on in labour. Feeling in control in S2 was most likely among those women who had had the type of birth experience that they had hoped for; and those who had strong advocates to help with decision-making. Although women said that they had exercised a degree of control, most also described their experiences as being dominated by decisions made by health professionals – a theme that resonated with S1. Sometimes they felt these decisions had been made for good reason, but sometimes they referred to the existence of hospital protocols, or hospital convenience, or medical need to avoid potential litigation. Although there were a few notable exceptions, most women did not feel party to the big decisions (instrumental deliveries or emergency Caesareans).

Most women in S2, as in S1, said they were satisfied with the care they received in labour (satisfaction was high for 59% in S1 and 49% in S2), but satisfaction with individual carers (midwives, doctors, anaesthesiologists) varied considerably, and many women described both poor and excellent care.

Not having seen the person who delivered their baby before, and experiencing constant shifts in personnel during labour, were sources of discontent for S1 women. Despite policy changes, most of the S2 women did not experience continuity of care, either in terms of having previously met the carers who were with them in labour, or in having the same carer/small team of carers look after them. Multiple carers often meant conflicting information. When continuity of carer during labour was achieved, it was normally praised, although the carer's personality was deemed the most crucial factor.

V. AFTERBIRTH

In S1 the average length of stay in hospital was just under nine days compared with 2.4 days in S2. The main rationale for the policy of booking all new mothers for a prolonged hospital stay in the 1970s was for them to achieve competence in changing, washing and feeding their babies. By the second study, increasing the availability of hospital beds had become the overriding factor. Other key differences include the high routine use of sleeping pills and other medication in S1, as well as the practice of placing babies in the nursery after birth. Rates of dissatisfaction with midwife care after birth were approximately a quarter in both studies. There was considerable overlap with respect to reasons for dissatisfaction on the postnatal ward: complaints about environmental and structural factors (noise, light, restrictions on partner visiting); a lack of information and explanation; contradictory advice; insufficient practical support:

(S2, 'GT', 32 years, Lawyer, married)
The day after she was born, there was a paediatrician and there was a midwife who came to check me, but other than that nothing happened so nobody came to tell me anything about breastfeeding, about how to take care of my baby. Nothing.

The widespread use on postnatal wards of mobile phones and personal electronic entertainment in S2 may aid individual women, but it contributes a new and poorly controlled source of disturbance. For those in S2 who had Caesarean sections or were unwell for other reasons, these issues had a particular impact. Some in both studies described neglect, for example being unable to access anti-sickness medication, and being left with a constantly crying baby whom they were unable to pick up or feed:

(S2, 'AA', 32 years, Accounts officer, married, (emergency C-section))
[My husband] had to go about 10 o'clock and left me on my own. I'm sitting there, I'm panicking 'cause I can't feel anything... They put the baby in the cot and he was crying and I said, 'please could you be able to sort him out because I can't move?'

With increased Caesarean rates, these experiences are now much more common than they were. In S1, camaraderie often developed between the women during their nine day postnatal stay, and this helped them to cope. The much briefer stays in S2 did not allow for this mutual help to develop, but some women tried to take control over their situation by paying for a private room. Ironically, however, this often created another problem – a feeling of isolation and of being forgotten by staff. One woman discharged herself, and the partner of another attempted to negotiate an extension to visiting hours in order to support his very unwell partner, but was removed by security guards. Women who had babies in the midwife-led birthing unit were able to have their partner stay overnight with them, in a room that was not shared with other mothers.

In both studies, women reported receiving mixed messages about breast feeding from professionals in hospital and community settings. On the postnatal ward, they felt pressure from staff to use formula supplements. In S2, this advice was sometimes couched in terms of the risk to babies' health of not being 'topped up' in this way. Women in both studies said they felt criticised and undermined, physically 'manhandled', and confused by inconsistent advice and information. The accounts of those in S2 who felt they 'failed' at breastfeeding are striking in the way that they portray feelings of shame and guilt:

> (S2, 'EP', 32 years, Marketing executive, married (stopped breastfeeding after 8 weeks))
> I should have just stuck myself in the middle of the town square and whipped myself on the back to deal with the guilt, it was dreadful, utter, utter guilt.

In many ways, the impact on women in S2 of 'failing' to breastfeed seemed to parallel the impact of a 'bad' birth in S1.

Women in both studies were very keen to get out of hospital. Looking back, some of those in S2 regretted not being more assertive about the problems on the postnatal wards. The structure of community care that was in place for S1 women offered most of them regular visits from midwives and then health visitors. However, for S2 women, professional support from community staff was often inadequate; for example, there was often a gap of several days between leaving hospital and a first midwife visit. Most women only had three such visits at the most, with limited continuity of care. A woman with an infected Caesarean wound described her postnatal care, once home:

> (S2, 'RL', 42 years, Project planner, single)
> I had him on Wednesday, I went home on Sunday, (…) The first visit of the midwife was on the Monday, and then they asked me if I could come to [local] drop-in centre, so I went there on Friday to have him checked, and by that time I was pretty sure it was properly infected, I was in so much pain and it was oozing like mad, so it was really not nice. So I had her have a look at it, and she said, 'well you've got to go and see the GP straight away'. That was a week after, or more than a week after I'd already thought I don't think this is right.

VI. SOCIAL SUPPORT

In maternity hospitals in the 1970s, paternal presence during labour and birth was not the accepted custom it is now. 'Husbands' had to sign a form in the study hospital saying that they would sit at the head of the bed, would leave immediately if staff asked them to, and that they understood they were present at their own risk. Complaints of women being left alone in labour were consequently not uncommon. By the time of the second study, not only were partners expected to be there, but other relatives and friends were acceptable as well. A few middle class women also paid to have doulas (non-medically trained labour supporters). Mothers of a number of the women attended the birth, alongside the partner where there was one. In most of these cases, the women were young, from a minority ethnic culture or single. Sisters and best friends were also present, especially where mothers were overseas or no longer alive. One young African woman, whose mother lives abroad, was partnered by her sister and best friend throughout her labour, which lasted over 36 hours:

> (S2 – 'SN', 24 years, Student, single)
> My friend was like, 'move around to make it, it can come out'. I said 'no ways, I can't, I don't feel like moving around'. They helped me a lot. None of them, they didn't sleep, because every time the pain is come, rubbing my back. The whole time since I was there, they didn't leave the hospital.

At the time of the first study, there was no governmental support for paid paternity leave. At S2, partners were entitled to two weeks' paid leave and 13 weeks of unpaid parental leave, though, like a third of fathers nationally (Equality and Human Rights Commission, 2009), some of the fathers of S2 babies did not take even the two weeks' paid leave.

Once they were out of the protected medical environment, mothers in S1 without wider family support were often faced abruptly with looking after the baby alone during the day, as their partners went straight back to work. At S2, most mothers, whether single or in partner relationships, spent little time alone in the first two weeks after leaving hospital. A majority of women with partners spent the initial two weeks of their partner's leave just with him, then in about a third of these cases her mother (or parents) came to stay once the partner had returned to work. Another pattern – in around a further quarter of cases – was where the woman's mother and/or other family members stayed from the outset while the partner was on leave, an arrangement that created tension in some instances, while in other instances women felt doubly supported. Some minority ethnic fathers took leave from work later, leaving early support to female family members, as a British-born Pakistani woman below describes:

> (S2, 'LM', 38 years, FE college lecturer, married)
> I'll be coming here [to my mother's flat] and I'll have my mum and my sister, I'll feel fine.
> **So you'll be coming here from the hospital?**
> Yeah... in our culture generally a mother goes to her parents first... first 30, 40 days. (...) [It's] a cultural thing, protecting your child and ... also because of the mother, it gives her a chance to recuperate so she has her family, her mother, sister, to help. (...) My husband will have his two weeks paternity leave when I go back to [our] flat.

A number of the younger women in the S2 sample also lived with their families, or stayed with their parents on leaving hospital. Most of these women were single or their partners lived elsewhere. One women paid for the support of a maternity nurse at home in the early days after the birth.

VII. THE INFORMATION REVOLUTION

For information, women in the 1970s relied mainly on booklets handed out by GPs and hospital clinics. Since then there has been an explosion of advice literature on pregnancy, childbirth, and parenthood, and a greatly enhanced general media coverage. The main change, though, has been the development of the internet. Nearly all the S2 women used the internet. Some said that this enabled them to access information, for example about the development of the fetus, that they found reassuring:

> (S2, 'LL', 23 years, Unemployed, has partner, living separately)
> During the early stages I didn't know anything they was explaining, I came straight home and I was on the net to try and find an explanation for what was wrong with me. (This has been) brilliant because I found out that if they couldn't find a fetal pulse it didn't necessarily mean there was no baby, just meant that you weren't pregnant enough for them to see it....That put my mind at rest straightaway.

Another equally important use of the internet was for social support, with discussion forums and email groups enabling women to confer about common problems and sometimes organise to meet up. On the debit side, it was sometimes difficult for women to work out which information was useful in helping them to make decisions. For example, information about particular hospitals is available on the internet, but this is hugely varied in topic and quality. A small number of S2 women mentioned that they had used the internet to help them decide where to have their babies (usually in the light of the GP's recommendation).

The way in which women in S2 used the internet echoes the findings of other studies in this area. An American survey found that three quarters of pregnant women use the internet for accessing information about pregnancy and birth; 16% of first-time mothers considered it their most important information source (Romano, 2007). In this and other studies (see eg Dickersin, 2006; Larsson, 2007; Szwajcer et al., 2005), women used the internet in early pregnancy to get questions answered before they went public about their pregnancies. The internet also allows women to seek information anonymously on private topics (eg concerns about breasts, bowels, bladders, vaginas) (Plantin and Daneback, 2009).

An interesting question is whether this expansion of accessible information about pregnancy and birth has altered women's relationship to medical authority. Comparing women's experiences with doctors in our two studies suggests that, as others (see Freedman, this volume) report, the increased emphasis on information and choice has probably decreased the mismatch between women's expectations and experiences of birth management. Women now were less likely than before to allow doctors to 'do' things to them (for example, internal examinations, induction of labour) without explanation, but they do not seem any more likely to challenge medical decisions about birth management. The culture of choice is more a rhetoric about choice than a sign that women have become equal partners with doctors in deciding the shape of their maternity care. This may be partly because most of the information women can access is not presented in such a way that it enables them to discuss the effectiveness of particular interventions, and even when it is, most women do not feel confident in using it to contradict health professionals (Wiggins and Newburn, 2004).

Take-up of antenatal and parenting classes was similar in the two studies; about three quarters of S2 women attended hospital classes, and about half private ones (some did both). The S2 women's classes seemed to focus mostly on birth, with most describing them as a useful source of information. Private classes (usually run by the National Childbirth Trust), attended almost exclusively by middle class women, functioned to facilitate social groups of first time mothers and were enormously valued for this. Amongst other relevant sources of knowledge, previous experience with babies was greater (50%) in S1 than in S2 (32%), reflecting a reduction in women who serve 'an apprenticeship of mothering' (Miller, 2005). S2 women also valued information and advice from their own mothers less. Women have greater expectation of their partners' involvement in pregnancy and childcare and their own mothers are not so readily accessible now, being more likely to be engaged in paid employment and/ or less likely to be living nearby, compared with in the 1970s. Because the second study included Black and minority ethnic women, there is a contrast of cultures here, with women in this group being more likely to regard their mothers as authorities on motherhood.

VIII. CONCLUSION

The two studies we discuss in this chapter include a total of 412 interviews with 103 women. This is an enormous amount of data, and we have only been able to draw on a small proportion. Data collection and analysis in the second study are still ongoing. Nonetheless, certain patterns are emerging. The transition to motherhood remains a process which is subject to a high degree of 'medicalization', that is, definition as hazardous and under the control of medical professionals (Fox and Worts, 1999). However, discourses around risk and choice are now considerably more sophisticated than they were (Possamai-Inesedy, 2006). The focus on 'woman-centred' care provides something in-between a guarantee and an illusion of control for women becoming mothers for the first time. Despite a background of an official shift towards women's rights to choose the pattern of maternity care, there was little evidence of women in the second study being able to make meaningful informed choices. Although rhetoric and procedures have changed (eg more emphasis on choice, scans and Caesarean sections, fewer episiotomies and sleeping pills), the experience for women may not be very different with regard to medical control. This finding is in line with those of other, larger studies (see eg Redshaw et al., 2007) and a recent systematic review of UK studies of first-time motherhood (Brunton et al., 2010). Green and colleagues' (2003) study, like ours, found a complex pattern, in which similar levels of satisfaction hid increased dissatisfaction among some women about greater use of obstetrical procedures, and increased satisfaction among others who reported greater feelings of control. The changing cultural context of choice also throws some light on our findings on the experiences of women who 'fail' to breastfeed; a theme also reported by others (see eg Shakespeare et al., 2004). The increased promotion of breastfeeding renders it the healthy, risk-free route and consequently the only acceptable 'choice' for a 'good mother'. The cultural context is one which emphasizes an ideal of 'intensive motherhood' that conflicts with the practical realities of many mothers' lives (Lee, 2008). Thus, women who 'fail' at breastfeeding may experiences a range of negative emotions and struggle to maintain a positive sense of self (Lee, 2007; Ryan et al., 2010).

Medical technology now has an accepted place in the process of becoming a mother, even for those women who view pregnancy and childbirth as primarily 'natural' (Green and Baston, 2007; Kornelsen, 2005). Some aspects of the 'technologisation' of reproduction are potentially worrying, for example, the increasing use of ultrasound scans (Redshaw et al., 2007) and the rise in the use of commercial 'boutique' scans (Independent Advisory Group, 2010). But, from a sociological point of view, the evidence of women's narratives today suggests a more complex version of the old dichotomy between 'natural' and 'medicalised' childbirth in which the dominant cultural view is one of childbirth as a medical event (Brubaker and Dillaway, 2009). Conversely, current policy in relation to infant feeding insists that it ought to be a natural process, with the locus of control remaining with the mother. This may help to explain why lack of success with breastfeeding impacts negatively on identity more powerfully than 'failure' to give birth naturally.

A major shift between the two studies is the rise in the use of private services throughout the process of becoming a mother: extra scans, private rooms, doulas, maternity nurses, breastfeeding supporters. These additional services, almost completely absent in the first study, were used predominantly by middle class women in the hope that they would enhance or ease their experience. For some this additional support seemed to be successful in achieving these aims. Notably though, for others, the experiences of birth or breastfeeding remained challenging and traumatising, despite these additional resources.

With the rise in information sources about labour and birth in the last three decades (including documentary channels where births can be viewed constantly), we expected that the 'shock' element of the experience would be reduced among women in the second study compared to the first. This was not so. Perhaps childbirth is always shocking because it is always unpredictable, or perhaps there are aspects of the social and/or medical treatment of women as mothers which make the process of becoming a mother in our culture emotionally uncomfortable.

ACKNOWLEDGEMENTS

The first study, 'The transition to motherhood: social and medical aspects of first childbirth' was funded by the (then) Social Science Research Council in 1974-9. The second study, 'Women's experiences of childbirth: continuities and discontinuities in social and medical aspects of first childbirth', is supported by the BUPA Foundation from 2007-11.

REFERENCES

Arms, S. (1975). *Immaculate Deception*. New York: Bantam Books.

Barbour, R. S. (1990). Fathers: The Emergence of a New Consumer Group. In *The Politics of Maternity Care* (ed. J. Garcia, R. Kilpatrick, and M. Richards), pp. 202–16. Oxford: Clarendon Press.

Brubaker, S.J. and Dillaway, H.E. (2009). Medicalization, Natural Childbirth and Birthing Experiences. *Soc Compass* **3/1**, 31–48.

Brunton, G., Wiggins, M., Oakley, A. (2011) *Becoming a Mother: A Research Synthesis of Women's Views on the Experience of First-time Motherhood*. London: EPPI-Centre, Social Science Research Unit, Institute of Education. http://www.ioe.ac.uk/study/departments/ssru/37968.html

Cartwright, A. (1979). *The Dignity of Labour?* London: Tavistock.

Cosslett, T. (1994). *Women Writing Childbirth*. Manchester: Manchester University Press.

Davies, C. and Charles, N. (2002). The Piano in the Parlour: Methodological Issues in the Conduct of a Restudy. *Sociol Res Online.***7**(2), http://www.socresonline.org.uk/7/2/davies.html.

Department of Health (2007). *Maternity Matters: Choice, Access and Continuity of Care in a Safe Service*. London: Department of Health.

—— (2009). *Commissioning Local Breastfeeding Support Services*. London: Department of Health.

Dickersin, S. S. (2006). Women's Use of the Internet: What Nurses Need to Know. *J Obstet Gynecol Neonatal Nurs.***35**, 151–156.

Dykes, K. and Stjernqvist, K. (2001). The Importance of Ultrasound to First-time Mothers' Thoughts about their Unborn Child. *J Reprod Infant Psyc.***19**(2), 95–104.

Equality and Human Rights Commission (2009). *Working Better: Fathers, Family and Work – Contemporary Perspectives.* Manchester: Equality and Human Rights Commission.

Expert Maternity Group (1993). *Changing Childbirth: Part 1: Report of the Expert Maternity Group.* London: HMSO.

Fox, B. and Worts, D. (1999). Revisiting the Critique of Medicalized Childbirth: A Contribution to the Sociology of Birth. *Gender Soc.*13 (3), 326–346.

Furness, M.E. (1990). Fetal Ultrasound for Entertainment? *Med J Australia.* 153(7),371.

Garcia, J., Bricker, L., Henderson, J., Martin, M-A., Mugford, M., Nielson, J. and Roberts, T. (2002). Women's Views of Pregnancy Ultrasound: A Systematic Review. *Birth.* **29** (4), 225–250.

Government Statistics Service (2005). NHS *Maternity Statistics, England: 2003–4.* London: Department of Health.

Green, J., Baston, H.A. (2007). Have Women Become More Willing to Accept Obstetric Interventions and Does this Relate to Mode of Birth? Data from a Prospective Study. *Birth.* **34**(1), 6–13.

Green, J., Baston, H., Easton, S., McCormick, F. (2003). *Greater Expectations? Summary Report.* University of Leeds: Mother and Infant Research Unit.

Independent Advisory Group on Non-ionising Radiation (2010). *Health Effects of Exposure to Ultrasound and Infrasound.* London: Health Protection Agency.

King's Fund Centre (1993). *Maternity Care: Choice, Continuity and Change.* London: King's Fund.

Klein, J.G., Brown, G.T., Lysyk, M. (2000). Replication Research: A Purposeful Occupation Worth Repeating. *Can J Occup Ther.* **67**(3), 155–161.

Kornelsen, J. (2005). Essences and Imperatives: An Investigation of Technology in Childbirth *Soc Sci Med.* **61**, 1495–1504.

Larsson, M. (2007). A Descriptive Study of the Use of the Internet by Women Seeking Pregnancy-related Information. *Midwifery.* **25**, 14–20.

Lee, E. (2007). Health, Morality and Infant Feeding: British Mothers' Experiences of Formula Milk Use in the Early Weeks. *Sociol Health Ill.* **29** (7), 1075–1090.

—— (2008). Living with Risk in the Age of 'Intensive Motherhood': Maternal Identity and Infant Feeding. *Health Risk Soc.* **10**(5), 467–477.

Macfarlane, A., Mugford, M., Henderson, J., Furtado, A., Stevens, J., Dunn, A. (2000). *Birth Counts: Statistics of Pregnancy and Childbirth. Vol 2, Tables.* London: The Stationery Office.

Miller, T. (2005). *Making Sense of Motherhood: A Narrative Approach.* Cambridge: Cambridge University Press.

—— (2007). 'Is This What Motherhood is All About?': Weaving Experiences and Discourse through Transition to First-time Motherhood. *Gender Soc.* **21** (3), 337–358.

Neuliep, J.W. (1991). *Replication Research in the Social Sciences*. Newbury Park, CA: Sage Publications.

Oakley, A. (1979a). *Becoming a Mother*. Oxford: Martin Robertson, reprinted under the title *From Here to Maternity*. Harmondsworth: Penguin, 1981, reprinted with new Introduction, 1986.

—— (1979b). A Case of Maternity: Paradigms of Women as Maternity Cases. *Signs*. **14**,607–631.

—— (1980). *Women Confined: Towards a Sociology of Childbirth*. Oxford: Martin Robertson.

—— (1982). Normal Motherhood: An Exercise in Self-control? In *Controlling Women* (eds. B. Hutter and G. Williams), pp. 79–107. London: Croom Helm.

Oakley, A., Chamberlain, G. (1981). Medical and Social Factors in Postpartum Depression. *J Obstet Gynaecol*. **1**, 182–187.

Plantin, L. and Daneback, K. (2009). Parenthood, Information and Support on the Internet. A Literature Review of Research on Parents and Professionals Online. *BMC Fam Pract*. **10**, 34.

Possamai-Inesedy, A. (2006). Confining Risk: Choice and Responsibility in Childbirth in a Risk Society. *Health Sociol Rev*. **15** (4), 406–414. http://www.biomedcentral.com/1471-2296/10/34

Redshaw, M., Rowe, R., Hockley, C., and Brocklehurst, P. (2007). *Recorded Delivery: A National Survey of Women's Experience of Maternity Care 2006*. Oxford: NPEU.

Romano, A.M. (2007). A Changing Landscape: Implications of Pregnant Women's Internet Use for Childbirth Educators. *J Perinat Ed*. **16**, 18–24.

Ryan, K., Bissell, P. and Alexander, J. (2010). Moral Work in Women's Narratives of Breastfeeding. *Soc Sci Med*. **70**, 951–958.

Shakespeare, J., Blake, F. and Garcia, J. (2004). Breast-feeding Difficulties Experienced by Women Taking Part in a Qualitative Interview Study of Postnatal Depression. *Midwifery*. **20** (3), 251–260.

Szwajcer, E.M., Hiddink, G.J., Koelen, M.A. and van Woerkum, C.M. (2005). Nutrition-related Information-seeking Behaviours before and throughout the Course of Pregnancy: Consequences for Nutrition Communication. *Eur J Clin Nut*.**59** (Suppl.1), S57–S65.

Wiggins, M. and Newburn, M. (2004). Information Used by Pregnant Women, and their Understanding and Use of Evidence-based Informed Choice Leaflets. In: *Informed Choice in Maternity Care* (ed. M. Kirkham), pp 147–168. Hampshire: Palgrave Macmillan.

Zander, L. and Chamberlain, G. (1984). *Pregnancy Care for the 1980s*. London and Basingstoke: Macmillan.

2

Changing Medical Birth Rites in Britain: 1970–2010

FRANÇOISE BARBIRA FREEDMAN

I. INTRODUCTION: ANALYSING MEDICAL BIRTH RITES

THERE IS NO human birth without ritual. Birth, copulation and death – what TS Eliot calls the 'brass tacks of human experience' – are accompanied with ritual activity and provide the greatest source of imagery in art. The earliest evidence of fertility and funeral rites around 40,000 BC has been used as a marker of human culture. Birth rituals make statements on particular understandings of how we enter the world, and implicitly, how we leave it. They provide scripts that are liable to variation in performance and manipulation for various ends. They mark changes on the bodies of mothers and infants. Like other forms of ritualised behaviour, birth rituals are open to various styles of interpretation.

Birth rituals start with the social announcement of pregnancy and extend to what Wendy James (2003) has called 'the placing of the newborn': that is, the public recognition of the baby as human and his/her gradual introduction into society. Should the mother or baby die, rituals of misfortune are called for. Van Gennep coined the phrase 'rite de passage' (1909) to denote sets of rituals that express and produce a change of status within the life cycle. These typically include three phases: separation or liminality, transition and new integration into the social milieu. He observed that these phases are not developed to the same extent in all rites de passage and that particularly in the case of the first child, the transition phase from woman to mother is dominant. In the same way that myths are situated outside history, in ancestors' time, rituals are perceived in the present as unchanging although they are in constant evolution, upholding a seemingly stable social and moral order.

In this chapter, my concern is with changing medical birth rites in Britain in the last four decades. This is a period when expectations of biomedicine's abilities to guarantee a live birth have been firmly associated with births in hospitals (Peel Report, 1970). In spite of evidence-based national initiatives such as Changing Childbirth (1993) following the Cumberledge Report, and the 2007 guidelines for normalising birth, public debates still reflect divided opinions on risk and safety regarding the place of birth. Today, while women officially have choice about home births and attendance by midwives (whether community midwives or independent midwives), only a small minority of 1% to 5% according to regions, nearly all of them categorised as 'low risk', opt for home delivery compared with 0.5% in 1990. An examination of the succession of Committees shows a marked break between 1980 (Short, 1980) when the focus on perinatal death was still dominant, and 1992 (Winterton, 1992) with a main preoccupation for the quality of care in normal pregnancy and birth, albeit still in hospitals. The perception of birth and, increasingly, fertility as medical processes rather than social ones has gained firm hegemony regardless of income, class or ethnic affiliations. While British women gained equal access to pain relief in childbirth – a remarkable advance since the 1940s – in the last four decades new social forms of secularity, multiculturalism and consumerism have also been associated with a greater inequality of women in a disintegrating welfare state. Birth rituals associated with the medical management of childbirth in hospitals, however, are standardised for all women in NHS maternity services, with social differences arising more in prenatal and postnatal approaches to care. While some features of these 'obstetric rites' have become part of cosmopolitan maternity care and evolve in a global context, others are idiosyncratic in national health systems.

The definition of ritual in anthropology is as vexed as that of culture, kinship or myth, yet we cannot do without this elusive concept because it refers to a particular form of social events that we implicitly recognise. In the broadest definition that encompasses not only human rituals but also animal behaviour displays, all ritual actions are formal, stylised and repetitive. Contention arises with attempts to differentiate rituals from other formal performances on the basis of encoded meanings that are more or less shared by participants to produce symbolic communication. The medical birth rites I comment on are instances of 'secular rituals'(Moore and Meyerhoff, 1977): their overlap with religious rituals (when the lives of mother or baby are in danger) is now determined by the private religious affiliation and choice of parents rather than officially Christian or Jewish, Muslim, Buddhist, Hindu. The mere mention of 'obstetric rituals' invites reactions from medical practitioners ranging from amused scepticism to outright dismissal: formal repetitive acts are essential to the efficacy of procedures in protocols, interventions are rational for the benefit of patients. Labelling some of these interventions as 'rituals' implies both a questioning of their rationale and a disconcerting projection of encoded meanings. Reference to ostensibly life-saving procedures on obstetric wards as 'birth rituals' may seem provocative, even shocking. Following Rappaport

(1999, p. 24), I use a broad definition of ritual as 'the performance of more or less invariant sequences of formal acts and utterances not entirely encoded by the performer'. It is generally accepted that action is first and foremost in ritual (Humphrey and Laidlaw, 1994) but the socially meaningful aspects of the repetitive actions in ritual, what is encoded and how it is encoded, are open to discussion and interpretation. Actions are seen by all as right and proper best practice. What separates sheer protocols from rites is best made apparent to participants when shared meanings are acknowledged or once the rationale for proper actions has become obsolete. For example, holding newborns upside down by the ankles and slapping their bottoms to make them utter a healthy cry, unquestioned up to the 1980s, would be abhorrent to new parents in today's Britain. In the period 1970–2010, I consider both obstetric procedures that can be exposed as ritual actions after being discarded and current procedures that are more opaque in their ritual quality.

Actors may or may not be aware of the ritual quality of 'naturalised actions', particularly within medical practice. This quality may come to the fore in retrospect, when the rationale for the action has been exposed as unfounded. Yet in ritualised behaviour there is a distinctive quality of the agents' awareness of their actions in relation to perceptions of these actions by others (Goffman, 1972). In this respect it is useful to distinguish between 'ritualisation' (a term borrowed from ethology) and ritual (a classic anthropological concept). Human beings share with animals a communicative world that depends upon gestural routines. Ritualisations occur when particular behaviours are standardised as vehicles of expression and behavioural patterns become set and socially valued, functioning as devices for storing and transmitting information. Making and preserving order, determining relative status within groups as well as signalling and communicating intentions are functions of animal ritualisations. These meaningful routines however can become obsolete when circumstances change: for example, Wells, Huxley and Wells (1937, p. 199) first explained how the domestic dog's turning round on a rug is a non-functional relic of a ritualisation that was useful in the wild.

Obstetric rituals range from ritualisations that mostly pass unnoticed as they arise and are modified in time (for example, doctors no longer entering labouring cubicles unannounced or midwives now asking women permission to carry out routine procedures) to explicit rituals (for example, fathers now being expected to cut their newborns' cords ceremonially).

Medical interventions are presented as rational – if not evidence-based – and beneficial in the light of calculated risks and desired outcomes. Discussing the ways in which general values and norms related to risk, normality, gender, family are expressed and negotiated between medical practitioners and pregnant women/couples offers an avenue to better understand life-cycles in a culture of bio-medicine coupled with technology. In this chapter I trace and question the way in which changing birth rites are inscribed in the epistemic practices of biomedicine with a persistent reductionist and positivistic value orientation yet without consistent evidence.

Birth rites are never just concerned with babies: all rites de passage (birth, initiation, death) carry implications for social reproduction. Birth rites involve overlapping multiple contexts such as other life-cycle rituals, definitions of personhood and gender, body politics. The protocols for transforming women into compliant patients in labour wards both differ from and are similar to general hospital routines of patient admission. Rituals of crisis management also have an overlap across the wards; uniforms signal and structure the interaction between doctors of different statuses (consultants, senior and junior registrars, anaesthetists), midwives and parturient women in ways that are familiar even to those who have no previous experience of hospitals.

Steering clear of systems, cultures and societies as reified entities, questions are drawn from the borderline between medical procedures and birth rites: when does a procedure become a rite? How does the rationalisation of procedures, whether normalised through policy or generalised use, impinge on their perception as rituals? How does the standardisation and resulting enforcement of procedures hide or reveal their ritualistic qualities? Where are the main areas of resistance and contention in the medical management of childbirth? Which birth rituals are made hyper-visible and positively encouraged by doctors, while others remain invisible? When doctors endorse new medical rituals, are they aware of doing so? In my attempt to address these questions I look at the historical dynamics of how standardised practices have arisen and fallen into disuse within the frame of birth as a 'rite de passage' from first hospital appointments to home transfer of mother and baby.

II. CHANGES IN MEDICAL BIRTH RITES

Three sets of medical birth rites, corresponding to the liminality, transition and integration phase of Van Gennep's rites of passage, are of particular interest for tracing historical change over the period 1970–2010. First, fetal ultrasound imaging has become established as a bio-social marker of pregnancy. I focus in particular on the 20 week scan. Second, the increasing use of epidural analgesia and anaesthesia as a main form of pain relief in childbirth points to broader social changes in the perception of bodies and pain. Trends to control and yet to create 'natural scenarios' of birth, with a tension between statistical and ideal norms, will also be examined. Finally, fathers' attendance in childbirth has been normalised over just four decades in Britain while becoming a feature of cosmopolitan obstetrics and the global culture of parenting. This dramatic change has gone largely unchallenged while fathers' participation in labour and birth has been endorsed as a cultural norm.

(a) Fetal ultrasound imaging: The 20 week 'scan' as an established bio-social marker of pregnancy in Britain

In the last four decades, technology related to imaging has transformed medicine. In obstetrics, scans have become a major diagnostic tool not just in relation to possible fetal abnormalities but also to determine the due date, the position of the placenta and presentation and maturity before birth. The obstetric 'trumpet' of the pre 70s is now a relic. Ultrasound scanners (as well as fetal heart monitors during labour) act as standardised mediators between nature and society. They differentiate cosmopolitan obstetrics from pre-modern locations where they are conspicuously absent from maternity care. In the words of Bruno Latour (1993, 106):

> [I]n constituting their collectives – of humans and non humans – some mobilise ancestors, lions, fixed stars and the coagulated blood of sacrifice; in constructing ours, we mobilise genetics, zoology, cosmology and haematology... But those are sciences, the moderns will exclaim, horrified at this confusion.

While early scans (11–14 weeks) aim at detecting pathologies, the 20 week scan has gradually assumed the socially accepted part of making pregnancy visible in the community of the British pregnant couple. In North America, earlier scans also serve as markers (Sandelowski, 1994) and this trend may develop in Britain in years to come. Both parents-to-be are generally present for this scan as an event announced to family and friends, who will anticipate seeing the 'baby's first picture'. Cutting across class and ethnicity boundaries, the symbolism of this picture as a token of a viable, bio-medically sanctioned 'baby' is now well established. The scan is a turning point in that the printed image offers a social confirmation and tangible image of the pregnancy. Couples who prefer not to know the sex of their baby are now rare. Parents often give a name to their sexed baby following the scan and start referring to their baby by name in social interactions. Scans produce the first picture in the baby album, the start of a personal identity and also the start of medical records. Parents are now aware of babies yawning, hiccupping and sucking their thumbs in utero: the interest and involvement of new fathers are manifested in media representations of pregnant couples announcing the event jointly. Here is a recent email announcement: 'we had our 20 week scan today which was just so beautiful to see Jacob's little baby brother Solomon here in front of us on the screen. All is well here and the pregnancy is going well'.

Pregnancy tests are now routinely done at home by women or couples, using widely available kits before obtaining a formal confirmation of pregnancy from general practitioners. Commercial enterprises capturing fetal images through fetal 3D ultrasound without physicians' involvement have proliferated since the early 2000s through 'direct to consumer' marketing on the internet and in shopping centres all over the world offering special bonding ultrasound experiences (Lauredhel, 2009). The fetal scans that British parents to be regard as authoritative, however, are those booked and done in hospitals. Concomitant with technological improvements in ultrasound scanning since the 80s, there has been a shift from a descriptive to a more functional approach in fetal imaging including fetal biometry and biophysical score (Yagel and Valsky, 2008). By showing a pregnant woman's womb, her fetus, and the hospital scanner's frame together in one image, a sonogram initiates the mediating role of machines in pregnancy and birth under medical control. Sonograms convey to parents the normality of this mediation located in hospitals. Ultrasound imaging has invaluable therapeutic applications in medicine and the value of routine prenatal scanning for detecting fetal malformations and chromosomal abnormalities is unquestionable (Romosan, Henriksson, Rylander et al., 2009).   In this chapter I am specifically concerned with the way in which fetal scans have recently assumed a unique function in socially integrating clinical intervention and a baby's identity. The hospital scan plays an explicit mediating role in both revealing and promoting the creation of a special relationship with the fetus by the parents together rather than just confirming the woman's pregnant status.

Linda Layne (2002) has written eloquently about the 'social and biological work' that mothers invest in the emotional early construction of their baby's identity and the drama of loss in case of miscarriage. Given the recent trend to a later gestational age, pregnancy loss is increasingly common and heartfelt in the case of wished for babies whose personhood was sometimes outlined even before the confirmation of pregnancy. 'Making a baby' can be an intense personal project for women and couples. In the case of loss, the sonogram then becomes a cherished memento of a baby who was not born but nevertheless was acknowledged and loved. Actual and virtual support groups have arisen to meet the needs of sufferers of pregnancy loss. Terminations of pregnancies prompted by abnormalities are now conducted in hospitals with a ritual script; the mother or couple are treated more as if it were a birth with an acknowledgement of their grief. Trained counsellors, whether on a voluntary basis or as maternity professionals, take time with parents. In the case of late terminations parents have an option of burying the fetus. A trend to avoid late abortions after 20 weeks in the UK is not just due to earlier viability of fetuses but also to the growing social recognition – linked with sonograms – that the baby's identity has already been shaped.

The great deal of emotional investment around the first marker scan can be related not only to changing demographic trends towards smaller families and to the concomitant greater value given to babies, particularly those conceived by older mothers, but also to the increasing perception of the fetus as co-patient with his/her mother in maternity care. The concept of fetal patienthood emerged in the USA in the 1970s (Layne 2006) yet it continues to raise social, political and legal issues (Casper 1998; Morton, 2004; Williams, 2005). Genetic counselling has gained social acceptance over the 80s and 90s. Given the trend towards medically managing pregnancy at ever earlier stages, the 20 week scan provides parents with a visible social-medical stamp of approval but also a platform for the closer monitoring of fetal growth.

As ritual markers initiating the pre-birth parenting phase, sonograms also equalise the status of pregnancies resulting from assisted conception with other pregnancies. Parents can then join childbirth preparation classes and other activities together with an experience of 'natural' normality. In establishing the risk status of pregnancies, particularly in relation to the position of the placenta and to fetal presentation, sonograms play a gate-keeping role in relation to women's options of where and how to give birth.

Throughout pregnancy, both normal and pathological physiological processes are assessed in relation to images that medical practitioners and technicians decipher for parents, increasingly involving them in negotiating risk and normality. The routine use of 3D ultrasound technology in obstetrics is mostly unchallenged on account of its clinical applications (Yagel and Volsky, 2008) in spite of earlier review articles exposing possible hazards of ultrasound imaging in the 80s and 90s (Petchesky, 1987; Richards, 1989; Georges, 1996). While the Royal College of Obstetricians and Gynaecologists' Working Party on Ultrasound Screening for Fetal Abnormalities reported in 1997 that the objectives of routine ultrasound scanning 'include psychological support', structured reviews demonstrated the absence of experimental evidence of links between fetal images, maternal attachment and positive attitudes towards health during pregnancy (Baillie et al., 1999; Nabhan and Faris, 2010). While the hospital scan serves as a ritualised bio-social threshold of pregnancy in hospital, once normality has been established parents make increasing use of the technology to enhance the visibility of their babies in utero. Parents' films of their growing fetuses are now proliferating on You Tube.

(b) Intra Partum Rituals

Following the public announcement of their pregnancies, approximately half of British pregnant women seek some instruction about how to approach labour and birth, whether in an NHS hospital or privately. Information about obstetric procedures they can expect to undergo is conflated with statistical norms yet presented within an overall framework of 'choice' and with reference to enduring ideal norms of 'physiologic labour' and delivery (midwives' terms). The ritual dimension of 'childbirth education' in all its current social and cultural forms in Britain is relevant to the historical evolution of the management of labour but it lies outside the scope of my present concern with medical birth rituals. It is worth noting however that the mismatch between pregnant women's expectations and the management of their births has been reduced over the last two decades (Kitzinger et al., 1988), showing British women's greater acceptance of standard medical procedures. As the caesarean section rate has risen to over 20% of all births in Britain and the use of epidural analgesia has become routine, medical interventions in childbirth affect the majority of parturient women in Britain in spite of successive government supported initiatives to 'normalise birth'. In the same way that breastfeeding is an ideal norm widely endorsed but flouted by women's practical choices of formula feeding, WHO directives to lower the C-section rate to below 15% are not adhered to despite solid research evidence that complications are associated with higher rates. The standardisation of obstetric interventions associated with hospital births in the UK in the last four decades is an absurdly broad topic. Looking at intra partum rites, I will consider the concept of 'embodiment' (Csordas, 1994), looking at parturient women's bodies as the 'existential ground' for culture, with particular reference to the management of pain in labour. In all cultures, rituals operate with what Merleau Ponty (1945) first called 'inscriptional meanings of the body' (praktognosia). Repetitive patterned behaviours culturally shape bodies and in doing so they transfer 'naturalised' cultural values. As embodied, values remain invisible up to the time when the boundaries of the perceived danger associated with the body practices are displaced within the process of social change. For example, the pubic shaving and administration of enema that ritually marked the prepping of women admitted to labour wards in Britain in the 70s has now nearly completely disappeared from hospital protocols to transform the newly confined woman into a patient. Devoid of its hygienic rationale – still upheld in some European maternities – the practice is distasteful to British women today in spite of the rising fashion of pubic hair waxing. Besides admission to a bed, notes, routine temperature and blood pressure tests, the attachment of women's bodies to an electronic fetal monitor has become the normative marker for initiating the 'transition phase' of birth rites in hospital. Like fetal ultrasound imaging, electronic fetal monitoring has become entrenched in standard maternity care protocols without scientific endorsement. Controversies about the detrimental effects of monitoring on labour outcomes have been ongoing since the 1980s, consistently pointing to 'Contradictions between Practice and Research' (Haggerty, 1999) on the basis of randomized controlled trials (MacDonald et al., 1985; Thacker et al., 1995; Banta and Thacker 2001) and comprehensive reviews of both research and practice (Thacker et al., 2006; Macones et al., 2008). In spite of cautions called for by professional associations including the American College of Obstetricians and Gynecologists regarding the reliability, validity and efficacy of electronic fetal monitoring (EFM), 83% of labouring women in the United States were monitored electronically in 1996. The 2008 National Institute of Child Health and Human Development Workshop Report on EFM included 'the relationship to clinically relevant outcomes' in its research recommendations. In the meantime, technological improvements have aimed at increasing the patient-friendly quality of monitoring. Recent contraptions to increase women's mobility during monitoring include a waterproof battery operated monitor for women who labour in water.

For the purpose of this chapter, my interest lies in the analysis of ritualised markers rather than in discussing the rationality of routine fetal monitoring. The fact that the rationality of this practice has been so widely questioned however is relevant to my argument. Why has their use been so compelling in spite of evidence mounted by a rare alliance of medical professionals, researchers, midwives and labouring women? While the use of hospital gowns, pubic shaving and bed confinement constrained women's bodies in both a practical and symbolic way, monitors hook them more directly yet more insidiously to an externally validated time-frame and performance dictated by apparently impersonal decision making criteria (McCourt, 2009). Monitors also produce paper traces that can be used as evidence in case of litigation. The non-negotiable, imperative application of monitors to all women admitted to labour wards stands on the boundary between procedure and rite. It is precisely this rigid standardisation that gives away its ritual quality: it defuses subsequent questioning of procedures and enlists passive compliance from obstetric patients. Many writers on birth have commented on the compulsive staring at monitor screens by women in labour, particularly by those under epidural anaesthesia, as if the monitors sustained rather than traced the process of labour. As monitoring became ubiquitous and dominant, individualised and homely features, such as clothes and hospital décor, were increasingly permitted and even encouraged. 'Marking the stage', a process identified by Audrey Richards in her pioneering anthropological study of Bemba birth rituals (1956, pp. 161–2) is effected by linking bodies and machines in a way that is congruent with other aspects of medical care and consistent with other behavioural patterns in our culture. On this 'stage' marked by the mandatory use of monitors, questioning obstetric protocols is as futile as the questioning of fertility dances in front of male elders by educated nubile girls in Nigeria. Irrefutability and inescapability are central to the rite de passage.

Cultural norms related to time (induction policies, partograms, labour management guidelines) determine the majority of medical interventions in childbirth (McCourt, 2009). Once monitored, women labour under strict conditions of timely performance. For a majority of British women, labour needs to be augmented with synthetic oxytocin administered intravenously as a drip. The interplay between the augmentation of labour and the need for additional pain relief caused by more intense and frequent uterine contractions is widespread, most frequently resulting in the use of epidural analgesia. The current standardised management of pain in hospital births, as reflected in perinatal surveys, is therefore the use of 'soft' sources of pain relief (tens machine, body practices, immersion in birthing pool, entonox) followed by an epidural. While the use of injected opiates (pethidine, meptid) during labour has diminished in the last four decades, entonox, the popular 'gas and air' (introduced 1938) has remained a favourite form of pain relief in the hands of British midwives who are keen to promote 'physiologic labour' and to avoid the higher rate of instrumental deliveries associated with epidurals. The active role of midwives in the management of labour in British maternity hospitals, albeit increasingly under threat (Kirkham, this volume) may explain the lower use of epidurals in Britain in comparison with other countries of the European Union except the Netherlands.

The reduction or elimination of pain in childbirth has been among the concerns of medical practitioners for over a century, well before safe motherhood was consolidated in Britain in the 1950s. A discussion of obstetric birth rites in Britain cannot be undertaken without considering doctors' prescriptive mandate for alleviating human pain coupled with the increasing general social expectation that women's reproductive cycle and indeed the human life cycle can and should be 'managed' as freely from pain as possible. The perennial objective of obstetric rituals is the sight of a happy mother holding a healthy baby and the pain of childbirth is possibly the greatest source of fear and concern for pregnant women. Notwithstanding the haphazard use of chloroform and scopolamine as innovations that filtered from the upper classes to mid-society in the early twentieth century in Britain, the gradual expectation of total pain relief as part of the medical management of labour over the course of the twentieth century marks a historical break from earlier times. The immense historical benefit of knowing that reliable modes of pain relief are routinely available in British hospitals cannot be overlooked even if it is consistent with a more widespread use of pain relief in all areas of medicine on the basis of advances in both pharmacology and anaesthetic procedures. Obstetric anaesthesia has been at the forefront of applications of epidural anaesthesia.

There is however a cultural dimension in the experience of pain, including childbirth pain. As Mauss noted long ago (1936), 'there is no such thing as natural behaviour'; any natural expression is culturally determined. In contrast with Amazonian bodies that are culturally shaped by a resilience that may include ritually induced pain, our bodies are conditioned to expect means of suppressing pain. The sequence of monitoring, labour augmentation and pain relief in the most common form of epidural analgesia in childbirth constitutes a set of rites in that these procedures are based on cultural assumptions that are difficult to disentangle from the rationality of alleviating pain and suffering. The call for intervention may be primary. The analysis of medical control-cum-management of childbirth and the female reproductive cycle has been extensive since Emily Martin's *Woman in the Body* (1989). That this control is achieved through ritualised sequences of behaviour, which as such may be as invisible to medical practitioners as they are to their female patients, has been less salient.

Following Goffman's pioneering insights on rituals of mundane social interaction (1972) and ethnographic insights gained across cultures (Richards, 1956; Lewis, 1980), we need to look at the production and interpretation of signs that underscore the patterned behaviours for all participants. As Rappaport (1999) pointed out, in ritual the formal acts are always invested with morality and expressions of a conventional order. In the transition phase of birth rites de passage, when actions are most transformative to effect a change of status from woman to mother, two aspects of patterned behaviour can best throw light on the contours of ritual: as previously mentioned, obsolete rules and interventions throw light on temporality in the rationality of medical procedures. Resistance is another area that may expose fault lines in hegemonic protocols.

(i) Obsolete obstetric rites of transition

In their seminal paper, Margaret Mead and Niles Newton (1967) were the first to expose the irrational character of two systematic obstetric procedures and to show their ritual aspects: episiotomy and 'nil by mouth', the abstention of food and drink during labour. After a review of all available evidence on episiotomy, Newton found that claims that episiotomies caused less discomfort, blood loss and injuries than perineal tears during childbirth were not supported by controlled studies. The prevention of uterine prolapse later in life could not be confirmed. After noting that delivery with an intact perineum was a common occurrence in the Netherlands, the authors suggested that the routine practice of episiotomy in American hospitals was 'in keeping with the prevailing culturally determined philosophy of labour speeding'. Four decades later, a systematic review of episiotomy in obstetric care in the United States (Viswanathan et al., 2005) reached the same conclusions. The study could only attribute the variation in the episiotomy rate from under 10% to over 70% in different countries to the fact that 'cultural differences still exist in the medical world'. The policy of 'nil by mouth' was founded on the slim risk of inhaling vomitus under anaesthesia. A cross-cultural survey revealed the American policy to be extreme and confirmed the character of these procedures as 'two strongly entrenched customs:... it is not necessary to accept them as biological necessities when they are actually culturally determined'. While episiotomy ceased to be performed routinely in Britain on the basis of the evidence that Newton referred to during the 1980s, it continues to be routinely performed in other European countries such as Italy (Sartore, 2004) in disregard of comprehensive randomised controlled testing. The status of episiotomy as a ritualised bodily inscription of change from woman to mother (some activists have described it as 'Western genital mutilation') is made apparent by its obsolescence in countries where the practice has been discontinued in response to documented evidence of its lack of clinical justification.

(ii) Water birth: the invention of an alternative birth script

Between the mid eighties and the mid nineties, labouring in water ceased to be an obstetric anathema and gradually became an option available in British maternity units. Water birth can be seen as an alternative birth script supported by midwives for low risk parturient women and based on resistance to the numerous interventions associated with augmented labour, epidural analgesia and supine birth positions on delivery beds. Parturient women's naked bodies in birthing pools against the backdrop of painted ocean murals invite a perception of undisturbed nature. Women who labour and give birth in water with little or no pain relief claim agency in managing pain within the dominion of the care of midwives. The 'stage' set by birthing pools overtly challenges the tenets of control through partograms and active management of labour. Women who complete their labour and birth in water, however, are such a small minority that they are not a threat to the statistical norm of compliance to exogenous forms of pain relief. The utopian images that inspire birthing in water, particularly those of ocean births, offer extreme contrasts to medically managed births in the form of powerful images: in the wild, outside social boundaries, childbirth can be free, spontaneous, unscripted.

Paradoxically, the greater acceptance of water birth facilities in British maternity hospitals has also been associated with a widening gap between 'active management' of birth and 'active birth'. The national guidelines for normalising birth (NICE, 2007) have rekindled midwives' commitment to reduce unnecessary interventions. Since the mid 90s however, many midwives have voted with their feet by withdrawing from patterns of medical management that were not congruent with traditional midwifery skills of empowering women to give birth with bodies de-coupled from technology (Ball et al., 2002; Kirkham, this volume). The ritualised sequence of hospital birth marked by monitoring and augmentation of labour accompanied by epidural analgesia has been consistently shown to raise the incidence of instrumental deliveries (by forceps or ventouse) and emergency C sections (Thacker et al., 1995; Banta and Thacker, 2001; Thacker et al. 2006). Evaluations of maternal morbidity associated with instrumental deliveries have prompted midwives to call for better woman-centred care. At the same time, there has also been an incentive for obstetricians to offer women more patient-friendly and 'caring caesareans'. While British women in their majority still perceive hospitals as the safer place of birth for them and their babies and are prepared to compromise between the medical management of their labour and an ideal of birth with minimal intervention, midwives have been more directly exposed to internal contradictions between ideal norms and standardised obstetric procedures in their practice.

Challenging notions of risk and normality from a radical critical perspective inevitably produces an entrenched clash of paradigms related to 'who controls childbirth' (Savage, 2007). Current dominant practices within biomedicine indicate that the ritualisation of medical intervention as described above will move one step further in the direction of the 'caring caesarean' as a standardised global cultural script that will also prevail in British maternity hospitals rather than one step back towards more effective support of midwifery led 'physiologic labour'.

(c) Postpartum 1970–2010: A Shift from Medical to Social Rites

The symbolic act of midwives carrying newborns and formally handing them over to parents at the main door of the hospital, the threshold between ritual space and public space, was discontinued in Britain in the 1990s. For two decades this act had marked the completion of the transition from woman to mother in British maternity hospitals. New mothers are now given charge of their newborns on postnatal wards from birth and are encouraged to actively care for them. While before the 1980s babies were immediately cleaned, weighed, tested and dressed before being handed to mothers, more widespread 'baby friendly' practices (UNICEF, 1994) reflect the evidence-based priority given to early physical contact between mother and newborn. In 2009, 52 Baby Friendly accredited maternity hospitals in Britain implemented 'rooming in'. It is clear to all in retrospect that the multiple reasons given for the separation of mother and newborn before the 1990s did not amount to a coherent rationale. The accumulation of evidence showing the detrimental effects of early separation clearly point to a formal ritualisation. As the routine administration of silver nitrate drops became obsolete, that of vitamin K became normative. While newborns are still swaddled in blue and pink blankets that mark gender in a quaint tradition in many British maternity hospitals, they are also individualised with garments and soft toys among an array of cards, flowers and web announcements signalling a 'home' network prevailing over the hospital birth stage. In the last four decades, the 'integration' phase following birth has become remarkably un-scripted and its association with hospitals as sites of care has decreased considerably, with a postpartum hospital stay reduced from 14 days to an average of two days in the absence of complications.

A third notable area of change is the social expectation that fathers should play a supportive and nurturing role before, during and after birth. Indeed the marked increase in fathers' overall presence and involvement from the first scan in hospital to the home postpartum over the last four decades is perhaps the most salient evolving cultural pattern in the current staging of birth rites in British maternity hospitals.

(d) Fathers in Childbirth: 1970–2010

Historical accounts of fathers' participation in childbirth remind us that the social setting of birth has changed again and again over time in Britain alone. What is notable in the recent period is the apparent encouragement (or at least tolerance) by both obstetricians and midwives of the involvement of fathers on the labour ward and even in theatre, as part of medical birth rites.

Birth was changed in Britain in the 1970s not only when hospital births became normative but also when fathers were encouraged to be present at the birth of their babies in hospitals. It is not entirely clear how fathers came to be officially invited on labour wards in the 70s. Women's pressure groups claimed success but articles and correspondence in the Lancet indicate that doctors closed ranks with little internal dissent in making this recommendation. The presence of fathers in childbirth was seen as a positive reinforcement of family formation and an aid to fill gaps in care (Enkin et al., 1995). Fathers' attendance in childbirth spread as a cultural norm through the entire social spectrum and in all parts of the United Kingdom including Northern Ireland within less than twenty years between 1980 and 2000 (Smith, 1999). In 2002, 93% of British men living with their partners attended their children's births (Kiernan and Smith, 2003). The progressive interconnection between behavioural pattern, norm and rite is of particular interest in the institutionalisation of this change (Blackshaw, 2009). Fathers' socially expected involvement in birth ranges from the transfer of parturient women to maternity hospitals to constant support during labour and delivery, with a ritual climax of the cutting of the cord. Stories of fainting men spice up midwifery care but midwives also welcome men's attendance. Fathers are handed over their newborns for skin-to-skin contact if mothers are not available after interventions. New fathers have become more visible in TV documentaries and sit-com representations of birth in Britain. These developments could not be expected from earlier studies of fatherhood. They may be the most remarkable changes in patterns of early parenting in the context of changing patterns of employment, gender role expectations and the intensified significance of joint parenting for non-married couples. Whereas men in waiting rooms and corridors fitted neatly Van Gennep's phase of liminality, living their transition to fatherhood in isolation, men on the labour ward are protagonists in what Victor Turner calls 'the ritual process' (1969). The concomitance between the medicalisation of childbirth in hospitals and the involvement of fathers seems to have gone largely unnoticed in the literature related to the management of childbirth. This may be due to the fact that men in attendance have not impinged in any way on obstetric scenarios. Reed (2005) comments on the unquestioned authority of obstetricians, male or female, at times when decisions need to be made, while some male obstetricians enlist fathers' consent more specifically before interventions.

With differences predicated on the relative importance given to technology in hospital births and home births, the ritualised role of new fathers appears to be uniform in all the optional places of birth in Britain: hospitals, birth units and home. Fathers' support during the sometimes long-term intensive care of premature babies is now also socially expected. Among male obstetricians who have championed the reduction of unnecessary medical interventions in childbirth and opposed the obstetric scripts described above as harmful to mothers, babies and society at large, Frederick Leboyer and Michel Odent (1999) have both taken a stance against the ritualised participation of fathers in childbirth. For different reasons, they both see this participation as disruptive to women's physiological needs in labour and delivery. The practice, however, is clearly here to stay. To meet a growing social need in the effective support not only of parturient women but also of couples during labour, trained birth supporters ('doulas') can now be hired to care for both new mother and new father during labour and after birth. Further social implications are likely to unfold in time as a greater variety of family configurations, parental roles and support roles are more openly represented in the media.

III. CONCLUSIONS

At any point in space and time, the embodied quality of ritual can be highlighted. In rites of passage, change of status is marked by divesting persons not just from their social attributes but also from physical identity markers. Initiands can be dressed or painted as marginal beings such as ghosts, ancestors or other non-humans. Many traditional birth rites share elements in common with funeral rites. In the culture of biomedicine, hospitals have become simultaneously the locus of birth and death. The active medical management of human birth and death in hospitals has developed in parallel. The emergence of ritualised patterns of behaviour in hospital care around the beginning and end of the life cycle has remained mostly invisible to both medical practitioners and their patients under the guise of rational procedures that alleviate pain and conform to best therapeutic efficacy.

From conception to delivery and beyond, biomedicine now relies more on signs recorded by machines than on clinical observation, symptoms and subjective experience. The production and interpretation of these signs have reset the 'stage' of birth with new sequences of formal patterned behaviour that are no less ritualised than others in space and time. The social and moral meanings associated with these formal patterns are not deliberately encoded by any of the actors (except perhaps doctors' explicit endorsement of fathers' attendance in childbirth with the aim of enabling new family units). Machine-produced signs and evidence have altered the boundaries between birth rites and both doctors and patients' rights in the shaping of selfhood for babies and also for their parents. In a cross cultural perspective, however, changing medical birth rites in Britain indicate the extent to which technological input in the birth process has also enhanced human relations, most particularly with regards to cooperation between parents and their greater affective investment in their babies before and after birth.

Since the early medicalisation of childbirth in Europe in the 18th century, prescribed birth scripts have matched prevailing assumptions among doctors that for the majority of women's bodies the birth process needs to be speeded up and assisted in order to achieve optimal outcomes. The ambiguity between biomedicine's humanitarian relief of suffering and its fundamental assumption that female human bodies are generally deficient have continued to shape obstetric protocols as new technologies were introduced in the last four decades. This is irrespective of the increasing body of research produced by midwives and others outside clinical practice, confirming the viability of alternative models of care. It is the combination of these cultural assumptions and of routine forms of care presented as unquestionably right, that adds a 'ritual' quality to dominant obstetric scenarios above and beyond therapeutic interventions. The resistance of women who choose water births, home births or even in extreme cases resort to unlawful unassisted deliveries exposes cultural perceptions of women's bodies implicitly associated with normative obstetric practices in biomedicine. While a majority of women accept the current medical norm of successive caesarean sections following a first emergency section, a minority perceive this norm as unfounded in the light of available evidence. Once a path of resistance has been consolidated to the extent that a change of policies is called for on the basis of reviewed evidence, the arbitrary quality of particular norms and procedures – as in the cases of episiotomy and nil by mouth – places them firmly in the category of (obsolete) rites. Until then however it is legitimate to refer to a ritualisation of obstetric procedures for which documented evidence of clinical or other benefits is not available or refuted by recent research.

Ritual actions operate both on the social and individual levels and the two cannot be understood separately. The dissonance between feminist critiques of the 'technocratic model of birth' (Davis-Floyd, 1994) and the choices made by the majority of birthing women calls for an anthropological enquiry in the sense of 'an empirical exploration of the historical and cultural conditions for the articulation and implementation of values' (Marcus and Fisher, 1986, p. 167).

An enquiry into the historical evolution of medical birth rituals reveals trends at the intersection of science, technology and society. In the long historical negotiation of power around birth between doctors and midwives, new balances have been achieved and undermined in turn. Aspects of this process are conscious, others not. Just like shamans, but mostly unbeknown to them, obstetricians officiate with socially powerful symbols integrated in rites that arise both from them and around them. In Britain in the last four decades, fathers have been encouraged to act as new ritual agents and mediators in the birth process without challenging medical hegemony. Opening the doors of 'the clinic' to fathers may have inadvertently brought back onto the 'ritual stage' powerful emotions that medical rites in previous decades contrived to contain or exclude through more clearly set sequences of liminality, transition and integration of parturient patients. In the same way that 'cutting the cord', a symbolic act endowed with social meanings across cultures, has gained a new significance among current medical birth rites in Britain, other rites will inevitably develop to shape emerging new forms of selfhood. As umbilical cords become perceived in relation to stem cells and research throws new light on the placenta, it is possible that these body parts, discarded without consideration in the last decades in the medical birth scenario, may be involved in novel ways in the ritualised shaping of selfhood around childbirth.

Ritualisation of birth in Britain, early 1970s

Phase in rite de passage	Sequential markers	Procedure into rite
Liminality	First appointment with consultant	Notes set till due date, mother only
	Hospital education	Parentcraft classes 4–6 weeks, for mother only
	Onset of labour	Induction
	Labour prepping	Shaving & enema Hospital gown Confinement to bed
Transition	Labour augmentation	Routine ARM Routine glucose drip + oxytocin
	Pain relief	Routine use of opiates and entonox
	Delivery of baby	Routine episiotomy
	Timing	Partograms introduced
	Placenta & cord	Immediate cord clamping Routine ergometrin for third stage management
	Mother & baby	Controlled contact
	Father	Majority of fathers in waiting room, changing to fathers attending delivery but not labour
Re-integration with new status	Family & friends in hospital	Controlled visits
	Postpartum care and education	4 to 14 days
	Infant feeding	Routine use of formula in nursery, 4 hourly breast feeding routine
	Terms of address	Use of the term 'mum'
	Discharge	Formal handing over of newborn to parents
	Social integration	Daily visits by midwife followed by health visitor. Social help if needed

Ritualisation of birth in 2010 Britain

Phase in rite de passage	Sequential markers	Procedure into rite
	Late termination of pregnancy or loss	Couple involved in hospital rites
	Hospital visit	Couples involved
	Labour prepping	Electronic fetal monitoring (20 mins mandatory), mobility possible in principle
Transition	Labour augmentation	Routine oxytocin drip
	Pain relief	Routine use of entonox and epidurals Mobile epidurals since 1995 Birthing pools available since late 90s
	Delivery of baby	Intervention as statistical norm (instrumental or C section) with ideal norm of spontaneous delivery
	Timing	Partograms with extensive midwives' record keeping
	Placenta & cord	Routine syntometrin
	Mother & baby	Ideal norm of immediate / sustained contact-negotiating delayed routine interventions on newborns
	Father	Norm of father's attendance in labour and at delivery
Re-integration with new status	Family & friends in hospital	Free visits to mother with baby
	Postpartum care and education	1 to 4 days
	Infant feeding	Ideal norm of breast-feeding Feeding on demand Day and night on ward
	Terms of address	Use of 'mum' evolving to use of first name
	Discharge	Professional signatures
	Social integration	4 visits by midwife followed by health visitor's checks

REFERENCES

Baillie, C., Hewison, J. and Mason, G. (1999). Should Ultrasound Scanning in Pregnancy be Routine? *Journal of Reproductive and Infant Psychology* **17**(2), 149–157.

Ball, L., Curtis P. and Kirkham, M. (2002). *Why Do Midwives Leave?* London: Royal College of Midwives.

Banta, D. and Thacker, S. B. (2001). Historical Controversy in Health Technology Assessment: The Case of Electronic Fetal Monitoring. *Obstetrical & Gynecological Survey* **56** (11), 707–719.

Blackshaw, T. (2009). Fathers and Childbirth. In *The Social Context of Birth*. (ed. C. Squire) pp. 215–235. Abingdon: Radcliffe Publishing Ltd. (second edition).

Burri, R. V. and Dumit, J. (eds.) (2007). *Biomedicine as Culture: Instrumental Practices, Technoscientific Knowledge and New Modes of Life*. London: Routledge.

Casper, M.J. (1998). *The Making of the Unborn Patient. A Social Anatomy of Fetal Surgery*. New Brunswick: Rutgers University Press.

Csordas, T. (ed.) (1994). *Embodiment and Experience*. Cambridge: Cambridge University *Press*.

Davis Floyd, R. (1994). The Technocratic Body: American Childbirth as Cultural Expression. *Social Science and Medicine* 56(9),1913–31.

Douglas, M. (1970). *Natural Symbols: Explorations in Cosmology*. London: Barrie & Rockcliff, Cresset Press.

Douglas, M. (1973). *Implicit Meanings: Essays in Anthropology*. London: Routledge Kegan Paul.

Enkin, M., Keirse, M. J. N. C ., Neilson, J., Crowther, C. (1995). *A Guide to Effective Care in Pregnancy and Childbirth*. Oxford: Oxford University Press.

Foucault, M. (1976). *The Birth of the Clinic*. London: Routledge

Georges, E. (1996). Fetal Sound Imaging and the Production of Authoritative Knowledge in Greece. *Medical Anthropology Quarterly* 10(2),157–175.

Goffman, E. (1972). *Encounters: Two Studies in the Sociology of Interaction*. London: Penguin books.

Good, B. J. (1990). *Medicine, Rationality and Experience: An Anthropological Perspective*. Cambridge: Cambridge University Press.

Haggerty, L. A. (1999). Continuous Electronic Fetal Monitoring: Contradictions between Practice and Research. *Journal of Obstetric, Gynecologic and Neonatal Nursing* 28 (4), 409-416.

Humphrey, C. and Laidlaw, J. (eds.) (1994). *The Archetypal Actions of Ritual*. Oxford: Oxford University Press.

James, W. (2003). *The Ceremonial Animal*. Oxford: Oxford University Press.

Keating, P. and Cambrosio, A. (2003). *Realigning the Normal and the Pathological in Late Twentieth Century Medicine.* Massachusetts Institute of Technology.

Kiernan, K. and Smith, K. (2003). Unmarried parenthood: new insights from the Millenium Cohort Study. *Population Trends* **114**, 26-33. London: Office of Population, Censuses and Surveys.

Kitzinger, J. Green, J.M. and Coupland, V.A. (1988). *Great Expectations: A Prospective Study of Women's Expectations and Experiences of Childbirth.* University of Cambridge: Centre for Family Research.

Latour, B. (1993). *We Have Never Been Modern. Hemel Hampstead, UK: Harvester* Wheatsheaf.

Latour, B. (2005). *Reassembling the Social: An Introduction to Actor Network Theory.* Oxford: Oxford University Press.

Lauredhel (2009). Recreational Obstetric Ultrasound Advert, Serenity Spa, Wollongon Australia. Hoyden About Town blog, 13 September. Franchising the Womb: Selling *Fetal Imaging*: Hoyden About Town.

Layne, L. (2002). *Motherhood Lost: The Cultural Construction of Miscarriage and Stillbirth in America.* New York: Routledge.

Layne, L. (2006). Pregnancy and infant loss support: A new feminist, American, patient movement. *Social Science and Medicine* **62**(3), 602–613.

Lewis, G. (1980). *Day of Shining Red: An Essay on Understanding Ritual.* Cambridge: Cambridge University Press.

Lock, M. and Gordon D. (eds.) (1988). *Biomedicine Examined.* Dordrecht: Kluwer Academic Publishing.

MacDonald, D., Grant, A., Sheridan-Pereira, M., Boylan, P and Chalmers, I. (1985) The Dublin Randomized Controlled Trial of Intrapartum Fetal Heart Rate Monitoring. *Am.J. Obstet. Gynecol.* **152**(5), 524–39.

Macones, G., Hankins, G., Spong, C., Hauth, J and Moore, T. (2008).The 2008 National Institute of Child Health and Human Development Workshop on Electronic Fetal Monitoring: Update on Definitions, Interpretations and Research Guidelines. *Journal of Obstetric, Gynecologic and Neonatal Nursing.* **37**(5), 510–515.

Marcus, G. E. and Fisher, M.J. (1999). *Anthropology as Cultural Critique: An Experimental Moment in the Human Sciences.* Chicago: University of Chicago Press.

Martin, E. (1989). *Woman in the Body: A Cultural Analysis of Reproduction.* Milton Keynes: Open University Press.

Mauss, M. (1973) (1936) Techniques of the Body. In *Economy and Society* **2**, 70–88.

McCourt, C. (2009). *Childbirth, Midwifery and Concepts of Time.* Oxford: Berghahn Books.

Mead, M. and Newton, N. (1967) Cultural Patternings of Perinatal Behavior. In *Childbearing: its Social and Psychological Aspects* (eds. S.A. Richardson and A.F. Guttmacher), pp. 142–245. New York: The Williams & Wilkins Company.

Merleau Ponty, M. (1945). *Phénoménologie de la Perception.* Paris: Gallimard.

Morton, C.H. (2004). Baby's First Picture: Ultrasound and the Politics of Fetal Subjects. *Journal of Health Politics, Policy and Law* 29(1), 156–159.

NICE 2007 *Clinical Guidelines CG45.* National Institute for Health and Clinical Excellence, NHS. February 2007.

Moore, S. and Meyerhoff, B. (eds.) (1977). *Secular Ritual.* Amsterdam: Van Gorcum.

Nabhan, A. and Faris, M. (2010). High Feedback Versus Low Feedback of Prenatal Ultrasound for Reducing Maternal Anxiety and Improving Maternal Health Behaviour in Pregnancy. *Cochrane Database of Systematic Reviews 2010, Issue 4. Art. No.: CD007208. DOI:10.1002/14651858.CD007208.pub2.*

Odent, M. (1999). Is the father's participation at birth dangerous? *Midwifery Today* 51, 23–25.

Peel Report, (1970). Standing Maternity and Midwifery Advisory Committee *Domiciliary Midwifery and Maternity Bed Needs: Report of a Sub-committee.* London: HMSO. ISBN: 0113202563

Petchesky, R. P. (1987). Fetal Images: The Power of Visual Culture in the Politics of Reproduction. *Feminist Studies* 13(2), 263-292.

Rappaport, R. A. (1999). *Ritual and Religion in the Making of Humanity.* Cambridge: Cambridge University Press.

Reed, R. K. (2005). *Birthing Fathers: The Transformation of Men in American Rites of Birth.* New Brunswick: Rutgers University Press.

Richards, A. I. (1956). *Chisungu: A Girls' Initiation Ceremony among the Bemba of Zambia.* London: Tavistock.

Richards, M. P.M. (1989). Social and Ethical Problems of Fetal Diagnosis and Screening. *Journal of Reproductive and Infant Psychology* 7(3), 171–185.

Romosan, G., Henriksson, E., Rylander, A. and Valentin, L. (2009). Diagnostic Performance of Routine Ultrasound Screening for Fetal Abnormalities in an Unselected Swedish Population in 2000–2005. *Ultrasound in Obstetrics and Gynecology* 34(5), 526–533.

Sandelowski, M. (1994). Separate but Less Unequal: Fetal Ultrasonography and the Transformation of Expectant Mother/Fatherhood. *Gender & Society* 8(2), 230–245.

Sartore, A., De Seta, F., Maso, G., Pregazi, R., Grimaldi, E. and Guaschino, S. (2004). The Effects of Mediolateral Episiotomy on Pelvic Floor Function After Vaginal Delivery. *Obstetrics & Gynecology* 103(4), 669–673.

Savage, W. (1985). *A Savage Enquiry.* London: Virago Press.

Savage, W. (2007 (1985)). *Birth and Power: 'A Savage Enquiry' Revisited. An examination of freedom and control within the medical profession.* London: Middlesex University Press.

Short Report, (1980). *Second Report from the Social Services Committee, Perinatal and neonatal mortality.*(Session 1979/80, HC 663). London: HMSO. ISBN:0102976805.

Smith, J. (1999). Antenatal Classes and the Transition to Fatherhood: A Study of some Fathers. *MIDIRS—Midwifery Digest.* 9(3), 327–330.

Thacker, S. B., Stroup, D.F. and Peterson, H.B. (1995). Efficacy and Safety of Intrapartum Electronic Fetal Monitoring: An Update. *Obstetrics & Gynecology* 86 (4), Part 1.

Thacker, S. B., Stroup, D. and Chang, M. (2006). *Cochrane Database Syst Rev.* (3): CD000063.

Turner, B. S. (1987). *Medical Power and Social Knowledge.* London: Sage.

Turner, V. (1969). *The Ritual Process: Structure and Anti-Structure.* Ithaca: Cornell University Press.

UNICEF, (1994). UK Baby Friendly Hospitals Initiative. Maternity Best Practice Standards.www.unicef.org.

Van Gennep, A. (1909). *Rite de Passage: Étude systématique des rites de la porte et du seuil, de l'hospitalité, de l'adoption, de la grossesse et de l'accouchement, de la naissance, de l'enfance, de la puberté, de l'initiation, de l'ordination, du couronnement.* Paris: É. Nourry.

Viswanathan, M., Hartmann, K., Palmiery, R et al. (2005). *The Use of Episiotomy in Obstetrical Care: A Systematic Review.* Evidence Report/ Technology Assessment No112. Agency for Health Care Research and Quality, U.S. Department of Health and Human Services.

Wells, H., Huxley, J. and Wells G. (1937). *The Science of Life: A Summary of Contemporary Knowledge about Life and its Possibilities.* Volume VII: *How Animals Behave.* London: Cassell.

Williams, C. (2005). Framing the Fetus in Medical Work: Rituals and Practices. *Social Science and Medicine* 60(9), 2085–95.

Winterton Report (1992). House of Commons Health Select Committee. *Second Report on the Maternity Services.* Vol.1: *Report together with Appendices and the Proceedings of the Committee.* ISBN: 0102830924. Vol.2: *Minutes of Evidence.* ISBN:0102838925. Vol.3: *Appendices to the Minutes of Evidence.* London: HMSO ISBN: 0102897921

Yagel, S. and Valsky, D. (2008). From anatomy to function: the developing image of ultrasound evaluation. *Ultrasound in Obstetrics and Gynecology* 31(6), 615–617.

3

Are Doctors Still Improving Childbirth?

SUSAN BEWLEY & LIN FOO

A 39 year old with twins and two previous caesareans had a complication of placenta invading through the uterus. A large team of surgeons, anaesthetists, interventional radiologists, theatre assistants, midwives, high dependency unit and neonatal intensive care ensured safe delivery of her premature twins. The 14 litre haemorrhage was controlled with a hysterectomy and massive blood transfusion. The doctors saved her life but high maternal age, twins and previous caesareans are causes of abnormal placentation. There are diminishing rates of return despite rising rates of childbirth interventions: Does medical innovation and intervention eventually cause problems that other interventions are then required to solve?

I. INTRODUCTION

WOMEN HAVE GIVEN birth, and died alongside their babies, since a time before written records. Pregnancy and labour experiences have shifted with societal norms and maternity advancements. We thrive, reproduce (or not) and eventually die as part of a life cycle. Dawkins (1989) reflected on biogenesis – the principle that life only arises from pre-existing life. Provided an individual reproduces before death, genes are immortal. Hence a pure biological measure of successful childbirth is the number of children outliving us at our death. Natural selection honed our complex physiology; human suffering and wastage were discounted by evolution. Examining this in the context of primates, 'Mother Nature' eloquently describes the huge maternal resource investment into pregnancy, lactation and early child-rearing (Hrdy, 1999). Females inevitably make trade-offs between quality and quantity of offspring, and humans are distinguished by an extreme length of infant-dependency.

Doctors intervene to improve mother or child survival with minimal morbidity or mortality. Understandably, doctors fear natural birth, particularly at home, as they deal with fatal complications that require hospital facilities. They tend to dismiss iatrogenesis: adverse outcomes caused by medical intervention. This chapter explores whether doctors have improved, or continue to improve, childbirth outcomes, as well as exploring their rationale for action. Maternal mortality ratios (MMR) are used as the primary measure of obstetric value, and we highlight a recent trend of rising MMR in the developed world. Does this suggest a limit to medical benefit: perhaps doctors are no longer doing more good than harm?

II. MATERNAL MORTALITY RATIOS

The International Classification of Diseases, Injuries and Causes of Death defines maternal death as the death of a woman while pregnant or within 42 days of termination of pregnancy, from any cause related to or aggravated by the pregnancy or its management but not from accidental or incidental causes.

This encompasses women of all gestational ages or outcome of pregnancy that presumably would have lived if not pregnant. The international definition of Maternal Mortality Ratio (MMR) is the number of direct and indirect deaths per 100,000 live births (see Table 1). The UK examines deaths up to a year (including late deaths), and has the advantage of live and stillbirth records. Hence, national data define MMR as the number of direct and indirect deaths per 100,000 maternities.

There is no standard measurement of maternal deaths globally. Compounding factors include lack of accurate records (an estimated two-thirds of the world's population reside where health services data are lacking or highly biased) and classification errors such as failing to record pregnancy status in adult female death. Half of excess calculated maternal deaths in the United States compared to Britain in the early 1900s were due to differences in classification or methods of data collection (Tandy, 1935). These historical misrepresentations make it difficult to compare regional trends.

(a) MMR Worldwide

MMR differs widely between developing and developed regions (450 vs. 9 maternal deaths/100,000 live births) with 14 countries having MMRs over 1000 (WHO, 2010). Globally, nearly 40% of childbearing women deliver without a trained attendant, and a significant minority receives little or no antenatal care. 85% of all maternal deaths occur in sub-Saharan Africa and South Asia, where more than half the births are not attended by trained personnel (Figure 1; Khan et al., 2006). Whilst basic care can be given to and by illiterate people using pictograms, doctors cannot work without an array of civic and medical

Table 1: Definitions of maternal death

Maternal death (CEMD)	Any death which occurs during or within one year of pregnancy, ectopic pregnancy or abortion which is directly or indirectly related to these conditions
Direct maternal death	A death resulting from obstetric complications of the pregnancy state (pregnancy, labour and puerperium), from interventions, omissions, incorrect treatment, or from a chain of events resulting from any of the above
Indirect maternal death	A death that resulted from previously existing disease, or disease that developed during pregnancy and which was not due to direct obstetric causes, but which was aggravated by the physiological affects of pregnancy. These include cases of self harm as a consequence of postnatal depression
Fortuitous (coincidental)	A death that occurs from unrelated causes which happen to occur in the pregnancy or puerperium, *ie* some malignancies, domestic violence, road traffic accidents, etc. They are also important causes of death from the aspect of wider public health
Late death	A death that occurs between 42 days and one year after abortion, miscarriage or delivery that is due to direct or indirect maternal causes. Late fortuitous deaths can sometimes also be important

Source: International Classification of Diseases (ICD code 9)
World Health Organisation/ Eurostat definition for comparative purposes:
A maternal death is defined as the death of a woman while pregnant or within 42 days of termination of pregnancy, irrespective of the duration and site of the pregnancy, from any cause related to or aggravated by the pregnancy or its management but not from accidental or incidental causes.

resources, of which transport systems are key. Standards of care cannot be improved without monitoring, and a Lancet series (Setel et al., 2007) on the basic human right of birth and death registration highlighted the lack of such infrastructure in some countries.

Many resource-poor countries suffer emigration of skilled medical, nursing and midwifery personnel that distorts the accountability between doctors and improvements in childbirth: would the changing rates observed in many countries be better or worse but for medical emigration? It is unclear who takes credit for improvements in global maternal mortality or is held responsible for enormous variations. In 2000, the UN pledged to cut 75% of maternal deaths by 2015 (Millennium Goal 5, MDG5). Ten years on, the Secretary-General reports that MDG5 is the farthest off target; MMR remains an indicator of the rich-poor divide, both between and within regions (Ban, 2010). The UN report

Figure 1: Maternal deaths worldwide

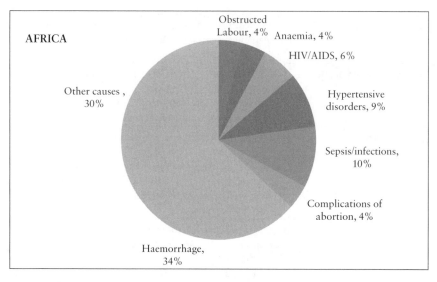

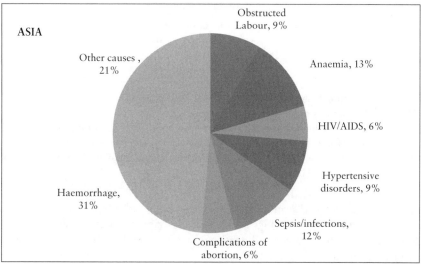

Reprinted from The Lancet, Vol 367, Khan KS et al., *WHO Analysis of Causes of Maternal Death*, p. 106, Copyright (2006), with permission from Elsevier.

Giving Birth Safely is largely a Privilege of the Rich highlighted the fact that 99% of the estimated 536,000 annual maternal deaths occurs in developing countries (UN, 2009). A recent publication (Hogan et al., 2010) reported an MMR yearly decline of 1.3%, whereas a 2.5% drop is needed to meet MDG5 target. It is postulated that MMR decline could have reached 2.2% without HIV.

(b) Historical MMR in the UK

MMR is useful for surveillance and benchmarking, and for looking at the history of obstetrics. The dramatic early 20th century decline in UK MMR (Figure 2)

Figure 2: Maternal Mortality in England and Wales 1847-2002

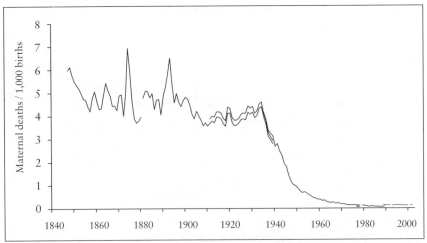

Reproduced from Why Mothers Die (2000-2002), Alison Macfarlane, 'Confidential Enquiries into Maternal Deaths: developments & trends from 1952 onwards', p. 297.

reveals the hidden and often unappreciated continuing medical contribution to low UK mortality today. MMR in the developing world today is reminiscent of UK MMR in the 1920s. Historic classification of UK maternal deaths documents the main causes in the early 1900s as infection, toxaemia and haemorrhage (similar to developing countries today). It is widely accepted that UK MMR fell due to: the introduction of sulphonamides and penicillin; a decline in alpha-haemolytic streptococcus virulence; the introduction of ergometrine; blood transfusions and flying obstetric squads for obstetric haemorrhage; better care and co-operation between obstetricians and midwives as well as improvements in obstetric education (Loudon, 2001).

(c) Recent MMR in UK and Resource-rich Countries

Presently, UK mothers die in childbirth for different reasons. The latest Confidential Enquiry into Maternal Death for 2003–05 (CEMACH, 2007) records cardiac disease as the leading cause overall (48 cases), with the main killers of the past – infection (eg HIV, TB) and haemorrhage causing 16 and 14 deaths respectively. UK MMR has not decreased since the 1980s, but has increased slightly (Figure 3). Indirect deaths (mainly underlying medical and psychiatric causes) have overtaken direct deaths. Doctors believe there is stricter governance on invasive procedures, more rational practice based on scientific evidence, as well as advocacy towards patient power and choice. Developing countries are encouraged to model their women's health policies on the UK as a gold-standard of maternity care (Drife, 2002).

Figure 3: UK Maternal mortality rate in last 21 years

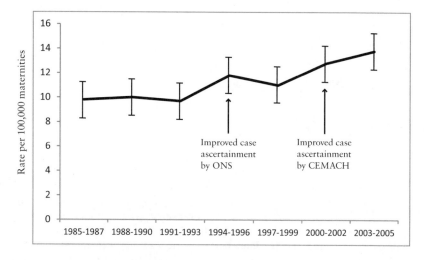

Reproduced from Saving Mother's Lives (2003-2005), Gwyneth Lewis and Alison Macfarlane, 'Which mothers died, and why', p. 22 (2007) with the permission of the Centre for Maternal and Child Enquiries.

The continuing slow rise in MMR might suggest a retreat in the battle against maternal death, and the UK is not alone. Maternal mortality in the USA in 1950 was 83.3 deaths/100,000 live births, which had fallen ten-fold by 1990 to 8.2, but by 2005 was 15.1. The National Centre for Health Statistics suggests the 84% rise over 15 years (1990–2005) (NCHS, 2007) is due to methodological changes in reporting and data processing. A TV news report refers to a forthcoming Californian publication about a tripling of MMR in a decade (Johnson, 2010). A rise in maternal mortality in the Netherlands is explained partly by ascertainment (Schutte et al., 2009). Hogan (Hogan et al., 2010) reported rises in MMR in the US, Denmark, Austria, Canada and Norway, although cautioned that it might be due to better reporting.

III. THE DOCTOR'S ROLE IN CHILDBIRTH

Doctors are a product of human intelligence. Obstetrics is a surgical specialty dealing with the care of pregnant and postpartum women (from the Latin *obstare* 'to stand by'). Medical professions, particularly obstetrics, anaesthesia and neonatology, are justified on the basis that they avoid, or minimise, maternal and child death and damage. Historical 'proof' of their value was the fall in MMR, though other outcome measures exist (eg fertility control or infertility treatment, perinatal mortality and morbidity, life expectancy and long-term wellbeing). All women need support in labour (preferably a trained attendant), but only a minority need doctors. UK services rely on midwives to ensure most babies are delivered safely with minimal intervention. As a limited resource, doctors should, in theory, only become involved in risky births when normal boundaries are crossed or management exceeds midwifery competencies.

In examining the doctor's role in childbirth, we should consider the biological purpose and the social role of medicine. Birth means much more than mere biogenesis, or genetic heritage. It is a personal experience for all involved. Many women view it as a rite of passage or even a ritual they experience in order to be labelled a 'mother' (Freedman, this volume).

The medical profession has been accused of 'hijacking' the triumph of birth – the vogue being a 'medicalised' as opposed to a 'natural' birth. The majority of women in the developed world deliver in hospitals surrounded by clinicians and technology, and fewer consider it a natural physiological process. The new notions of 'choice' and 'control' (Cumberlege, 1993) are somewhat contradictory to usual understandings of physiology. Doctors are seen as advocating, or being requested to provide, interventions that may be unnecessary, resulting in medical over-management with detrimental effects. Unfortunately, this view is aggravated by indictments that obstetricians intervene for personal gain, whether monetary (eg private practice) or pride.

(a) Probabilities Rather than Certainties

How do doctors work? Essentially, medical expertise is the ability to diagnose from a list of possibilities, achieved by considering multiple sources of information (symptom history, examination findings, test results including the 'test of time'), followed by the formulation of a likely prognosis and plan. The accuracy is re-appraised continuously based on emerging findings, ideally with time periodicity dependent on the degree of illness. All judgments have a degree of uncertainty. Screening or diagnostic tests have sensitivities and specificities that are less than 100% though these concepts are not well understood by all doctors or the lay public. Positive and negative predictive values change with the prevalence of disease in a population. Thus, applying a medical lens to whole populations inevitably leads to over-diagnosis (too many false positives). This is an explanation for some current disillusionment with screening programmes. Giving all women a treatment that is not required will result in lesser benefits and increasing side effects, compared with focusing treatment on the relevant sick population.

Applied to obstetrics, there should be no expectation of 100% diagnostic and therapeutic accuracy. There exists a trade-off between chance of benefit and risk, both at an individual and population level. 'Number needed to treat' (NNT) is one way of expressing this trade-off. For example, 100 elective caesarean sections (CS) are needed to avoid one dead or immediately seriously damaged breech baby compared with labour and vaginal delivery (Hofmeyr and Hannah, 2003; Hannah et al., 2004). Many women, midwives and obstetricians would think this 1% risk justifies elective CS despite a 30% increase in maternal mortality and morbidity. Unfortunately, we do not know which breech babies could have been delivered safely, nor which CSs were unnecessary. As vaginal breech delivery disappears, maternal deaths associated with breech elective CS are rising (Schutte et al., 2007). Is the pendulum swinging too far? Harm may be caused in pursuit of absolute safety.

IV. THE LAW OF DIMINISHING RETURNS

We propose that medical intervention is subject to the law of diminishing returns (see Figure 4). This established economic concept asserts that if one factor of

Figure 4: The law of diminishing returns

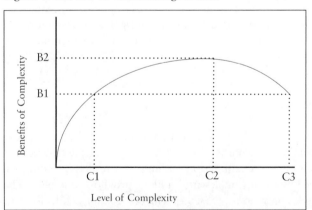

Reprinted from Joseph A. Tainter, The Collapse of Complex Societies (1988), with permission from Cambridge University Press.

production (eg financial investment in maternity services, number of doctors or CS rate) is increased while other factors (eg numbers of women giving birth) are held constant, the resulting increase in output (eg lives saved) will rise rapidly, level-off and then decline. Initially, the effort required to save lives or diminish suffering is low (C1) but becomes increasingly costly (C2). Eventually any further efforts actually cost more than the returns (C3) — a negative marginal return. The 'law of diminishing returns' in medicine translates to the risks of an intervention overtaking the benefits as the threshold for application falls. Consequently, instead of doing 'more of the same', innovation is required to continue to provide a positive return.

V. MEDICAL INTERVENTION IN CHILDBIRTH

We now explore why and to what extent doctors intervene in childbirth, touching on several factors including obstetric culture, patient's wishes, and personal boundaries for a 'safe, normal' birth.

How do women, midwives and doctors define a 'normal' birth (Figure 5), when this has so many dictionary meanings? As illustrated in Figure 6, many more women suffer morbidity than die – death constituting the 'tip of the iceberg'. Doctors aim to stop women climbing the iceberg and to return them to normal health or lesser morbidity categories. Three women might lose a life-threatening amount of blood after birth: one dies without help (eg an anaemic unattended woman without access to care), another dies despite the availability of intervention (eg Jehovah's witness refusing blood transfusion), whereas a third recovers with treatment. Different trajectories could be drawn from prior risk categories depending on professional skill mix or obstetrician's and midwives' personal or professional cut-offs for thresholds.

Cut-offs are necessary in health systems to classify primary, secondary and tertiary centre health care needs. It is sensible to keep normal women under primary healthcare teams while well, and only refer patients with symptoms or signs to secondary care, reserving the most challenging cases for specialist consultants and tertiary centre services. This ensures overall best outcomes, economy of resources, and most patients avoid unnecessary intervention from 'over-specialised' services. As illustrated in the satiric story 'The Gatekeeper and the Wizard' (Mathers and Hodgkin, 1989), primary care gatekeepers work best in populations with low prevalence of disease and high specificity tests. Specialists work best with high prevalence populations and high sensitivity tests. Specialists are good at picking out what is wrong if there is truly something abnormal (high positive predictive value), but not so good at picking out patients that are not ill (low negative predictive value for 'normality'). The benefit:harm ratio of doctors is better with the sick than the 'worried well'.

Figure 5: What does normal mean with respect to birth?

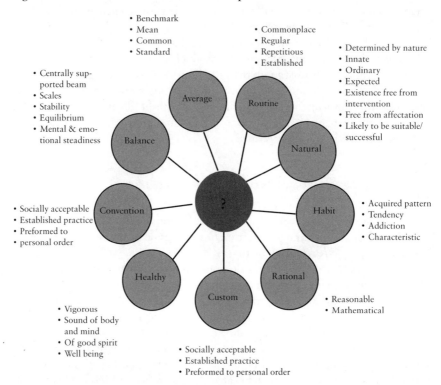

Drawn from an original idea of Ms Christina McKenzie with thanks.

Figure 6: The 'iceberg' of maternal death and morbidity

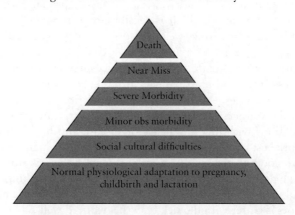

Different cut-offs can be used to define primary, secondary or tertiary boundaries where referrals can be made to doctors or other interventions applied.

(a) Obstetric Culture

Birth has never been safer, yet many obstetricians consider that 'no birth is safe except in retrospect' with its connotations; firstly, that childbirth is a dangerous time for mother and baby alike, and secondly, that no one could guarantee a 'safe' birth until afterwards – as exemplified by a quote from a leading Canadian practitioner, 'Nature is a bad obstetrician' (Wagner, 2000). Midwives, conversely, emphasise the normal physiological processes of pregnancy, childbirth and early mothering responses and draw attention to the harms of injudicious interference, centering their practices on a confidence in the ability of women's bodies to give birth, the art of 'doing nothing' skillfully and 'watchful waiting' (Cragin and Kennedy, 2006). 'Normal' and 'abnormal' are dichotomies used by the competing professions, whereas 'optimal birth' is a more recent and potentially unifying paradigm (Downe, 2008; Donna, 2010).

(b) Leaving Birth Alone, or to Midwives

A recent Cochrane review of 11 trials involving 12,276 randomised women shows that midwife-led care is successful (Hatem et al., 2008). Women with midwife-led care were 8 times more likely to be attended at birth by a known midwife; 21% less likely to lose their baby before 24 weeks; 9% less likely to have regional analgesia; 14% less likely to have instrumental birth; 18% less likely to have an episiotomy and significantly more likely to have a spontaneous vaginal birth, initiate breastfeeding, and feel in control during childbirth. The authors concluded that midwifery-led care confers benefits for pregnant women and should be recommended.

(c) Birth Setting

Doctors disdain home birth, as treatment may be delayed or compromised by out-of-hospital settings (eg obstructed labour, eclampsia, haemorrhage). However, they tend to ignore or dismiss iatrogenesis (eg poor and fragmented communications between hospital staff, high induction and CS rates, hospital acquired infections, and drug complications). The difference between planned and unplanned out-of-hospital settings bedevils methodological analysis, and clearly transport times factor into births that are far-away from hospital facilities. The acrimonious disputes about facts and the safety of home birth (outlined by the National Institute for Health and Clinical Excellence, NICE, 2007) remains a turf-war and few obstetricians are well-versed or trained to support home births.

(d) Overuse of Medical Interventions

Historically, increased MMR was strongly associated with enthusiastic surgical interference in normal labour. At the end of the 19th century, obstetrics formed a major part of general practice. A busy GP would often apply forceps rather than wait for normal delivery. In response to a plea in the British Medical Journal (1906) for conservatism, several GPs attacked elaborate aseptic precautions as unnecessary, and normal delivery as impossible, for 'civilised' women. One wrote 'I use chloroform and the forceps in every possible case, and have done so for many years' (Mears, 1906). The attitude of unnecessary intervention was one of the reasons MMR in Britain in 1935 was the same as at the beginning of Queen Victoria's reign. Across the Atlantic, a 1920s American obstetrician advocated instrumental delivery and anaesthetising all women in late labour in his paper *The prophylactic forceps operation* (DeLee, 1920).

Why would doctors choose excessive rather than reasonable intervention? Reasons vary from perceived 'safe practice' to fear of litigation or personal gain. Some evidence for the former comes from a widely misquoted survey of UK obstetricians, in which a minority was identified as choosing an elective CS in preference to vaginal delivery even in normal circumstances (Al-Mufti et al., 1997), despite UK data showing that an elective CS presents a 2.84-fold risk of maternal death compared to a vaginal delivery (Hall and Bewley, 1999). Death is so rare that it is unlikely to be decisive, but all other morbidities rise in parallel (eg intensive care admission, use of blood transfusion, length of stay, readmissions etc.). The belief that CS is safer could also stem from 'defensive obstetrics', largely influenced by the after-effects of litigation. One survey shows that 82% of physicians opted for CS to avoid negligence claims (Birchard, 1999). Performing a CS takes the risk away from the doctor and imposes it on the mother and baby (Wagner, 2000). After things go wrong doctors are more commonly criticised for doing too little than too much. Hence, some perform unnecessary interventions rather than leave matters alone.

(e) Rising Harm from Rising Caesarean Section Rate

An extensive literature recognises the over-promotion of CS. As with any other major abdominal surgery, CS carries the risk of bleeding, anaesthetic reactions, damage to organs (eg urinary bladder, accidental extension of uterine incision) and infection (20% of women develop pyrexia after CS, primarily due to iatrogenic infections (Wagner, 2000)). There is no evidence that a national CS rate over 7% saves lives (Enkin et al., 1995), but the optimal rate quoted by the World Health Organisation is 10–15% (WHO, 1985). There are many countries where CS rates are even higher. Taking 15% as a medically justified rate, Belizan et al.,(1999) calculated that over 850,000 unnecessary CSs were being performed in Latin America. A recent Lancet publication reports China's CS rate at a staggering 46% (Lumbiganon et al., 2010), thought to be due to a mixture of social, medical and institutional factors (Sufang et al., 2007). Up to 50% of the CSs were requested by mothers, but doctors still have to agree to operate, so are still instrumentally the 'cause' of the recent trend. These interventions are a burden to health systems with limited economic resources, and provide unnecessary risks to women and neonates. In a study using WHO global survey data (Villar et al., 2006), rates of CS (after adjustment for risk factors) were positively associated with post-partum antibiotic treatment and severe maternal mortality and morbidity, indicating that high CS rates do not necessarily deliver better care.

(f) Maternal Choice

Sometimes maternal-doctor conflict exists, whereby a woman does not agree or comply with advice. At a trivial level, this might be a woman not taking iron tablets or attending for scans. A more serious refusal would be the life-saving blood transfusion for the woman suffering massive haemorrhage or the hydropic fetus (in-utero cardiac failure sometimes caused by anaemia). Whilst obstetricians may feel entitled to use heavy-duty moral pressure to persuade pregnant women to undergo treatment, they cannot act against refusal in a woman deemed competent as this would constitute assault.

It is quite another matter when doctors act with maternal consent and yet cause avoidable harm. Surely women are entitled to believe that 'if my [trusted] professional is willing to act this way, it must be for my benefit, otherwise it would not be contemplated?'. It is not possible to pass all responsibility onto patients whilst 'first of all, do no harm' remains a central professional tenet (GMC, 2006). Stark choices about positive and negative 'rights' are enacted when women desire multiple embryo transfer causing riskier pregnancies. Should professional concern extend beyond the immediate intervention? There are competing issues: the risk of complications from multiple pregnancy in a desperate woman with significant medical conditions versus conforming to her wishes when she feels it is her body, her embryos and her choice.

Although doctors and patients weigh up actions by examining all possible positive and negative outcomes, they are rarely utilitarians. It is not a question of adding and subtracting percentage risks of very different outcomes that either occur or not. Doctors, even with the best intentions, can be unaware of their ability to balance good versus harm.

(g) Payment

Patient choice and demands may be best examined within private practices where patients might be likelier to receive what they request. In Southern Brazil, more than half of private sector patients 'choose' CS. Operation rates are directly related to the woman's income, and inversely related to her degree of risk (Barros et al., 1986). This finding could suggest that women choose CS when they can afford it, rather than when it is needed. However, other anthropological studies show that doctors working in several institutions subtly influence patients' requests, fitting in with their schedules and maximising earning capacity (Murray, 2001).

(h) Fear

One common explanation for patients choosing CS is fear of childbirth. Indeed, it may be rational to fear all forms of childbirth (Bewley and Cockburn, 2002), but possible to overcome this. In a study of women with a severe fear of childbirth, 62% who initially chose CS because of their phobias converted to a vaginal delivery after therapeutic intervention with a senior midwife and cognitive behaviour therapy (Saisto et al., 2001). This outcome demonstrates how patient choice can be influenced by provision of information and counselling. However the situation equally can be manipulated if obstetricians want women to 'choose' CS. Obstetricians too may be fearful, which is understandable if inexperienced or poorly trained. Doctors without faith in women's capacity to deliver normally will more obligingly assent to CS than home birth 'choices'. Their belief that CS may be 'safer' can be reflected in the way they counsel women. In a post-natal study in Chile, 70% of women surveyed in a private clinic had a CS, but only 18% of them 'wanted' it (Murray, 2000).

(i) Pain

Has the innovation of effective pain relief made pain less bearable? Women's perception of labour pain rates highly on scoring systems, comparable with amputation (Melzack, 1984). A woman's behaviour when in pain is influenced by her personal and cultural values (Melzack, 1973). Some view labour as an opportunity to demonstrate feminine strength and stoicism, while others tap into all avenues of medical therapy to ensure pain is minimised as much as possible. Many different meanings associated with pain, including those of resilience, overcoming and triumph, may be denied to women who do not experience 'normal' birth. With these unpredictable factors, it is understandably difficult to gauge individual pain levels: doctors are influenced by their own pre-conceptions of pain thresholds and management.

Midwifery authors have questioned standard notions about pain, especially those held by doctors and obstetric anaesthetists (who feel duty-bound to relieve pain). Regional analgesia undoubtedly reduces pain effectively, although there is a 5% chance of failure. Its use increases fetal malposition (19% vs. 4% without epidural; Lieberman et al., 1996) and instrumental delivery with forceps or ventouse (Anim-Somuah, 2005). The use of general anaesthesia in emergency deliveries has diminished, but the rate of CS continues to rise, as if the increasing imme-diate safety of an operation justified the lowering of the threshold for its indica-tion. An analysis of National Sentinel CS Audit data showed that 1 in 29 women in the UK still deliver their babies while unconscious (O'Sullivan, 2003), not great-ly different from the 1950s. Anaesthetic deaths continue to appear in the CEMD.

A 'menu' approach to pain relief may set up an expectation of use. The Royal College of Obstetricians and Gynaecologists (MacLean, 2001) and NICE (NICE, 2007) have recommended that clinicians should explore their own distress at witnessing labour and women in pain, and involve themselves in the 'working with pain framework'.

VI. MMR & DECLINING MATERNAL HEALTH

As demonstrated, a host of factors influence how and why doctors intervene in childbirth. We now consider our primary measure, MMR, to determine whether they are still improving childbirth outcomes. Our starting point is that, despite medical advancements in the last two decades, there is no decline in UK MMR, rather a static or rising trend (Figure 3).

The population of UK childbearing mothers is changing in terms of age, ethnicity, multiple pregnancies, co-morbidities and increasing inequalities. These factors are all well known drivers of MMR, and maternity services need greater productivity to keep up with the new challenges, whether of total numbers of patients, co-morbidities or expectations. Health inequalities travel hand-in-hand with social inequalities: the Marmot Review noted that more needs to be done, not only within medicine, but across all 'social determinants of health' (Marmot, 2010).

Undoubtedly, improved methods of data collection contribute to any rise in MMR. However, the UK has had stringent and improving records of maternal death since the early 1950s, hence better ascertainment is unlikely to solely account for this increase. Similarly, whilst partly attributing the MMR rise to ascertainment, the Dutch maternal mortality study (Schutte et al., 2009) also cited rising maternal age, IVF, immigration, language barriers, rising CS rates, and co-morbidities as contributing factors.

(a) Ethnicity

The UK has a longstanding ethnic minority population and has recently experienced large-scale immigration. There are insufficient data on migration statistics for delivered women eg how long they had been in the UK, the circumstances under which they arrived, and links with previous and subsequent pregnancies. This creates a crucial gap in our understanding of maternal deaths, especially as the number of direct and indirect deaths of immigrant women increased (4 deaths in 1997–99, 36 in 2003–05). Examination of this sub-group revealed that a number of pregnant women or girls were not identified by health services until too late. One 14 year old Bangladeshi (brought in as a young bride) had her first contact when 6 months pregnant and 'too ill to have sex with her husband'. She spoke little or no English and died within days of tuberculosis (CEMACH, 2007). Her death illustrates how cultural and language barriers can obstruct healthcare input for vulnerable women and the trend of migration means that tropical diseases will feature more. Doctors and maternity services that are unable to keep up with changing population demands and disease spectra will certainly run into higher rates of maternal mortality and morbidity.

(b) Age

The 'changing face of motherhood' (Stuart, 2006) and ageing maternity population is shown in Figure 7. In the UK the average age of childbirth is increasing: over 15% of all maternities in 2003–2005 were in women aged 35–39 years (CEMACH, 2007) compared to 6% during the mid-1980s. Despite earlier menarche, effective contraception and legal abortion instrumentally raise the age of childbearing. The recent innovation of assisted conception does not help the majority of couples experiencing the rise in infertility, and contributes new risks (see chapters by Braude and by Daly, this volume).

The prevalence of most medical conditions increases with age. About one-quarter of pregnant women aged >45 years have a chronic medical condition

Figure 7: Demographic shift in maternal age of childbearing

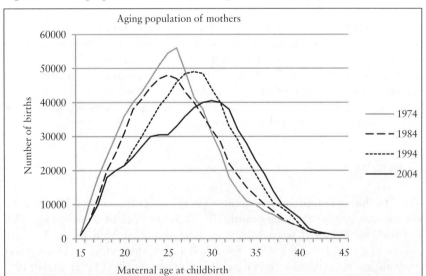

Source: Office of National Statistics

(Dildy et al., 1996). Indirect deaths arising from pre-existing medical conditions now outnumber direct deaths in the UK, underlining the contribution of physical or psychological co-morbidities on pregnancy outcome. Rising age probably contributes to cardiac disease becoming the leading cause of maternal death.

(c) Co-morbidities Increase with Age

Many studies link maternal age with increased co-morbidities (Table 2). A retrospective cohort study showed that the incidence of pre-eclampsia/toxaemia (PET) in women aged >40 is approximately doubled compared with that in women aged 20–29 (Vigil-De Gracia et al., 2004). PET is associated with fetal complications such as growth restriction and stillbirth. Maternal complications include cerebro-vascular accident, and death. There is a 2–5 fold increase in gestational diabetes in women aged >40 compared with women in their 20s (Dhanjal, 2009). Gestational diabetes is associated with higher chances of instrumental delivery and postpartum haemorrhage. Risks to the baby include growth restriction, congenital malformations and perinatal death. Obesity (Body Mass Index ≥30) has increased dramatically in developed countries over the past two decades, and USA maternal weights at booking rose by 20%

Table 2: Adverse effects of age on reproduction on four aspects of women's health

Gynaecological	Conception and implantation
Premature menopause	Reduced fertility
Sexually transmitted infections	Miscarriage and ectopic
Pelvic inflammatory disease	Chromosomal anomaly
Endometriosis	Birth defects
Fibroids	More multiples – natural and assisted
Cervical surgery	More IVF and worse outcomes
Other acquired medical problems	**Pregnancy outcomes**
Obesity	Increased stillbirth and neonatal death
Essential hypertension (including pregnancy-induced)	Malpresentation Prematurity
Diabetes (including gestational)	Pre-eclampsia
Heart disease	Intrauterine growth retardation
New diagnoses (eg cancer, lupus, antiphospholipid syndrome, liver, renal etc.)	Placenta praevia
Post surgery (eg cosmetic breast, hernia, varicose vein)	Venous thrombosis
	Caesarean section
	Morbidity and maternal death

From Nwandison, M. and Bewley, S.(2006) 'What is the right age to reproduce?' *Fetal Medicine and Maternal Review*, 17 (3), 185-204. © Cambridge Journals, reproduced with permission.

over a period of 20 years (Lu et al., 2001). The incidence of obesity increases significantly with age; in 2003, one third of UK women aged 35–54 years were overweight (Dhanjal, 2009). Maternal obesity is associated with hypertension, thromboembolism, cardiac disease, gestational diabetes and postpartum haemorrhage. Fetal risks from maternal obesity include stillbirth, macrosomia and neural tube defects.

The risk of fetal loss (stillbirths, ectopics, and miscarriages) follows a J-shaped curve if plotted against maternal age, sharply increasing after age 35 (Nybo Andersen et al., 2000). Even adjusting for confounding factors (pre-existing medical conditions, race, parity, BMI, education, marital status, previous adverse obstetric outcomes) and controlling for the use of assisted reproductive technology (ART), maternal age of ≥40 years is still an independent risk factor for gestational diabetes, placental abruption and praevia as well as perinatal mortality (Cleary-Goldman et al., 2005).

Maternal age is now also linked with nulliparity. In the UK, 20% of nulliparous women were found to be ≥40 (Gilbert et al., 1999). Maternal parity influences outcome: women in first pregnancies have different risks from those of the same age on their second or third pregnancies.

The law of diminishing returns predicts that marginal returns from a factor of production begin to progressively decrease as the factor is increased, in contrast to what might be expected (*ie* more input, more output). Despite increasing efforts, the worsening trends of MMR in the developed world could represent a 'marginal negative return'. Whether directly or indirectly, doctors are a factor in the production of this negative return. Developed countries may have passed the pinnacle of women's healthcare. By doing 'more of the same', the balance of needs vs. demands is upset. As a result, and almost inevitably, continuing as we are will result in doing more harm than good.

VII. WHY THE DEMOGRAPHIC SHIFT IN MATERNAL AGE?

In an ostensibly 'risk-averse' society, riskier pregnancy may be a paradoxical result of improved childbearing outcomes. Doctors, women's health services and national policies may drive the trend of older mothers. Women access better contraception, safer abortions, as well as family planning advice. These measures are all designed to avoid the dangers of excess and uncontrolled fertility, but inevitably result in women having babies at an older age, simply by providing some flexibility in the 'timing' of children.

Many women in the developed world need to work, pay off debt or seek a career or lifestyle geared towards acquiring independence and financial and social stability. Few can achieve this when young and many put off child-bearing until they are older and more settled, allowing them the time and freedom to pursue other aims. The interviews Daly undertook offer further interesting views on why women defer childbirth (see Daly, this volume).

In 2006–7, 76% of UK women ≤50 years were using at least one method of contraception (ONS, 2007) which reduces the number of pregnancies, especially at extreme reproductive ages, and allows women to have children when they are ready. Women receive mixed messages in the media rather than consistent information about contraception through their most fertile years. Confusing messages might lead them to be unperturbed until they later experience an inability to conceive, miscarriage, less healthy pregnancy or one of the serious complications that increases with age. Fertility declines as women age (Braude, this volume); 20% of conceptions in women ≥35 result in fetal loss (Nybo Andersen et al., 2000), rising to over half by the early 40s. As Daly elucidated, assisted reproductive technologies (ARTs) may provide false security (Daly, this volume). Women are shocked to realise the low success rates, perhaps being less well informed when planning their lives. IVF cannot compensate for delays in childbearing, and success depends on the number and quality of eggs obtained for fertilization. The age of the oocyte (egg) is the best outcome predictor; live birth rates decrease as the woman's age increases (30% for women <35, 15% for women >40 and <5% for women aged 43; HFEA, 2008).

Recent technological advances are oocyte and embryo freezing. Couples can choose to freeze embryos during their more fertile years for use at a later time. Live birth rates from frozen embryos are generally half that of fresh embryos, so logically couples wanting the best chances of childbearing would be better advised to proceed with pregnancy rather than store embryos and postpone childbearing. Oocyte freezing has the advantage that the woman does not have to have a partner. However, it is technically more difficult, and only a few hundred births have been reported worldwide, with no long-term outcomes. Even if a woman used her younger eggs, this cannot overcome the aged uterus, circulation and body.

Childlessness, intentional or not, is on the increase: 1 in 5 women born in 1963 are childless compared with 1 in 8 born in 1933 (ONS, 2009). Women should not be bullied into having children; some may simply not wish to have children and some may only desire them at a later age. Support for women who do want children has changed in terms of partner commitment, marriage stability, proximity of family, financial and work demands, ageing grandparents and neighbourly communities. Delayed childbearing might be a logical trade-off against these conflicting pressures.

VIII. POOR NEONATAL OUTCOMES

Although less obvious, there are suggestions that the law of diminishing returns operates for baby outcomes. For example, prematurity rates are rising, and the causes include many medical interventions (Muglia and Katz, 2010). Also, there is a loss of association between the perinatal mortality rate (PNMR) and higher CS rate (CSR) (Matthews et al., 2003).

In the USA between 1990 and 2006, there was a 20% rise in live preterm births, both spontaneous and iatrogenic (Muglia and Katz, 2010). Causes include maternal ageing, higher rates of twin conception, IVF, obesity, and cervical surgery (Shennan & Bewley, 2006). The rate of preterm CSs has increased from 33% to 50% over the past decade without a similar change in maternal risk profiles. This might indicate a lowered threshold for preterm CS (Muglia and Katz, 2010); doctors perhaps finding it easier to counsel women for a 'cautious' CS, rather than the possibility of 'watchful waiting' going awry.

A loss of association between PNMR and CSR was observed in Dublin (Figure 8; Matthews et al., 2003), where the fall in PNMR lessened as CSR increased beyond 15%. This is not an isolated finding: the WHO advocates national CSR of 10–15% as the balance-point between risk of harm from no or minimal intervention, and the risks of a caesarean. Many countries have higher rates and few national health agendas advocate cutting down on interventions. Governments seem keener to promise more optimal and modern medical practice, which the public translate as 'more is better'.

Figure 8: Evidence for diminishing returns for babies? Loss of association of perinatal mortality with higher CS rates

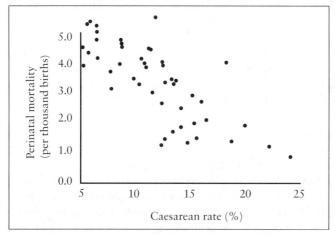

Adapted from Matthews et al. Rising caesarean section rates: a cause for concern? BJOG 1999; 319:1397–400.

With more CSs comes more neonatal iatrogenic harm, eg the increased risk of unexplained antenatal stillbirth after a previous CS (Smith et al., 2003). This risk may be attributable to a damaged uterus or abnormal placentation. There is well-known animal and human evidence of iatrogenic harm to babies who do not experience labour and vaginal delivery. Labour induces respiratory & metabolic adaptation, influences long term lung function and affects maternal behaviour and bonding. There is a neonatal argument for planned elective CS to be performed after the onset of labour especially for 'soft' indications (eg maternal wishes). Presently, few women are fully informed of the benefits of labour versus pre-labour CS.

Unfortunately, there still exists much ambiguity on long term outcomes in relation to all the choices and procedures around birth. Elective CS, cord clamping (thought to induce anaemia and mild hypoxia) and many other childbirth practices might have child development effects, which are presently unknown. It is too early and the issues are too complex to speculate on the population consequences of maternal ageing and the current increase in medical intervention on longer term outcomes for children and adult health.

IX. CONCLUSION

Although not responsible for global inequalities, and with notable exceptions, doctors have made slow progress in highlighting avoidable maternal death and improving childbirth worldwide. MMR in the developing world could be viewed as a structural problem: women are dying from acquired morbid states (eg infection), which could be combated were sufficient infrastructures in place (eg transport, antenatal support, emergency obstetric and blood transfusion services). The solutions seem simple: to follow established health models in countries that have dramatically reduced MMR. However, there are hurdles of political will, leadership, resources and economic instability. The HIV epidemic has contributed to maternal mortality, and universal access to anti-retrovirals by 2010 (declared at the Gleneagles G8 summit) is another as yet undelivered promise.

In the developed world, mothers rarely die of infection or haemorrhage. Here, doctors offer reproductive choices designed to increase lifespan and reduce suffering, yet these options have collateral damaging effects. We are witnessing a new era of infertility, riskier pregnancies and adverse obstetric outcomes. Medical techniques that gave women some reproductive control (*ie* contraception and safe abortion) have been followed by successful treatments for impaired reproduction, paradoxically leading to more demands for medical intervention. These new problems might be harder to solve, as there is no precedent medical model to guide us. High levels of complexity in developed countries make it increasingly difficult to deliver extra medical benefit.

If the law of diminishing returns does apply to maternal and perinatal health within complex societies, then fantastic innovation, rather then stagnation of attitudes and policies is needed to reverse the negative returns such as mortality. The use of antibiotics and blood transfusions previously transformed medicine: both revolutionary ideas for their time, they came at a period of great need with high national mortality rates. Conceivably a similar radical innovation is needed to maintain maternity care within a complex system which has gone too far. It is difficult to envisage this advancement, perhaps because the idea that in developed countries maternity services are worsening has not yet sunk in: hence we are not actively seeking solutions.

Certain suggestions could be made, the adoption of which might slow the decline of maternal health in resource-rich countries. Public health could do more to educate and promote general health, fitness, fertility, and the avoidance of co-morbidities that threaten pregnancy. The public should understand that excessive intervention is harmful, and that there is a time clock not only to bear children, but to do so safely. This resonates in the adage that maternity care starts pre-conception, with emphasis on optimising social, environmental and behavioural variables. 'Social policy is indivisible from health policy' (Marmot, 2010), and as the Marmot review indicated, social differences still perturb healthcare for women of lower social status, despite their residence in a developed country. Women need better control for sustainable life prospects (eg career, higher educational training). Greater flexibility within employment, training programmes, insurance, and mortgage policies could allow women to fulfill potential and achieve security, without having to trade off child-bearing.

Doctors are only part of a package that makes childbirth safe; yet they tend to discount iatrogenesis and the importance of primary maternity care. Medical education could be adapted for trainees to understand the midwifery curriculum and 'normal' birth outside of hospitals, and thereby feel more confident to support it. Governance for doctors should also do more to protect and promote minimal intervention; providing obstetricians with security in their decisions to 'leave pregnancy alone' (in optimal conditions), without being penalised for responsibly under-utilising the technology at their disposal.

It is important to educate doctors about the dangers of over-intervention and how prejudices, culture, personal beliefs or motivations might cause unnecessary harm. Their professional behaviour has great influence on outcomes, and they must skillfully guide patients around the fine lines of risk and benefit. They need expert evidence-based practice, tempered with self-reflection – even though this is not emphasised during their training, and perhaps experience is required to truly acknowledge the limits of medicine.

The complex physiology of pregnancy and childbirth cannot be changed. It is only by using a public health lens to look at the antecedents, associations and context of pregnancy and applying an evidence-base to maternity care systems that medicine can deliver improvements in outcomes.

REFERENCES

Al-Mufti, R., McCarthy, A. and Fisk, N. M. (1997). Survey of Obstetricians' Personal Preference and Discretionary Practice. *Eur J Obstet Gynecol Reprod Biol* 73, 1–4.

Ban, K. (2010). *Keeping the Promise: A Forward-looking review to promote an agreed action agenda to achieve the Millennium Development Goals by 2015*; Report of the Secretary-General, 64th Session, Agenda Item 48 and 114: United Nations.

Barros, F. C., Vaughan, J. P. and Victora, C. G. (1986). Why so Many Caesarean sections? The Need for a Further Policy Change in Brazil. *Health Policy Plan* 1, 19–29.

Belizan, J. M., Althabe, F., Barros, F. C. and Alexander, S. (1999). Rates and Implications of Caesarean Sections in Latin America: Ecological Study. *BMJ* 319, 1397–400.

Bewley, S. and Cockburn, J. (2002). Responding to fear of childbirth. *Lancet* 359, 2128–9.

Birchard, K. (1999). Defence Union Suggests New Approach to Handling Litigation Costs in Ireland. *Lancet* 354, 1710.

CEMACH. (2007). *Saving Mothers' Lives: Reviewing maternal deaths to make motherhood safer 2003–2005 (VIIth Report)*: Confidential Enquiry into Maternal and Child Health. London.

Cleary-Goldman, J., Malone, F. D., Vidaver, J., Ball, R. H., Nyberg, D. A., Comstock, C. H., Saade, G. R., Eddleman, K. A., Klugman, S., Dugoff, L. et al. (2005). Impact of Maternal Age on Obstetric Outcome. *Obstet Gynecol* 105, 983–90.

Cragin, L. and Kennedy, H. P. (2006). Linking Obstetric and Midwifery Practice with Optimal Outcomes. *J Obstet Gynecol Neonatal Nurs* 35, 779–85.

Cumberlege, J. (1993). Changing Childbirth (Cumberlege Report): Department of Health. London: HMSO.

DeLee, J. (1920). The Prophylactic Forceps Operation. *Am J Obstet Gynecol*, 1: 34–44.

Dhanjal, M. (2009). The Older Mother and Medical Disorders of Pregnancy. In *Reproductive Ageing*. Bewley S, Ledger W, Nikolaou D eds. pp. 367. London: RCOG Press.

Dildy, G. A., Jackson, G. M., Fowers, G. K., Oshiro, B. T., Varner, M. W. and Clark, S. L. (1996). Very Advanced Maternal Age: Pregnancy after Age 45. *Am J Obstet Gynecol* 175, 668–74.

Donna, S. (2010). *Optimal Birth – What, Why and How – A Reflective, Narrative Approach Based on Research Evidence* Chester: Fresh Heart Publishing.

Downe, S. (2008). *Normal Childbirth: Evidence and Debate*. London: Churchill Livingstone.

Drife, J. (2002). *Lessons from the Confidential Enquiry in the UK, in Maternal Morbidity and Mortality*. London: RCOG Press.

Enkin, M. W., Keirse, M. J., Renfrew, M. J. and Neilson, J. P. (1995). Effective Care in Pregnancy and Childbirth: A Synopsis. *Birth* 22, 101–10.

Gilbert, W. M., Nesbitt, T. S. and Danielsen, B. (1999). Childbearing beyond Age 40: Pregnancy Outcome in 24,032 Cases. *Obstet Gynecol* 93, 9–14.

GMC. (2006). Good Medical Practice: Duties of a Doctor. http://www.gmc-uk. org/guidance/good_medical_practice/duties_of_a_doctor.asp.

Hall, M. H. and Bewley, S. (1999). Maternal Mortality and Mode of Delivery. *Lancet* 354, 776.

Hannah, M. E., Whyte, H., Hannah, W. J., Hewson, S., Amankwah, K., Cheng, M., Gafni, A., Guselle, P., Helewa, M., Hodnett, E. D. et al. (2004). Maternal Outcomes at 2 Years after Planned Cesarean Section Versus Planned Vaginal Birth for Breech Presentation at Term: The International Randomized Term Breech Trial. *Am J Obstet Gynecol* 191, 917–27.

Hatem, M., Sandall, J., Devane, D., Soltani, H. and Gates, S. (2008). *Midwife-led versus other Models of Care for Childbearing Women*. Cochrane Database Syst Rev, CD004667.

HFEA. (2008). *A Long-term Analysis of the HFEA Register Data (1991–2006)*. Human Fertilisation and Embryology Authority. London.

Hofmeyr, G. J. and Hannah, M. E. (2003). *Planned Caesarean Section for Term Breech Delivery*. Cochrane Database Syst Rev, CD000166.

Hogan, M. C., Foreman, K. J., Naghavi, M., Ahn, S. Y., Wang, M., Makela, S. M., Lopez, A. D., Lozano, R. and Murray, C. J. (2010). Maternal Mortality for 181 Countries, 1980–2008: A Systematic Analysis of Progress towards Millennium Development Goal 5. *Lancet* 375, 1609–23.

Hrdy, S. (1999). *Mother Nature: A History of Mothers, Infants and Natural Selection*. New York: Pantheon.

Johnson, N. (2010). Chart: Tracking Maternal Mortality Rates; http:// californiawatch.org/health-and-welfare/chart-tracking-maternal-mortality-rates: May 2010.

Khan, K. S., Wojdyla, D., Say, L., Gulmezoglu, A. M. and Van Look, P. F. (2006). WHO Analysis of Causes of Maternal Death: A Systematic Review. *Lancet* 367, 1066–74.

Lieberman, E., Lang, J. M., Cohen, A., D'Agostino, R., Jr., Datta, S. and Frigoletto, F. D., Jr. (1996). Association of Epidural Analgesia with Cesarean Delivery in Nulliparas. *Obstet Gynecol* 88, 993–1000.

Lu, G. C., Rouse, D. J., DuBard, M., Cliver, S., Kimberlin, D. and Hauth, J. C. (2001). The Effect of the Increasing Prevalence of Maternal Obesity on Perinatal Morbidity. *American Journal of Obstetrics and Gynecology* 185, 845–849.

Lumbiganon, P., Laopaiboon, M., Gulmezoglu, A. M., Souza, J. P., Taneepanichskul, S., Ruyan, P., Attygalle, D. E., Shrestha, N., Mori, R., Nguyen, D. H. et al. (2010). Method of Delivery and Pregnancy Outcomes in Asia: the WHO Global Survey on Maternal and Perinatal Health 2007–08. *Lancet* 375, 490–9.

MacLean, A. S., RW. Thronton, S. (2001). *Pain in Obstetrics and Gynaecology*. London: RCOG Press.

Marmot, M. (2010). Fair Society, Healthy Lives – Marmot Review, http://www.marmot-review.org.uk/.

Mathers, N. and Hodgkin, P. (1989). The Gatekeeper and the Wizard: A Fairy Tale. *BMJ* 298, 172–4.

Matthews, T. G., Crowley, P., Chong, A., McKenna, P., McGarvey, C. and O'Regan, M. (2003). Rising Caesarean Section Rates: A Cause for Concern? *BJOG*. 110, 346–9.

Mears, F. C. (1906) Midwifery of the Present Day *BMJ*. 1,773.

Melzack, R. (1973). *The Puzzle of Pain*. Harmondsworth, U.K: Penguin Books.

—— (1984). The Myth of Painless Childbirth (the John J. Bonica lecture). *Pain* 19, 321–37.

Muglia, L. J. and Katz, M. (2010). The Enigma of Spontaneous Preterm Birth. *N Engl J Med* 362, 529–35.

Murray, S. F. (2000). Relation between Private Health Insurance and High Rates of Caesarean Eection in Chile: Qualitative and Quantitative Study. *BMJ* 321, 1501–5.

NCHS. (2007). *Trends in the Health of the Americans*. – National Centre for Health Statistics, Hyattsville, United States.

NICE. (2007). Intrapartum Care: Management and Delivery of Care to Women in Labour; http://www.nice.org.uk/CG55.

Nybo Andersen, A. M., Wohlfahrt, J., Christens, P., Olsen, J. and Melbye, M. (2000). Maternal Age and Fetal Loss: Population Based Register Linkage Study. *BMJ* 320, 1708–12.

O'Sullivan, G., Bewley, S. (2003). Rapid Response: Unconscious Birth; http://www.bmj.com/cgi/eletters/327/7415/587. *British Medical Journal* 327, 587.

ONS. (2007). *Contraception and Sexual Health 2006/7; Omnibus Survey Report no.33,*.Office of National Statistics (United Kingdom).

—— (2009). *Rise in UK Fertility Continues* (Office for National Statistics, United Kingdom). http://www.statistics.gov.uk/cci/nugget.asp?ID=951.

Saisto, T., Salmela-Aro, K., Nurmi, J. E., Kononen, T. and Halmesmaki, E. (2001). A Randomized Controlled Trial of Intervention in Fear of Childbirth. *Obstet Gynecol* 98, 820–6.

Schutte, J. M., Steegers, E. A., Santema, J. G., Schuitemaker, N. W. and van Roosmalen, J. (2007). Maternal Deaths after Elective Cesarean Section for Breech Presentation in the Netherlands. *Acta Obstet Gynecol Scand* 86, 240–3.

Schutte, J. M., Steegers, E. A., Schuitemaker, N. W., Santema, J. G., de Boer, K., Pel, M., Vermeulen, G., Visser, W. and van Roosmalen, J. (2009). Rise in Maternal Mortality in the Netherlands. *BJOG* 117, 399–406.

Setel, P. W., Macfarlane, S. B., Szreter, S., Mikkelsen, L., Jha, P., Stout, S. and Abouzahr, C. (2007). A Scandal of Invisibility: Making Everyone Count by Counting Everyone. *Lancet* 370, 1569–1577.

Smith, G. C., Pell, J. P. and Dobbie, R. (2003). Caesarean Section and Risk of Unexplained Stillbirth in Subsequent Pregnancy. *Lancet* **362**, 1779–84.

Stuart, J. (2006). The Changing Face of Motherhood. *The Independent*, 2nd December, London.

Sufang, G., Padmadas, S., Fengmin, Z., Brown, J.J. and Stones, R.W. (2007). Delivery Settings and Caesarean Section Rates in China. *Bulletin of the WHO*. **85(10)**, 733–820.

UN. (2009). United Nations Publications – Giving Birth Safely is a Privilege of the Rich; http://findarticles.com/p/articles/mi_m1309/is_1-2_46/ai_n42723732/.

Vigil-De Gracia, P., Montufar-Rueda, C. and Smith, A. (2004). Pregnancy and Severe Chronic Hypertension: Maternal Outcome. *Hypertens Pregnancy* **23**, 285–93.

Villar, J., Valladares, E., Wojdyla, D., Zavaleta, N., Carroli, G., Velazco, A., Shah, A., Campodonico, L., Bataglia, V., Faundes, A. et al. (2006). Caesarean Delivery Rates and Pregnancy Outcomes: The 2005 WHO Global Survey on Maternal and Perinatal Health in Latin America. *Lancet* **367**, 1819–29.

Wagner, M. (2000). Choosing Caesarean Section. *Lancet* **356**, 1677–80.

WHO. (1985). Appropriate Technology for Birth. *Lancet* ii, 436–37.

—— (2010). http://www.who.int/making_pregnancy_safer/topics/maternal_mortality/en/index.html: World Health Organisation.

4

The Midwife-Mother Relationship[1]

MAVIS KIRKHAM

B IRTH IS ABOUT relationships, it is also the entry to society and the rites and management of that entry demonstrate our values as a society. This chapter aims to explore firstly the potential of the midwife-mother relationship and secondly, the tensions between relationships around birth and our organisations, which embody values of hierarchy, efficiency, technology and expert authority.

There seem to be two different views on the purpose of the midwife-mother relationship, springing from the very different discourses of organisations and of women. There are considerable tensions between the rites which organisations adopt to manage risk or finance and the rights of women to a birth setting where they can feel calm and secure.

From the organisational viewpoint, the midwife-mother relationship is the medium through which the service is provided. The service works best where relationships work well, but organisational aims assume and do not seek to foster relationships, rather they focus on measurable outcomes which are generalised to cover all service users and all eventualities. There is, therefore a real tension between the crafting of systems for healthcare organisations and the crafting of care for individuals within those systems (Sennet, 2008).

(a) With Woman: Affirmation and Safety

Women want midwives who listen to their concerns as well as monitoring their clinical condition (Edwards, 2005; Kirkham and Stapleton, 2001), thus focusing on their social and personal situation as well as their physiology. This has been shown by many studies, whether the women are at high (Berg,

---

[1] This chapter is developed from Chapters 1 & 14 in Kirkham M. (ed) *The Midwife-Mother Relationship*, 2nd Edition with permission of the publishers Palgrave Macmillan.

2010) or low (Edwards, 2005) obstetric risk, poor and disadvantaged (Gaudion and Homeyard, 2010), from ethnic minorities (eg Bharj and Chesney, 2010) or midwives themselves (Kirkham et al., 2006). Being heard validates and affirms us, showing respect which is the first step towards trust. When the midwife shows trust in the woman and her ability to birth her baby, this has a profound impact on the woman and her self confidence. 'Trust invites reciprocal trust: there are virtuous spirals' (O'Neill, 2002 p. 25), networks of trust which can be developed over the course of a pregnancy and career.

Women also want to feel safe at a time of vulnerability. Their definition of safety around birth is likely to be much wider than a clinical definition both in time and in embracing the emotional and physical health of their whole family (Edwards, 2005). Midwives can hold safe space in which women can forge relationships and can birth their babies. This can start with friendship building in antenatal groups where women learn from and grow to support each other (Leap, 2010). It becomes vitally important in labour where the woman needs to feel safe enough to 'enter an altered state of consciousness' in which the mind can let go and allow the body to be in control (Anderson, 2010).

Midwives often work hard to establish relationships with women they have not met before and are unlikely to meet again and to help them to feel safe. Midwives put varying degrees of 'emotion work' (Hunter and Deery, 2009) into such relationships, which women see as making a real difference to them. Women have described midwives as 'caring and empowering' as opposed to 'uncaring and discouraging' (Halldorsdottir and Karsldottir, 1996) or 'warm professional' versus 'cold professional' (McCrea and Crute, 1991).

In a busy service with fragmented care it is difficult, frustrating and emotionally draining to be consistently caring, empowering and warm. Where there is continuity of care much more can be achieved: time can be spent building trust during the pregnancy so that, when the woman comes to labour midwife and mother can calmly focus on the labour.

> There was a kind of silence in the relationship, a stillness which was very important. And we'd done all the talking in the build up. So the talking was done. I felt confident that she [midwife] knew where I was coming from and vice versa. It was like we'd done all our dress rehearsal – what if ... what if ... And on the day there was nothing left to say really. So it just felt very calm, and I think that was the most important thing (Edwards, 2010)

Such calm is 'aspired to by women and birth partners' (Huber and Sandall, 2009; p. 613) and is associated with greater satisfaction with birth.

> Relational continuity is perfectly placed to create calm as it tends to foster a sense of familiarity and enables all parties to get to know what to expect from one another. It also facilitates calm because conflicting advice is minimised and midwives are able to build their confidence and wisdom by learning from the repercussions of their own actions.

The calm behaviour of midwives also helps, as much as their words, to convince women that their experience is normal and this prevents anxiety and panic and helps women to cope.

(b) Social Outcomes

Birth is a classic rite of passage (Kirkham, 2007; Van Gennep, 1960) and trust is essential in the liminal phase of massive physical and social change, which is inevitably a time of great vulnerability. The creation of 'virtuous spirals' of trust in the face of vulnerability should therefore be of primary importance to those who attend women through these rites. Such spirals, networks (Gilligan, 1982) or webs of support and trust take time to spin.

When midwives can develop relationships with women and listen to them they engage with wider relationships (Kirkham, 2010). Continuing reciprocal relationships nurture mother and midwife (McCourt and Stevens, 2009). Support networks are established and extended and power moves from the professional towards the mother as she develops knowledge and confidence in her ability to birth and to mother her baby. The development of sustaining relationships around birth, rather than short term coping strategies (Kirkham, 2007), supports and models new dimensions of reciprocal support for mothers and midwives. It also offers more sustainable ways of living our professional and family lives.

Where women feel they were supported to fully engage with their childbearing, they can look back on this experience as evidence of their own strength when they later face challenges as mothers (Edwards, 2005). This is important because,

> Birth is not only about making babies. Birth is also about making mothers – strong, competent, capable mothers who trust themselves and know their inner strength. (Rothman, 1996: p. 253)

Emerging from the rite of passage with self confidence and a group of local friends with babies of the same age gives women a good start on the challenges of motherhood. This is possible where maternity care is local, is offered on a small enough scale to feel human and continuity of care is valued. For midwives this provides a secure group of colleagues small enough to know each other well and the autonomy which makes such a difference to occupational health (Marmot, 2004). The mutual support and job satisfaction such midwives experience appears to protect them from high levels of occupational stress and burnout (McCourt and Stevens, 2009; Sandall,1997). Thus anxiety is lessened, social capital is increased and clinical outcomes improved.

The circumstances where midwifery achieves most tend to be those where a much broader view of health is taken than is usually measured in clinical outcomes. Such a view includes families' own priorities and the development of community networks and support. This is entirely appropriate for a service which can have such long-term impact upon the health of families. Such a social, rather than a narrowly medical model of birth facilitates true community development.

(c) Good Midwifery Care

Three main ingredients for positive outcomes of maternity care are repeatedly cited:

> [A] close personal and trusting relationship with a midwife in a one-to-one caseload model; a strong belief in childbirth as normal physiology; a familiar environment for birth that enhances and supports the normalcy of childbirth. (Pairman, 2006, p 85).

The characteristics of *'Birth Models that Work'* developed from cases in many countries (Davis-Floyd et al., 2009) make a longer list, which centres on the three main ingredients which Sally Pairman developed in New Zealand. This list includes 'creative use of appropriate technologies and modalities that work to support normal birth', 'cultural appropriateness and sensitivity' and 'mutually respectful and collaborative relationships' amongst care providers. The last point of this list underpins the others.

> Regional and national organisations and communication networks that support this work, which include major consumer components that can generate political support and facilitate practitioner in their abilities to humanise care. (Davis-Floyd et al., 2009, p. 23)

Such networks seem crucial, especially when there is tension between the aims of individuals or between parts of a service and of the service as a whole. Other points are included in definitions of good care concerning its knowledge base in research evidence and women's self-knowledge. But most definitions of good care see the midwife as 'working alongside' or with individual women, as 'guardians' of the birth process (Page and McCandlish, 2006, p. xiii) and of the social and geographical space within which the rite of passage occurs (Fahy et al., 2008). Such wording highlights the agency of the mother and fosters her growth into a 'strong, competent, capable mother'. It is acknowledged that behind all these grand aims must lie that of avoiding harm to mother, baby or family.

(d) The Social Context

Any relationship is influenced by its context and this is certainly true for the midwife/mother relationship. The social context of those involved, their values, beliefs and social obligations affect what the two parties bring to their relationship. For the mother this context includes the wider society's values concerning birth and the childbearing experiences of her friends and family.

'Women birth as they live' (Hastie, 2008, p. 83) and many women have little experience of the confidence and strength which good midwifery can foster. This may be because of economic or social deprivation, or it may be because their experience is largely passive and/or stressful, and this deeply influences their expectations of birth. Our society is not full of images of strong birthing women but of fearful pain from which passive women are rescued by medicine and technology. Childbearing women are largely seen as passive, whether as patients being rescued from their suffering, or as consumers choosing from a menu they did not design.

Within the political and economic values of our society consumption is seen as economically crucial. Thus childbearing women are defined in relation to the service they use, rather than by their social role as new mothers. The commodification of maternity services has led to concepts of customer choice, and informed choice has become a big issue in maternity care. Yet 'there is a fragile element within the notion we call 'informed choice' (Leap, 2010). Such choice assumes static alternatives yet the process of birth is dynamic and changing.

> I have found that in many situations raising the notions of 'uncertainty' has led to more fruitful discussions than has pursuing the idea of 'informed choice'. Embracing uncertainty sometimes brings a sense of calm…This is not about engendering a passive fatalism but more about enabling women to learn to trust that they will cope with whatever comes their way. (Leap, 2010, p. 5)

The other, major limitation on women's choice is that the service provider controls the menu and with centralisation ensuring only one service provider in most areas, and the powerful professional concept of the 'right choice', options are limited for many women (Kirkham and Stapleton, 2001; Oakley et al., this volume). There are very impressive exceptions to this trend but they are exceptions.

How birth is seen in our society impacts upon the midwife too. She is also influenced by her commitments as a professional and as an employee.

(e) The Policy Context

Maternity care policy documents over the last 20 years appear to fit well with good midwifery. In 1992 the House of Commons Health Select Committee Maternity Report (1992) concluded that a medical model of care should no longer drive the maternity services. The recommendations of *Changing Childbirth* (Department of Health, 1993) addressed the individuality of women's needs, their need for information, involvement and choice in the planning of their care, continuity of carer, accessibility of services and privacy. Support within an ongoing relationship with a midwife was emphasised. The aims were to be achieved within 5 years. A number of highly innovative pilot schemes followed, most seeking to achieve continuity of care, many funded by Department of Health grants. Despite many excellent evaluations, most of these pilot schemes ended when their funding finished. There was no requirement that service providers implement *Changing Childbirth* and it faded into history, leaving many midwives and childbirth campaigners disillusioned. It did however influence subsequent policy documents and the language used around maternity care.

Maternity Matters (Department of Health, 2007) is the current policy document. It stresses the aims of 'positive experiences for everyone', 'a wider choice in maternity care' and 'the need for flexible services with a focus on the needs of the individual' (p. 2). It is also cheering to see specific mention of these issues as applied to childbearing women from 'our most deprived communities'. This document lays down 'choice guarantees' to be achieved by the end of 2009 (p. 5) but that date has now passed and although a monitoring framework for its implementation is part of the document (p. 26), the choice guarantees have not been achieved in many areas.

The National Institute for Health and Clinical Excellence Clinical Guideline on Intrapartum Care (NICE, 2007) has considerable implications for the midwife-mother relationship, not least for the clear statement on the need for 'supportive one-to-one care' (p. 7). 'This guideline offers best practice advice' (p. 6) and states that women and families' views concerning their care should be 'sought and respected' and stresses the importance of informed decision-making, good communication and involving the woman in flexible care. The guidance given is clear and detailed and helpful to midwives, especially with regard to outmoded practices. Nevertheless, guidelines can come to be seen as rules and midwives now have to justify any deviation from these edicts (Griffiths, 2009). The 'best practice' title of such guidelines carries great authority, despite the rhetoric of consumer choice.

Our society is one where problems are defined and solved by experts with specialist knowledge. For birth, and most of life's rites of passage, the technical specialists are medical. Association with the technical carries a degree of status and the midwifery role has tended to become something between a handmaiden and a willing technical assistant to obstetric practice, at the same time as endeavouring to maintain the traditional role with women. Midwifery has a long tradition of taking on tasks cast off by medicine or seen by doctors as essential but inappropriate or too time-consuming to do themselves. The recent rise of the manager as expert has greatly influenced the work of midwives and doctors, creating for both professions more tasks, less autonomy and awareness of the values they hold in common.

(f) The Maternity Services Context: Centralisation, Standardisation and Anxiety

Centralisation of maternity services has been going on for many years, first with the hospitalisation of birth, then with the movement of community midwifery services out of local government public health services and recently with the closure of small maternity hospitals.

Most midwives work in hospitals which are hierarchically organised and this organisation has been reinforced by the requirements of obstetric technology. Within a hierarchical model of maternity care, it is hard for midwives to trust mothers when they feel themselves to be controlled rather than trusted. Midwives cannot empower women where they themselves feel disempowered. Despite policy statements which expect midwives to support women in exercising choice, they increasingly lack the opportunity to exercise choice and control or to have experienced facilitation in their work and thereby to have developed the necessary skills. This leaves us very vulnerable and unwilling to give up what power we have.

Childbearing women became patients and later 'consumers' of maternity services, still a relatively passive role for life's most creative act. Many surveys of their views contain graphic descriptions of being on a conveyor belt, not a place where relationships flourish. This industrial model of care profoundly changed midwives' relationships too and priority had to be given to pleasing power-holders within the institution rather than mothers who passed through it relatively rapidly.

Midwives are employed by hospitals and deployed to fit the needs of the industrial model of care. For many years midwives staffed wards; now with staff shortages and pressures on resources, they are frequently moved to 'plug the gaps' in the service. Relationships with women and with colleagues are thereby further fragmented within the working day, which many midwives dislike and which causes some to leave midwifery (Ball et al., 2002).

Ensuring smooth patient flow is a key management issue in our large maternity hospitals. This has led to the creation of specialist midwifery roles to ease bottlenecks in that flow. Triage is a good example; a system originally developed to deal with battlefield casualties is now used to control the flow of admissions to labour wards. Thus the woman's experience is further fragmented and at a point of especial vulnerability she is briefly processed by another stranger who she will not meet again.

Another key factor in modern maternity care is the move to standardise and control clinical practice. This is seen in the rise of micro-management and the growth of rules, whether they are called policies, procedures, protocols or guidelines, which must be followed or careful attention paid to justifying any deviation. Rites thereby acquire a rightness (Freedman, this volume). Such a philosophy of managerial control is justified as enhancing safety for childbearing women. Yet it invokes a very narrow definition of safety: a live mother and baby at the end of a defined clinical episode. The requirements of the Clinical Negligence Scheme for Trusts (CNST) link guidelines to the cost of insurance for Trusts (NHS Litigation Authority, 2008) and thereby add a further economic imperative to the many pressures to standardise care. The rituals of these requirements give staff the security afforded by risk management, but can be seen as protecting the organisation rather than its users or clinicians for whom it can increase risk (Edwards, 2005).

Such micro-management focuses the attention of midwives on the rules, however named, rather than on the women in their care and the complexities of their childbearing. Nadine Edwards (2005) examined 'the risk of focussing on risk' which the mothers she interviewed saw as generating anxiety and fear and undermining confidence for their midwives and themselves.

> My experience of antenatal care was that they make you anxious and then try to reassure you. (Edwards, 2005, p. 113)

Such focussing on informing women of specific risks also distracts staff attention away from discussing the complexities of coping with uncertainty.

As rules have proliferated, so have the opportunities to get things wrong and clinical practice has become increasingly fearful. Midwifery practice and education generate fears of doing the wrong thing, and more importantly of not doing all the small, required right things. Such constant anxiety as to the details of practice ritual is destructive in two ways. Firstly it distracts from the individual woman and the midwife's relationship with her. Secondly it inhibits the synthesis of clinical knowledge and the development of higher levels of skill by clinicians who have developed manual and relationship skills through practice and engagement. Fear can be useful as skilled awareness that things are not as they should be (Becker, 1997). Constant worry as to whether we have done the ever-changing 'right' thing corrodes our ability to pick up small cues as to future problems: the well honed skills in noticing slight differences which are often described as intuition. Such worry therefore undermines clinical judgement.

As Jean Robinson observed of maternity services,

> What we sense most is fear. Fear of loss of control, loss of power and loss of dominance. Without these they do not know how to function...The inflexible system, in which they have had to work for so long, does not allow them to respond in any other way. (Robinson, 2003, p. 719)

This is a sad indictment of our need to ensure women make the 'right' choices and completely ignores the fact that 'without informed refusal, informed consent cannot exist' (ibid, p. 719; Oakley et al., this volume).

In an era where economic efficiency is required of public services and health care is seen as a market service, resources are of crucial importance. Staff time is money and midwifery establishments tend to be pared in the face of financial pressures. This creates a situation where, even when hospitals have their full staffing establishment, and this is rarely the case, midwives on the ground experience a shortage of staff. Midwives certainly think that shortage of midwives and of other resources makes maternity care less safe in England (Kirkham et al., 2006; Smith et al., 2009). Midwifery vacancy rates are rising. (NMC, 2010). The RCM annual survey of UK heads of midwifery service (quoted in RCOG et al., 2007, p. 5) shows that a growing majority hold the view that the number of funded midwifery posts in their Trust is not adequate for the level of work undertaken. This situation is exacerbated by the failure of Trusts to specifically earmark extra government funding for maternity services and for increasing the number of midwives, which has often not reached those services (Guardian, 2009).

Midwives are also leaving midwifery mainly because they cannot practice as they would wish and as they were trained to do. Those who leave tend to be younger and better educated that their colleagues, exactly those who should be the future of the profession (Ball et al., 2002). For those who stay, relationships with clients provide a major source of job satisfaction (Kirkham et al., 2006), and those relationships become more difficult as staff shortages increase and midwifery work becomes ever more fragmented.

When midwives feel overwhelmed with work, they focus on getting through tasks as quickly as possible with minimal engagement (Bharj and Chesney, 2010; Deery and Kirkham, 2007; Dykes, 2009). They do not have time to listen.

The tasks midwives are required to do are increasing, as is the paperwork required to demonstrate that these tasks are done. Time is rationed, for mothers and midwives. This industrial approach to time and tasks also demonstrates a linear approach to time very different from that experienced by new mothers. Though often treated as inevitable, this model itself carries many risks including 'the risk of rushing' (Edwards, 2005, p. 121).

The mother in labour, or breastfeeding her baby, experiences time as cyclical, lived in response to the activities of her uterus or her baby, not the clock (McCourt, 2009). Similarly, where there is an on-going relationship between the midwife and mother, time can be used in response to the mother's needs. When time can be invested in getting to know each other and establishing trust, issues will be revealed when the mother feels safe enough to raise them. This is very different from the endless list of questions which must be asked on booking, some so intrusive that I wonder how many women answer them truthfully. In an on-going relationship, time will be invested in preparation for labour and new motherhood. Where time is thus used responsively, more time may not be needed, but both parties will need flexibility to respond to each other. A mother recently told me of useful advice given by a midwife: 'watch your baby, not the clock'; the midwife also expressed the wish that she could do the same thing and 'watch the woman, not the clock'. Sadly, current levels of control and surveillance make this difficult to achieve and such investment of time is only directly beneficial to the midwife where she continues to provide care for that woman.

(g) Contradictions and Tensions

The way in which maternity care is organised creates and sustains great contradictions. Birth is usually a joyous event and midwifery can be hugely rewarding. Yet there is real danger that present systems of maternity care spread anxiety, fear and passivity rather than confidence and joy, without enhancing safety. Such systems cannot be sustainable, since they make mothers unhappy and midwives leave or become 'obedient technicians' (Deery and Hunter, 2010).

The midwife-mother relationship can improve short term clinical and long term social outcomes. This is done through the fostering of trust and the building of a network of sustaining relationships. The rhetoric of policy documents advocates this. Yet the managerial need to control and the fear which permeates the service disempowers both women and midwives and keeps caesarean section rates high (see Bewley and Foo, this volume). The need to limit expenditure limits midwife numbers; fewer midwives are linked with more caesareans which cost more than normal deliveries financially and physically. The perverse incentives of Payment by Results reward this (O'Sullivan and Tyler, 2009). Thus the gap between policy rhetoric and clinical reality is reinforced by the way the service is funded and the costs of CNST.

The industrial model of care prevents midwives listening to women, and thereby prevents relationship, with all its positive potential. So often midwives, giving fragmented care, pressed for time and unheard themselves, dash through their working day, attending to prescribed tasks rather than to the concerns of individuals. This prevents midwives from hearing women's concerns and prevents women from voicing their needs, out of sympathy with the midwife who is 'so busy'. This and other coping strategies, such as stereotyping women (Kirkham and Stapleton, 2001) or fragmented care (Menzies Lyth, 1988) or dissociation (Garrett, 2010), whilst saving time and defending us from anxiety (Menzies Lyth, 1988), also 'defend' us from relationship and thereby impoverish all concerned. The more we cope like this the more we reinforce the habits of an oppressed group (Freire, 1972) which responds to pressure to internalise oppressive values (Roberts, 1983; Heagarty, 1996) and then tends to act them out upon colleagues and clients (Leap, 1997; Stapleton et al., 1998). Through the latter half of the twentieth century many midwives would have identified their relationship with obstetrics as oppressive, now the economic values of NHS management put considerable pressure upon both professions.

From a midwifery viewpoint, much of the service context of maternity care in this country is the opposite of what we know works best. This is not the fault of individual managers, midwives or obstetricians. The values underpinning the service assume but do not value relationships.

> The documented but seemingly invisible quality of care that can be provided by midwives is difficult to promote in the neoliberal market place because midwifery is labour, skill and time intensive and much of what it achieves remains hidden, and is therefore inefficient in terms of monetary profit. (Edwards, 2008, p. 465)

Given the emphasis on social capital in some areas of public health, I wonder whether this has to be the case, even within current values. Nevertheless, there are major issues in the politics of practice which centre around the movement of power towards childbearing women.

Within a health service where experts carry authority and patients are relatively passive, 'bringing childbearing woman and midwives together in relationships in which the midwife "works with" rather than "doing to or for"' (Page, 2003) is unusual, though it can have very positive results. Nevertheless, such collaboration does not carry the status of medical technology and has ensured the relatively humble position of midwifery relative to obstetrics within the NHS. Yet all of us need a degree of autonomy and women who need much obstetric and medical care in pregnancy also benefit from midwifery care to counteract the medical tendency to 'focus on risk rather than the person'. Marie Berg found that these women sought from their midwives 'mutuality, trust, ongoing dialogue, enduring presence, and shared responsibility' and concluded that,

> Childbearing women at high risk live in an extremely vulnerable situation. It is crucial that midwifery and medical care exist on equal terms for the women's sake. (Berg, 2010)

So, rather than being seen as opposing models of care, collaboration between obstetrics and midwifery can help all concerned. There are excellent examples of good collaboration between caseholding hospital midwives and obstetricians who support that model of midwifery care as in St Georges Hospital, Sydney Australia. (Brodie and Homer, 2009). Sadly, the historically acquired coping habits of midwives and the hierarchical structures of the NHS do not favour collaboration as equals. But with good leadership and a degree of autonomy for midwives this can be changed (Homer et al., 2001; Homer et al., 2008; Leyshon, 2004; Page, 1995).

Where services are centralised and standardised, and run for maximum economy, management, far from striving for excellence, tends to see it as an opportunity for cost-cutting or even to fear it as fuelling demand for better services (Page, 1997). We hear the tragic arguments for closing birth centres or case-holding practices on the grounds of 'equity', meaning the lowest common denominator of service provision. This approach has the sad result of lowering all our expectations of maternity services.

There are excellent examples of midwifery care in this country. Yet where the midwifery model works best it is also most vulnerable to financial cuts and extending management control. An international study of *Birth Models that Work* (Davis-Floyd et al., 2009) includes two English examples of such excellent care: The Albany Midwifery Practice which has recently had its contract with Kings College Hospital terminated because 'we feel that we need to bring all our services in line with the same national clinical and safety guidelines and standards' (Reed, 2010, p. 5) and a freestanding birth centre which, like all similar birth centres has been repeatedly threatened with closure (Walsh, 2007).

(h) Ways Forward

There are now plenty of clinical examples and research evaluations which show what midwifery care can achieve in small scale settings where relationships can develop, be they case holding projects (McCourt and Stevens, 2009), birth centres (Kirkham, 2003; Walsh 2007) or independent midwifery (van der Kooy, 2009). Women at high and low obstetric risk can have good clinical outcomes, high satisfaction with their care and feel safe without feeling passive. The social outcomes described above can be achieved. If the midwife follows the woman, rather than staffing the conveyor belt, it is possible to keep relationships on a human scale, with one to one care, even within large hospitals (Homer et al., 2008). This involves much reorganisation and rethinking and is a real management challenge, but it can be done. Where it is only partially done, the changed part within a larger system is always vulnerable.

There are situations where the political aims of midwifery have been acknowledged and, to varying degrees achieved on a much larger scale. 'In order to "work with" it is necessary to establish a relationship of equality and reciprocity and power sharing such as midwifery partnership' in New Zealand. (Pairman, 2010). New Zealand midwifery has established itself as a 'profession that recognises its primary commitment is to the women it attends and consciously works to put control over childbirth into the hands of women' (Pairman, 2010).

> When articulating midwifery as a partnership of equal status midwives have redefined the accepted view of professionalism. Instead of seeking to control childbirth, midwifery seeks to control midwifery, in order that women can control childbirth. Midwifery must maintain its women-centred philosophy to ensure that its control of midwifery never leads to control of childbirth (Guilliland and Pairman, 1995, p. 49).

In New Zealand independent midwives can be Lead Maternity Carers (LMC), paid by the health service and offering continuity of care.

> Because of the individual nature of the relationship, midwifery's practice of partnership is a personal one between the woman and the midwife ...Because midwifery recognises the social context of all women, the partnership is also a political one at both a personal and organisational level (Guilliland and Pairman, 1995, pp. 7–8)

Such a model was achieved as a result of a long political campaign, largely by women as service users. (Donley, 1989), who continue to play a crucial role.

A similar model is now being piloted by Independent Midwives UK and two NHS Trusts (van der Kooy, 2009 and www.independentmidwives.org.uk). It enables independent midwives to provide care for individual women contracted through the NHS. By this means any woman could access independent midwifery care without having to pay for it privately, independent midwives would have access to NHS facilities for their clients, and insurance for independent midwives would be available through the NHS. This model skilfully builds upon market options, which have been widely used in some areas of the NHS but not, as yet, in maternity care.

There are wider organisational models which may fit better with a public service and which could be used in health care. Jane Jacobs proposes that there are two moral systems: commercial and guardian. It may well be that the values and practices which suit commercial activity do not fit the 'guardian' activities of public services where loyalty and generosity are traditionally valued (Jacobs, 1992) and the same generosity could be applied to the use of time in caring relationships. Or it may be that the market values underpinning the organisation of the modern NHS are out of date in the real marketplace. Some management writers value workers' autonomy, flexibility and trust far more than does the NHS. Fairtlough (2005) states that there are 'Three ways of getting things done: hierarchy, heterarchy and responsible autonomy' and health services tend to suffer from 'the hegemony of hierarchy' (ibid, p. 7). Accountability is a key characteristic of responsible autonomy where central control is replaced by more self-sufficient sub-units. Fairtlough suggests that 'responsible autonomy may be the better alternative to hierarchy in Guardian organisations' (ibid, p. 60). It is interesting that these alternative ways of organising foster the relationships and the autonomy which are pre-requisites for good midwife-mother relationships.

The contradictions and tensions within NHS maternity care show that change is needed. Such change would need to involve the underlying values of the service, not just its policy rhetoric. We have sufficient evidence to know that placing the midwife-mother relationship at the centre of care could improve outcomes for all concerned. The pilot studies have been done, the organisational will to change is all that is now needed.

REFERENCES

Anderson, T. (2010). Feeling Safe Enough to Let Go: The Relationship between a Woman and her Midwife in the Second Stage of Labour. In *The Midwife-Mother Relationship*. *Second edition*. (ed. M.Kirkham) Basingstoke: Palgrave Macmillan.

Ball, L., Curtis, P. and Kirkham, M. (2002) *Why Do Midwives Leave?* London: Royal College of Midwives.

Becker, G. de (1997) *The Gift of Fear.* London: Bloomsbury.

Berg, M. (2010) Midwifery Relationships with Childbearing Women at Increased Risk. In *The Midwife-Mother Relationship*. *Second Edition*. (ed. M.Kirkham). Basingstoke: Palgrave Macmillan.

Bharj, K. and Chesney, M. (2010) Pakistani Muslim Women and Midwives' Relationships: What Are the Essential Attributes? In *The Midwife-Mother Relationship*. *Second Edition*. (ed. M. Kirkham). Basingstoke: Palgrave Macmillan

Brodie, P. and Homer, C. (2009) Transforming the Culture of a Maternity Service: St George Hospital, Sydney, Australia. In *Birth Models That Work*, pp.

187–212 (eds. R.E. Davis-Floyd, L.Barclay, B-A. Daviss, and J.Tritten). Berkeley: University of California Press.

Davis-Floyd, R. E., Barclay, L., Daviss, B-A. and Tritten, J. (2009) *Birth Models That Work*. Berkeley: University of California Press.

Deery, R. and Kirkham, M. (2007) Drained and Dumped on: The Generation and Accumulation of Emotional Toxic Waste in Community Midwifery, In *Exploring the Dirty Side of Women's Health* (ed. M.Kirkham) pp. 72–83. London, New York: Routledge.

Deery, R. and Hunter, B. (2010). Emotional Work and Relationships in Midwifery. In *The Midwife-Mother Relationship. Second Edition*. (ed. M.Kirkham.) Basingstoke: Palgrave Macmillan

Department of Health (1993). *Changing Childbirth: Report of the Expert Maternity Group*. London: HMSO.

—— (2007). *Maternity Matters: Choice, Access and Continuity of Care in a Safe Service*. London:DOH.

Donley, J. (1989). Professionalism: The Importance of Consumer Control over Childbirth. *New Zealand College of Midwives Journal*, September, 6–7.

Dykes, F. (2009). 'No Time to Care': Midwifery Work on Postnatal Wards in England. In *Emotions in midwifery and reproduction*. (eds. B. Hunter and R. Deery.) pp. 90–104. Basingstoke: Palgrave Macmillan.

Edwards, N. P. (2005). *Birthing Autonomy: Women's Experiences of Planning Home Birth*. Abingdon: Routledge.

—— (2008) Safety in Birth; The Contextual Conundrums Faced by Women in a 'Risk Society', Driven by Neoliberal Policies. *MIDIRS Midwifery Digest* **18,4**, 463–470.

Edwards, N. P. (2010) 'There's so much Potential and for whatever Reason It's not Being Realised.' Women's Relationships with Midwives as a Negotiation of Ideology and Power. In *The Midwife-Mother Relationship. Second Edition*. (ed. M.Kirkham). Basingstoke: Palgrave Macmillan.

Fahy, K., Foureur, K. and Hastie, C. (eds.) (2008) *Birth Territory and Midwifery Guardianship*. Sydney: Books for Midwives, Elsevier.

Fairtlough, G. (2005). *The Three Ways of Getting Things Done. Hierarchy, Heterarchy and Responsible Autonomy in Organisations*. Bridport, Dorset: Triarchy Press.

Freire, P. (1972). *The Pedagogy of the Oppressed*. Harmondsworth: Penguin.

Garrett, E. F. (2010) *Survivors of Childhood Sexual Abuse and Midwifery Practice. CSA, Birth and Powerlessness*. Oxford: Radcliffe.

Gaudion, A. and Homeyard, C. (2010) The Midwife-mother Relationship where there is Poverty and Disadvantage. In *The Midwife-Mother Relationship. Second edition*. (ed. M.Kirkham). Basingstoke: Palgrave Macmillan.

Gilligan, C. (1982). *In a Different Voice*. Cambridge MA: Harvard University Press.

Griffiths, R. (2009). Maternity Care Pathways and the Law. *British Journal of Midwifery.* **17**, 5, 324–325.

Guardian (2009) Funding Gap Puts Maternity Reform at Risk. Dec 22, p1.

Guilliland, K. and Pairman, S. (1995). *The Midwifery Partnership: A Model for Practice.* Wellington New Zealand, Monograph Series 95/1, Department of Nursing and Midwifery, Victoria: University of Wellington.

Halldorsdottir, S. and Karlsdottir, S. I.. (1996). Empowerment or Discouragement: Women's Experience of Caring and Uncaring Encounters during Childbirth. *Health Care for Women International* **17**, 361–379.

Hastie, C. (2008). The Spiritual and Emotional Territory of the Unborn and Newborn Baby. In *Birth Territory and Midwifery Guardianship.* (eds. K. Fahy, K.Foureur and C.Hastie). Sydney, Books for Midwives: Elsevier

Heagarty, B. V. (1996). Reassessing the Guilty: the Midwives Act and the Control of English Midwives in the Early Twentieth Century. In *Supervision of Midwives.* (ed. M.Kirkham). Hale: Books for Midwives.

Homer, C., Brodie, P. and Leap, N. (2001) *Establishing Models of Continuity of Midwifery Care in Australia. A Resource for Midwives.* Sydney: University of Technology Sydney, Centre for Family Health and Midwifery.

—— (2008) *Midwifery Continuity of Care.* Sydney: Churchill Livingstone, Elsevier.

House of Commons (1992) *Health Committee Second Report, Session 1991–2: Maternity Services.* London:HMSO.

Huber, U. S. and Sandall, J. (2009). A Qualitative Exploration of the Creation of Calm in a Continuity of Carer Model of Maternity Care in Inner London. *Midwifery* **25**, 613–621.

Hunter, B. and Deery, R. (eds.) (2009). *Emotions in Midwifery and Reproduction.* Basingstoke: Palgrave.

Jacobs, J. (1992). *Systems of Survival. A Dialogue on the Moral Foundations of Commerce and Politics.* London: Hodder and Stoughton.

Kirkham, M. (ed.) (2003). *Birth Centres: A Social Model for Maternity Care.* Elsevier Science,:Oxford.

——(ed.) (2004). *Informed Choice in Maternity Care.* Basingstoke: Palgrave Macmillan.

—— (ed.) (2007). *Exploring the Dirty Side of Women's Health.* Abingdon: Routledge.

—— (ed.) (2010) *The Midwife-Mother Relationship. Second edition.* Basingstoke: Palgrave Macmillan .

Kirkham, M., Morgan, R.K. and Davies, C. (2006) *Why Midwives Stay.* London: Department of Health.

Kirkham, M. and Stapleton, H. (eds.) (2001). *Informed Choice in Maternity Care: An Evaluation of Evidence Based Leaflets.* York:NHS Centre for Reviews and Dissemination.

Leap, N. (1997). Making Sense of 'Horizontal Violence' in Midwifery. *British Journal of Midwifery* 5(11), 689.

—— (2010). The Less We Do the More We Give. In *The Midwife-Mother Relationship. Second edition.* (ed. M.Kirkham). Basingstoke: Palgrave Macmillan.

Leyshon, L. (2004). Integrating Caseloads across a whole Service: The Torbay Model. *MIDIRS Midwifery Digest* **14, 1,** Supplement 1, S9–S11.

Marmot, M. (2004) *Status Syndrome.* London: Bloomsbury.

McCourt, C. ed. (2009). *Childbirth, Midwifery and Concepts of Time.* Oxford: Berghahn Books.

McCourt, C. and Stevens, T. (2009) Relationship and Reciprocity in Caseload Midwifery. In *Emotions in Midwifery and Reproduction.* (ed. B.Hunter. and R.Deery). Basingstoke: Palgrave.

McCrea, H. and Crute, V. (1991). The Midwife/Client Relationship: Midwives' Perspectives. *Midwifery* 7(4), 183–192.

Menzies Lyth, I. (1988) *Containing Anxiety in Institutions. Selected Essays Vol 1.* London: Free Association Books.

NHS Litigation Authority (2008) *Clinical Negligence Scheme for Trusts. Clinical Risk Management Standards for Maternity Care.* London:Willis.

National Institute for Health and Clinical Excellence (2007). *Clinical Guideline 55. Intrapartum Care.* London: NICE.

Nursing and Midwifery Council (2010). *Support, Supervision and Safety.* London: NMC.

O'Neil, O. (2002). *A Question of Trust.* Cambridge: Cambridge University Press.

O'Sullivan, S. and Tyler, S. (2009). New Arrangements for Payment by Results. *Midwives* June/July; 36–37

Page, L. (2003). One-to-one Midwifery: Restoring the 'with Woman' Relationship in Midwifery. *Journal of Midwifery and Women's Health* 48(2), 119–125.

—— (1997). Misplaced Values: in Fear of Excellence. *British Journal of Midwifery* 5(11), 652–654.

—— ed. (1995) *Effective Group Practice in Midwifery: Working with Women.* Oxford: Blackwell.

Page, L. and McCandlish, R. (2006) *The New Midwifery: science and sensitivity in practice.* Edinburgh: Churchill Livingstone/Elsevier.

Pairman, S. (2006). Midwifery Partnership: Working 'with' Women. In *The New Midwifery: Science and Sensitivity in Practice* 2nd edition (ed. L.A. Pageand. R. McCandlish R.), pp.73–96. Edinburgh: Churchill Livingstone/Elsevier.

—— (2010). Midwifery Partnership: a Professionalising Strategy for Midwives In *The Midwife-Mother Relationship.* 2nd edition. (ed. M. Kirkham) Basingstoke: Palgrave Macmillan

Reed, B. (2010) 'Choices are not choices if you are not allowed to make them for yourself.' *The Practicing Midwife* 13(1), 4–5.

Roberts, S. J.(1983) Oppressed Group Behaviour: Implications for Nursing. *Advances in Nursing Science* July, 21–30.

Robinson, J. (2003) Professional Fear: A Barrier to Consent. *British Journal of Midwifery* 11(12), 719.

Rothman, K. B. (1996). Women, Providers and Control. *JOGNN* 25(3), 253–6.

Royal College of Obstetricians and Gynaecologists, Royal College of Midwives, Royal College of Anaesthetists and Royal College of Paediatrics and Child Health (2007). *Safer Childbirth. Minimum Standards for the Organisation and Delivery of Care in Labour.* London: RCOG Press.

Sandall, J. (1997). Midwives' Burnout and Continuity of Care. *British Journal of Midwifery* 5(2), 106–111.

Sennett, R. (2008) *The Craftsman.* New York: Yale University Press.

Smith, A. H. K., Dixon, A. L., and Page, L. A. (2009). Health Care Professionals' Views about Safety in Maternity Services. *Midwifery* 25(1), 21–31.

Stapleton, H., Duerden, J., and Kirkham, M. (1998). *Evaluation of the Impact of the Supervision of Midwives on Professional Practice and the Quality of Midwifery Care.* London: English National Board.

van der Kooy, B. (2009). Choice for Women and Choice for Midwives – Making it Happen. *British Journal of Midwifery* 17(9), 524–525.

Van Gennep, A. (1960). *The Rites of Passage* London: Routledge.

Walsh, D. (2007) *Improving Maternity Services, Small is Beautiful – Lessons from a Birth Centre.* London: Radcliffe Publishing Ltd.

Part 2:

Status and Consequences of Birth

5

The Loneliness of Status: The Legal and Moral Significance of Birth

JONATHAN HERRING[1]

I. INTRODUCTION

THE MOMENT OF birth has a dramatic impact on the legal status of the fetus. It is the moment when the fetus moves from the rather murky legal status of the 'unborn' to the more certain world of being a person and entitled to all the legal rights that people have. Birth is selected because it is seen as the moment when the characteristics of the fetus are such that the baby becomes a person. It has the added appeal for lawyers of being readily susceptible to proof.

The significance that the law attaches to birth has been the subject of sustained criticism from writers from a range of perspectives. Charles Foster (2009) argues:

> Autonomy bestows its decisive favours on the adult woman rather than the 24-week fetus she carries, on the ground, apparently, that the fetus is on one side of the woman's vagina rather than the other. The mere geographical situation of the fetus means that it has no autonomy rights at all. A journey of a few centimetres would stamp it with the awesome imprimatur of autonomy and so invest it with the draconian protection of the English law ....

His implied question: why should the few centimetres make such a difference to the status of the fetus?, with its implied answer: 'none at all'; has a wonderful logic, but is, it will be argued, a fearsome error.

[1] I am grateful for the comments of participants at the seminars behind this book, but also of participants of seminars at the Faculty of Law, Birmingham University and HeLEX, Oxford University.

Ken Mason (1998, p. 108) a doctor and medical lawyer has written this:

Medically speaking, however, the fact of birth is not especially material. Certainly, the fetus in utero depends upon its mother but, had it been born, say, two days earlier, its chances of survival would, in normal circumstances, have been no different; it is, therefore, illogical to make an absolute distinction between the potential for life of a mature fetus and a neonate.

Peter Singer (1979, p. 108) a leading opponent of 'pro-life' views argues:

… the fetus/baby is the same entity whether inside or outside the womb, with the same human features (whether we can see them or not) and the same degree of awareness and capacity for feeling pain. A prematurely born infant may well be *less* developed in these respects than a foetus nearing the end of its normal term. It seems peculiar to hold that we may not kill the premature infant, but may kill the more developed foetus. The location of a being – inside or outside the womb – should not make much difference to the wrongness of killing it.

These views will be rejected in this chapter. It will accepted that their basic premise: that the intrinsic qualities of the foetus are unchanged by birth is essentially correct; but it will be argued that it is not status based on individual characteristics which should generate legal and moral rights. Rather these should flow from relationships. Before exploring this, the law on the changing status at birth needs explaining.

II. THE LAW

Birth marks a crucial transition in the legal status of the fetus. Prior to the birth the fetus holds a somewhat ambiguous position but afterwards it is a legal person with the full protection of the law. Baker P sought to summarise the law in *Paton v BPAS*, 1978:

The fetus cannot, in English law, in my view, have any right of its own at least until it is born and has a separate existence from the mother.

That is, a debatable statement of the law. Lord Mustill more accurately in *Attorney-General's Reference (No 3 or 1994*, 1998) explained the foetus was 'a unique organism' and 'protected by the law in a number of different ways'. In saying this he rejected an argument that the fetus should be regarded as equivalent to a leg of the mother. So, the fetus is not a person entitled to rights, but it is something entitled to some kind of protection. Protection can be found in the criminal and civil law.

(a) The Fetus in Criminal Law

Prior to birth a fetus is not a person for the purposes of the criminal law. Killing a fetus cannot be the offence of murder. If, however, the child is injured in utero, is born alive and dies sometime later of those injuries, a conviction of murder or manslaughter can lie (*Attorney-General's Reference (no 3 of 1994)*, 1998). In *R v Tait*, 1990 a man who said to a pregnant woman 'I am going to kill your baby' was not guilty of committing the offence of threatening to kill a person (Offences Against the Person Act 1861, s. 16) because the fetus was not a person. In *Re J*, 2006 an argument that a pregnant woman who was leaving the country was committing child abduction was rejected for the same reason.

This does not mean the fetus is unprotected by the criminal law. The fetus is protected by the offences of unlawfully procuring a miscarriage under section 58 Offences Against the Person Act ,1861 and the offence of child destruction under Infant Life (Preservation) Act, 1929. These are not minor offences. They carry a potential life sentence. In respect of both statutes no offence is committed if the procedure is rendered lawful by the Abortion Act, 1967. The 1929 Act was passed specifically to deal with the scenario where a child was killed in the birthing process. Prior to the Act such a killing would not be a miscarriage nor murder and so would not amount to a criminal offence. The Act was designed to cover this loophole. However, it seems that there is still some uncertainty in a case where an abortion procedure results in a child being born alive. In one case a child aborted at 23 weeks lived for 36 hours. Her death was simply recorded as caused by prematurity and the coroner recorded death by want of attention (Inquest on Infant Campbell, 1983). No criminal proceedings were brought. In another case a prosecution was brought against a doctor who allowed a living abortus to die in a sluice room, but the Magistrates determined that there no case to answer (*R v Hamilton*, 1983). The official Guidance from the Royal College of Obstetricians (1996, p. 8) states clearly that

> When abortion is induced at a gestation at which the fetus, after birth, might be capable of remaining alive by breathing through its lungs, it is imperative that the fetal heart is arrested before delivery, that is part of the legal abortion and is not murder.

This makes it clear that stopping the fetal heart before delivery is permitted, but does not state the position where that does not happen. It seems that if the child is delivered capable of living, then it would be a crime to kill it, but there has been no prosecution of such a case.

(b) The Fetus in Civil Law

For the purposes of civil law personhood also starts at birth. However, the significance of this is lessened because 'there is a well-established rule of civil law that an unborn child shall be deemed to be born whenever its interests require it' (Whitfield, 1998). The use of this legal fiction enables the law to offer protection to those in utero, without denying the significance of birth. A good example of the fiction in operation is that if a person dies leaving a gift to his children, but one of the children is *'en ventre de sa mère'* then she will be deemed born and therefore be able to claim the gift. Similarly, a child once born can sue for injuries she suffered while a fetus (Congenital Disabilities (Civil Liability) Act 1976, s. 1(1)). It was explained in *Burton v Islington HA*, 1993 that the fetus on being injured had a potential claim, which on birth generates an actual claim. The crucial point is, however, that had the fetus not been born no claim could be brought on its behalf.

Prior to birth it is not possible to bring claims in the courts in the name of the fetus in order to prevent an abortion or control the actions of the mother (*Paton v BPAS*, 1979). A fetus cannot be made a ward of court (*Re F* (In Utero), 1988). Nor can the fetus claim rights under the European Convention on Human Rights (*Vo v France*, 2004). Heilbron J. in *C v S*, 1988 summarised the legal position in this way:

> The authorities, it seems to me, show that a child, after it has been born, and only then in certain circumstances based on his or her having a legal right, may be a party to an action brought with regard to such matters as the right to take, on will or intestacy, or for damages for injuries suffered before birth. In other words, the claim crystallises on the birth, at which date, but not before, the child attains the status of a legal persona, and thereupon can exercise that legal right.

(c) What Is Birth?

The precise legal definition of birth is unclear (Fovargue and Miola, 1998). Proof of birth seems to require two things. First, that the whole of the baby's body be outside the outside the womb (*R v Poulton*, 1832). Second, the child must have an existence which is independent of the mother (*R v Enoch*, 1833). That is generally taken to mean that the child has an independent circulation from the mother and breathes independently of her (*Rance v Mid-Downs Health Authority*, 1991). However, neither of these requirements is absolute. A child has been treated as born even though he or she has not drawn breath (*R v Sellis*, 1837) and even though the umbilical cord has not yet been severed (*R v Crutchley*, 1837). In *Rance v Mid-Downs Health Authority* (1991), the phrase 'capable of being born alive' in the 1929 Infant Life (Preservation) Act was said to mean 'breathing and living by its breathing through its lungs alone, without deriving any of its living or power of living by or through its connection to its mother.' However in *Re A* (Conjoined Twins) (2001) the Court of Appeal emphasised the requirement of living independently of the mother, rather than breathing independently. That was an important point in that case because Mary, one of the conjoined twins involved, was not able to breathe independently from her sister and had not been able to since birth. The court were keen to reject any argument that she was not a person. In *R v Poulton* (1832), Littledale J stated:

> With respect to the birth, the being born must mean that the whole body is brought into the world ... Whether the child was born alive or not depends mainly upon the evidence of the medical men.

It may be, therefore, that precisely what counts as birth depends on a range of factors: breathing, heartbeat and independent circulation (R v Iby, 2005). All of these can indicate a birth and there is no single criterion. Just as with the definition of death, lawyers seem tempted to fudge the question of when birth occurs, and leave it to medical expertise.

III. THE TRADITIONAL APPROACH TO LEGAL STATUS

To many commentators the starting point for determining the significance of birth and a host of other pregnancy issues is the moral status of the fetus. As Mary Anne Warren (1997, p. 3) has written:

> To have moral status is to be morally considerable, or to have moral standing. It is to be an entity towards which moral agents have, or can have, moral obligations. If an entity has moral status, then we may not treat it in just any way we please.

Typically commentators list particular characteristics of personhood in order to ascertain whether or not the fetus has the status of being a person. At this point the debate breaks down into the well-documented pro-life v pro-choice camps. Typical of the pro-life position would be this comment (George, 2008, p. 1):

> The adult human being that is now you or me is the same being who, at an earlier stage, was an adolescent and, before that, a child, an infant, a fetus, and an embryo. Even in the embryonic stage, you and I were undeniably whole living members of the species Homo sapiens. We were then, as we are now, distinct and complete – though, in the beginning, developmentally immature – human organisms. We were not mere parts of other organisms.

As the fetus contains the entire genetic material of the adult it will become it has the hallmark of humanity and is a person. Under such a view birth is of relatively little moral significance. The fetus acquired the status of person much earlier.

By contrast there are those who argue that the features of personhood are factors such as those listed by Joseph Fletcher (1979, p. 15):

(1) Minimal intelligence
(2) Self-awareness
(3) Self-control
(4) A sense of time
(5) A sense of futurity
(6) A sense of the past
(7) The capability to relate to others
(8) Concern for others
(9) Communication
(10) Control of existence
(11) Curiosity
(12) Balance of rationality/feeling

(13) Idiosyncrasy change/changeability
(14) Neo-cortical function.

As the fetus lacks such features, or only has them to a limited extent, it cannot claim the moral or legal status of personhood. There is little agreement as to when these characteristics are acquired. For some it will be in the later stages for pregnancy, although for others it is not until sometime after birth that these characteristics are displayed sufficiently to grant personhood (Singer, 1979). Birth, however, is rarely regarded as being significant because it has little effect on the capabilities of the fetus.

(a) Status

A central claim of this chapter is that the focus on status as the source of legal rights and obligations is misguided. Martha Nussbaum (1999, p. 62) explains why she believes the individual should be the basic unit for political thought:

> It means, first of all, that liberalism responds sharply to the basic fact that each person has a course from birth to death that is not precisely the same as that of any other person; that each person is one and not more than one, that each feels pain in his or her own body, that the food given to A does not arrive in the stomach of B.

It will be immediately apparent that what she says is not true of the fetus. The pain of the mother can affect the child and the food given to the mother certainly can arrive in the stomach of the fetus.

The argument of this chapter will be that legal rights and duties should flow from relationship, not individual status. This claim is not as radical as might at first be thought. Consider, for example, parental rights. Although at one time parental rights and responsibilities flowed from the status of being a parent, defined biologically, many family lawyers would now argue that they flow from the nature of the relationship between the person and child. Hence parental responsibility, which incorporates the rights and responsibilities of parenthood, is not restricted to parents but can be acquired by anyone with whom the child lives and can be exercised by anyone with care of the child (Gilmore, Herring and Probert, 2009). Further, where there is a dispute over the upbringing of a child, the person who has the closest social relationship with the child will have the strongest say over the child's upbringing. Again, this is a complex issue and the law has been greatly simplified in the comments above. However, a good case can be made for saying that it is the doing of parenthood that creates the rights and responsibilities, rather simply being a parent (Masson, 2006). 'Parental rights' flow from the relationship between adult and child rather than being inherent in the status of being a parent.

Before exploring the possibility of developing a relational understanding of birth I will explain further why the individualised status model is particularly inappropriate in the context of pregnancy.

(b)The Problems in Seeing Fetal/Baby Status Individualistically

An approach which considers the moral and legal status of the fetus as flowing from its inherent characteristics is objectionable for a number of reasons.

First, it ignores the biological reality of interconnection between the fetus and the pregnant woman. They share fluids and space. There is no clear point at which the fetus ends and the woman begins. The health and well-being of the fetus can impact on the pregnant woman's well-being in both physical and psychological terms, and the reverse is also true (see Herring and Chau, 2007 for a discussion of the biology). Any attempt to consider the fetus outside the context of the pregnant woman utterly fails to acknowledge the corporeal intertwining that pregnancy involves and presents the fairy-tale image of the fetus living in a cosy house inside the mother.

Second, considering the fetus alone fails to capture the circumstances in which the fetus came into being. The woman has gone through profound biological changes in order to bring the fetus into being (Nelson, 2004). The fetus depends entirely on her for everything necessary for life. Continuing with the pregnancy will have a profound impact on her and those in relationship with her. The circumstances of the creation and nurturance of the fetus are sidelined by a focus on current fetal characteristics.

Third, the kind of factors listed by Fletcher as indicating personhood emphasise viability, consciousness and self-determination. This privileges autonomy over other important aspects of human life (Effron, 2005). Our identity and sense of self comes more from our relationships with others than out of characteristics inherent within us. People's definition of themselves: sister, environmentalist, fan of curling, reflect their relations with others, rather than an individualised sense of identity. Throughout our lives it is our relationships that are essential to physical, mental and emotional well-being, and indeed existence. We do not define ourselves in terms of status, viability, consciousness or self-determination, but rather relationships (Herring, 2009). We should do the same for fetuses.

Finally, considering fetal status downgrades the weight attached to the interests of the woman. The woman is not simply a fetal container (Annas, 1986). Yet that is how she is seen if one seeks to determine the status of the fetus in isolation. Barbara Katz Rothman (1986) writes of:

> the reigning medical model of pregnancy, as an essentially parasitic and vaguely pathological relationship, [which] encourages the physician to view the fetus and mother as two separate patients, and to see pregnancy as inherently a conflict of interests between the two. Where the fetus is highly valued, the effect is to reduce the woman to what current obstetrical language calls the 'maternal environment'.

IV. JUSTIFYING A RELATIONAL APPROACH

We cannot, I have argued, consider the status of the fetus in isolation from the woman. Rather our discussion should focus on the relationship between the pregnant woman and fetus and others. I will explain shortly the reference to others. But first I wish to develop the point that our focus must be on the relationship between pregnant woman and fetus. They are both two and one. Any dealings with the fetus must be mediated by the woman; and some dealings with the woman will need to be mediated through the fetus. Dworkin (1993, p. 55) puts it this way:

> [H]er fetus is not merely 'in her' as an inanimate object might be, or something live but alien that has been transplanted into her body. It is 'of her and is hers more than anyone's' because it is, more than anyone else's, her creation and her responsibility; it is alive because she has made it come alive.

The interconnection formed by pregnancy causes a blurring of boundaries and can alter the identity of the individual. As Elvey (2003, p. 203) explains:

> [T]he pregnant body … calls into question these assumptions of separateness and sameness. When I am pregnant, 'my' body is both 'I' and 'not I', mine and not mine. The boundaries of the body shift as the pregnant body creates its own expanding space. While the skin stretches the boundary between the body and its outside is continually renegotiated, until in birth the inside enters the outside. The pregnant body is, moreover, two or more under the influence of a third, the placenta, through the agency of which self and other are interconnected.

Of course, not every woman will perceive a pregnancy in the way described, but the impact of pregnancy on identity, whatever that is, cannot be captured by a model which pits the interests of the mother and fetus against each other, as the traditional fetal status approach does.

The most significant argument in favour of the relational approach is that it requires law and ethics to reflect the experiences and understanding of pregnant women. Many pregnant women do not regard pregnancies as involving a clash between their rights and those of the fetus. A relational approach is able to take account of the particular circumstances and characteristics of the case, rather than focussing on the abstracted status of the fetus. The dilemma for many feminist advocates is that if the fetus is given a legal status this will impact negatively on women seeking abortion, but if the fetus is not given a status this may work against the interests of women who are happily pregnant and seeking legal rights to protect the pregnancy. By focussing on the nature of the relationship between the parties we can justify different legal and ethical responses to wanted and unwanted pregnancies and better reflect the nuances of the situation and how pregnant women themselves understand their pregnancy.

A common argument justifying abortion is that the fetus has no interests and so the woman is entitled to remove it. However, this fails to appreciate the complex responses of women who undertake abortions. While abortion may be seen by some women as equivalent to the cutting of hair or removal of growth, in fact the evidence suggests that for most women the abortion decision is a decision made about the relationship. The decision is made on the basis of what is appropriate for both the mother and the fetus (Ludlow, 2008). Consider, for example, these comments from three women who had abortions (taken from Hainsberg, 1995):

> I do not wish to have a child at the present time in light of my age, my social situation as a single person and my moral values as I want to provide for a child in a serene stable family environment in which there is no violence … .

> It is taking a life. Even though it is not formed, it is the potential, and to me it is still taking a life. But I have to think of mine, my son's, and my husband's [lives]. And at first I thought it was for selfish reasons, but it is not. I believe that, too, some of it is selfish. I don't want another one right now; I am not ready for it… . [But I cannot be] so morally strict as to hurt three other people with a decision just because of my moral beliefs.

> I am a junior in college and am putting myself through because my father has been unemployed and my mother barely makes enough to support the rest of the family. I have promised to help put my brother through when I graduate next year and it's his turn… . There is no way I could continue this pregnancy because of my responsibilities to my family.

As these reports show, the decision to abort is not necessarily taken as a 'selfish' one, nor is it necessarily taken from perspective that the fetus is 'nothing'. Further, they show how the abortion decision is taken in the context of their relationship with their fetus and those around them. These perspectives can be captured by the relationship-based approach in a way the status-based approach cannot.

The relational model requires a consideration of the emotional issues raised. These too can change on birth. Gillian Hadfield (1998, p. 1257) writes of those who focus on choice in the abortion decision:

> Who are these people who populate the economist's … imaginatio[n], who calmly assess the alternatives available according to a stable set of internally consistent preferences and proceed to select the obvious choice, who apparently feel no passion or emotion, who do not worry about whether they are choosing well, who never feel trapped by their choices, and who never discover over time more about themselves and their understanding of their choices? Where is love, duty, fear, self-doubt, and power?

The abstracting of the pregnancy decision into a weighing up of competing interests 'enables the presentation of the woman as selfishly pursuing her own desires while denying that the fetus has any meaning to her at all' (Bridgeman and Millns, 1998, p. 83). An approach which seeks to understand the obligations and rights that flow from the relationships can be better nuanced in considering the emotions that can govern such a decision and what rights and responsibilities can be expected as a result? A relational approach can recognise that pregnancy can create responsibilities for pregnant woman. It enables the decisions about pregnancy and parenthood to be placed in the real murky world of relationships where sometimes things go wrong and sometimes they go right. The world of family life where being a parent is sometimes about survival, rather than reaching the highest ideals of a parent; where weighing up nicely the competing moral interests makes no sense when everything is going crazy and control over life is a long lost fiction.

We need to consider the relationship between not only the pregnant woman and fetus, but also between them and those around them. The pregnant woman herself is in relationship with others and her identity and relationship with the fetus is shaped by others. For example, her understanding of what an abortion is; her understanding of the choice, indeed the nature of the choice itself, are all shaped by the values and practices of the community of which she is a part. There is growing evidence of the links between abortion and domestic violence (Romito et al., 2009), and that provides a powerful backdrop against which to consider the obligations that are imposed upon pregnant women. To seek to consider the correct legal and moral obligations facing a pregnant woman, without an appreciation of the wider social and personal contexts she is in, is misguided.

Adopting a relational approach would mean that it would not be appropriate to consider questions based on observations about 'fetuses' in general. Instead we would need to consider the appropriate legal and moral response to the relationships between fetus, the pregnant woman, others in relationship with her and the wider society. It flows from this that, for example, the rights and responsibilities that a pregnant woman has would differ greatly in the case where pregnancy was desired and where the pregnancy was unwanted. They might also differ depending on social contexts or the set of personal relationships the pregnant woman was in. The nature of the relationship will affect what responsibilities may be imposed upon the community and those close to the woman. This has important implications for the provision of health care for pregnant woman and for social and financial support from the wider community and from the father (Collier, this volume; Wise, 2008).

(a) Developing a Relational Approach to the Significance of Birth

Adopting a relational approach will provide insights into the legal regulation of pregnancy and the issues surrounding abortion (Seymour, 2000). I would use it to develop an argument for a liberal law on abortion. However, the focus of this chapter is on the issue of birth. It will be argued that birth marks a significant change in the relationship between the fetus, woman and others. The relational approach provides a strong explanation for the significance the law attaches to birth.

First, we must recall the biological realities of pregnancy which are ended, or significantly altered, following birth. Pregnancy makes enormous personal demands upon the woman. The pain, bodily interconnection and invasion which occur during pregnancy and which should, on my approach, play such a significant role in determining legal and moral responses to the pregnant woman-fetus relationship are dramatically changed at birth (Dickenson and Bewley, 1999). Of course, following birth there is often still considerable pain interconnection and bodily interconnection caused by the mother-baby relationship, but there are of a different nature and kind.

Second, birth ends the blurring of identity that pregnancy can cause. Margaret Anne Little (1999) emphasises the significance of the intercorporality involved in pregnancy:

> To be pregnant is to be *inhabited*. It is to be *occupied*. It is to be in a state of physical *intimacy* of a particularly thorough-going nature. The fetus intrudes on the body massively; whatever medical risks one faces or avoids the brute fact remains that the fetus shifts and alters the very physical boundaries of the woman's self. To mandate continuation of gestation is, quite simply, to force continuation of such occupation.

This blurring of the body, the self and identity, is fundamentally changed on birth. Again, it is not claimed that following birth the woman returns to her 'former self'. The blurring of boundaries between parent and child continues after birth, but it becomes a different blurring.

Third, as argued above, it is important to see pregnancy within the wider social context. A relational model requires a consideration of the rights, obligations and responsibilities not only of the pregnant woman and the fetus, but also of the wider society. The nature of the obligations of society and others are also dramatically changed by birth. The social and political dynamics which play such a role in forming an understanding of what it is to be pregnant change, as the woman becomes regarded as a mother. A new set of expectations and norms are created concerning what it is to be a 'good mother' (Herring, 2007). As this social role changes so too do the obligations that flow from the relationship.

Another obvious change caused through birth is that care of the child by people other than the pregnant woman becomes more feasible. Staughton LJ in *Re F (In Utero)*, 1988 made the obvious point in explaining why a fetus could not be made a ward of court:

> The court cannot care for a child, or order that others should do so, until the child is born; only the mother can.

Birth enables there to be treatment of the child by others, without directly interfering on the body of the woman. As Mary Anne Warren (1989) argues:

> Birth is morally significant because it marks the end of one relationship and the beginning of others. It marks the end of pregnancy, a relationship so intimate that it is impossible to extend the equal protection of the law to fetuses without severely infringing women's most basic rights. Birth also marks the beginning of the infant's existence as a socially responsive member of a human community. Although the infant is not instantly transformed into a person at the moment of birth, it does become a biologically separate human being. As such, it can be known and cared for as a particular individual. It can also be vigorously protected without negating the basic rights of women.

Finally, the enormity of the birthing process itself changes the relationship between the parties. Dickenson and Bewley (1999) have written that

> The fetus cannot enjoy rights until the pregnant woman elects to endow it with the Status of an autonomous agent, cannot enjoy life until the pregnant woman *gives* it life.

This captures the important point that the woman through the labour and birth causes this significant change in the relationship between woman and child.

To summarise the argument, I have argued that moral rights and obligations during pregnancy should flow from the relationship, rather than the status of the fetus. The significance of birth lies not in the change in the capacities of the fetus, but in the dramatic impact it has upon the relationship between pregnant woman and fetus.

(b) Difficulties of a Relational Approach

There will be concerns about the relational approach adopted in this chapter. The chapter has applied a relational approach to the significance of birth, but leaves a host of other pregnancy issues unanswered (see Scott, this volume). Other commentators have looked at some of these issues using a relational approach (eg Seymour, 2000; Morgan, 1996), but space prevents me doing so here. For some readers there may be a concern that in talking in terms of a relationship between a pregnant woman and the fetus, I am implicitly accepting that the fetus has some kind of status or interests, which will work against the interests of pregnant women (Bewley, 1994). I do not mean to accept that. By relationship I mean to focus on concrete matters such as what each party has done for each other in the past and future burdens that will be incurred in the relationship. I do not mean my approach to shut off the conclusion that the fetus has done nothing for the pregnant woman and the circumstances of their relationship give rise to no obligations from the pregnant woman at all. From a rather different view point, the relational approach might be said to load the dice against the fetus who, inevitably, cannot contribute to the relationship. The relational approach, it might be said, inevitably downplays the claims of the fetus. This argument, however, assumes that the central claim that obligations arise from relationship is incorrect. If the relational approach is the correct approach to take and using it means that the fetus has no claims on the pregnant woman, its conclusion is not a reason for rejecting it. Finally, it might be said that status is an inherent part of a relationship. A person relates to someone in a certain way because of their status. A person's relationship to another person will be deeply affected by whether or not they are their child, for example. So we cannot avoid the issue of addressing status because that is central to the relationship. However, pregnancy gives us a fine example of why that is not so. The widely differing attitudes and responses of pregnant women towards their fetus indicate that it is not the status of the fetus which is important in their relationship. Women's relationships with their fetuses differ greatly. That is something that the relational approach is able to capture well, but is lost with an approach based on status.

V. CONCLUSION

The law has struggled to determine the precise nature of the fetus. It has been more confident in determining that on birth an important change of legal status takes place: from fetus to person. Many writers have found the significance attached to birth hard to justify. The status of fetus, they argue, has not changed because its inherent characteristics do not change significantly on birth. This chapter has argued that this approach is mistaken. The law should focus on the relationship between the pregnant woman, the fetus and those around them. From this perspective the moment of birth marks a clear change in the relationship between woman and child and justifies a change in the nature of obligations between them. This chapter, therefore, seeks to provide a justification for the current law on the significance of birth.

The traditional focus on status explains why the law has struggled to determine the legal position of the fetus and provide a satisfactory explanation for the significance of birth. As Catherine Mackinnon (1991) puts it: 'The fetus is in the pregnant woman's body, but it is also "of" her in that it is interconnected with her in many intricate and intimate ways'. This makes ascertaining the intrinsic qualities of the fetus not only impossible, but meaningless. Not only that, but the wider set of relationships the pregnant woman is in and the broader social context are invisible when the focus on fetal status. (Donchin, 2001).

Catriona Mackenzie (1992) has written of the way those academic discussions on abortion:

> have focused philosophical and moral reflection away from the contexts in which deliberations about abortion are usually made and away from the concerns and experiences which motivate those involved in the processes of deliberation. The result is that philosophical analyses of abortion often seem beside the point, if not completely irrelevant, to the lives of the countless women who daily not only have to make moral decisions about abortion but, more importantly, who often face serious risks to their lives in contexts where abortion is not a safe and readily accessible procedure.

Much the same could be made about the legal regulation of pregnancy and parenthood generally. It is this which, for me, most strongly calls for a relational approach. The abstracted weighing of the interests of the fetus/baby and woman pays no account of the complex interactions between them; and between them and those who are in relationship with them.; not to mention to the broader social context which has such an impact on the actual and perceived moral and legal obligations that are imposed. We need to move from an idealised analysis and listen to voices of women faced with pregnancy decisions and decisions concerning birth and children. There we usually find not the language of status, rights, viability or choice: but the language of despair; ecstasy; interconnection and guilt. The language is that of relationships: seeking to do the right thing 'for everyone'. It is there we need to start the legal and moral analysis of pregnancy and find the significance of birth.

REFERENCES

Annas, G. (1986). Pregnant Women as Fetal Containers. *Hastings Centre Report* **16**, 13–14.

Bewley, S. (1994). Legal Frameworks to Prevent Harm in-utero. *Medical Law International* **1**, 227.

Bridgeman, J. and Millns, A. (1998). *Feminist Perspectives on Law*. London: Sweet and Maxwell.

Dickenson, D. and Bewley, S. (1999). Abortion, Relationship, and Property in Labour: A Clinical Case Study. *Cambridge Quarterly of Healthcare Ethics*, **8**, 440–448.

Donchin, A. (2001). Understanding Autonomy Relationally. *Journal of Medicine and Philosophy* **26**, 4–15.

Dworkin, R. M. (1993). *Life's Dominion*. New York: Alfred Knopf.

Effron, R. J. (2005). Dependence, Identity, and Abortion Politics. *NYU Journal of Law & Liberty* **1**, 1108–1133.

Elvey, A. (2003). The Material Given: Bodies, Pregnant Bodies and Earth. *Australian Feminist Studies* **18**, 199–209.

Fletcher, J. (1979). *Humanhood: Essays in Biomedical Ethics*. Buffalo, NY: Prometheus Books.

Foster, C. (2009). Medical Law too often Doffs its Cap to the Doctor's White Coat. *The Times*, 21 May 2009.

Fovargue, S. and Miola, J. (1998). Policing Pregnancy. *Medical Law Review* **6**, 265–296.

George, R. P. (2008). Embryo Ethics. *Daedalus* **137**, 23–25

Gilmore, S., Herring, J. and Probert, R. (2009). Parental Responsibility – Law, Issues and Themes. In *Parental Responsibility and Responsible Parenting* (ed. R. Probert, S. Gilmore and J. Herring), pp. 1–20. Oxford: Hart.

Hadfield, G. (1998). An Expressive Theory of Contract. *University of Pennsylvania Law Review* **146**, 1235–1285

Hanisberg, J. (1985). Homologizing Pregnancy and Motherhood: A Consideration of Abortion. *Michigan Law Review* **94**, 371–418.

Herring, J. (2007). Familial Homicide, Failure to Protect and Domestic Violence: Who's the Victim? *Criminal Law Review* 923–933.

Herring, J. (2009). Relational Autonomy and Rape. In *Regulating Autonomy: Sex, Reproduction and Family* (ed. S. Day Sclater, F. Ebtehaj, E. Jackson and M. Richards), pp. 53–71, Oxford: Hart.

Herring, J. and Chau P.-L. (2007). My body. Your body. Our bodies. *Medical Law Review* 15, 34–61.

Little, M. O. (1999). Abortion, Intimacy and the Duty to Gestate. *Ethical Theory and Moral Practice* 2, 295–312.

Ludlow, J. (2008). Sometimes, it's a Child *and* a Choice: Toward an Embodied Abortion Praxis. *NWSA Journal* 20, 26–50.

Mackenzie, C. (1992). Abortion and Embodiment. *Australian Journal of Philosophy* 70, 136–155.

Mackinnon, C. (1991). *Towards a Feminist Theory of the State*. Cambridge MA: Harvard University Press.

Mason, K. (1998). *Medico-Legal Aspects of Reproduction and Parenthood*. Aldershot: Dartmouth.

Masson, J. (2006). Parenting by Being; Parenting by Doing. In *Freedom and Responsibility in Reproductive Choice* (ed. J. Spencer and A. du Bois-Pedain). Oxford: Hart.

Morgan, L. (1996). Fetal Relationality in Feminist Philosophy: An Anthropological Critique. *Hypatia* 11, 47–70.

Nelson, E. (2004). Reconceiving Pregnancy: Expressive Choice and Legal Reasoning. *McGill Law Journal* 49, 593–634.

Nussbaum, M. (1999). *Sex and Social Justice*. New York: Oxford University Press.

Romito, P., Escriba-Aguir, V., Promicino, L., Lucchetta, C., Scrimin, F. and Molzan, J. (2009). Violence in the Lives of Women in Italy who Have an Elective Abortion. *Women's Health Issues* 19,335–343.

Rothman, B. K. (1986). When a Pregnant Woman Endangers her Fetus. *Hastings Centre Report* 16, 24–25.

Royal College of Obstetricians and Gynaecologists (1996). *Termination of Pregnancy for Fetal Abnormality in England, Wales and Scotland*. London: Royal College of Obstetricians and Gynaecologists.

Seymour, J. (2000). *Childbirth and the Law*. Oxford: Oxford University Press.

Singer, P. (1979). *Practical Ethics*. Cambridge: Cambridge University Press.

Turan, J. (2009). Violence in the Lives of Women in Italy who Have an Elective Abortion. *Women's Health Issues* 19, 335–34

Warren, M. A. (1989). The Moral Significance of Birth. *Hypatia*, 4, 46–65.

—— (1997). *Moral Status*. Oxford: Oxford University Press.

Wells, C. and Morgan, D. (1991). Whose Foetus Is It? *Journal of Law and Society* 18, 431–445.

Whitfield, A. (1998). Actions Arising from Birth in *Principles of Medical Law* (ed. A. Grubb), pp. 650–713. Oxford: Oxford University Press.

Wise, P. (2008). Transforming Preconceptional, Prenatal, and Interconceptional Care into a Comprehensive Commitment to Women's Health. *Women's Health Issues* **18**, 13–18.

Cases

Attorney-General's Reference (No 3 or 1994) [1998] AC 245

Burton v Islington HA [1993] QB 204

C v S [1988] QB 135

Campbell, Inquest on Infant, Stoke on Trent 19 October 1983.

Paton v BPAS [1978] 2 All ER 987

R v Crutchley [1837] 7 C & P 814

R v Enoch [1833] 5 C & P 539

R v Hamilton The Times 16 September 1983

R v Iby [2005] 63 NSWLR 278

R v Poulton [1832] 5 C & P 329

R v Sellis [1837] 7 C & P 850

R v Tait, [1990] 1 QB 290

Rance v Mid-Downs HA, 1991

Re A (Conjoined Twins) [2001] Fam 147

Re F (In Utero) [1988] Fam 122

Re J [2006] EWHC 2199 (Fam)

Vo v France [2004] 2 FCR 577

Legislation

Abortion Act 1967

Congential Disabiltiies (Civil Liability) Act 1976, s. 1(1)

Infant Life Preservation Act 1929

Offences Against the Person Act 1861

6

Refusing Medical Treatment during Pregnancy and Birth: Ethical and Legal Issues

ROSAMUND SCOTT

I. INTRODUCTION

I T IS WELL-KNOWN that pregnant women typically do all they can to promote the wellbeing of the fetuses they are carrying. Sometimes however, although rarely, fetal medical needs may be problematic for a pregnant woman, to the extent that she wishes to refuse treatment apparently needed by the fetus (see further Bewley and Kirkham, both this volume). This was the case in *Re S*, English law's first 'caesarean' decision, which occurred 18 years ago by means of a hearing that lasted about 18 minutes. Here Sir Stephen Brown P. had to decide whether it would be lawful for doctors to override the refusal on religious grounds (S was a Born Again Christian), of a fully competent 30-year-old woman to undergo an emergency caesarean section. Without a declaration it would have been a criminal and tortious assault to touch the woman without her consent, even if it was deemed to be in her (or her fetus's) best interests. The surgeons considered the operation necessary to save the lives of both the woman and the fetus, which was in a position of 'transverse lie', and the declaration was granted. Following *Re S* there was a series of high-profile and controversial cases in which the competence of pregnant women generally in the treatment context appeared at times to be in doubt (for example, *Re L*, (1997); *Rochdale (NHS) Trust v C*, (1997); *St George's Healthcare NHS Trust v S, R v Collins and others, ex parte S*, (1998)). Five years later, however, the legal right of a competent pregnant woman to refuse any medical treatment or surgery for the fetus was established in *Re MB* (1997).

In *Re MB*, however, the Court of Appeal observed that ethical dilemmas remain about why a woman – particularly an apparently voluntarily pregnant one – should have this right in the light of the possible harm to the fetus or the future child she carries. Accordingly, I offer some brief reflections on aspects of the maternal-fetal relationship within the treatment context, with a view to considering the moral justification for a pregnant woman's legal right to refuse medical treatment, in Section III of this chapter. The court in *Re MB* was also puzzled (even embarrassed, perhaps) by aspects of the relationship between the right to refuse treatment when pregnant, on the one hand, and the law of abortion on the other, but said nothing further about this. Moreover, since third parties do have legal duties not to harm the fetus, duties instantiated in the tort of negligence, one might also ask why a pregnant woman does not. I address aspects of the relationship between the law regarding the right to refuse treatment in pregnancy, abortion and prenatal injury in Section IV (see also Scott, 2002).

In Section II, I discuss in more detail the decisions in *Re S* and *Re MB*.

II. THE 'CAESAREAN CASES'

a) The Current Law

When *Re S* was heard (*ex parte*) there was no prior English authority directly on point. Two months earlier however, in *Re T (Adult: Refusal of Treatment)* (1992), in which a 34-week pregnant Jehovah's Witness in the first stages of labour refused a blood transfusion, as subsequent to the forthcoming caesarean section, following discussions with her mother, Lord Donaldson MR had suggested a 'possible qualification' to the autonomy of a competent adult where respecting a treatment refusal may lead to the death of a viable fetus. By granting the declaration that it would be lawful to operate on S without her consent, Sir Stephen Brown P., in effect, took up the invitation to allow such an exception. Yet his judgment – of less than one page – does little to reveal what Lord Donaldson MR had described as a situation of 'considerable legal and ethical complexity'. This is one of the shortcomings, of course, of emergency and also *ex parte* decision-making. Although he sought to bolster his judgment with reference to then recent American authority on point in *Re AC* (1987), in fact he was misinformed about the state of the US case law (*Re AC* had been overturned in 1990: *Re AC* (1990)), and so *Re S* was not in fact in line with the most recent US authorities, although it was compatible with earlier US decisions involving similar fact patterns.

English law had the opportunity to revisit the caesarean issue several times in the aftermath of *Re S*. In all of the subsequent cases competence to consent to or refuse medical treatment was in issue. It was not until *Re MB* in 1997 that the principle was established of a competent woman's right to refuse any medical or surgical treatment needed by the fetus, although in that case the court deemed the woman, who had a needle phobia which rendered her unable to consent to the needle that was the precondition to the general anaesthetic, incompetent. In my view, this was the correct decision, since Miss MB clearly wanted the caesarean, but found herself unable to consent to the anaesthetic that preceded it. Her autonomy, then, was aided by a decision to operate on her without the consent she was, in fact, unable to give.

Turning to explore the principle of the decision in *Re MB* Lady Justice Butler-Sloss stated:

> The law is, in our judgment, clear that a competent woman who has the capacity to decide may, for religious reasons, other reasons, or for no reasons at all, choose not to have medical intervention, even though… the consequence may be the death or serious handicap of the child she bears or her own death. …The fetus up to the moment of birth does not have any separate interests capable of being taken into account when a court has to consider an application for a declaration in respect of a caesarian section operation.

In essence, the given legal reason for the equivalence in rights of the pregnant and the non-pregnant woman lies in the fetus's lack of legal rights, or 'legal personality', such that the courts have no power to take its needs into existence before birth, at least against the pregnant woman. In concluding this, the court cited case-law such as *Re F (in utero)* (1988), concerning a failed attempt to ward a fetus on the grounds of the lifestyle of its mother, and *Paton v UK* (1980), in which the (then existing) European Commission essentially held that the fetus does not have a right to life under Article 2 of the European Convention on Human Rights. This position was recently affirmed by the European Court of Human Rights in *Vo v France* (2004). The court in *Re MB* also noted that the law relating to prenatal injury, on which I touch below, supported at most third-party liability for prenatal harm (with an exception for harm occurring as a result of negligent driving in the pregnant woman's case).

b) The Reliance on the Fetus's Lack of Legal Personhood

The court in *Re MB* might also have referred to the right to respect for private and family life under Article 8 of the European Convention on Human Rights ('ECHR'), now incorporated into English law under the Human Rights Act 1998 ('HRA' 1998), and would certainly have done so if the case had been heard after that Act came into force in 2000. It is now clear that Article 8 is a very powerful article in the medical treatment context. Generally, it protects the right of the competent adult to refuse medical treatment, though there has been no subsequent case-law explicitly confirming this in the context of pregnancy. Yet, apart from reiterating that the fetus is not a legal person, *Re MB* did not address the question of why a pregnant woman – who is not identical to one who is not pregnant – should have the same right as any other competent woman to refuse medical treatment. This is symptomatic of the extent to which the court placed reliance, in its reasoning, on the bald fact of the fetus's lack of legal personality, rather than engage in a consideration of the significance of a woman's rights that are called into play in the medical treatment context. The latter approach can be found in case-law in the United States. For instance, in *Baby Boy Doe* (1994) (a caesarean case heard in the Appellate Court of Illinois) Presiding Justice DiVito, in explaining the significance of the right to refuse treatment, stressed that a woman's interests in self-determination and bodily integrity are 'deeply personal', citing US Supreme Court case law from another medical context (that of persistent vegetative state, considered in *Cruzan v Director, Missouri Department of Health* (1990)). I discuss this and related case-law further below.

In reality, the rule that the fetus lacks legal rights has in fact emerged because of the impact that the ascription of fetal rights would have on a pregnant woman. In this sense the denial of fetal legal personhood is ultimately a choice against coercion of pregnant women. Although the extent to which a woman's interests and rights in self-determination and bodily integrity would be affected by an attempt to protect the fetus will depend upon the nature of the restriction or invasion in question, the denial of fetal legal personhood is effectively recognition that, as Mary Ann Warren (1989, p. 112) has put it, '[t]here is room for only one person with full and equal rights inside a single human skin'. In *Re MB*, however, there is no discussion of the reasons for the fetus's lack of legal personhood. This can make the decision's reliance on this point seem like something of a *technicality*. In turn, this is unfortunate when such significant interests, particularly in life and health, may be at stake on the fetus's part. Further, given the rather technical appearance of the rule that the fetus has no legal personality, it is perhaps not surprising that English judges appear to struggle, on occasion, to acknowledge something, in law, about the 'value' of fetal life. For instance, in the caesarean case of *St George's Healthcare NHS Trust v S, R v Collins and others, ex parte S* (1998), Judge LJ observes '[w]hatever else it may be, a 36-week foetus is not nothing; if viable it is not lifeless and it is certainly human'. I return to this point about 'fetal value' in my conclusions. In general, it is important that the reasons for the fetus's lack of legal personality are the subject of reflection at significant judicial moments as well as in academic commentary.

In the light of what may appear a rather technical solution to the issue before the court, and even though the fetus's lack of legal personality can in fact be explained with reference to highly significant points of principle and policy, in *Re MB* Butler-Sloss LJ is acknowledging that ethical dilemmas remain about a pregnant woman's treatment refusal rights. It was not thought appropriate for a court of law to address this issue. Yet, as she virtually admits, a reconciliation of the law and ethics by means of a moral justification of the law is desirable. This is particularly so in the light of the widespread public awareness of the issue that attended the caesarean cases, as well as the increasing scope for interventions to benefit the fetus, both of which may in the future put pressure on a pregnant woman's legal right to refuse medical treatment. This highlights the need for some consideration of the moral justification of this legal right.

This is also desirable given the extent to which competence has been in issue in the caesarean cases and the way the legal test to rebut an adult's presumed competence under the Mental Capacity Act 2005, which includes a 'weighing element', may play out in this context, for instance as maternal concerns or risks versus fetal medical needs. Thus, despite the inclusion of a 'diagnostic threshold', so that the presumption that an adult has capacity can only be rebutted if a mental impairment or disturbance is affecting the ability to make a decision (sections 2 and 3), it is not inconceivable that third-party judgments about the apparent 'irrationality/immorality' of a woman's reasons for refusing medical treatment may illegitimately come to bear on the determination of her competence to decide treatment issues for herself.

Another reason why thinking about the moral justification of the law is helpful is that in *Re MB* Butler-Sloss LJ sanctioned the use of persuasion by third parties, but offered no guidance on this issue. Indeed, after the decision, one health professional who was interviewed described how in most cases there was a consensus of views about treatment between pregnant women, obstetricians and midwives, but in those few cases where this was not so 'heavy duty persuasion usually works' although, at the end of the day, the 'woman's wishes' must be accepted (Anon, 1998). In fact, the lack of guidance about the appropriate place and extent of persuasion in *Re MB* is highly problematic because excessive use of persuasion might itself breach a pregnant woman's rights in this context: the ECHR, incorporated into English law by the HRA 1998, 'is intended to guarantee not rights that are theoretical or illusory but rights that are practical and effective' (*Airey v Ireland*, 1979–80). By comparison, the place of persuasion in relation to the legal right to *abort* has been the subject of intensive scrutiny in US Supreme Court case-law as in *Planned Parenthood of Southeastern Pennsylvania v Casey* (1992). I return to the place of persuasion in my conclusions.

I now offer some thoughts about moral aspects of the maternal-fetal relationship in the treatment context. There is only scope for a brief sketch here.

III. MORAL ASPECTS OF THE MATERNAL-FETAL RELATIONSHIP IN THE TREATMENT CONTEXT

a) The Moral Status of the Fetus

It seems unlikely that there will ever be agreement on the moral status of the fetus. On the one hand, then, offering any thoughts on this issue might be thought to have little point. On the other, if any thoughts are to be offered on the question of the moral justification of the legal position that a pregnant woman has the right to refuse medical treatment, some consideration of the fetus's moral position is unavoidable. What moral claims, if any, does the fetus have?

As is well-known, there is a range of moral positions on this issue. For example, on a potentiality account of moral status, the embryo has full moral status from the moment of conception (Finnis, 1973). On many other views, its status is either non-existent or very low when compared with that of a three- or six-month fetus, such that it lacks moral rights. On some moral views also, the fetus lacks these. For instance, if personhood is deemed morally significant, then since even a relatively advanced fetus lacks many of the features associated with personhood, such as rationality and self-consciousness, it is not a moral person and so lacks moral rights (Warren, 1973).

Although both the potentiality account and the personhood account entail the notion of rights, it is worth recalling that moral duties do not have to correlate with rights, in the sense that arguably there is a domain of what have been called 'imperfect obligations' which may be owed to others regardless of whether they possess rights. If this is so, then if the fetus lacks moral rights, this is not determinative of the moral question of our treatment of it.

In my view, the embryo's and fetus's moral status increases gradually. This is typically called a 'gradualist' account, one that is favoured by various others (Feinberg, 1989; Kennedy, 1992; Dworkin, 1994). It is also an approach that is reflected in the law relating to abortion, given the increased stringency of the grounds under the Abortion Act 1967 (as amended by the Human Fertilisation and Embryology Act 1990) (the 'AA 1967') section 1. A weakness of this approach may seem that it involves no clear concepts, such as 'potentiality' or 'personhood' and that one cannot point to any particular moment, such as conception or viability or the last week before birth, as deciding the moral status of the embryo or fetus. Yet I tend to think that the more one reflects on the moral status of each, the less satisfactory the potentiality account at one end or the personhood account at the other, or the identification of some intermediate marker, such as the fetus's attainment of viability, can ever be. Importantly, this may be because I consider that, at least when we are thinking about reproductive autonomy, the question of the moral status of the fetus is necessarily, and primarily, a question about the relationship between the fetus and a pregnant woman (see also Herring, this volume). It is worth stressing the considerable significance of this point. (This is not to deny that others may also have a moral relationship with the embryo or fetus, such as health professionals or fathers.) So what does a gradualist approach mean in this context?

In essence, the longer a pregnancy has been allowed to develop, the greater must be the justification – or the more serious the reason – on the woman's part for compromising the life or health of the fetus. Another way of expressing this is to say that a woman's reasons for refusing medical treatment must be that much more serious. Attractively, the approach allows for an interplay of maternal and fetal interests: by definition it looks both to the fetus and to the pregnant woman who carries it. This is highly appropriate to the maternal-fetal relationship. Further, since a gradualist approach is not concerned with whether the fetus has moral rights but instead with the imperfect duties that may be owed it, it has a moral sensitivity to the developmental and physically dependent story that is the fetus's journey into the world. And since it acknowledges the possibility that a woman's serious reasons may justify compromising the fetus's position, it recognises the physical, emotional and other burdens of pregnancy for her.

This approach can be refined to apply to the future child (understood here as 'the child who will be but is not yet born', rather than, as it were, the fetus which might die as a result of non-treatment) who may subsequently be born with damage suffered *in utero*. In this case, a woman's reasons for refusing treatment must relate particularly to her body (which will likely be the case especially where invasive treatment is in issue), given that the most important distinguishing feature between a born child and a future but as yet unborn child is that the latter is *in utero* until birth.

Having briefly discussed the fetus, I now touch on a pregnant woman's interests in the treatment setting. There is only scope for a brief sketch here.

b) The Moral Interests that Underlie a Woman's Right to Refuse Treatment

The moral right to refuse medical treatment is underpinned by a person's moral interests in bodily integrity and in self-determination (understood here as an interest in making important personal choices). Arguably, both of these interests can be derived from the value of autonomy (following in part Raz, (1986)). Since at least a voluntarily pregnant woman has chosen to bring a child into the world, what are usually thought of as absolute moral rights for non-pregnant adults might reasonably be thought of as *prima facie* rights in her case, because (unless it is thought that the fetus or future child has no moral claims, as some may indeed consider) she also has at least *prima facie* moral duties to the fetus or the future child. But when does she retain the right to refuse treatment, and when does she have the duty to submit to it?

Here it may be helpful to think, so far as we can, about whether a woman's *reasons* for seeking to exercise her right to refuse medical treatment are serious. When we try to do this, however, we see that judging seriousness (in non-trivial cases) is inherently problematic because the reasons a woman has for refusing medical treatment will be very personal. Indeed, since the medical treatment context generally invokes a patient's very personal interests and rights in self-determination and bodily integrity – and so a woman's reasons for refusing treatment will typically be related to the way the proposed treatment impacts on these interests – then how would we judge when, if ever, a woman has the duty, moral or legal, to accept medical treatment for the fetus? In my view, this *is* the problem, in effect, of the maternal-fetal conflict within the medical treatment context and it lies at the heart, not only of an ethical analysis of the conflict, but also of the relevant law. As I see it, then, the maternal-fetal conflict is a problem which lies at the interface between rights and duties, both moral and legal. On this analysis there are important conceptual links between the ethics and the law which mean that the problem is not *primarily* one inhering in the legal enforcement of moral obligations, as there has been a tendency to suppose. In my view, therefore, apart from some very obvious cases where reasons may be trivial, seriousness may be something that has in some sense to be taken on trust.

I shall briefly hint at these difficulties by considering a pregnant woman's relationship to the fetus, first in terms of her rights and second, her duties. Thinking about the extent of her rights, we can focus on her interest in self-determination (in making important personal choices) and different kinds of reasons for refusing medical treatment. One example is the religious reason. As foreshadowed above, the moral difficulty here is how to weigh a very personal reason, one we do not share, against the moral claims of the fetus. In essence, we can either challenge the seriousness of that reason, and so potentially disrupt the role of religion in the pregnant woman's life, or we must respect the place of religion in her life – perhaps because we recognise that religion is a 'construct which gives meaning to people's lives' (Savulescu, 1994). In this way, even though we might not think a woman's religious reasons serious ourselves, we would have to recognise the seriousness of the reasons for her.

By contrast, a woman who for no apparent reason refuses to take a pill which has no adverse side-effects for her (such as folic acid) might be thought clearly not to be justified in exercising her moral right to refuse treatment, so that in effect we could say that she has the moral duty to take the pill. Interestingly, the lack of a serious reason for not taking the pill, with its implication that she has the duty to do so, is connected with the point that doing so could not be said *seriously* to invoke her interest in self-determination (recall, this concerns deep personal choices) or bodily integrity (impinged minimally by the ingestion of the pill).

We can also try to look at the maternal-fetal relationship through the lens of the idea of duty, focusing on the idea of a duty being owed 'through the body'. Is there a duty to have a caesarean section apparently needed by the fetus, just as Thomson considered whether there is a duty to continue a pregnancy (Thomson, 1971)? Thinking about this, in my view we encounter considerable difficulties if we try to determine the existence and extent – in effect, the reasonableness – of a very bodily (indeed extraordinary) duty, to aid another. For example, the case of *Rochdale (NHS) Trust v C*, (1997) concerned a woman who, like her fetus, was also at risk of death without a caesarean. She had previously experienced a caesarean birth and, most strikingly, said she 'would rather die' than have another. This very strong feeling was apparently more significant than the particular issues of 'back pain' and 'pain around the scar' which she also raised. In other words, what is significant about C's case, I think, is not that she was offering the latter as reasons which she thought sufficient to justify her own and the fetus' death, but rather that she actually felt she would prefer to die than have another caesarean. (It is worth noting here that a bad birth experience can be the result of both 'natural' and surgical delivery.) C was in fact deemed incompetent. This kind of case reveals, I think, the limitations of attempts to analyse a pregnant woman's duties to the fetus in terms of Good Samaritan arguments, since these typically concern duties in the course of daily conduct. Similarly, the idea of a pregnant woman's duty to accept a caesarean for her fetus's sake is wrongly characterised as an instance of an 'ordinary neighbourly duty' to help another, as John Finnis would likely describe it given his work on abortion (Finnis, 1973), since by definition such 'ordinary' duties do not involve extraordinary bodily invasions.

Indeed, travelling along the spectrum of possible positive duties, we can move away from the notion of a positive duty being owed in the treatment context 'through the body', as it were, to the notion of positive duties toward others in the realm of what we might call 'general conduct', the reasonableness of which appears *somewhat* easier to determine: the reasonableness of an able-bodied rescuer jumping into a slow-flowing river to save a child is an example. By contrast, moving on to negative duties not to harm others in the course of general conduct, these are arguably the clearest: for instance, it is not difficult to say that a negative moral duty clearly lies not to knock the child into the river in the first place.

However, the women in the maternal-fetal cases are typically voluntarily pregnant, and it might be objected that they therefore have absolute positive duties entailing large and even extraordinary burdens to the fetuses they are carrying. For instance, although Joel Feinberg criticises the view that negative duties are more stringent than positive ones, he argues that positive duties are indeed less stringent where social organisation would make the imposition of strict positive duties on everyone chaotic but that some people, such as firemen and pregnant women, have undertaken extensive positive duties that entail running exceptionally high risks (Feinberg, 1984).

In my view, however, beginning a pregnancy is not just the assumption of a chosen social role with associated social duties but rather is a choice to create another human being. Pregnant women (and their partners) cannot choose another way to have a child (subject to irrelevant exceptions). Given the very real personal significance to the woman (and partner) of reproduction, it might be thought unjust to say that either a pregnant woman must accept any treatment required by the fetus, in particular the seriously invasive and, for some, religiously problematic caesarean section, or not become pregnant and have a child. In this light, her positive duties to assist the fetus are arguably less stringent than the negative ones not unintentionally to harm it. I refer to this as the 'social context' of pregnancy.

In the next and final section of the chapter I consider the case for a maternal legal duty of care, as well as the reconciliation of the law relating to maternal refusal of medical treatment with the law on abortion.

IV. RECONCILING A PREGNANT WOMAN'S LEGAL RIGHT TO REFUSE MEDICAL
TREATMENT WITH THE LAW OF TORT AND ABORTION

a) A Maternal Prenatal Duty of Care?

Under section 1 of the Congenital Disabilities (Civil Liability) Act 1976 (the 'CDA 1976') if a child is born disabled due to certain specified occurrences it may have a cause of action (derived from a duty owed to its parents) in respect of the wrongful act against a third party, but not against its mother, except in relation to her negligent driving. Why should this be so? Reflection on this question requires that we think about why a maternal prenatal duty of care is inappropriate, if it is.

The above discussion of the difficulty, in certain cases at least, of determining when a woman's *prima facie* moral rights in the treatment context should 'give way' to a duty to accept treatment on the fetus's behalf also foreshadows the difficulty that we would have, for the purposes of the tort of negligence, of determining the standard of any 'prenatal maternal duty of care'.

In the medical treatment context, the difficulty stems from the fact that a pregnant woman's *rights* are invoked. To attempt to define the 'reasonable pregnant woman' in the treatment context therefore involves the problematic task of seeking to assess the strength of very personal interests and reasons. The tort of negligence, focused as it is on deterring and compensating in respect of harm to others occurring in the arena of general conduct, is ill-placed to do this. Not surprisingly then, the Appellate Court of Illinois in *Baby Boy Doe* (1994) considered that a pregnant woman does not have a legal duty to submit to a caesarean because of the extensive impact this would have upon her life, but especially on her rights. The case drew on the earlier decision in *Stallman v Youngquist* (1988) in which the Illinois Supreme Court held that a pregnant woman did not owe a duty of care to her fetus in respect of unintentional prenatal injuries. The *Stallman* court emphasised the uniqueness of the relationship between a pregnant woman and her fetus, observing (per Cunningham J):

> No other plaintiff depends exclusively on any other defendant for everything necessary for life itself. No other defendant must go through biological changes of the most profound type, possibly at the risk of her own life, in order to bring forth an adversary into the world.

By contrast with the difficulty of establishing the extent of a maternal duty to submit to medical treatment or surgery, determining a standard of care would be less difficult in relation to possible instances of maternal conduct which may harm the fetus, such as negligent driving, smoking, excessive alcohol consumption or drug abuse. The idea of a moral duty not to engage in these activities is in fact an example of a negative duty not to harm the future child, in relation to which the determination of unreasonableness would often be fairly clear. In this light, there is a *prima facie* case for the imposition of a tortious duty not to engage in such conduct, in the same way that third parties can be liable for harm to the fetus/future child of a pregnant woman by their negligent conduct. In relation to third parties, it is worth noting that they are detached (that is, not physically attached) from the fetus. In turn this means that the rule that the fetus is not a legal person is of no import when we think about their potential liability.

Turning first to the case of negligent driving, in relation to which a woman's interests in self-determination and bodily integrity are not invoked, there is a good case for legal liability for negligently caused harm to the fetus. In this light, it is right that in England a woman can be liable for harming her fetus by her negligent driving under the CDA 1976, a position influenced by the existence of compulsory third-party insurance in the road-traffic accident context. By comparison, the Supreme Court of Canada arguably unnecessarily rejected maternal liability for negligent driving in *Dobson v Dobson* (1999).

Moving beyond negligent driving, should there be potential liability for maternal use of drugs, cigarettes and excess alcohol? In effect, should pregnant women be liable for negligently caused harm in the way that detached third parties can be in various ways? As indicated above, and in the light of the wholly unjustified nature of the harm that might occur in these ways, especially, to the future child, there is a good *prima facie* case for the imposition of such liability. However, arguably social problems giving rise to addiction would make it hard to be sure that such a duty was appropriate or fair. I am alluding here also to problems that may be associated with voluntariness in women's lives, particularly women who may have been the subject of some kind of abuse. In Canada, the Supreme Court rejected just such liability in *Winnipeg Child and Family Services (Northwest Area) v DFG* (1997), arguing that the idea of imposing legal duties upon a pregnant woman could intrude upon a 'woman's right to make choices concerning herself' (per McLachlin J). As it happens, the issue in that case (solvent abuse) was an instance of what I have called general conduct and does not invoke the key moral interests that are at play in the treatment context. In fact, this is implicitly acknowledged by the majority in *Winnipeg*, which observed that it 'may be easy to determine that abusing solvents does not add substantial value to a pregnant woman's well-being and may not be the type of self-determination which deserves protection...' (per McLachlin J). In effect, then, the court's reasoning is much more convincing when applied to the situation of maternal refusal of medical treatment, which will likely invoke a woman's valuable moral and legal interests in self-determination and/ or bodily integrity, or to activities of value to the woman. I am thinking here of the demands placed on her by her family commitments or her work.

Overall, however, there are a number of broad policy considerations that weigh against the imposition of tortious duties as regards a woman's general conduct, including the idea that the imposition of a legal duty could intrude heavily into the privacy of a pregnant woman's life, since she can never be 'alone' during pregnancy. This argument brings into play her right to respect for private and family life under Article 8 of the ECHR. As the Supreme Court of Illinois strikingly observed in *Stallman* v *Youngquist*, unlike the third-party tortfeasor whose conduct may harm the fetus, it is a pregnant woman's 'every waking and sleeping moment which, for better or worse, shapes the prenatal environment which forms the world for the developing fetus', something that is not a 'pregnant woman's fault' but 'a fact of life'. This is another way of expressing what I have called the 'social context' point above, but this time in relation to the application of the law. In essence, to decide that pregnant women owe tortious duties of care to their fetuses would make the woman and her fetus 'legal adversaries from the moment of conception until birth'. There is much discussion in the literature of the way in which this would be an unwise policy choice that may well be harmful to prenatal health since pregnant women may be deterred from seeking prenatal care, lest their addictive or other habits become known (Johnsen, 1986).

b) The 'Illogicality' of the Absolute Right to Refuse Treatment but the Limited Options to Abort?

An important question the court left open in *Re MB* was how to understand the relationship between a pregnant woman's right to refuse medical treatment and the law on abortion. Towards the end of its judgment, the court observed that it was 'illogical' that, on the one hand, a competent pregnant woman can refuse medical treatment even at the point of birth but that, on the other, abortions after 24 weeks are illegal in English law except on certain grounds (noted below). On this point, however, the court simply observed that this 'appears to be the present state of the law'.

In English law, as is well known, there is in fact no right to abort at any time. Rather, abortion is legally permissible on the basis of certain grounds, and the law becomes more restrictive after 24 weeks (Section 1 of the AA 1967). Under the so-called 'social ground', up until 24 weeks a woman can terminate a pregnancy if two doctors have formed a good-faith view that there is a greater risk to her physical or mental health in going to term than in termination. After 24 weeks, abortion is only available on the basis that an abortion is necessary to prevent serious permanent injury to her physical or mental health, or to reduce a risk to her life, or where there is a substantial risk that the subsequently born child will be 'seriously handicapped', all grounds also potentially available before 24 weeks.

What is the legal effect of this change at 24 weeks? The most important question, for our purposes, is whether this increased restriction on access to abortion amounts to the imposition of positive legal duties to aid the fetus. In reality, the reduced access to the possibility of abortion after 24 weeks amounts only to the imposition of a more stringent negative duty not to harm, in particular not abort, rather than a positive duty to benefit the fetus. Further, given that abortion law prioritises a pregnant woman in some cases over her fetus even after 24 weeks (at least in relation to the need to prevent serious permanent mental or physical injury or to reduce the risk to her life), it could be reasoned that this assists in confirming a woman's right to refuse medical treatment. This is in the sense that we could highlight the difficulties of third parties – doctors or judges – in making judgments about the physical, psychological or spiritual questions that could arise in relation to treatment issues, in comparison with the purely medical issues arising in relation to the protection of the woman's life or the prevention of grave or permanent injury to her after 24 weeks in the abortion context. The latter, of course, are judgments that doctors are qualified to make regarding post-24 week abortions (see Scott, 2007, Ch 2). In such cases, they are working within a predetermined legal framework in which a woman's rights are not in issue. In turn, this would give further weight to allowing pregnant women the scope to decide these issues in the treatment context.

A further way of reconciling these two areas of law could argue that, given that in English law a pregnant woman has opportunities to abort in the first two-thirds of pregnancy (at least if she satisfies the 'social ground'), increased restrictions upon access to abortion are appropriate after this time. In contrast, as part of the social context argument with regard to the idea of a woman's duties toward the fetus, the need for treatment such as a caesarean arises unpredictably, if not necessarily completely unforeseeably, at the last moment of pregnancy. This means that safe avoidance thereof could only be achieved by abstaining from reproduction. In this way, for the law to hold the caesarean section, or such like, to be a matter of legal duty would be both unsympathetic and unjust toward pregnant women.

A final point, however, might be made about the relationship between these two areas of law and the thought that in one case there is a legal right and in the other there is not. Of course, a pregnant woman's right to refuse medical treatment 'grew out' of the idea of any competent adult's right to refuse treatment. By contrast, the law of abortion is governed by statutory defences to what would otherwise be a crime (Offences Against the Person Act 1861, sections 58 and 59). Thinking about the relationship between the two areas of law then, we could attend, not to the law on abortion after 24 weeks, but rather the law before it. In particular, I am thinking of the case for at least a time-limited legal right to abort, on the basis that women could be trusted to make judgments about terminations themselves. Even if not all women would make this judgment in a reflective manner, the thought that many or most would might be thought to justify the case for at least a limited legal right to abort in English law.

V. CONCLUSIONS

In my view, a pregnant woman cannot fairly be said to have the legal duty, in becoming pregnant, to make extraordinary sacrifices on the fetus's behalf. This is not to say that she does not have a moral duty to 'do all she can'. This much is only reasonable. Yet doing all she can will involve doing all those things that she does not have serious reason to refuse to do (including serious doubts grounding such reasons). In other words, to say that she must 'do all she can' is at the same time to allow for the constraints of her religious faith or her concerns and fears in relation, for instance, to invasive surgery.

Once begun (and not terminated), a pregnancy is something which, in a very real sense, 'happens' to a pregnant woman. In addition, the task of the reproduction of the species is one that falls principally upon women. These factors suggest that justice is broadly served by recognising how important it is for women to have as much control as possible over medical treatment issues in this process. Generally, of course, discussion with third parties about treatment options and choices is likely to enhance a pregnant woman's autonomy. In the unlikely event that a woman's reasons for refusing treatment appear trivial or ill-considered, a delicate judgment, there should be a place for discussion and counselling. This would, in a sense, allow recognition of the point that the fetus's life has value – despite its lack of legal rights – and of the potential for harm to the future child where refusal of treatment would result in harm rather than fetal death. In these circumstances, attempts at persuasion by third parties would be morally acceptable: the reason is that where a woman's reasons are obviously trivial or in some way ill-considered, maternal self-determination (and with it the deep values a woman might hold) is not meaningfully invoked. In such cases, a woman's *prima facie* moral right has clearly 'given way' to the claims of the fetus, and she would unjustifiably claim and exercise a moral and legal right to refuse the treatment. However, coerced (especially surgical) treatment is unwise for a range of moral, legal and policy reasons. It therefore seems appropriate that English law gives pregnant women the right to refuse medical treatment. This position values pregnant women. Overall, it must be hoped that it will be the most beneficial approach for unborn children.

REFERENCES

Airey v *Ireland* [1979-80] 2 EHRR 305
Re AC [1987] 533 A2d 611 (DC App 1987)
Re AC 573 A2d 1235 (DC App 1990)
Baby Boy Doe, 632 NE2d 326 (Ill App 1 Dist 1994)
Cruzan v Director, Missouri Department of Health Led2d 224(1990)
Dobson v *Dobson* [1999] 2 Can SCR 753
Re F (in utero) [1988] 2 All ER 193
Re L [1997] 1 FCR 609
Re MB, 8 Med LR 217 [1997]

Paton v *UK* [1980] 3 EHRR 408

Planned Parenthood of Southeastern Pennsylvania v *Casey*, 120 LEd 674 [1992]

Rochdale (NHS) Trust v *C* [1997] 1 FCR 274

Re S (Adult: Refusal of Treatment) [1992] 4 All ER 671

Stallman v *Youngquist*, 531 NE2d 355 (Ill 1988)

St George's Healthcare NHS Trust v *S, R* v *Collins and others, ex parte S* [1998] 3 All ER 673

Re T (Adult: Refusal of Treatment) [1992] 4 All ER 649

Vo v *France*, Judgment of 8 July 2004, Application no. 53924/00

Winnipeg Child and Family Services (Northwest Area) v *DFG* [1997] 152 DLR (4th) 193

Abortion Act 1967 (as amended by the Human Fertilisation and Embryology Act 1990)

Congenital Disabilities (Civil Liability) Act 1976

Human Rights Act 1998

Mental Capacity Act 2005

Anon, Interviewed on BBC 1 News at 9pm, 7 May 1998 (No name given)

Dworkin, R., (1993). *Life's Dominion: An Argument about Abortion and Euthanasia.* London: Harper Collins

Feinberg, J., (1979). Abortion. In *Freedom and Fulfillment* (ed. J. Feinberg), pp. 37–75. Princeton: Princeton University Press, 1992

—— (1984). The Moral and Legal Responsibility of the Bad Samaritan, pp. 175–196. In *Freedom and Fulfillment* (ed. J. Feinberg), Princeton: Princeton University Press, 1992

Finnis, J., (1973). The Rights and Wrongs of Abortion: A Reply to Judith Thomson. *Phil. & Pub. Aff.* 2, 117–145

Johnsen, D., (1986). The Creation of Fetal Rights: Conflicts with Women's Constitutional Rights to Liberty, Privacy, and Equal Protection. *Yale Law Journal* **95**, 599

Kennedy, I., (1992). A Woman and her Unborn Child. In *Treat Me Right* (ed. I. Kennedy), pp. 364–384. Oxford: Oxford University Press

Raz, J., (1986) *The Morality of Freedom.* Oxford: Clarendon Press

Savulescu, J., (1994) Rational Desires and the Limitation of Life-Sustaining Treatment. *Bioethics*, 8 (3) *Bioethics*, 191–222

Scott, R., (2002). *Rights, Duties and the Body: Law and Ethics of the Maternal-Fetal Conflict.* Oxford: Hart Publishing

—— (2007). *Choosing Between Possible Lives: Law and Ethics of Prenatal and Preimplantation Genetic Diagnosis.* Oxford: Hart Publishing

Thomson, J.J., (1971). A Defence of Abortion. *Philosophy & Public Affairs* **1**, 47–66

Warren, M.A., (1973). On the Moral and Legal Status of Abortion. *The Monist* **57**(1), 43–61

—— (1989). The Moral Significance of Birth. *Hypatia* **4**, 3

7

The Consequences for Preterm Infants of Antenatal Glucocorticoid Treatment

ALISON J FORHEAD AND ABIGAIL L FOWDEN

I. INTRODUCTION

FROM CONCEPTION TO delivery, modern medicine has improved both fertility and the survival of mothers and their babies. For example, increasing numbers of infants are born following use of assisted reproduction technologies, and the survival rate of babies delivered prematurely has risen over the last 20 to 30 years, in part as a result of antenatal glucocorticoid treatment (AGT) of their mothers (Braude, this volume; Norman et al., 2009). Clinical use of AGT helps to prepare the fetus for its premature transition from the uterus to the outside world by accelerating some of the maturational processes that would have occurred naturally with delivery at full term. Whilst AGT is clearly beneficial for the immediate survival of the preterm baby, its consequences in the longer term remain largely unknown. A number of human and animal studies have shown that the environment before birth is important in determining the development and health of the offspring after birth, both in the short and longer term. In human populations, low birth weight, often an indicator of a poor environment in the uterus, is linked to increased neonatal mortality and morbidity, and to a greater susceptibility to diseases such as type II diabetes, obesity, hypertension and coronary heart disease in adulthood (Barker, 1994). Similarly, in experimental animals, and consistent with the human observations, low birth weight is associated with a failure to thrive and with abnormalities in cardiovascular and metabolic function in later life. Together, these epidemiological and experimental studies have led to the concept that environmental factors during pregnancy, such as the level of nutrition, oxygen and circulating hormones, interact with the genes inherited at conception to determine the physiology of the developing fetus with consequences for its health after birth. The process by which these factors, acting at critical periods of development, exert organisational effects that persist throughout life is known as 'developmental' or 'intrauterine programming' (Lucas, 1991). Given that more preterm babies are surviving as a result of AGT, the question arises whether they too might suffer adverse 'developmental programming'? This review will examine the use of AGT as a successful treatment for the effects of preterm delivery and, using examples from experimental animal models, will consider the short- and long-term consequences of this treatment for infants born preterm.

II. MATURATION OF THE FETUS AND THE IMPORTANCE OF GLUCOCORTICOIDS

Towards term, the organs and physiological systems of the mammalian fetus mature to prepare for the transition from the uterus to the outside world. Before birth, the fetus relies on the placenta and mother for its nutritional, respiratory and excretory needs and hence at birth, substantial changes in the structure and function of fetal organs are necessary in order to sustain independent life. In particular, the lungs need to mature sufficiently to take the first breath. Many of the changes in maturation that occur in the fetus near term are mediated by hormones produced by the fetus itself. Glucocorticoids are key regulators of fetal maturation. These steroid hormones are secreted by the fetal adrenal gland and levels in the blood of the fetus rise gradually towards term and particularly during the stress of labour and vaginal delivery (see Figure 1). Glucocorticoids have a wide range of actions on the structure and function of fetal organs (Fowden et al., 1998). They promote differentiation of specific cell types and the expression of key genes and proteins essential for normal maturation. For example, in the lungs, glucocorticoids activate the synthesis of surfactant, a biological detergent that reduces surface tension and enables expansion of the lungs at birth and thus the first breath (Bolt et al., 2001). The importance of glucocorticoids in preparing the fetus for birth is demonstrated by the respiratory problems and lung diseases, such as respiratory distress syndrome, seen in preterm babies born before the normal rise in circulating glucocorticoids has occurred. In addition, some aspects of lung development are impaired in babies born by elective Caesarean section, rather than vaginal delivery, because there is less activation of stress hormones, such as glucocorticoids and adrenaline, in the neonate (Bewley and Foo, this volume; Ramachandrappa and Jain, 2008).

III. ANTENATAL GLUCOCORTICOID THERAPY FOR PRETERM INFANTS

In England and Wales, preterm delivery before 37 weeks affects 7–8% (1 in 13) of human pregnancies. This figure includes rates of approximately 6% for singleton and 53% for multiple births (Office for National Statistics, 2005). Indeed, the incidence of prematurity has risen in recent years in association with increased obstetric intervention and a greater number of teenage mothers, older mothers, assisted conceptions and multiple births (Slattery and Morrison, 2002). To date, there is no effective clinical measure to prevent spontaneous preterm delivery, primarily because the mechanisms that trigger labour in women remain poorly understood. Premature birth is the most common cause of neonatal mortality in the developed world: prematurity and its complications contribute to around 25% of all neonatal deaths. The survival rate of the preterm infant depends upon its gestational age and birth weight. Using data collected in 2005 in England and Wales, the percentages of preterm babies surviving to one year of age were 5% at 22 weeks, 16% at 23 weeks, 42% at 24 weeks, 65% at 25 weeks and 76% at 26 weeks of gestation (Moser et al., 2007). Premature infants suffer from a range of postnatal complications which affect underdeveloped organs such as the lungs, gut, brain and eyes (respiratory distress syndrome, necrotising entercolitis, intraventricular haemorrhage and retinopathy). They are also at greater risk of cerebral palsy and other neurological and visual handicaps than babies born at normal term. One in ten babies born preterm will have a permanent disability such as lung disease, cerebral palsy, deafness or blindness. Advances in obstetric and neonatal care have meant that the survival of the premature infant has improved markedly, albeit with the possibility of long-term disability.

Figure 1. Circulating levels of a naturally-occurring glucocorticoid (cortisol) in fetuses of different animal species towards term. Redrawn from Fowden et al., 1998.

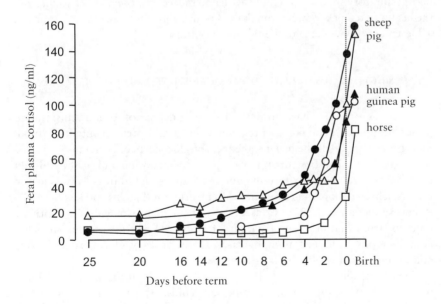

For the last 30 to 40 years, synthetic glucocorticoids have been prescribed for women at risk of preterm delivery. Normally, the placenta inactivates natural, maternally-produced glucocorticoids, thereby protecting the fetus from premature exposure to their high circulating levels. However, synthetic glucocorticoids are not inactivated and so readily cross the placenta. They also have a longer duration of action and are more potent than the natural glucocorticoids.

Sir Graham (Mont) Liggins (1969) was the first to propose the use of AGT to increase the rate of organ maturation, especially the lungs, in the fetus at risk of preterm delivery. In experiments primarily designed to investigate the role of glucocorticoids in triggering the onset of labour in sheep, he demonstrated that AGT improved lung function in lambs that were delivered preterm. These findings led directly to the first and largest randomised controlled trial of AGT (Liggins and Howie, 1972). This trial showed that AGT markedly reduced the incidence of respiratory distress syndrome and improved the survival of premature infants. Since then, several studies have confirmed the beneficial effects of AGT on mortality and morbidity in the preterm infant. In a recent Cochrane Review, Roberts and Dalziel (2006) analysed data from 21 studies involving 4,269 infants and concluded that a single dose of AGT reduced neonatal mortality by approximately one-third and the incidence of conditions such as respiratory distress syndrome, brain haemorrhage and inflammation of the gut by 35–55%. Preterm infants delivered after AGT were also less likely to need respiratory support and intensive care. Indeed, the use of AGT to improve the health outcomes of premature babies is arguably one of the most important achievements in medicine in the twentieth century.

IV. SINGLE VERSUS MULTIPLE DOSES OF ANTENATAL GLUCOCORTICOIDS

The success of AGT has, however, led to a degree of over-enthusiasm in prescribing glucocorticoids to pregnant women and preterm infants. Initial reports suggested that the beneficial effects of glucocorticoids on maturation of the lungs diminished over time between its administration and birth, and that the reduction in neonatal mortality and morbidity induced by AGT was lost in infants delivered more than seven days after treatment (Liggins and Howie, 1972; Roberts and Dalziel, 2006). Consequently, if pregnant women given synthetic glucocorticoids did not deliver within a few days of treatment, clinicians gave additional doses. Indeed, in many cases, repeat doses of glucocorticoids were administered on a weekly basis until delivery.

There is conflicting evidence from clinical trials about the short- and long-term effects of multiple doses of glucocorticoids. In particular, it is unclear whether repeat doses of glucocorticoids improve lung function in the neonate above that seen after a single dose, and whether there are adverse consequences of multiple doses for growth and the development of the brain and nervous system. A Cochrane Review examined data from 5 trials of repeat AGT and concluded that there were reductions in the incidence and severity of neonatal morbidity, including respiratory distress syndrome, in women treated with multiple doses of glucocorticoids (Crowther et al., 2007). There was, however, no difference in neonatal mortality, or in the incidence of neonatal chronic lung disease, for women given one or more than one dose of AGT.

In an observational cohort study, two or more doses of AGT did not improve neonatal survival or respiratory outcomes above those seen in women given a single dose, but repeat AGT was associated with a significant reduction in body weight and head circumference of the newborn infant (French et al., 1999). Most recently, a randomised controlled trial compared the effects of multiple doses of AGT with a placebo in women who did not deliver within 2 to 3 weeks of all receiving a single AGT (Murphy et al., 2008). No additional benefit of repeat doses of glucocorticoids on respiratory or other outcomes was observed in the babies. At delivery, however, the infants exposed to multiple doses of AGT were shorter, lighter in body weight and had a smaller head circumference than those exposed to the placebo after the initial single dose. In the course of promoting the maturation of fetal organs, glucocorticoids tend to reduce cell proliferation and promote cell differentiation and functional activity, and so can slow general body growth. Some of the growth-retarding actions of the glucocorticoids may also be mediated by adverse effects on the transfer of nutrients across the placenta. Repeat doses of AGT have been shown to reduce placental weight at delivery, such that placental weight decreases with increasing numbers of AGT doses (Sawady et al., 2007).

Several studies have investigated the effects of single and repeat doses of AGT on aspects of development of the brain and nervous system in the longer term. The surviving premature infants that participated in the first trial of AGT carried out by Liggins and Howie (1972) have been followed up in a series of studies. At 4 and 6 years of age, a single dose of AGT did not appear to affect cognitive development or progress at school (MacArthur et al., 1981, 1982). Similarly, no adverse consequences for growth, cognitive and motor development, behaviour or achievement at school have been observed in 10 to 12 year old children exposed to a single dose of AGT (Schmand et al., 1990; Smolders-de Haas et al., 1990). Prenatal exposure to multiple doses of AGT, however, has been linked with an increased incidence of hyperactivity, distractibility, aggressive and destructive behaviour, and other neurodevelopmental abnormalities in children aged 2 to 6 years (French et al., 2004; Spinillo et al., 2004). In contrast, Wapner et al. (2007) and Crowther et al. (2007) failed to demonstrate any effect of repeat AGT on the incidence or severity of respiratory disease, behavioural problems, neurosensory disability or on other physical or cognitive measures in children at 2 to 3 years of age. There was, however, a significant increase in the number of children assessed for attention problems in the repeat AGT group (Crowther et al., 2007). Both higher and lower rates of cerebral palsy have been reported in pre-school children exposed to multiple doses of glucocorticoids before birth (French et al., 2004; Wapner et al., 2007).

In the light of these findings and those from experimental animal studies, clinicians have been advised by medical governing bodies to be more cautious in the administration of repeat doses of AGT. The Royal College of Obstetricians and Gynaecologists (RCOG 2004, 2009) advises a single dose of AGT for all women at risk of spontaneous or iatrogenic (ie caused unintentionally by the clinician) preterm birth or for whom an elective caesarean section is planned prior to 38 weeks of pregnancy.

In the past, preterm infants were also routinely given synthetic glucocorticoids in early postnatal life to prevent or treat chronic lung disease. Both the dose and the duration of glucocorticoid exposure were significantly greater for postnatal compared with antenatal treatments. In recent years, however, the use of glucocorticoids in postnatal life has been reduced as there is evidence to show that this treatment increases the risk of cerebral palsy and impairs neuromotor and cognitive function in childhood (Barrington, 2001; Halliday et al., 2009a, 2009b; Yeh et al., 1998, 2004). In addition, advances in the clinical care of women at risk of preterm delivery and their babies have reduced the severity of lung disease after birth, and therefore, postnatal glucocorticoid treatment is largely reserved for seriously ill premature babies who are still reliant on a ventilator after several weeks.

V. ANIMAL MODELS USED IN STUDIES OF ANTENATAL GLUCOCORTICOID TREATMENT

A range of experimental animal models has been used to study the pre- and postnatal consequences of AGT for the structure and function of organ systems in the offspring. However, some caution is needed in extrapolation of the findings from these studies to human pregnancy. First, there are differences among species in the availability of glucocorticoids and these can influence their effectiveness in the body. Exposure of the fetus to antenatal glucocorticoids depends on their transfer across the placenta; on their rate of breakdown in maternal, placental and fetal tissues; and on the sensitivity of target organs to them. These factors vary with the gestational age of the fetus and the stage of organ development, and between humans and non-human animal models. For instance, the sensitivity of organs to glucocorticoids shows patterns of development that are highly species-specific, especially in organs such as the brain (Pryce, 2008).

Second, although the sequence of key stages of development in organs such as the lungs and brain are relatively similar among animal species, the specific timings of these developmental changes differ between those species that deliver offspring that are relatively mature (precocious) and those producing immature offspring (altricial). In altricial species, like rodents, organ development and maturation are delayed relative to precocious species like humans and especially farm animals. For example, rodent pups are much less mature at birth than the human neonate and, in terms of brain development, rat pups at 2 weeks of postnatal age are considered equivalent to the human fetus at term (Clancy et al., 2007).

Third, the relatively short length of gestation in rodent species means that, in experimental studies, the duration of glucocorticoid exposure as a fraction of overall gestation is long relative to that in other animal species. For this reason, the sheep fetus is commonly used as an experimental animal model for the human, as it has a longer period of gestation than the rat and the timing of the development of many organs and physiological systems resembles that of the human fetus. Similarly, the guinea pig is born relatively mature and shows similar patterns of organ development to the human infant. Non-human primates, such as rhesus monkeys and baboons, are less commonly used for ethical and financial reasons, but are arguably a more appropriate animal model for translation to clinical medicine. Animals with longer gestational lengths, however, also have longer life-spans and periods of prepubertal development, which can make studies of the long-term consequences of AGT more prolonged and expensive.

Fourth, glucocorticoids may have effects on the mother, placenta and fetus that are specific to particular animal species. For instance, in the sheep placenta, glucocorticoids activate an enzyme that is not found in the human placenta. Activation of this enzyme by glucocorticoids near term leads to the production of other steroid hormones by the placenta in sheep. Therefore, the extent to which the effects of the glucocorticoids are direct and/or mediated by changes in hormones produced by the placenta needs to be considered.

Finally, many of the experiments using animals to study the effects of AGT on the development of the fetus and neonate have used higher doses of glucocorticoids than those used in clinical practice. Indeed, experimental design has varied widely among studies using animal models, in terms of the dose, route, timing and duration of glucocorticoid treatment and of the outcomes measured. While it is important to consider all of these factors when interpreting the results from experiments using animals, it is unquestionable that these studies can provide a wealth of information that would be impossible to obtain from clinical studies alone. Indeed, animal models have demonstrated that AGT causes changes to the physiology of the offspring in ways that, largely, resemble the observations in humans, and have suggested that there may be adverse effects in the longer term. They have also provided evidence for some of the underlying mechanisms responsible.

VI. EFFECTS OF ANTENATAL GLUCOCORTICOID TREATMENT ON THE GROWTH AND NEURODEVELOPMENT OF THE FETUS AND NEONATE IN ANIMAL MODELS

As in the human infant, maternal glucocorticoid treatment has been shown to promote maturation in both the structure and function of the fetal lungs in several animal models (Bolt et al., 2001); however, it can also cause growth retardation and other developmental abnormalities in the fetus.

(a) Non-human Primates

For some time, AGT has been known to impair the overall growth of the fetus and, specifically, to reduce head circumference and brain weight in non-human primate species (Johnson et al., 1979; Novy and Walsh, 1983). A number of studies have since focussed on the effects of glucocorticoids on specific regions of the brain, such as the hippocampus. The hippocampus is an important part of the brain that is involved in cognitive functions, such as learning, memory and spatial orientation, and in the control of the blood levels of the natural glucocorticoids. In the human fetus, the hippocampus is known to be sensitive to glucocorticoids from mid-gestation, which makes it a target for the actions of AGT (Noorlander et al., 2006). In pregnant rhesus monkeys, single and repeat AGT, at clinically relevant or higher doses, influences the normal development of the fetal hippocampus (Uno et al., 1990). When the fetuses were studied either preterm or near term, AGT was associated with reductions in the numbers of specific types of nerve cells within the hippocampus and with degeneration of the interconnections between nerve cells. These effects were greater with higher doses, and more damage was observed in the fetuses exposed to multiple doses of AGT compared with those exposed to one dose.

Abnormalities have also been reported in the cerebral cortex, the outermost region of the brain important for memory, language and consciousness, of non-human primate offspring exposed to synthetic glucocorticoids before birth. When multiple doses of AGT were given to pregnant baboons, the differentiation of nerves in the developing cerebral cortex of the fetus were affected in ways that may impair their functional connections with other nerves (Antonow-Schlorke et al., 2003).

(b) Other Animal Models

Studies undertaken on rodents, guinea pigs and sheep have led to broadly consistent conclusions. First, AGT results in lower body weight in the newborn offspring. Thus, a single dose to pregnant rats led to the birth of smaller pups with reduced head diameter and fewer brain cells (Bruschettini et al., 2006; Scheepens et al., 2003). The higher the dose of AGT, the more pronounced the effect, and repeat AGT doses also decreased the body weight of rat pups at birth (Levitt et al., 1996; Nyirenda et al., 1998; O'Regan et al., 2004). Offspring of mice exposed to a single dose of glucocorticoids were also born smaller (Noorlander et al., 2008). Similarly, both single and repeat doses of AGT to pregnant ewes reduced the growth of the fetus, and repeat doses caused a greater reduction in fetal body weight than a single dose (Ikegami et al., 1997; Jobe et al., 1998). Both treatment regimes also caused a decrease in the weight of the placenta at term (Jobe et al., 1998).

Second, AGT has consequences for the development of the brain and nervous system. A single dose of AGT had no effect on overall brain weight in preterm sheep fetuses, but did reduce the size of the cerebral cortex (Huang et al., 1999). By term, however, total brain weight in the fetuses exposed to a single dose was lower than in the control fetuses. In contrast, repeat doses of AGT reduced total brain weight and a variety of other measures of brain size both preterm and at term (Huang et al., 1999), and was accompanied by other abnormalities in the development of the central nervous system. These included delays in the maturation of the retina of the eye and myelination of the optic nerve (Dunlop et al., 1997; Quinlivan et al., 2000). Myelination is an important process by which an insulating layer of fat and protein (myelin) is formed around nerve fibres to allow rapid conduction of nerve impulses, and appears generally impaired in sheep fetuses exposed to multiple doses of AGT (Antonow-Schlorke et al., 2009). Impaired myelination can have serious functional consequences: for example, it has been observed in the nerve tract connecting the two hemispheres of the brain where it is likely to affect the integration of behaviour, attention and cognition (Huang et al., 2001). Some of the effects of AGT on the fetal brain diminished with increasing age of the fetus and were temporary after single, but maintained after multiple, doses. In a series of experiments in the guinea pig, repeat AGT influenced the sensitivity of the fetal brain to various hormones in a manner that depended on the dose of AGT, the region of the brain and sex of the fetus (Andrews et al., 2004; Dean and Matthews, 1999). Varying single doses of AGT have also been shown to lower blood levels of the natural glucocorticoids in the fetus (McCabe et al., 2001).

Overall, experimental studies using animal models have demonstrated that synthetic glucocorticoids have marked effects on growth patterns and the development of the brain and nervous system in the fetus.

VII. PROGRAMMING EFFECTS OF ANTENATAL GLUCOCORTICOID TREATMENT ON ADULT PHYSIOLOGY

Epidemiological studies in human populations worldwide have demonstrated that a low birth weight predisposes an individual in adult life to the development of diseases, such as type II diabetes, dyslipidaemia (abnormal levels of blood fats), hypertension (high blood pressure) and coronary heart disease (Barker, 1994). Since both synthetic and high levels of natural glucocorticoids can retard the growth of the fetus, they have been proposed as one mechanism by which size at birth, and the environment before birth, can programme metabolic and cardiovascular disease. Indeed, a number of experimental animal studies have shown that exposure to glucocorticoids before birth has long-term consequences for the structure and function of organs, and for overall physiology and health, in the adult animal.

(a) Non-human Primates

The offspring of rhesus monkeys treated with multiple doses of AGT, that show abnormalities in the development of the hippocampus in fetal life (Uno et al., 1990), have been studied as juvenile and adult animals. In juvenile life, the resting levels of natural glucocorticoids, and their response to stress, were increased, probably due to impaired regulation by the hippocampus (Uno et al., 1994). Indeed, in adulthood, the hippocampus in the monkeys exposed to glucocorticoids before birth was 20–30% smaller than that in the control animals (Uno et al., 1994).

In vervet monkeys, AGT had no effect on birth weight, but did slow the growth rate of the infants during postnatal life (de Vries et al., 2007). At 1 year of life, the offspring that had been exposed to the higher doses of AGT had impaired control of blood glucose levels. They also had higher blood pressure and showed an exaggerated stress response compared with control animals. These alterations in metabolism and blood pressure resemble the early signs of diabetes and cardiovascular disease seen in human subjects.

(b) Other Animal Models

There is increasing evidence from studies in rodents that AGT has consequences for various aspects of behaviour and physiology in adult life. The smaller offspring of mice given a single dose of AGT had a shortened life-span and, in adult life, had reduced cell proliferation in the hippocampus and impaired spatial learning (Noorlander et al., 2008). Likewise, offspring of rats treated with AGT showed hyperactive behaviour, exaggerated stress responses and altered signalling systems in the brain (Muneoka et al., 1997). Furthermore, AGT was associated with abnormalities in the development of an area of the brain involved in motivation and reward processes, the nucleus accumbens (Leao et al., 2007). Reductions in the size of the nucleus accumbens, in the total number of neurones, and in the rate of cell division were observed in juvenile rats exposed to AGT before birth, and the findings were more pronounced in male than in female animals.

In rats, AGT has been shown to cause an increase in blood pressure in the offspring in postnatal life (Levitt et al., 1996; Ortiz et al., 2001; Woods and Weeks, 2005). This effect may be an indirect consequence of reduced food intake in the mother during pregnancy, because, in one study, AGT suppressed maternal food intake by 30% and when control mothers were fed with the same (lower) amount of food, high blood pressure was also observed in the offspring (Woods and Weeks, 2005). In juvenile and adult life, the offspring of rats treated with AGT also show differences in metabolic and hormone function, and the nature of many of these changes depends on the sex of the offspring (Franko et al., 2010; O'Regan et al., 2004). In the long term, exposure to AGT causes a reduction in the sensitivity of organs to insulin and poor control of blood glucose, both of which are changes indicative of the development of diabetes (Levitt et al., 1996; Nyirenda et al., 1998). Some of the programming effects of AGT can also persist to the next generation of animals with both maternal and paternal transmission. In rats, offspring of mothers or fathers exposed to AGT as fetuses were smaller at birth, and, in adulthood, showed impaired control of blood glucose (Drake et al., 2005).

In sheep exposed to single and multiple doses of AGT, a number of studies have subsequently examined metabolic and hormonal function in the offspring in postnatal life. The reduction in brain weight observed in lambs born after AGT was maintained in adult animals (Moss et al., 2005). The juvenile and adult offspring of ewes given AGT showed impaired sensitivity to insulin and poor glucose tolerance, and other early indicators of diabetes (Moss et al., 2001; Sloboda et al., 2005). Similar programmed reductions in brain to body weight ratio have been reported in the juvenile offspring of guinea pigs given AGT (Liu et al., 2001). These animals were also found to have sex-specific differences in the hormonal response to a stressful stimulus, and, in adult life, blood pressure was increased in male offspring (Banjanin et al., 2004; Liu et al., 2001).

Therefore, the prenatal use of synthetic glucocorticoids in experimental animal studies has shown marked and widespread effects in the offspring, not only before birth, but also into postnatal life. The exact nature of the effects depends on the animal species and on the sex and postnatal age of the offspring. In many cases, the postnatal outcomes of AGT can vary as the animal ages. Moreover, some of the effects may then be transmitted to the next generation.

VIII. MECHANISMS BY WHICH ANTENATAL GLUCOCORTICOID TREATMENT MAY PROGRAMME ADULT DISEASE

Much current research is focussed on determining how AGT can influence the development of the fetus in a way that has consequences for its physiology and risk of disease in later life. Several different mechanisms have been proposed, each working at a different, but inter-related, 'biological level' within the body (Figure 2). First, at the molecular level, glucocorticoids can determine whether certain genes of the fetus are expressed or not. Changes in gene expression which occur at the time of glucocorticoid treatment can influence fetal growth and development with long-term consequences for the physiology of the offspring. In addition, glucocorticoid exposure in the uterus can trigger changes in gene expression after birth, either during normal life events, such as birth, puberty,

Figure 2. Mechanisms by which AGT may programme physiology and disease in postnatal life.

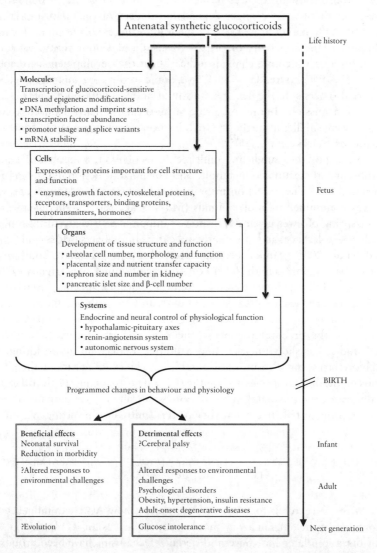

pregnancy and ageing, and/or in response to particular environmental challenges unique to the individual. These altered patterns of gene activity that are seen some time after glucocorticoid treatment may result from specific physiological traits that are programmed at the time of exposure. Alternatively, they may arise from glucocorticoid-induced structural changes in the organisation of the fetal genome, which permanently modify gene expression without any change in the DNA code, a process known as epigenetics. These epigenetic modifications can, therefore, provide a 'memory' of events before birth that persists into adult life and even across generations (Fowden and Forhead, 2009). For example, adult rats exposed to AGT as fetuses have a permanent epigenetic change to the gene that encodes the binding site of natural glucocorticoids in their kidneys, which affects expression of this gene and the sensitivity of the organ to these hormones (Wyroll et al., 2007).

Second, at the cellular level, glucocorticoids can influence the fetal production of proteins that are important for normal cell functions such as signalling, metabolism, growth and differentiation (Fowden and Forhead, 2004). These actions can result in changes to the sensitivity of organs to various hormones and nerves. Third, at the level of the organ, glucocorticoids can affect the number and types of cells present which can, in turn, lead to changes in the structure and function of the organ. For instance, adult vervet monkeys exposed to glucocorticoids before birth have a lower number of cells that secrete insulin in the pancreas (de Vries et al., 2007). Finally, at the level of the whole body, the programming effects of AGT on various hormones and nerves will affect the regulation of blood pressure and blood glucose levels with consequences for the supply of nutrients, growth factors and other blood-borne signalling molecules to all organs in both fetal and postnatal animals. Furthermore, changes in the levels of these molecules may mediate some of the effects of AGT on the growth and development of organs and their function in later life. Therefore, at the time of treatment and long after, glucocorticoids are able to trigger a cascade of action from the molecules to the physiological systems of the offspring with consequences for its life history (Figure 2).

At all these different levels of control, some of the actions of glucocorticoids on the organs of the fetus may be direct and others may be indirect, via the actions of other hormone systems influenced by AGT. For example, the suppressive effects of AGT on fetal growth may be partly due to changes in the expression of insulin-like growth factors in the fetus and placenta (Fowden, 2003; Gatford et al., 2008). Furthermore, in sheep, AGT has been shown to increase levels in the fetal circulation of hormones such as insulin, leptin and thyroid hormone (Forhead et al., 2007; Franko et al., 2007; O'Connor et al., 2007). These hormones may contribute to the maturational actions of glucocorticoids on the lungs of the fetus, but may also be partly responsible for the effects on the development of the brain and other tissues. In addition, AGT may change the balance between factors which can damage tissues (such as highly reactive oxygen radicals) and the factors that can limit them (such as antioxidants), and thereby influence exposure of the fetus to damage by oxidative stress. In preterm human infants, recent studies have shown that AGT is associated with lower umbilical levels of an antioxidant and with a transient increase in oxidative damage (Verhaeghe et al., 2009). Oxidative damage to developing organs caused by AGT is likely to have important consequences for pre- and postnatal development. Overall, it is important to note that the glucocorticoids may programme changes in physiology either (1) by causing changes to the structure and function of organs at the time of exposure that persist into later life and/or (2) by causing changes that increase the likelihood of abnormalities developing under the influence of specific environmental conditions that occur in late life. Indeed, in young and adult individuals exposed to glucocorticoids before birth, it may be possible to modify lifestyle, in terms of diet, stress and mental and physical activity, to minimalise the development of abnormalities and disease.

IX. LONG-TERM CONSEQUENCES FOR PRETERM HUMAN INFANTS EXPOSED TO ANTENATAL GLUCOCORTICOID TREATMENT

The programming effects of clinically administered AGT on the development of diseases later in adult life, such as diabetes and coronary heart disease, are in the early stages of investigation. The surviving premature infants from the first clinical trial of AGT (Liggins and Howie, 1972) are now in early middle age and have been followed up in a series of studies. Overall, in individuals at age 30, a single dose of AGT has not been shown to have any long-term consequences for lung function or prevalence of wheeze or asthma (Dalziel et al., 2006); for cognitive functioning, working memory and attention, psychiatric morbidity (anxiety, depression, schizophrenia) or health related quality of life (Dalziel et al., 2005a); or for blood pressure, blood lipid profile, prevalence of diabetes or history of cardiovascular disease (Dalziel et al., 2005b). However, oral glucose challenge tests have indicated a degree of insulin resistance in the AGT group of subjects (Dalziel et al., 2005b). In addition, a small but significant increase in blood pressure has been reported in children at 14 years of age after exposure to a single dose of AGT (Doyle et al., 2000). The individuals recruited into these studies are still relatively young and as they age, it will be important to continue to monitor various health outcomes and the incidence of disease in adult life. In the future, this will be especially pertinent for individuals exposed to multiple doses of glucocorticoids before birth. At present, it is still too soon to known whether the improved survival rates of preterm infants treated with glucocorticoids come at a cost of increased morbidity and mortality in later life.

In summary, the development and use of AGT in pregnant women at risk of preterm delivery is a good example of a medical procedure that has obvious clinical benefit in the short term, and yet undetermined, but potentially adverse, consequences for the long-term health of the offspring. Certainly the evidence from animal models indicates that it is vital to continue to review current practice and monitor outcomes following AGT. While clinicians and parents are rightly concerned with the immediate survival of the preterm infant, the wider implications of this treatment on health outcomes in the future need to be considered by society more generally. It may also be necessary to provide clear information and counselling for the prospective parents. These discussions may prove challenging because, even if adverse outcomes were detected following AGT, there is still a risk-benefit balance to be calculated between the short- and long-term effects of this therapy. Clearly, the ability to diagnose reliably those pregnancies at highest risk of preterm delivery, and to prevent spontaneous preterm delivery, would help to reduce unnecessary glucocorticoid treatment. Paradoxically, it is those individuals that were not born as prematurely as expected and were exposed to repeat, and potentially unnecessary, doses of AGT that may be at greatest risk of the adverse consequences of glucocorticoids. Clinicians are becoming more aware of the long-term effects of AGT and are monitoring outcomes to enable risk:benefit ratios to be calculated. Can the same be said of other medical procedures used during conception and pregnancy, such as *in vitro* fertilisation or embryo freezing? In order to elucidate the nature and extent of the programming effects of these types of clinical treatments, it is important that adequate documentation is available to allow patient follow-up. This may be particularly relevant in the field of assisted reproduction technologies where clinical procedures continue to develop without information on the long-term consequences for the physiology of the offspring.

REFERENCES

Andrews, M. H., Kostaki, A., Setiawan, E., McCabe, L. and Matthews, S. G. (2004). Developmental Regulation of 5-HT$_{1A}$ Receptor mRNA in the Fetal Limbic System: Response to Antenatal Glucocorticoid. *Dev. Brain Res.* **149**, 39–44.

Antonow-Schlorke, I., Schwab, M., Li, C. and Nathanielsz, P. W. (2003). Glucocorticoid Exposure at the Dose Used Clinically Alters Cytoskeletal Proteins and Presynaptic Terminals in the Fetal Baboon Brain. *J. Physiol.* **547**, 117–123.

Antonow-Schlorke, I., Helgert, A., Gey, C., Coksaygan, T., Schubert, H., Nathanielsz, P. W., Witte, O. W. and Schwab, M. (2009). Adverse Effects of Antenatal Glucocorticoids on Cerebral Myelination in Sheep. *Obstet. Gynecol.* **113**, 142–151.

Banjanin, S., Kapoor, A. and Matthews, S. G. (2004). Prenatal Glucocorticoid Exposure Alters Hypothalamic-Pituitary-Adrenal Function and Blood Pressure in Mature Male Guinea Pigs. *J. Physiol.* **558**, 305–318.

Barker, D. J. P. (1994). *Mothers, Babies and Disease in Later Life.* London: BMJ Publishing Group.

Barrington, K. J. (2001). The Adverse Neuro-developmental Effects of Postnatal Steroids in the Preterm Infant: A Systematic Review of RCTs. *Biomed. Central Pediatrics* **1**, 1.

Bolt, R.J., van Weissenbruch, M. M., Lafeber, H. N. and Delemarre-van de Waal, H. A. (2001). Glucocorticoids and Lung Development in the Fetus and Preterm Infant. *Pediatr. Pulm.* **32**, 76–91.

Bruschettini, M., van den Hove, D. L. A., Gazzolo, D., Steinbusch, H. W. M. and Blanco, C. E. (2006). Lowering the Dose of Antenatal Steroids: The Effects of a Single Dose of Betamethasone on Somatic Growth and Brain Cell Proliferation in the Rat. *Am. J. Obstet. Gynecol.* **194**, 1341–1346.

Clancy, B., Finlay, B. L., Darlington, R.B. and Anand, K. J. S. (2007). Extrapolating Brain Development from Experimental Species to Humans. *Neurotoxicity* **28**, 931–937.

Crowther, C. A., Doyle, L. W., Haslam, R. R., Hiller, J. E., Harding, J. E. and Robinson, J. S. (2007). Outcomes at 2 Years of Age after Repeat Doses of Antenatal Corticosteroids. *New Engl. J. Med.* **357**, 1179–1189.

Crowther, C. A. and Harding, J. E. (2007). Repeat Doses of Prenatal Corticosteroids for Women at Risk of Preterm Birth for Preventing Neonatal Respiratory Disease. *Cochrane Db. Syst. Rev.* CD003935.

Dalziel, S. R., Lim, V.K., Lambert, A., McCarthy, D., Parag, V., Rodgers, A. and Harding, J. E. (2005a). Antenatal Exposure to Betamethasone: Psychological Functioning and Health Related Quality of Life 31 Years after Inclusion in Randomised Controlled Trial. *Brit. Med. J.* **331**, 665–676.

Dalziel, S. R., Walker, N. K., Parag, V., Mantall, C., Rea, H. H., Rodgers, A. and Harding, J. E. (2005b). Cardiovascular Risk Factors after Antenatal Exposure to Betamethasone: 30-year Follow-up of a Randomised Controlled Trial. *Lancet* **365**, 1856–1862.

Dalziel, S. R., Rea, H. H., Walker, N. K., Parag, V., Mantell, C., Rodgers, A. and Harding, J. E. (2006). Long Term Effects of Antenatal Betamethasone on Lung Function: 30 Year Follow up of a Randomised Controlled Trial. *Thorax* **61**, 678–683.

Dean, F. and Matthews, S. G. (1999). Maternal Dexamethasone Treatment in Late Gestation Alters Glucocorticoid and Mineralocorticoid Receptor mRNA in the Fetal Guinea Pig Brain. *Brain Res.* **846**, 253–259.

Doyle, L. W., Ford, G. W., Davis, N. M. and Callanan, C. (2000). Antenatal Corticosteroid Therapy and Blood Pressure at 14 Years of Age in Preterm Children. *Clin. Sci.* **98**, 137–142.

Drake, A. J., Walker, B. R. and Seckl, J. R. (2005). Intergenerational Consequences of Fetal Programming by in Utero Exposure to Glucocorticoids in Rats. *Am. J. Physiol.* **288**, R34–R38.

Dunlop, S. A., Archer, M. A., Quinlivan, J. A., Beazley, L. D. and Newnham, J. P. (1997). Repeated Prenatal Corticosteroids Delay Myelination in the Ovine Central Nervous System. *J. Maternal-Fetal M.* **6**, 309–313.

Forhead, A. J., Jellyman, J. K., Gardner, D. S., Giussani, D. A., Kaptein, E., Visser, T. J. and Fowden, A. L. (2007). Differential Effects of Maternal Dexamethasone Treatment on Circulating Thyroid Hormone Concentrations and Tissue Deiodinase Activity in the Pregnant Ewe and Fetus. *Endocrinology* **148**, 800–805.

Fowden, A. L., Li, J. and Forhead, A. J. (1998). Glucocorticoids and the Preparation for Life after Birth: Are there Long-term Consequences of the Life Insurance? *P. Nutr. Soc.* **57**, 113-122.

Fowden, A. L. (2003) The Insulin-like Growth Factors and Feto-placental Growth. *Placenta* **24**, 803–812.

Fowden, A. L. and Forhead, A. J. (2004). Endocrine Mechanisms of Intrauterine Programming. *Reproduction* **127**, 515–526.

—— (2009). Hormones as Epigenetic Signals in Developmental Programming. *Exp. Physiol.* **94**, 607–625.

Franko, K. L., Giussani, D. A., Forhead, A. J. and Fowden, A. L. (2007). Effects of Dexamethasone on the Glucogenic Capacity of Fetal, Pregnant and Non-pregnant Adult Sheep. *J. Endocrinol.* **192**, 67–73.

Franko, K. L., Forhead, A. J. and Fowden, A. L. (2010). Differential Effects of Prenatal Stress and Glucocorticoid Administration on Postnatal Growth and Glucose Metabolism in Rats. *J. Endocrinol.* **204**, 319–329.

French, N. P., Hagan, R., Evans, S. F., Godfrey, M. and Newnham, J. P. (1999). Repeated Antenatal Corticosteroids: Size at Birth and Subsequent Development. *Am. J. Obstet. Gynecol.* **180**, 114–121.

French, N. P., Hagan, R., Evans, S. F., Mullan, A. and Newnham, J. P. (2004). Repeated Antenatal corticosteroids: Effects on Cerebral Palsy and Childhood Behaviour. *Am. J. Obstet. Gynecol.* **190**, 588–595.

Gatford, K. L., Owens, J. A., Li, S., Moss, T. J. M., Newnham, J. P., Challis, J. R. G. and Sloboda, D. M. (2008). Repeated Betamethasone Treatment of Pregnant Sheep Programs Persistent Reductions in Circulating IGF-I and IGF-Binding Proteins in Progeny. *Am. J. Physiol.* **295**, E170–E178.

Halliday, H. L., Ehrenkranz, R. A. and Doyle, L. W. (2009a). Early (< 8 days) Postnatal Corticosteroids for Preventing Chronic Lung Disease in Preterm Infants. *Cochrane Db. Syst. Rev.* CD001146.

—— (2009b). Late (> 7 days) Postnatal Corticosteroids for Chronic Lung Disease in Preterm Infants. *Cochrane Db. Syst. Rev.* CD001145.

Huang, W. L., Beazley, L. D., Quinlivan, J. A., Evans, S. F., Newnham, J. P. and Dunlop, S. A. (1999). Effect of Corticosteroids on Brain Growth in Fetal Sheep. *Obstet. Gynecol.* **94**, 213–218.

Huang, W. L., Harper, C. G., Evans, S. F., Newnham, J. P. and Dunlop, S. A. (2001). Repeated Prenatal Corticosteroid Administration Delays Myelination of the Corpus Callosum in Fetal Sheep. *Int. J. Neurosci.* **19**, 415–425.

Ikegami, M., Jobe, A. H., Newnham, J., Polk, D. H., Willett, K. E. and Sly, P. (1997). Repetitive Prenatal Glucocorticoids Improve Lung Function and Decrease Growth in Preterm Lambs. *Am. J. Resp. Crit. Care M.* **156**, 178–184.

Jobe, A. H., Wada, N., Berry, L. M., Ikegami, M. and Ervin, M. G. (1998). Single and Repetitive Maternal Glucocorticoid Exposures Reduce Fetal Growth in Sheep. *Am. J. Obstet. Gynecol.* **178**, 880–885.

Johnson, J. W., Mitzner, W., London, W. T., Palmer, A. E. and Scott, R. (1979). Betamethasone and the Rhesus Fetus: Multisystemic Effects. *Am. J. Obstet. Gynecol.* **133**, 677–684.

Leao, P., Sousa, J. C., Oliveira, M., Silva, R., Almeida, O. F. X. and Sousa, N. (2007). Programming Effects of Antenatal Dexamethasone in the Developing Mesolimbic Pathways. *Synapse* **61**, 40–49.

Levitt, N. S., Lindsay, R. S., Holmes, M. C. and Seckl, J. R. (1996). Dexamethasone in the Last Week of Pregnancy Attenuates Hippocampal Glucocorticoid Receptor Gene Expression and Elevates Blood Pressure in the Adult Offspring in the Rat. *Neuroendocrinology* **64**, 412–418.

Liggins, G. C. (1969). Premature Delivery of Foetal Lambs Infused with Glucocorticoids. *J. Endocrinol.* **45**, 515–523.

Liggins, G. C. and Howie, R. N. (1972). A Controlled Trial of Antepartum Glucocorticoid Treatment for Prevention of the Respiratory Distress Syndrome in Premature Infants. *Pediatrics* **50**, 515–525.

Lucas, A. (1991). Programming by Early Nutrition in Man. In *The Childhood Environment and Adult Disease. CIBA Foundation Symposium 156* (ed. G. R. Bock and J. Whelan), pp. 38–55. Chichester: Wiley.

Lui, L., Li, A. and Matthews, S. G. (2001). Maternal Glucocorticoid Treatment Programs HPA Regulation in Adult Offspring: Sex-Specific Effects. *Am. J. Physiol.* **280**, E729–E739.

MacArthur, B. A., Howie, R. N., Dezoete, J. A. and Elkins, J. (1981). Cognitive and Psychosocial Development of 4-Year-Old Children whose Mothers Were Treated Antenatally with Betamethasone. *Pediatrics* **68**, 638–643.

—— (1982). School Progress and Cognitive Development of 6-Year-Old Children whose Mothers Were Treated Antenatally with Betamethasone. *Pediatrics* **70**, 99–105.

McCabe, L., Marash, D., Li, A. and Matthews, S. G. (2001). Repeated Antenatal Glucocorticoid Treatment Decreases Hypothalamic Corticotrophin Releasing Hormone mRNA but not Corticosteroid Receptor mRNA Expression in the Fetal Guinea-pig Brain. *J. Neuroendocrinol.* **13**, 425–431.

Moss, T. J., Sloboda, D. M., Gurrin, L. C., Harding, R., Challis, J. R. and Newnham, J. P. (2001). Programming Effects in Sheep of Prenatal Growth Restriction and Glucocorticoid Exposure. *Am. J. Physiol.* **281**, R960–R970.

Moss, T. J., Doherty, D. A., Nitsos, I., Sloboda, D. M., Harding, R. and Newnham, J. P. (2005). Effects into Adulthood of Single or Repeated Antenatal Corticosteroids in Sheep. *Am. J. Obstet. Gynecol.* **192**, 146–152.

Muneoka, K., Mikuni, M., Ogawa, T., Kitera, K., Kamei, K., Takigawa, M. and Takahashi, K. (1997). Prenatal Dexamethasone Exposure Alters Brain Monoamine Metabolism and Adrenocortical Response in Rat Offspring. *Am. J. Physiol.* **273**, R1669–R1675.

Moser, K., Macfarlane, A., Chow, Y. H., Hilder, L. And Dattani, N. (2007). Introducing New Data on Gestation-Specific Infant Mortality among Babies Born in 2005 in England and Wales. *Health Stat. Q.* 35, 13–27.

Murphy, K. E., Hannah, M. E., Willan, A. R., Hewson, S. A., Ohlsson, A., Kelly, E. N., Matthews, S. G., Saigal, S., Asztalos, E., Ross, S., et al. (2008). Multiple Courses of Antenatal Corticosteroids for Preterm Birth (MACS): A Randomised Controlled Trial. *Lancet* 372, 2143–2151.

Noorlander, C. W., De Graan, P. N. E., Middeldorp, J., Van Beers, J. J. B. C. and Visser, G. H. A. (2006). Ontogeny of Hippocampal Corticosteroid Receptors: Effects of Antenatal Glucocorticoids in Human and Mouse. *J. Comp. Neurol.* 499, 924–932.

Noorlander, C. W., Visser, G. H. A., Ramakers, G. M. J., Nikkels, P. G. J. and de Graan, P. N. E. (2008). Prenatal Corticosteroid Exposure Affects Hippocampal Plasticity and Reduces Lifespan. *Dev Neurobiol* 68, 237–246.

Norman, J. E., Morris, C. and Chalmers, J. (2009). The Effect of Changing Patterns of Obstetric Care in Scotland (1980–2004) on Rates of Preterm Birth and its Neonatal Consequences: Perinatal Database Study. *PLoS Medicine* 6(9), e1000153.

Novy, M. J. and Walsh, S. W. (1983). Dexamethasone and Estradiol Treatment in Pregnant Rhesus Macaques: Effects on Gestational Length, Maternal Plasma Hormones, and Fetal Growth. *Am. J. Obstet. Gynecol.* 145, 920–931.

Nyirenda, M. J., Lindsay, R. S., Kenyon, C. J., Burchell, A. and Seckl, J. R. (1998). Glucocorticoid Exposure in Late Gestation Permanently Programs Rat Hepatic Phosphoenolpyruvate Carboxykinase and Glucocorticoid Receptor Expression and Causes Glucose Intolerance in Adult Offspring. *J. Clin. Invest.* 101, 2174–2181.

O'Connor, D. M., Blache, D., Hoggard, N., Brookes, E., Wooding, F. B. P., Fowden, A. L. and Forhead, A. J. (2007). Developmental Control of Plasma Leptin and Adipose Leptin mRNA in the Ovine Fetus During Late Gestation: Role of Glucocorticoids and Thyroid Hormones. *Endocrinology* 148, 3750–3757.

O'Regan, D., Kenyon, C. J., Seckl, J. R. and Holmes, M. C. (2004). Glucocorticoid Exposure in Late Gestation in the Rat Permanently Programs Gender-Specific Differences in Adult Cardiovascular and Metabolic Physiology. *Am. J. Physiol.* 287, E863–E870.

Office for National Statistics, press release 24 May 2007, based on 2005 data (http://www.statistics.gov.uk/pdfdir/preterm0507.pdf).

Ortiz, L. A., Quan, A., Weinberg, A. and Baum, M. (2001). Effect of Prenatal Dexamethasone on Rat Renal Development. *Kidney Int.* 59, 1663–1669.

Pryce, C. R. (2008). Postnatal Ontogeny of Expression of the Corticosteroid Receptor Genes in Mammalian Brains: Inter-Species and Intra-Species Differences. *Brain Res. Rev.* 57, 596–605.

Quinlivan, J. A., Beazley, L. D., Evans, S. F., Newnham, J. P. and Dunlop, S. A. (2000). Retinal Maturation is Delayed by Repeated, but not Single, Maternal Injections of Betamethasone In Sheep. *Eye* **14**, 93–98.

Ramachandrappa, A. and Jain, L. (2008). Elective Caesarean Section: Its Impact on Neonatal Respiratory Outcome. *Clin. Perinatol.* **35**, 373–393.

Roberts, D. and Dalziel, S. R. (2006). Antenatal Corticosteroids for Accelerating Fetal Lung Maturation for Women at Risk of Preterm Birth. *Cochrane Db. Syst. Rev.* CD004454.

Royal College of Obstetricians and Gynaecologists (2004) Antenatal Corticosteroids to Prevent Respiratory Distress Syndrome. Third edition, No.7.

—— (2009) Antenatal Corticosteroids to Prevent Neonatal Morbidity and Mortality. Draft fourth edition, No.7.

Sawady, J., Mercer, B. M., Wapner, R. J., Zhao, Y., Sorokin, Y., Johnson, F., Dudley, D. J., Spong, C. Y., Peaceman, A. M., Leveno, K. J., et al. (2007). The National Institute of Child Health and Human Development Maternal-Fetal Medicine Units Network BEARS Study: Impact of Repeated Doses of Antenatal Corticosteroids on Placental Growth and Histologic Findings. *Am. J. Obstet. Gynecol.* **197**, 281.e1-281.e8.

Scheepens, A., van de Waarenburg, M., van den Hove, D. and Blanco, C. E. (2003). A Single Course of Prenatal Betamethasone in the Rat Alters Postnatal Brain Cell Proliferation but not Apoptosis. *J. Physiol.* **552**, 163–175.

Schmand, B., Neuvel, J., Smolders-de Haas, H., Hoeks, J., Treffers, P. E., Koppe, J. G. (1990). Psychological Development of Children who Were Treated Antenatally with Corticosteroids to Prevent Respiratory Distress Syndrome. *Pediatrics* **86**, 58–64.

Slattery, M. M. and Morrison, J. J. (2002). Preterm Delivery. *Lancet* **360**, 1489–1497.

Sloboda, D. M., Moss, T. J., Gurrin, L.C., Newnham, J. P. and Challis, J. R. G. (2002). The Effect Of Prenatal Betamethasone Administration on Postnatal Ovine Hypothalamic-Pituitary-Adrenal Function. *J. Endocrinol.* **172**, 71–81.

Sloboda, D. M., Moss, T. J. M., Li, S., Doherty, D. A., Nitsos, I., Challis, J. R. G. and Newnham, J. P. (2005). Hepatic Glucose Regulation and Metabolism in Adult Sheep: Effects of Prenatal Betamethasone. *Am. J. Physiol.* **289**, E721–E728.

Smolders-de Haas, H., Neuvel, J., Schmand, B., Treffers, P. E., Koppe, J. G. and Hoeks, J. (1990). Physical Development and Medical History of Children Who Were Treated Antenatally with Corticosteroids to Prevent Respiratory Distress Syndrome: A 10-to12-Year Follow-up. *Pediatrics* **86**, 65–70.

Spinillo, A., Viazzo, F., Colleoni, R., Chiara, A., Cerbo, R. M. and Fazzi, E. (2004). Two-Year Infant Neurodevelopmental Outcome after Single or Multiple Antenatal Courses of Corticosteroids to Prevent Complications of Prematurity. *Am. J. Obstet. Gynecol.* **191**, 217–224.

Uno, H., Lohmiller, L., Thieme, C., Kemnitz, J. W., Engle, M. J., Roecker, E.B. and Farrell, P. M. (1990). Brain Damage Induced by Prenatal Exposure to Dexamethasone in Fetal Rhesus Macaques. I. Hippocampus. *Brain Res. Dev. Brain Res.* 53, 157–167.

Uno, H., Eisele, S., Sakai, A., Shelton, S., Baker, E., DeJesus, O. and Holden, J. (1994). Neurotoxicity of Glucocorticoids in the Primate Brain. *Horm. Behav.* 28, 336–348.

Verhaeghe, J., van Bree, R. and Van Herck, E. (2009). Oxidative Stress after Antenatal Betamethasone: Acute Downregulation of Glutathione Peroxidase-3. *Early Hum. Dev.* 85, 767–771.

de Vries, A., Holmes, M. C., Heijnis, A., Seier, J. V., Heerden, J., Louw, J., Wolfe-Coote, S., Meaney, M. J., Levitt, N. S. and Seckl, J. R. (2007). Prenatal Dexamethasone Exposure Induces Changes in Nonhuman Primate Offspring Cardiometabolic and Hypothalamic-Pituitary-Adrenal Axis Function. *J. Clin. Invest.* 117, 1058–1067.

Wapner, R. J., Sorokin, Y., Mele, L., Johnson, F., Dudley, D. J., Spong, C. Y., Peaceman, A. M., Leveno, K. J., Malone, F., Caritis, S. N et al. (2007). Long-term Outcomes after Repeat Doses of Antenatal Corticosteroids. *New Engl. J. Med.* 357, 1190–1198.

Woods, L. L. and Weeks, D.A. (2005). Prenatal Programming of Adult Blood Pressure: Role of Maternal Corticosteroids. *Am. J. Physiol.* 289, R955–R962.

Wyrwoll, C. S., Mark, P. J. and Waddell, B. J. (2007). Developmental Programming of Renal Glucocorticoid Sensitivity and the Renin-Angiotensin System. *Hypertension* 50, 579–584.

Yeh, T. F., Lin, Y. J., Huang, C. C., Chen, Y. J., Lin, H. C., Hsieh, W. S. and Lien, Y. J. (1998). Early Dexamethasone Therapy in Preterm Infants: A Follow-up Study. *Pediatrics* 101, E7.

Yeh, T. F., Lin, Y. J., Lin, H. C., Huang, C. C., Hsieh, W. S., Lin, C. H. and Tsai, C. H. (2004). Outcomes at School Age after Postnatal Dexamethasone Therapy for Lung Disease of Prematurity. *New Engl. J. Med.* 350, 1304–1313.

8

Fathers, Birth and Law

RICHARD COLLIER

I. INTRODUCTION

Policies focused on children and families have tended in the past to operate on the assumption that families are synonymous with mothers... However, fathers are becoming increasingly involved and their involvement with their children is important in contributing to child development, as well as being good for mothers. The Government wants to support and encourage fathers' involvement (DCSF, 2010, 113, para 6.6).

THE RELATIONSHIP BETWEEN fathers, law and social policy has been the subject of a rich interdisciplinary literature over the past decade. Work has explored the diverse and often contradictory nature of the ideas about fatherhood that circulate across a range of institutional and cultural contexts pertaining to law (see, for example, Collier and Sheldon, 2008; Dermott, 2008; Featherstone, 2009; Hobson, 2002). In a series of high profile public and political debates, meanwhile, the content and scope of fathers' legal rights and responsibilities has been linked to concerns about the changing nature of families and 'family life' (Barker et al., 2004; Burgess, 2007; Burgess and Russell, 2004). In the area of fathers' rights, contact and residence law, especially, a political policy conversation about fatherhood and law reform has become the focus of considerable attention (Collier, 2009; Collier and Sheldon, 2006; Ruxton and Baker, 2009). Somewhat less explored in contemporary debates about gender, law and parenting cultures, however, has been the issue of fathers and birth, an area in which recent social and legal developments have reshaped understandings of what Government might do to support and encourage fathers' involvement. I shall argue in this chapter that there has emerged within legal policy a new constellation of ideas about responsible fatherhood in law. This development has transformed, in significant and complex ways, legal understandings of fathers' relationship to birth.

II. FATHERS AND BIRTH: CONTEXTS

Questions about fathers and fatherhood are relevant to a wide range of ethical, legal, social, psychological and medical issues surrounding birth. Beyond the legal regulation of the birthing process itself, discussion of fathers and birth might encompass, for example, consideration of contraception, the relationship between men and health care, the significance of abortion, the role of service providers (see below) and the implications of treatment decisions in pregnancy for men. At a more general level, debates in this area have been marked by what Sally Sheldon and I have suggested elsewhere are questionable assumptions about men's relationship to human reproduction (Collier and Sheldon, 2008 Ch. 2). On closer examination, this has involved beliefs about men, birth and fatherhood that operate at three different levels.

First, in terms of the social practices that surround birth, as well as the legal frameworks that have historically regulated the birth process, there has been a cultural assumption that men play a secondary role in biological reproduction (Mander, 2004; Marsiglio, 1998). It is this downgrading of men's role in relation to birth, if not its invisibility, that the policy agendas around 'engaging fathers', detailed below, have sought to address.

Secondly, there has been a deeply entrenched, socially and legally pervasive assumption that the male body is, in the context of reproduction, compared with women, relatively invulnerable to the harms of the outside world (see further Daniels, 2006). The bodies of men in law, Sheldon (1999) has suggested, tend to be marked more by ideas of bodily absence and physical disengagement from reproduction, rather than any sense of corporeal presence, somehow non-permeable and 'safe' from the harms of the outside world (Thomson, 2007). Such depiction of men's bodies as signifying a tangential and contingent relation to gestation, fertility and reproduction has had particular significance in relation to the legal regulation of reproductive agency, freedom and responsibility. It has informed, for example, highly gendered constructions within law of antenatal responsibility, foetal harm and welfare (Daniels, 1997; Sheldon, 2006). This is evident in gendered constructions of responsible parenting in the context of foetal protection legislation such as the Congenital Disabilities (Civil Liability) Act 1976 (see further Collier and Sheldon 2008, Ch. 3).

Third, and finally, problematic assumptions about gender and sexuality have shaped social and legal attitudes to fathers and birth. This is evident in beliefs about the natural role of men as protectors of women and children and essentialist ideas about normative male (hetero) sexuality as somehow inherently, and unquestionably, virile. The latter has informed cultural attitudes to male infertility and im/potency (as a marker of manhood, as source of shame: Collier 1995, Ch. 4). Far from finding a reflective engagement with the idea of the 'sexed' male body in law (Collier, 1998; Thomson, 2007), these cultural conversations about fathers and reproduction tend to be shaped more by the notion of 'crisis' in masculinity (Clare, 2000). One feature of this crisis that has had particular resonance concerns a purported 'feminization' of men, whereby men's bodies, and parental role, have become somehow less 'manly', de-masculinized as a result of social, economic and technological changes (Colborn et al., 1997).

Debates around gender and contraception, abortion and fertility continue to be informed by these kinds of assumptions about men's bodies and relationship to reproductive responsibility. The legal and policy developments I chart in this chapter must be set against the backdrop of such understandings of reproduction as a matter of largely female expertise, responsibility and control. These social and legal frameworks around birth, however, have shifted considerably over the past decade or so. In the book *Fragmenting Fatherhood*, Sally Sheldon and I argue that fathers have, in fact, been reconstituted in law as a desirable presence within families via reference to three key themes (Collier and Sheldon, 2008). More specifically, there is a reconfiguration of interrelated beliefs about fathers as *heterosexual* (the sexual father), as family *breadwinners* (the worker father) and as embodiment of a particular kind of normative *masculinity*. Taken together, these developments have brought about a new constellation of ideas about what constitutes 'good' responsible fathering in law. In the remainder of this chapter, I shall outline how the idea of the father as uninvolved, secondary or tangential in birth has been challenged by social and legal shifts around parenting practices and cultures.

III. FATHERS, MARRIAGE AND BIRTH

Marriage has played a pivotal role in how law has historically attached men to their children (Probert, this volume). It has done so in ways that have interlinked beliefs about fatherhood to normative assumptions about masculinity and heterosexuality (see further Collier and Sheldon, 2008, Ch. 4). However, a complex amalgam of demographic, economic, cultural, technological and political changes has challenged the possibility of relying on marriage as a way of grounding legal fatherhood and the rights and responsibilities that have traditionally accompanied it. The recognition in law of civil partnerships (Civil Partnership Act, 2004), equality agendas around same-sex relations, for example around adoption (Adoption and Children Act, 2002), and changes in the law regulating assisted reproduction (Human Fertilization and Embryology Act, 2008) have reframed, in significant respects, normative ideas about legal parenthood, parental responsibility and heterosexuality. The new parenthood provisions set out in Part 2 of the latter piece of legislation, in particular, have removed the requirement that clinicians consider the future child's 'need for a father' when deciding whether a woman should be accepted for treatment services. This Act introduced changes to the status provisions of the Human Fertilization and Embryology Act 1990 that mean it is now possible for two women to be recognised as a child's legal parents. For some, these parenting provisions are 'another blow to fatherhood' (MacRae, 2009), legal reforms that reveal much about popular anxieties around the position of the father in families (McCandless and Sheldon, 2010).

It is important not to downplay the 'tenacious hold' of the 'sexual family form' in developments 'which might appear at first sight to herald its decline' (McCandless and Sheldon, 2010, p. 177). Shifts in case law around Parental Responsibility, not least in relation to lesbian couples, suggest fathers do continue to have an important symbolic role in families (Reece, 2009: see below). Nonetheless, one result of such legal reforms has not simply been to 'ratchet up' a well-established cultural and political debate about whether, and in what way, families 'need fathers'. This is a debate itself sharpened over the past decade by concerns about the social and legal consequences of divorce and rising levels of cohabitation. A hetero-normative understanding of family life, and a legal framework in which heterosexual marriage is the primary determinant of paternal responsibilities, has been challenged in significant respects by developments that have generated an increased emphasis within law on biological fatherhood and the biological and relational bonds between men and children.

Bound up with the increased focus in law, evident across diverse areas, on genetic links, Sheldon and I have referred elsewhere (2008) to a two-fold fragmentation and genetisation of fatherhood in the context of men and reproduction. If it was the case that in the past all aspects of fatherhood united in the person of one man (the mother's husband and child's genetic and social father), contemporary law appears marked more by an enhanced focus on the genetic link as grounding the rights and responsibilities associated with fatherhood (Smart, 2007). Set against the backdrop of a significant rethinking of the beneficial role of fathers in relation to child welfare and development (Burgess, 2007) there has emerged a view in law that a man's relationship with his children should be direct, and not mediated via his relationship with their mother. This has fed into an increased focus at both political and policy levels on the role of fathers in birth and the question of how law might encourage and promote fathers' responsibilities therein. This is a theme particularly evident within debates at the interface of fathers' 'earning and caring' responsibilities (O'Brien and Shemilt, 2003).

IV. EARNING AND CARING: FATHERS, BIRTH AND THE IMPORTANCE OF 'HITTING THE GROUND RUNNING'

Socio-legal work has charted the way ideas about fatherhood have been constructed via reference to a range of sexual divisions and gendered beliefs that have historically underpinned the cultural legitimacy of men's disengagement from child care, domestic labour and relations of dependency (Fineman, 1995; Fineman, 2004). Such a model of the father as breadwinner, however, enmeshed with ideas about fathers as detached or secondary to birth has been challenged by both social, economic and demographic changes (see Featherstone, 2009, pp.

128–9) and shifts in the contours of intimacy and personal life (Dermott, 2008; Giddens, 1992; Jamieson, 1998; Smart, 2007). Changing patterns of economic labour market participation (Crompton, 1999; EOC, 2007) and emergence of a policy paradigm based on the idea of the 'social investment' state (Jenson, 2004; Lister, 2006), in particular, have driven policy agendas seeking to 'bring fathers in the frame' (O'Brien, 2004). This theme was a central feature of New Labour policy in relation to families in the years from 1997–2010 (Annesley, 2001; Featherstone and Trinder, 2001). It is a policy aim, however, that operated at different levels, in different ways, depending on context (see further Collier, 2010a, Ch. 5), in which a redrawing of the relationship between fathers and birth has been central.

Much academic and policy discussion of New Labour's family and employment policy has focused on the issue of work-life balance and legal reforms seeking to promote women's employment and functional, 'balanced' family life within a new globalised economy (EHRC, 2009; Kilkey, 2006; Lewis and Campbell, 2007). Within this work-life debate, a repositioning of fathers' family practices and commitments has constituted men as a distinctive kind of 'social problem' within policy (Scourfield and Drakeford, 2002), notably as a potential obstacle to advancing equality agendas. This is an idea, however, that has had particular resonance within debates about how fathers connect to birth.

In the context of birth, politicians, policy makers and diverse organisations alike have argued that what is required are legal reforms directed at providing a more 'modern' progressive infrastructure of economic and social support that will promote the caring commitments of *both* parents within, and beyond, families (Lewis, 2000; O'Brien, 2005). The new framework of paternal involvement, part of a wider move from 'cash to care' in refocusing social policy (Hobson, 2002), has embraced questions about fathers involvement in both early years childcare and the antenatal period. As a result, there has emerged an apparent political consensus about the importance of the 'involved father' in the perinatal period. Supported by a growing research base charting fathers' own needs and expectations in this regard (Hatten et al., 2002; Lewis and Lamb, 2007), it is argued that by engaging with fathers around the point of birth, men will 'hit the ground running' in terms of accepting their responsibilities and promoting future participation in family life. Encouraging and facilitating greater paternal involvement around birth has become a key part of promoting both social responsibility and economic efficiency (see McCandless, this volume).

How, more precisely, has law been used to achieve this aim? Social policy has envisaged a key role for law, government and voluntary organisations alike (Daniel and Taylor, 2001; Williams and Roseneil, 2004) in making men 'better' fathers, linked to a belief that experts and expert knowledge have much to contribute to debates about fathering (Bristow, 2009; Changing Parenting Culture 2009/10). At both national and local levels, an infrastructure of funding support has sought to enable fathers' and parenting organisations to provide information about fatherhood, and encourage and promote involved, responsible fathering. The

Fatherhood Institute (formerly *Fathers Direct*) remains the most high profile of such organisations in the UK, with complex alignments to other parenting and fathers' groups (Bartlett et al., 2007; Burgess and Bartlett, 2004; Collier, 2009a, Ch. 5; Featherstone, 2009, pp. 140–142). The internet, meanwhile, provides a rich source of general and specific issue-focused advice for fathers from a diverse range of sources (for example, www.dads-space.com).

A rich body of law, meanwhile, has sought, in different ways, to promote father-inclusive practice across diverse areas of service delivery. To give no more than a flavour of the reforms introduced over the past decade, the Gender Equality Duty, created by the Equality Act 2006, places a duty on public authorities to be proactive in promoting equality of opportunity between men and women (Lewis, 2007). Public bodies are now required to publish an action plan for promoting gender equality, to undertake a 'gender impact assessment', gather information and consult on how their services will impact upon men and women, mothers and fathers. The Childcare Act 2006 requires Local Authorities in England and Wales to identify parents and prospective parents considered unlikely to use early childhood services (with fathers specifically mentioned) and work to facilitate access to those services. *Every Parent Matters* (DES, 2007) reinforces this concern, stating that fathers be offered as a matter of routine, irrespective of the degree of involvement they have had in the care of their children, the support and opportunities they need to play their parental role effectively.

A range of National Service Frameworks and practice guidance, meanwhile, places specific requirements on the need to include fathers and prioritise work with young and vulnerable fathers in the development of service provision around pregnancy and birth. In different ways, the Children's Centre Practice Guidance 2006 and guidance aimed at Teenage Parents (DH and DCSF, 2007) exemplify this concern about the importance of an active paternal role in relation to birth. The Teenage Pregnancy Guidance (DCSF, 2009) makes explicit reference to encouraging health and family services to engage proactively with fathers from pregnancy onwards. In February 2009, the announcement of the *Child Health Strategy* saw further recommendations about fathers' involvement in maternity services, including the provision of an 'Early Years Life Check' and use of an internet-based self-assessment tool for new dads (DH, 2009).

At the time of writing, in a political context shaped by economic concerns about budget deficit reduction, this agenda around fathers' engagement in birth shows no sign of slowing, notwithstanding forthcoming public sector funding cuts. This debate about fatherhood was a notable feature of the period up to the 2010 Election as political leaders sought to seize the initiative on family-friendly policy and express support for fathers. In the January 2010 *Support for All: The Families and Relationships Green Paper* (DCSF, 2010) enhancing support for fathers in relation to birth was explicitly seen by the then Labour Government as a key element of supporting families and family relationships (para 6.6). Thus, extra support from midwives, the provision of information packs on 'being a father', a father awareness campaign, a 'think Fathers' best practice guide and greater support from Children's Centres were just some of the initiatives proposed (DCSF, 2010, p. 114).

Government polices and clinical guidelines alike, in short, have sought to encourage health and family services to engage proactively with fathers from the point of pregnancy onwards. If we look closer, however, how have fathers, mothers and children figured in this evolving policy agenda? The document *Fathers and Family Health in the Perinatal Period*, published in January 2010, by the Fatherhood Institute, exemplifies arguments and assumptions about fathers' responsibilities that have shaped this debate (Fatherhood Institute, 2010). Paternal engagement in pregnancy and birth provides a key 'moment of intervention' in which fathers will re-evaluate their own health risk behavior and 'make more healthy choices and, when they receive emotional support, experience better physical and emotional health' (Fatherhood Institute, 2010, 3). The experience of both mothers and children will improve if fathers address, for example, their relationship with smoking and alcohol (Fatherhood Institute, 2010, pp. 3–4).

This reveals a very different approach to fathers' role in reproduction, and to the male body, from that outlined above. Men's reproductive vulnerability, and the responsibility of the individual *to do something about it*, is here explicitly recognised. It reflects a heightened focus within social policy around parenting on developing human capital, whereby men and women might adapt to new economic conditions and social risks (Bonoli, 2005). It is also indicative of a 'feminization' of health that sees fathers increasingly, like mothers, as a potentially at risk group, as vulnerable and in need of such help. Dominant forms of masculinity and men's practices have themselves become a barrier to promoting men's health, with early intervention therein a key way of reducing later State expenditure on health and crime.

The above developments have repositioned ideas about fathers' role and responsibilities in relation to birth in significant ways. As a result, key aspects of the traditional ideas about fathers, birth and gender outlined at the beginning of this chapter appear to be increasingly anachronistic in the era of the 'new father'. Yet what has also resulted, I argue in the following section, is a legal framework around fathers and birth that has, on closer examination, drawn upon contrasting and contradictory assumptions about gender neutrality, gender convergence and equality. These are themes that have become particularly clear in the context of debates about law, birth and the responsible father.

V. DIGGING DEEPER: FATHERS, MOTHERS AND THE RESPONSIBLE PARENT

No one model of 'new' fatherhood *or* paternal masculinity underscores these debates about fathers and birth. In their analysis of how a 'problem of men' informed an early phase of New Labour social policy, Scourfield and Drakeford

(2002) track significant differences in the deployment of the benefits of father engagement across areas of law. They note in relation to the perinatal period, and family law generally, a degree of policy optimism about fathers. In the home and family, policy has focused on encouraging and facilitating father involvement in birth, underscored by the assumption, reflected in numerous Ministerial and policy statements, not only that men are changing but also that men *want* to change. This perspective, in turn, highlights the institutional and organisational barriers to change, the cultural and legal obstacles to achieving 'active fathering' (Stanley, 2005). Here, law can both change the practices of individuals and organisations in socially desirable ways, and radiate clear messages about the appropriate scope of men's responsible parenting.

Outside the home, however, the debate appears somewhat different. Far from finding optimism about changing men, more traditional ideas of fathers as disciplinarians and gendered 'masculine' role models for children circulate within policy debates around, for example, youth crime, criminality, anti-social behavior and working with men (Featherstone et al., 2007). If a deficit model of fathering has been rejected inside the home, outside it a concern about men's individual and collective failure and lack of ability or commitment to engage in families, shapes policy debates in rather different ways. At times, intriguingly, politicians and policy makers alike slide (often in the same speech/report) between a simultaneous celebration and condemnation of contemporary fatherhood, deploying ideas about fathers' love and commitments, 'father absence' and irresponsibility (for example, in calls to 'shame' 'errant fathers': David Cameron, 2007).

Why is this significant? There is a complex history to the division between 'good dads/bad dads' (Furstenberg, 1988). It can be traced in recent times to policy concerns about 'troubled' masculinities that shaped the child support debates of the early 1990s (Williams, 1998), bound up with the assumptions about social class, race, ethnicity and sexuality that have historically shaped ideas about 'safe' and 'dangerous' fathers in law (Collier, 1998). As the important work of Val Gillies illustrates, questions of class, race, ethnicity and, indeed, geographical location remain important factors influencing family structures and women's and men's actual practices and *experiences* of parenting within specific locales and communities (Gillies, 2006). In relation to father involvement in the perinatal period, however, this raises intriguing questions about the limits of law in promoting fathers' responsibilities.

The dominant framework of engagement shaping the policy agenda outlined above has been one in which men, like women, need to be 'freed' from dominant oppressive gender categories (Ashe 2007, pp. 63–69). Such an approach begs the question, however, not only of whether men – and women – do want qualitatively different kinds of relationships with their children (see below), but also about the way the responsibilities of mothers and fathers have been depicted in these debates. Notwithstanding policies aimed at engaging men in social and health care provision around the perinatal period (Daniel and Taylor, 2001; Ghate et al., 2000; Lloyd et al., 2003), it would appear significant numbers of fathers do not see themselves as in need of support (Edwards and Gillies, 2004; Gillies, 2005). Contemporary experiences of 'intimate fathering', to use the sociologist Esther Dermott's term (2008), suggest that fatherhood continues to involve, for many men, a significant temporal and spatial trade-off between the domains of work and family (Crompton and Lyonette, 2008).

It is precisely the above attitudes that the engaging fathers agenda seeks to address. Any expansion of women's choices, certainly, will depend on a significant change in the behaviour of men in the home. However, there are dangers in pitching a policy aimed at 'changing men' in terms of men's 'choice' to change. What remains so difficult to see in legal-political exhortations about the promotion of a new individual responsibility for fathers is how choice is socially and structurally constrained, bound up within distinctive gendered rationalities and practices that are shaped by the relational networks, and material circumstances, in which individuals live (Barlow et al., 2002; Lewis and Guillari, 2005; Smart, 2007). For critics, therefore, the engaging fathers' agenda has been premised more on individualised, moral exhortations of change in the parenting practices of women and men. Moreover, concerns have been raised about the position of mothers in these debates and the complex relationship between the legal promotion of 'active fathering' and gender equality (Lewis, 2007). As Brid Featherstone has observed, it is most unlikely that 'good outcomes for children will ... be promoted by forcing father involvement against the wishes of mothers' (Featherstone, 2009, 131; also Ray Seward et al., 2006).

There has been a further tendency, Featherstone suggests, to downgrade the role and significance of mothers (who, in this model, need the importance of the father in birth explained to them) and the needs of children (who appear simply as outcomes of good parenting: Lister, 2006; Jenson, 2004). Thus, we find a view, not only that 'men need compensatory policies' but also that 'women [are] to blame for not allowing men to care' in the first place (Featherstone, 2009, p. 145). Such a charge may seem unfair given how father involvement in birth is seen, as above, as of direct benefit to mothers. However, this raises the question of whether women, and mothers especially, are being blamed for a failure to engage fathers in services that have historically been largely female dominated. It is women, and not men, who tend to be held responsible for the failure to control children, mothers, rather than fathers, who are more likely to be made the subject of Parenting Orders for example (Ghate and Ramalla, 2002). As in relation to the differential responsibilities of resident and non-residential parents in post-separation parenting, it would seem that although there are things fathers can do *wrong* in relation to the birth process, there is little they have to do which is *right*.

Additional questions have been raised about the reshaping of fathers' legal responsibilities in law in the context of birth. Recent proposals concerning (a) the reform of the law on unmarried fathers and birth registration (DWP 2008, 2007; McCandless, this volume; Sheldon, 2009), (b) developments in relation to what Reece (2009) has termed the 'degradation of parental responsibility' in case law and (c) policy attempts to manage the 'problem' of contact (Wallbank, 2009) exemplify, in different ways, more than a belief in law that 'fathers matter'. Nor, simply, a recognition that law has a role in promoting responsible fathering. They illustrate a growing recognition in law that parental responsibility has an important *symbolic* role in the therapeutic affirmation of fathers' identities as 'good parents' of their children (Reece, 2009). What is so difficult to see in much of the discussion of this institution of 'good' fatherhood at a legal policy level, however, is an engagement with fathering as a daily emotional, intimate practice. There is thus a 'gap', Bristow (2009) has observed, between the assumptions on the part of policy makers about what fathers should do and feel, and the realities of what are, for many, their everyday family practices.

This raises questions about the conceptual framing of debates about fathers, law and policy. As Aitken has noted (2005), notwithstanding the vast volume of research on contemporary fathering, there is in fact little theory or empirical data on how these everyday practices and the geographical 'spaces' of fatherhood are produced and gendered in specific, situated contexts (see also Marsiglio et al., 2005). Rather, a policy debate about law and fatherhood has rested upon problematic assumptions about the role of law in promoting fathers' responsibilities and the nature of parental responsibility itself (Reece, 2009; Sheldon, 2009). The micro-political realities of fatherhood, the everyday experiences of breadwinning, domesticity and child nurturing, 'occur at the interface of structure and individual agency within specific situated contexts' (Collier and Sheldon, 2008, p. 133; Marsiglio et al., 2005). Experiences of caring and the social responsibilities associated with fatherhood are mediated by individual biography and life history, bound up with the psycho-social dimensions of fathers' experiences in relation to birth (note, for example, Dermott, 2008).

These issues raise important issues about the process of men's identification as a 'father' in the perinatal period, especially in the context of shifting normative cultural messages about good fathering now conveyed by law detailed above. Recent work focusing on the emotional and affective dimensions of the interconnected lives of women, children and men, for example, would suggest that the shifting investments during the life course both women and men have in gendered categories around parenthood and intimacy are highly complex (Smart, 2007). With regard to the perinatal period, there is reason to believe that the normative messages about fatherhood contained in law may themselves be reshaping the contexts in which, in psychological terms, men come to identify as and feel *like* fathers at different moments in their lives. This is not just a matter of the moment of birth, most obviously, but also the period before, in planning for a child's future, in feeling a foetus move within a partner's body or witnessing movements through ultrasonography and so forth (Marsiglio 1998; Shapiro et al., 1995).

Set in the context of the growing medicalisation of birth (Barbira-Freedman, this volume), and the re-gendering of men's health discussed above, cultural and legal exhortations to be conscious of the potential vulnerability of male reproductive biology may have a number of consequences in making many more men aware of themselves as potential fathers long before birth. Sally Sheldon and I have noted elsewhere (2008) how diagnostic technologies and genetic knowledge have carved out a new context for fatherhood, a development that may ultimately be rendering the beginning of fatherhood as psychologically indeterminate as that of motherhood. At the same time, a new consciousness of risk and vulnerability amongst fathers is potentially heightening a perception that fathers, like mothers, are vulnerable parents, are in need of instruction, in need of being told 'how to be a good dad' (Lee, 2009).

VI. CONCLUDING REMARKS: MEDICALISING THE 'EXPECTANT FATHER'

This discussion of fathers and birth takes place against the backdrop of a heightened conversation about parenting as an object of political intervention and a growing concern about risk management and the regulation adult-child relations (Changing Parenting Culture, 2009/10; Furedi, 2003). The social and legal developments outlined above have occurred in the context of the rise of new 'intensive' parenting cultures marked by a reconstitution of the family as a site for the moral reassessment of the behaviour of both parents. A re-gendering of the relationship between fathers and birth has emerged at a nexus of developments in politics and society as much as any (undoubtedly significant) medical and scientific reframing of 'good' fatherhood. A neo-liberal concern to promote the privatisation of economic responsibilities in families and reduce public expenditure, meanwhile, runs through debates around fathers' responsibilities and law to a considerable, if often unspoken, degree, framing the positioning of fathers as both *cause of* and *solution to* a wide range of social problems.

Fathers, we have seen, have been encouraged to take on greater responsibility, not just for children but also for their own personal lives. It is noteworthy, however, that at a time when gender-neutral social care agendas have expanded and individualised ideas of parental responsibility, other, more established, collective social policies around care have contracted and are contracting (Lewis, 2007). An embedding of gender neutrality and formal equality in law has profoundly reshaped understandings of fathers' rights and responsibilities, and the politics of parenting (see Hunter, 2008; Wallbank et al., 2009). It is against this backdrop that we appear to have moved away from the position detailed at the beginning this chapter, one in which men's detachment, if not absence, from birth and early years childcare was accepted. Law has sought to increase expectations and change the practices of individuals, local authority and health care providers alike around the need to include and engage fathers, regardless of social background (Page and Whitting, 2008). Yet looking closer this debate has been pervaded by 'mixed messages' (Dey and Wasoff, 2006) about fatherhood, masculinity and parental responsibility, part of a policy agenda that has uncertain aims, encompassing simultaneously concerns about gender equality, child welfare and economic imperatives as well as some very different ideas about the nature of a normative paternal role.

ACKNOWLEDGEMENT

Discussion in this chapter explores ideas initially developed jointly with Sally Sheldon (Collier and Sheldon, 2008) and expanded on in subsequent work (Collier, 2010a). I am grateful to Sally for permission to draw on previous co-authored work here. Any errors are, of course, my own.

REFERENCES

Aitken, S. (2005). The Awkward Spaces of Fathering. In *Spaces of Masculinities* (ed. K.Horschelmann and B.van Hoven). London: Routledge.

Annesley, C. (2001). New Labour and Welfare. In *New Labour in Government* (ed.S Ludlam and MJ Smith). London: Macmillan.

Ashe, F. (2007). *The New Politics of Masculinity Men, Power and Resistance* (Routledge Innovations in Political Theory) London: Routledge.

Barker, G., Bartlett, D. Beardshaw, T. Brown, J., Burgess, A., Lamb, M., Lewis, C., Russell, G. & Vann, N. (2004). *Supporting Fathers: Contributions from the International Fatherhood Summit 2003*.The Hague, Early Childhood Development: Practice and Reflections Series, Bernard van Leer Foundation

Barlow, A., Duncan, S. and James, G. (2002). New Labour, the Rationality Mistake and Family Policy in Britain. In *Analysing Families: Morality and Rationality in Policy and Practice*(ed. A. Carling, S. Duncan and R. Edwards), London: Routledge.

Bartlett, D., Burgess, A. and Jones, K. (2007). *A Toolkit for Developing Father-Inclusive Practice*. London: Fathers Direct.

Bonoli, G. (2005). The Politics of the New Social Policies: Providing Coverage against New Social Risks in Mature Welfare States. *Policy and Politics* 33(3), 431–439.

Bristow, J. (2009). *Standing up to Supernanny*. London: Societas.

Burgess, A. (2007). *The Costs and Benefits of Active Fatherhood: Evidence and Insights to Inform the Development of Policy and Practice*. London: Fathers Direct.

Burgess, A. and Russell, G. (2004). Fatherhood and Public Policy. In *Supporting Fathers: Contributions From the International Fatherhood Summit 2003*(ed. G. Barker, D. Bartlett, T. Beardshaw, J. Brown, A. Burgess, M. Lamb, C. Lewis, G.

Russell & N. Vann.) The Hague: Early Childhood Development: Practice and Reflections Series, Bernard van Leer Foundation.

Burgess, A. and Bartlett, D. (2004). *Working with Fathers*. London: Fathers Direct.

Cameron, D. (2007) *BBC News*, 22 February 2007

Changing Parenting Culture (2009/10), a seminar series funded by the Economic and Social Research Council: http://www.parentingculturestudies.org/seminar-series/index.html, accessed 28 March 2009.

Clare, A. (2000). *On Men: Masculinity in Crisis*. London: Chatto and Windus.

Colborn, T., Dumanoski, D., Myers, J.P. (1997). *Our Stolen Future: How We are Threatening our Fertility, our Intelligence and our Survival*. New York: Plume Books, New York.

Collier, R. (1995). *Masculinity, Law and the Family*. London: Routledge.

—— (1998). *Masculinities, Crime and Criminology: Men, Heterosexuality and the Criminal(ised) Other*. London: Sage.

—— (2009) Fathers' Rights, Gender and Welfare: Some Questions for Family Law. *Journal of Social Welfare and Family Law* 31(4), 357–371

—— (2010a). *Men, Law and Gender: Essays on the 'Man' of Law*. London: Routledge.

—— (2010b). Masculinities, Law and Personal Life: Towards a New Framework for Understanding Men, Law and Gender. *Harvard Journal of Law and Gender* 33(2), 431–476.

Collier, R. and Sheldon, S. (eds) (2006). *Fathers Rights Activism and Legal Reform*. Oxford: Hart.

—— (2008). *Fragmenting Fatherhood: A Socio-Legal Study*. Oxford: Hart.

Crompton, R. (1999). *Restructuring Gender Relations and Employment: The Decline of the Male Breadwinner*. Oxford: Oxford University Press.

Crompton, R. and Lyonette, C. (2008). *Who Does the Housework? The Division of Labour Within the Home: British Social Attitudes 24th Report*. London: National Centre for Social Research/Sage.

Daniel, B. and Taylor, J. (2001). *Engaging with Fathers: Practice Issues for Health and Social Care*. London: Jessica Kingsley Publishers.

Daniels, C. (1997). Between Fathers and Fetuses: The Social Construction of Male Reproduction and the Politics of Fetal Harm. *Signs* 22(3), 579.

—— (2006). *Exposing Men: The Science and Politics of Male Reproduction*. Oxford: OUP.

Department for Children, Schools and Families (2009). *Getting Maternity Services Right for Teenage Mothers and Young Fathers*. London: DCSF.

—— (2010). *Support for All*. London: DCSF.

Department for Education and Skills (2007). *Every Parent Matters*. London: Department of Education and Skills.

Department of Health (2009). *Healthy Lives, Brighter Futures – The Strategy for Children and Young People's Health*. London: Department of Health.

Department for Health and Department for Children, School and Families(2007). *Parents Next Steps: Guidance for Local Authorities and Primary Care*. London: DH and DCFS.

Department for Work and Pensions (2007). *Joint Birth Registration: Promoting Parental Responsibility*, Cm 7160. London: DWP

Department for Work and Pensions WP (2008). *Joint Birth Registration: Recording Responsibility*, Cm 7293. London: DWP.

Dermott, E. (2008). *Intimate Fatherhood: A Sociological Analysis*. London: Routledge.

Dey, I. and Wasoff, F. (2006). Mixed Messages: Parental Responsibilities, Public Opinion and the Reforms of Family Law. *International Journal of Law, Policy and the Family* **20**, 225.

Edwards, R. and Gillies, V. (2004). Support in Parenting: Values and Consensus Concerning Who to Turn To. *Journal of Social Policy* **33**(4), 627–647.

Equal Opportunities Commission (2007). *Facts About Men and Women in Great Britain 2006*. Manchester: Equal Opportunities Commission.

Equality and Human Rights Commission (2009). *Working Better*. London: EHRC.

Fatherhood Institute (2010). *Fathers and Family Health in the Perinatal Period*. London: Fatherhood Institute.

Featherstone, B. (2009). *Contemporary Fathering: Theory, Policy and Practice*. Bristol: Policy Press.

Featherstone, B. and Trinder, L. (2001). New Labour, Families and Fathers. *Critical Social Policy* **21**(4), 534–536.

Featherstone, B., Rivett, M. and Scourfield, J. (2007). *Working With Men in Health and Social Care*. London: Sage.

Fineman, M. (1995). *The Neutered Mother, The Sexual Family and Other Twentieth Century Tragedies*. New York: Routledge.

—— (2004). *The Autonomy Myth*. New York: The New Press.

Furedi, F. (2003). *Therapy Culture: Cultivating Vulnerability in an Uncertain Age*. London: Routledge.

Furstenberg, F. (1988). Good Dads-Bad Dads: Two Faces of Fatherhood. In *The Changing American Family and Public Policy* (ed.AJ Cherlin). Washington, DC: Urban Institute Press.

Ghate, D. Shaw, C. and Hazel, N. (2000). *Fathers and Family Centres: Engaging Fathers in Preventative Services*. York: Joseph Rowntree Foundation.

Ghate, D. and Ramalla, M. (2002). *Positive Parenting: The National Evaluation of the Youth Justice Board's Parenting Programme*. London: Policy Research Bureau.

Giddens, A. (1992). *The Transformation of Intimacy.* Cambridge: Polity.

Gillies, V. (2005). Meeting Parents' Needs? Discourses of 'Support' and 'Inclusion' in Family Policy. *Critical Social Policy* 25(1), 70–90.

—— (2006). *Marginalised Mothers: Exploring Working Class Experiences of Parenting.* London: Routledge.

Hatten, W. Vinter, L. and Williams, R. (2002). *Dads on Dads: Needs and Expectations at Home and Work.* Manchester: Equal Opportunities Commission.

Hobson, B. (ed) (2002). *Making Men into Fathers: Men, Masculinities and the Social Politics of Fatherhood.* Cambridge: Cambridge University Press.

Hunter, R. (2008). *Rethinking Equality Projects in Law: Feminist Challenges.* Oxford: Hart.

Jamieson, L. (1998). *Intimacy: Personal Relationships in Modern Society.* Cambridge: Polity

Jenson, J. (2004). Changing the Paradigm: Family Responsibility or Investing in Children. *Canadian Journal of Sociology* 24(2), 169–181.

Kilkey, M. (2006). New Labour and Reconciling Work and Family Life: Making it Fathers' Business? *Social Policy & Society* 5, 167–175.

Lee, E. (2009). 'Pathologising fatherhood: the case of male Post Natal Depression in Britain'. In *Men, Masculinities and Health: critical perspectives* (ed. S. Robertson and B. Gough). Basingstoke: Palgrave

Lewis, C. (2000). *A Man's Place in the Home: Fathers and Families in the UK: JRF Foundations 440.* York: Joseph Rowntree Foundation.

Lewis, C. and Lamb, M. (2007). *Understanding Fatherhood: A Review of Recent Research.* York: Joseph Rowntree Foundation.

Lewis, J. (2007). Balancing Work and Family: The Nature of the Policy Challenge and Gender Equality: Working Paper for GeNet Project 9: *Tackling Inequalities in Work and Care Policy Initiatives and Actors at the EU and UK Levels, 2007* http://www.genet.ac.uk/projects/project9.htm, accessed 18 October 2008.

Lewis, J. and Guillari, S. (2005). The Adult Worker Model Family, Gender Equality and Care: The Search for New Policy Principles and the Possibilities and Problems of a Capabilities Approach. *Economy & Society* 34(1), 76–104.

Lewis, J. and Campbell, M. (2007). UK Work-Family Balance Policies and Gender Equality. *Social Politics* 14(1), 4–18.

Lister, R. (2006). Children (But Not Women) First: New Labour, Child Welfare and Gender. *Critical Social Policy* 26(2), 315–335.

Lloyd, N., O'Brien, M and Lewis, C. (2003). *Fathers in Sure Start: The National Evaluation of Sure Start (NESS)* London: Institute for the Study of Children, Families and Social Issues, Birkbeck, University of London.

MacRae, F. (2009). Another Blow to Fatherhood: IVF Mothers Can Name ANYONE as 'Father' on Birth Certificate – and It Doesn't Even Have to be a Man. *Daily Mail* 2 March 2009.

Mander, R. (2004). *Men and Maternity*. London: Routledge.

Marsiglio, W. (1998). *Procreative Man*. New York: New York University Press.

Marsiglio, W., Roy, K. and Litton Fox, G. (eds) (2005). *Situated Fathering: A Focus on Physical and Social Spaces*. Lanham, MD: Rowman & Littlefield.

O'Brien, M. (2004). Social Science and Public Policy Perspectives on Fatherhood. In *The Role of the Father in Child Development* (ed. M.E. Lamb). New Jersey: John Wiley.

—— (2005). *Shared Caring: Bringing Fathers into the Frame*. Manchester: Equal Opportunities Commission.

O'Brien, M. and Shemilt, I. (2003). *Working Fathers: Earning and Caring*. Manchester: Equal Opportunities Commission.

Page, J. and Whitting, G. (2008). *A Review of How Fathers Can Be Better Recognised and Supported Through DCSF Policy*. DCSF Research Report DCSF-RRO40, London: DCFS.

Ray Seward, R., Yeatts, D.E., Amin, I. and Dewitt, A. (2006). Employment Leave and Father's Involvement with Children: According to Mothers and Fathers. *Men and Masculinities* 8(4), 405–421.

Reece, H. (2009). The Degradation of Parental Responsibility. In *Responsible Parents and Parental Responsibility* (ed. R. Probert, S. Gilmore and J. Herring). Oxford: Hart.

Scourfield, J. and Drakeford, M. (2002). New Labour and the 'Problem of Men'. *Critical Social Policy* 22, 619–640.

Shapiro, J. Lee, Diamond, M.J. and Greenberg, M. (1995). *Becoming a Father: Contemporary, Social, Developmental and Clinical Perspectives*. New York: Springer.

Sheldon, S. (1999). *Re*Conceiving Masculinity: Imagining Men's Reproductive Bodies in Law. *Journal of Law and Society* 26(2), 129-143.

—— (2006). 'Reproductive Choice: Men's Freedom and Women's Responsibility? In *Freedom and Responsibility in Reproductive Choice* (ed. A. Pedain and J. Spencer). Oxford: Hart.

—— (2009). From 'Absent Objects of Blame' to 'Fathers who Want to Take Responsibility': Reforming Birth Registration Law. *Journal of Social Welfare and Family Law*, 31 (4), 373–389.

Smart, C. (2007). *Personal Life: New Directions in Sociological Thinking*. Oxford: Polity.

Stanley, K. (2005). *Daddy Dearest? Active Fatherhood and Public Policy*. London: Institute for Public Policy Research.

Thomson, M. (2007). *Endowed: Regulating the Male Sexed Body*. New York: Routledge.

Wallbank, J. (2009). Parental Responsibility and the Responsible Parent: Managing the 'Problem' of Contact'. In *Responsible Parents and Parental*

Responsibility (ed. R. Probert, S.Gilmore, S. and J. Herring). Hart Publishing: Oxford.

Wallbank, J., Choudhry, S and Herring, J. (2009) (eds). *Rights, Gender and Family Law.* London: Routledge-Cavendish.

Williams, F. (1998). Troubled Masculinities in Social Policy Discourses: Fatherhood. In *Men, Gender Divisions and Welfare* (ed. J Popay, J. Hearn and J. Edwards). London: Routledge.

Williams, F. and Roseneil, S. (2004). Public Values of Parenting and Partnering: Voluntary Organizations and Welfare Politics in New Labour's Britain. *Social Politics* **11**(2), 181–201.

Part 3:

After Birth

9

Recording Births: From the Reformation to the Welfare Reform Act

REBECCA PROBERT

I. INTRODUCTION

IN 1917 THE family lawyer W. Clarke Hall commented that, '[t]he obvious natural law that every child born into the world has a right to fatherhood, as well as to motherhood, has not yet been recognised' (Clarke Hall, 1917: 133). The year has a particular relevance for me – it was the same year that my grandmother's birth was registered: her mother was recorded as a domestic servant; her father – a blank.

This absence of information would have been the case for the majority of the 37,157 children born outside marriage in that year (Registrar-General, 1919, p. xxiii). Indeed, for most of the period under review the single most important factor influencing what was recorded about a child's birth was whether that birth occurred inside or outside marriage. This chapter therefore reviews the religious rite of baptism and the legal rite of registration and how the recording of information about legal parenthood has changed over that time, setting the rules in the context of demographic change and examples from primary sources.

Before doing so, three preliminary points need to be addressed: those of terminology, definition, and extent. Modern family lawyers eschew such terms as 'illegitimate' or 'illegitimacy', which have become legally and socially redundant. But when discussing the past, the deliberate avoidance of such terms would be equally anachronistic and would fail to convey the social opprobrium and legal disadvantages that such children laboured under. These – and other, still cruder terms – will be used where the context requires or original sources dictate.

The concept of illegitimacy is, by definition, linked to what the law regards as a valid marriage. Some writers have speculated that local custom may have played a role in defining marriage – and hence legitimacy – before the Clandestine Marriages Act of 1753 (Laslett, 1980a, p. 224); more recent research, however, confirms that the formalities required for a valid marriage were clearer and more concrete than has hitherto been appreciated, at least in the period under consideration (Probert, 2009). Custom can, therefore, be discounted as a variable in the definition of illegitimacy.

But whether or not a child was illegitimate was rather more complex than the question of whether the parents had gone through a legally-recognised ceremony of marriage by the time of the child's birth. Children whose parents had gone through such a ceremony might suddenly experience a change in status if the marriage was annulled. Children registered as legitimate might discover at a later stage that they were born as the result of an adulterous union, and that they had no biological link to the man recorded as their father. Perhaps more rarely, children born to a second union that was thought to be bigamous might find that they were legitimate after all if the first marriage was declared void. Those whose parents married after their birth, by contrast, would not have enjoyed any change in their own status for most of the period under review: English law did not allow legitimation by a subsequent marriage until 1926. Yet since the focus of this collection is on the rites associated with birth, changes in status resulting from such shifts of fortune will not be considered: the focus will be on the supposed status of the child at the time of birth.

This is also the measure of illegitimacy used by demographers, and so we should turn to considering the extent of illegitimacy in times past. This has fluctuated over the centuries, as well as from place to place (Levine and Wrightson, 1991), but until relatively recently such fluctuations have been within a fairly small range. While the illegitimacy ratio was rising over the course of the sixteenth century, it peaked at under 4 per cent before falling again in the seventeenth century, with a marked low of less than 1 per cent during the Commonwealth (Laslett, 1980b, p. 14; Wrightson, 1980). Over the course of the eighteenth century it rose from just under 2 per cent to a little over 5 per cent (ibid). While these are necessarily estimates in the absence of any formal system of recording births, they are consistent with the evidence from other sources (see eg Macfarlane, 1980; Cressy, 1999, p. 73).

The advent of civil registration in 1837 provided improved statistical information, and the middle years of the nineteenth century saw an increase to around 7 per cent. But both the number and the ratio then fell, with the result that the proportion of births outside marriage was smaller at the start of the twentieth century than at the end of the eighteenth. And apart from small spikes in the ratio (if not the number) of illegitimate births during each of the world wars, the ratio remained under 5 per cent until the 1960s. Since then, the increase has been rapid, with the latest figures showing that 45 per cent of children were born outside marriage in 2008 (ONS, 2009). While there may have been some under-registration in the past – of both legitimate and illegitimate births – it is implausible that this could have been so extensive as to account for the difference between, say, the mid-eighteenth century and the early twenty-first.

With these points in mind, let us turn to the way in which births have been recorded as either occurring inside or outside marriage and the extent to which such records operate as an indicator of legal parenthood.

II. BAPTISMS

While the modern system of civil registration of births dates only from 1837, there had been a system of recording a child's parentage for three centuries prior to that. Henry VIII's Chief Minister, Thomas Cromwell, had in 1538 ordered that each incumbent should keep

> one Book or Register, wherein he shall write the day and year of every wedding, Christening and Burial, made within your parish for your time… and also there insert every person's name, that shall be so wedded, christened and buried. (30 Hen VIII, 1538; for discussion see Szreter, 2007).

The impetus for this reform had been the dissolution of the monasteries, which had previously kept records of burials and marriages – although not, it would appear, baptisms (Burn, 1862, pp. 10–11). The Reformation therefore provides an appropriate starting point for a review of what was recorded when a child was born.

At this time what was being recorded was the religious rite of baptism, rather than the fact of the child's birth (save for the brief period of the Commonwealth, between 1653 and 1660, during which the other Cromwell ordered the registration of births). This did not, of course, mean that the authorities were any less assiduous in ensuring that baptism took place. Baptism was a key rite: it was, in the words of one scholar, 'the Gate or Entrance into Christianity itself … and without which, in the opinion of some men, … we cannot obtain everlasting salvation' (Ayliffe, 1726, p. 102). And although the date recorded in the register was that of the baptism rather than the birth, the two were usually close together in time: the Rubrick warned that baptism should be deferred no longer than the first or second Sunday after the birth. While there are occasional records of adolescents or even adults receiving baptism, for the vast majority of the population baptism relatively soon after birth was the norm.

In addition, in many cases the record of the baptism would contain the same basic information that one finds in modern registers of births – the names of the child and his or her parents. Unfortunately for historians, concern that the rite of baptism was carried out did not necessarily translate into careful recording of demographic detail. The lack of any specified form led to great variety in what was actually recorded. In some places incumbents chose to record only the father of a child. At Llansantffraid Glyn Ceiriog, the practice of one eighteenth-century incumbent was very variable, even if it originated in a desire for tidiness: for some time he tried to ensure that entries in the register occupied only one line. So if the wife's name was 'Ann' or 'Mary' there was usually room for this to be recorded; longer names, however, would simply be excluded if there was not sufficient room (Probert, 2009, p. 85).

And such variability was even more common if the child born was illegitimate. While the 1538 Act did not require the illegitimacy of a child to be recorded, this became common practice (Laslett, 1980b), underlining the importance of the issue for early modern society. In some cases the mere fact of baptism was recorded, with no mention of the child's parents. Such entries ranged from the sparse 'Harry, a base child, bap., 1580' and the even more condemnatory but no more informative 'Johan, the Daughter of a Harlott' to the more cheerful 'George Speedwell, a merry begot' and the positively romantic 'Craddock Bowe, love begot' (Burn, 1862, p. 84). Similarly, of Agnes Price we know no more than that she was 'base born in a barn' (ibid, p. 85). The fact that surnames were recorded for these latter children indicates that at least one parent was known. Other babies, however, were simply abandoned, and the name conferred on them could therefore offer no indication of their parentage – like 'Richard Monday' in George Crabbe's poem, *The Parish Register* (Dalrymple-Champneys and Pollard, 1988).

More usually, however, the name of at least the mother would appear. The luxury of a blank book allowed those recording a baptism to add their own comments if they thought fit. The register of Stepney for 1633 conscientiously explained the background to one particular entry:

> Alexander, Son of Katharine, Wife of Alexander Tuckey of Poplar, begotten she affirmed in the field on this side of the mud wall near the Gunne, about 9 of the o'clock at night; the father she knew not, but the said Alexander by them that brought the child to be baptized, requested that it might be recorded in his name. (Burn, 1862, p. 85)

And at Llansantffraid Glyn Ceiriog, in less informative but more vivid language, the clergyman used the pages of the baptismal register to fulminate against 'ye said wicked debauched animal Mary Roberts' as he noted the baptism of her fifth illegitimate child (Denbighshire Record Office, PD75/1/1, 18 January 1799; Clywd Family History Society, 1992, p. 14).

Of course, there was nothing to prevent the incumbent adding the name of the father – if he was known. At a time when an illegitimate child acquired a settlement for the purposes of the Poor Law in the parish of his or her birth, strenuous efforts were made to discover parentage, so that the father could be made to support the child. Midwives played a key role in the process of discovery (Cressy, 1999, p. 67). The licence granted to Bridget Kirby of Cropredy in 1726 was explicit as to what was expected:

> If you help to deliver any whom you suspect to be unmaryed you shall acquaint the Ecclesiastical Court of this Iurisdiction therewith and before you yield your assistance or helpe you shall perswade and by all lawfull means labour with them to declare who is the father of the said Child. (Peyton, 1928, p. xxv).

Given such 'perswasion', how common was it for a child to be recorded with the name of the mother alone? Studies of individual parishes may be misleading, given that the records may simply reflect the idiosyncrasies of the incumbent, or sometimes the presence of a particular family. For example, of the 180 couples who brought children to be baptised in the Scilly isles between 1734 and 1754, there were only seven mothers who were recorded as producing base or illegitimate children, but four of these were from the Barrisfield family. Even basing conclusions on collections of parishes may not resolve the difficulty, since parishes chosen for detailed demographic study inevitably tend to be those with the best-kept registers. What is needed is a study of a large number of parishes that have not been specially selected for particular attributes. The fact that many records are now available in electronic form renders this task rather easier than in the past: it was possible to draw up a cohort for the whole of Northamptonshire for the period 1730 to 1751 from an electronic index of births and baptisms (Clarke and Lyman-Clarke, 2007). In total, 847 instances of children being described as 'bastard', 'base', 'illegitimate', 'spurious', 'natural', 'reputed', 'supposed', 'misbegotten', or 'fathered out of wedlock' were traced. In the vast majority of cases – 623, or 74 per cent of the total – only the mother's name appeared in the register (Probert, 2009, p. 115).

With this as a base-line, it is possible to evaluate the typicality or otherwise of individual parishes. The parish of St Olave's in York has particularly full records for the period between 1770 and 1785: it also has a particularly high number of illegitimate baptisms – 26 per cent of the total – because of the presence of the poorhouse within its precincts. One would expect those mothers who were in the poorhouse to be the least likely to have any support from the father, and the proportion of cases in which no father was named was unsurprisingly high for this cohort, at 82 per cent. By contrast, at Holy Trinity Goodramgate, we have details of the fathers of 10 of the 16 infants who were described as illegitimate for the period between 1734 and 1754: this higher percentage may have been due to the fact that the incumbent was willing to baptise infants privately.

Such studies reflect the fact that births outside marriage in this period were almost invariably the result of 'slips' rather than the product of stable co-residential relationships (Probert, 2009, p. 115). Even where the mother did name a father, some incumbents were sceptical, prefacing the name given with phrases such as 'supposed' or 'as she saith'. Mothers did, however, prove more forthcoming when examined on oath by Justices of the Peace: in Rogers' study of bastardy examinations the identity of the father was disclosed in over 90 per cent of cases (Rogers, 1989).

It is clear, therefore, that the extent to which the rite of baptism operated as an indicator of legal parenthood was limited in the case of illegitimate children, whether this was due to the mother's refusal to disclose the name of the father or the incumbent's reluctance to enter the details in the register. In addition, such children had no legal entitlement to bear the name of either parent. As Sir William Scott commented in *Sullivan v Sullivan*:

The Court has had occasion to observe that it may in some cases be difficult to say what are the true names, particularly in the case of illegitimate children. They have no proper surname but what they acquire by repute; though it is a well known practice, which obtains in many instances, to give them the surname of the mother, whose children they certainly are, whoever be their father. However, if they are much tossed about in the world, in a great variety of obscure fortunes, as such persons frequently are, it may be difficult to say for certain what name they have permanently acquired.

(*Sullivan v Sullivan, falsely called Oldacre* (1818) 2 Hag Con 238; 161 *ER* 728, 254)

Yet while most illegitimate children took their mother's name, this was not an invariable practice. Some took the father's name – as in *Sullivan v Sullivan* itself.

In other cases children were recorded with a different surname to that of their mother even when the father was not named. And some children took the surnames of *both* parents – such double surnames marking them for life as born out of wedlock.

III. CIVIL REGISTRATION

Despite differences in practice in the registration of baptisms, it was not until the nineteenth century that attempts were made to introduce a more systematic approach.

Legislation passed in 1812 had required more detailed entries of baptisms to be made (52 Geo III c. 146), and one finds a greater degree of standardisation in the registers from this period. But the growth of nonconformism meant that the Anglican parish registers could no longer be relied upon as a comprehensive record of the community (Slack, 1987), despite the fact that many dissenters continued to use the parish church for key rites (Ambler, 1974; Probert, 2009). Moreover, a rapidly industrialising society demanded both improved statistical information of demographic trends and better proof of individual events. Not only were the birth registers of dissenters held inadmissible by the courts because of their unofficial nature, but, in addition, Anglican baptism records were held not to constitute evidence of the date or place of birth – or, indeed, of a child's legitimacy (Burn, 1862, pp. 229, 249).

In response to such demands, legislation was passed in 1836 introducing a system of civil registration (Wrigley and Schofield, 1989). Section 19 of the 1836 Act for the Registering of Births, Deaths, and Marriages set out the new requirement in clear terms: the father or mother of any child born should give notice of the birth to the Registrar of the District within 42 days. Yet the fact that religious objectives had been overtaken by bureaucratic and statistical concerns did not necessarily ensure the completeness of the register. The authorities' efforts to ensure that a child was registered with the names of both parents were distinctly half-hearted: a mother was not obliged to state the name of the father, with registrars being delicately advised that 'if the informant declines stating the name of the father, or there shall be reason to believe that the child is illegitimate, the Registrar shall not press inquiry on that subject' (GRO, 1838, p. 10).

Nor was there any means of ensuring the accuracy of the information given by the mother. At this time there was no requirement that the father be present at the time of registration or that he should give his consent. One petitioner to London's Foundling Hospital informed the authorities that the father of her illegitimate child had died before the birth: this did not prevent the baby being registered with his name (Barret-Ducrocq, 1989, p. 126).

It was, moreover, suspected at the time that there was widespread underreporting and misinformation in the context of illegitimate births. Some may never have been registered at all: illegitimate babies were more likely to be abandoned (on foundlings, see Adie, 2005) and infanticide offered another means of concealing an unwanted birth (Rose, 1986; Day Sclater, this volume). Others may have been recorded as legitimate, and the author Wilkie Collins was probably not the only man to use an alias when registering the birth of his illegitimate children. The National Association for the Promotion of Social Science estimated in 1867 that non-registration in parts of London might be between 15 and 33 per cent and that many illegitimate children were being registered as legitimate (Rose, 1986, p. 22).

But how accurate were such estimates of non-registration? Given the availability of census data with information about the occupants of households from 1841 onwards, it should, in theory, be possible to ascertain whether those listed in the census had actually been registered. A small exploratory study was therefore carried out to test this. For convenience, it drew on a published transcript of the 1851 census, relating to the Berkhamsted district of Hertfordshire (Goose, 1996).

However, investigating the completeness of registration is rendered difficult by the fact that the original registers are still not available for inspection: it is possible to order copies of the original certificates, but to undertake a cohort study by such means would be prohibitively expensive. The only viable option is therefore to check whether the name appears on the publicly-accessible index, using one of the searchable databases such as Free BMD (http://www.freebmd.org.uk). A second problem is finding a sufficiently large cohort of illegitimate children. A search for households headed by an unmarried mother with a child under the age of 13 – and so born after the advent of civil registration – yielded a mere seven mothers and nine children in a district of over 11,000 individuals. The workhouse in Great Berkhamsted supplied a further five mothers. A larger sample of 86 was gathered by identifying households consisting of a head, unmarried children, and grandchildren: this fits with the evidence that illegitimate children were more likely to be living with grandparents than with both biological parents (Robin, 1987; Gandy, 1978), although of course some of these grandchildren may have been the children of other, married but (at least on the night of the census) non-resident parents.

Overall, it was only possible to trace an entry in the BMD index for 71 per cent of those children. This does not, however, mean that almost 30 per cent of illegitimate births were not registered. There are many reasons why a particular entry might not be traced: one only needs to consider how many hands the data has passed through from the original informant (who may not have used a consistent spelling) to the current electronic form to appreciate the possibility of mistranscriptions rendering particular entries undiscoverable. That this, rather than non-registration, may be the problem is suggested by the fact that the proportion traced varies from parish to parish within the district. And perhaps the crucial point for current purposes is that these problems are not confined to the illegitimate: this was tested by carrying out a similar process for a matched sample of non-illegitimate children (chosen by taking the next child aged under 13 in the 1851 census). The proportion traced was not significantly higher for this group, at 77 per cent. Further evidence that Victorian estimates of non-registration of illegitimate births may have been exaggerated is provided by the impact of subsequent legal changes: registration was made compulsory in 1874, but although the total number of registered births rose, the number of those recorded as illegitimate continued to fall, contrary to the expectations of officials (Registrar-General, 1877, p. xxvi).

Whether or not the fact that a child was born illegitimate affected the likelihood of his or her birth being registered, it is clear that it continued to affect *what* was registered. Within the Berkhamsted sample, 73 per cent bore the same name as the head of the household (or, in the case of the workhouse, their mother), while 23 per cent had a different name, presumably that of the father, and four had joint surnames. The proportions are almost identical to those in the Northamptonshire cohort of a hundred years earlier. And it is likely that the 1874 Act would have exacerbated this trend by tightening the rules on who could register what information: the father of an illegitimate child was no longer entitled to register the birth, and his name could only be recorded at the joint request of both parents. This brought the rules relating to birth registration into line with the affiliation laws, which had been consolidated in the Bastardy Laws Amendment Act 1872 and required corroborative evidence of paternity before an order was made.

There were still of course a number of cases in which the register was misleading rather than simply incomplete. Margaret Penn's thinly-veiled autobiography noted the rumours circulating in the village that her father was a gentleman rather than the man her mother had married a mere five months before her birth in 1896 (Penn, 1979, pp. 6–9). And in 1918 Angelica, the daughter of Vanessa Bell, was registered with the name of Vanessa's husband Clive despite the fact that all parties knew her to be the child of Duncan Grant (Roiphe, 2008, p. 168).

With the introduction of the welfare state, many individuals faced the necessity of providing information about their age. The introduction of a short version of the birth certificate in 1947 was intended to avoid causing embarrassment to the illegitimate, and apparently led to a number of elderly individuals claiming the pensions to which they were entitled but which they had previously refrained from claiming because of reluctance to disclose their illegitimacy (James, 1957, p. 45). Some, however, resented its brevity: Sue Elliott, born in 1951 and subsequently adopted, described her birth certificate as a 'flimsy piece of toilet paper' which was 'brief to the point of insult':

> On it was my name, my sex, my date of birth and my country of birth... and that was all. Other people had much bigger and more self-important birth certificates stacked with interesting facts about occupations and places of birth. This deliberately uninformative piece of paper seemed to prove that there was something about me worth hiding. (Elliott, 2005, p. 17).

When she later obtained access to her full birth certificate, one crucial detail was still missing – no father was named (Elliott, 2005, p. 51).

This was still the common experience of children born outside marriage: as late as the 1960s sole registrations accounted for over 60 per cent of all births outside marriage (Smallwood, 2004). This may seem surprising given that a number of contemporary surveys of unmarried mothers revealed that a substantial proportion were living with the father. A sample of 1,142 infants born in Newcastle in 1947, for example, revealed 67 illegitimate children, of whom 27 were living with both parents 'as members of unofficial families.' (Spence, 1954, p. 144). Further surveys carried out in Leicester in 1949, in another, anonymous, Midland town in 1950 and in Birmingham in 1955 (MacDonald, 1956; Dewar, 1968, p. 40) found that around half of the mothers were living with the father at the time that the child was conceived. Of course, cohabitation at the time of conception did not guarantee cohabitation at the date of birth; more importantly, it should be borne in mind that these surveys focused on those unmarried mothers who had kept their child, and therefore excluded the significant proportion whose children had been adopted. In 1968 – the year in which the number of adoptions peaked – over a third of mothers of illegitimate children chose to give them up for adoption (Stockdale Report, 1972). Cohabitants thus accounted for only a minority of births outside marriage, but a cohabiting mother was better placed to keep her child than one who was not supported by the father.

This, however, was about to change. Births outside marriage rose from 10 per cent in the 1970s to 45 per cent in 2008, and this increase was largely accounted for by the increase in cohabitation, with joint registration being correspondingly common (Smallwood, 2004). Whether the name registered is that of the father or mother – or both – remains a matter of individual choice (and see Smart and Stevens, 2000, pp. 34–5) on the various factors that may play a role).

IV. REGISTRATION FOR ALL

The increase in joint registration has led to a closer scrutiny of those few remaining cases in which no father is named on the birth certificate. Kiernan and Smith's study of children born in 2001–2 found that where the child was born to cohabiting parents, all but three per cent were jointly registered (Kiernan and Smith, 2003). Of the 15 per cent of mothers who were not in a co-residential relationship at the time of the birth, high rates of joint registration were still observed among those who continued to be closely involved with the father, or who had lived with him at some point (81 per cent). Only among those who were not in a relationship at the time of birth did joint registrations fall to 27 per cent (see also Smallwood, 2004).

Yet the fact that almost 20 per cent of parents who were still 'closely involved' were not registering the birth of their child jointly might suggest that there is scope for joint registration to increase still further. So too might the figure, relied on by the government, to the effect that in 45 per cent of those cases where the birth was registered by the mother alone the father had regular contact with the child. Influenced by such considerations, it was therefore proposed that the father's name should be recorded on the birth certificate in all but exceptional cases (DWP, 2007; see eg Sheldon, 2009).

The expressed hope was that joint birth registration would encourage responsible parenting as well as conferring parental responsibility – and one form of responsible parenting in particular, namely the payment of child support. However, a shift in the rationale for reform was evident in the subsequent White Paper. This was published jointly by the DWP and the DCSF, and this time a greater emphasis on the rights of the child was evident:

> At the heart of our reforms is a desire to promote child welfare and *the right of every child to know who his or her parents are.* (DWP/DCSF, 2008: [6], emphasis added).

This reflected the responses from those who had replied to the earlier consultation paper: a number had argued that 'the right of a child to know his or her parentage should prevail over any objections by adults or difficulties in adult relationships' (DWP/DCSF, 2008: [17]; see also [25]). Such a rationale could be seen as reflecting a greater attentiveness to children's rights; one could also point out that it is rather easier to judge whether the reform has been a success if it is measured by the simple fact of registration. By contrast, if the aim of the scheme is to promote an ongoing relationship between the child and the parent, and responsible parenting, then there are many more opportunities for failure.

But if the reform is driven by the right of the child to know the identity of his or her biological parents, should it be open to either parent to oppose registration? The White Paper took the view that each parent should be able to insist upon the truth being established via paternity testing:

Where a mother wants the identity of a father to be recorded but this is against the wishes of the father, or the wishes of the father are not known, mothers will be allowed to identify the father of their child independently. At this point the father will be contacted and required to sign the birth register. Where the issue of paternity is denied or challenged, a paternity test will be required and the man concerned will be recorded as the father if his paternity of the child is established by such a test. (DWP/DSCF, 2008: [28])

This, however, was not what was enacted. In brief, the scheme envisaged by the Welfare Reform Act 2009 (much is left to be worked out in the regulations) requires a mother who attends the register office alone to provide information about the father, unless one of the exemptions applies. These are that the child has no legal father by virtue of s. 41 Human Fertilisation and Embryology Act 2008, or the father has died, or the mother does not know the father's identity or whereabouts, or the father lacks capacity (as defined by the Mental Capacity Act 2005) and so is unable to confirm whether he is the father, or the mother has reason to fear for her safety or that of the child if the father is contacted in relation to the registration of the birth. If none of these exemptions applies and the mother provides details of the father, he will then be contacted and required to confirm whether or not he is the father. Similarly, a man may attend and make a declaration that he is the father; and if the mother agrees, he can be named on the birth certificate.

Bainham has questioned whether these exemptions are consistent with the emphasis on the right of the child, arguing that welfare considerations (whether of the mother or of the child) are out of place in this context (Bainham, 2008). One might also suggest that different reasons would seem to justify different types of exemptions. If the father is dead or incapable, then the paternity of the child is unverifiable rather than unknown. As we have seen, before 1874 a mother would have been able to record the father's name in such cases: is the risk that this process would be abused sufficient to outweigh the desirability of ensuring the completeness of the register?

Similarly, in the case of the exemption based on the mother's fear of the father, the choice is not necessarily between non-registration on the one hand and the risk of violence on the other: might it not be possible to allow for the recording of such information without the father being contacted? After all, the likelihood of the mother falsely naming someone with a history of violence is small. Rather different considerations apply if the whereabouts of the father are currently unknown to the mother: it would be possible in this case for his identity to be recorded by the registrar for later verification, or indeed for an attempt to be made to trace his whereabouts. The final possibility, that the mother does not know the father's identity, could cover a range of scenarios: from 'not sure which' to 'no idea who he was'. The latter offers little scope for the identity to be discovered but is likely to be rarer; in the former case there would be the option of contacting the range of possible candidates – usually, one hopes, a reasonably short list.

There are, therefore, a number of ways in which the Act in its current form falls short of its professed aim of ensuring that all children know the identity of their parents. In addition, even where the mother does provide the father's name, there is no guarantee that it will be recorded on the register. The explanatory notes make it clear that while paternity testing could be used, 'nobody could be compelled to take part in such testing' and 'both the mother and the man to whom the test relates must consent to the test being carried out.' The right of the child to know their true parentage will thus still be dependent on the willingness of both parents to co-operate (or litigate).

One can understand why the New Labour Government of the time seized upon the rhetoric of the right of the child in its White Paper. Such a right, widely supported, seemed to offer a more convenient rationale for its proposed reforms, and a more easily achievable goal. But the scheme as enacted is a much-watered-down version of that initially proposed, and is unlikely to achieve its original aims. This is not to argue that a greater degree of compulsion should have been introduced, or that all children should be informed of their genetic identity: what should be recorded depends on the purpose that the system is intended to serve (and on this see McCandless, this volume). It is, rather, simply to point out that the reality did not match the rhetoric.

V. CONCLUSION

To draw parallels between the present and the past is a risky business, given that the context of having a child outside marriage in the twenty-first century is very different from that in the eighteenth or nineteenth, or even the first part of the twentieth century. Yet there does seem to be an element of continuity in the proportion of children for whom no father is recorded, even though such children now constitute a minority of those born outside marriage. One suspects that many of these fathers – from the Reformation to the present – were unknown or absent, dangerous or dead, or simply reluctant and refusing to be registered. And since these reasons will continue to result in sole registrations, even after the Welfare Reform Act, it is likely that the recording of births will continue, in a minority of cases, to be incomplete.

REFERENCES

Adie, K. (2005). *Nobody's Child: Who Are You When You Don't Know Your Past?*. London: Hodder & Stoughton.

Ambler, R.W. (1974). Baptism and Christening: Custom and Practice in Nineteenth Century Lincolnshire. *Local Population Studies* 12, 25–27.

Ayliffe, J. (1726). *Parergon juris canonici anglicani: or, a commentary, by way of supplement to the canons and constitutions of the Church of England*. London.

Ayres, J. (2003). *Paupers and Pig Killers: The Diary of William Holland: A Somerset Parson, 1799–1818*. Stroud: Sutton Publishing.

Bainham, A. (2008). What is the Point of Birth Registration? *Child and Family Law Quarterly* 20, 449.

Barret-Ducrocq, F. (1989). *Love in the Time of Victoria: Sexuality, Class and Gender in Nineteenth-Century London*. London: Verso, 1991, trans John Howe.

Burn, J.S. (1862). *The History of Parish Registers in England*. London: John Russell Smith.

Clarke, A. and Lyman-Clarke, K. (2007). *Northamptonshire Birth and Baptism Index*.

Clarke Hall, W. (1917). *The State and the Child*. London: Headley.

Clywd Family History Society (1992). *Llansanffraid Glyn Ceiriog parish registers 1754–1814*.

Cressy, D. (1999). *Birth, Marriage & Death: Ritual, Religion and the Life-Cycle in Tudor and Stuart England*. Oxford: Oxford University Press.

Dalrymple-Champneys, N. and Pollard, A. (eds) (1988). *George Crabbe: The Complete Poetical Works, Vol 1*. Oxford: Clarendon Press.

Department of Work and Pensions (2007). *Joint Birth Registration: Promoting Parental Responsibility*.

Department of Work and Pensions/Department for Schools and Families (2008). *Joint Birth Registration: Recording Responsibility*.

Dewar, D. (1968). *Orphans of the Living: A Study of Bastardy*. London: Hutchinson & Co.

Elliott, S. (2005). *Love Child: A Memoir of Adoption, Reunion, Loss and Love*. London: Random House.

Gandy, G.N. (1978). Illegitimacy in a Handloom Weaving Community: Fertility Patterns in Culcheth, Lancashire, 1781–1860 (unpublished DPhil dissertation).

Goose, N. (1996). *Population, Economy & Family Structure in Hertfordshire in 1851: Vol 1, The Berkhamsted Region*. Hatfield: University of Hertfordshire Press.

GRO (1838). *Regulations for the Duties of Registrars of Births and Deaths and Deputy Registrars*.

James, T.E. (1957). The Illegitimate and Deprived Child. In *A Century of Family Law* (ed. R.H. Graveson and F.R. Crane), pp. 39–55. London: Sweet & Maxwell.

Kiernan, K. and Smith, K. (2003). Unmarried Parenthood: New Insights from the Millennium Cohort Study. *Population Trends* 114, 26–33.

Laslett, P. (1980a). The Bastardy-prone Sub-society. In *Bastardy and its Comparative History* (ed. P. Laslett, K. Oosterveen and R. Smith), pp. 232–238 London: Edward Arnold.

—— (1980b). Introduction: Comparing Illegitimacy over Time and Between Cultures. In *Bastardy and its Comparative History* (ed. P. Laslett, K. Oosterveen and R. Smith), pp. 1–68 London: Edward Arnold.

Levene, A., Nutt T. and Williams, S. (2005). *Illegitimacy in Britain, 1700–1920.* Basingstoke: Palgrave Macmillan.

Levine, D. and Wrightson, K. (1991). *The Making of an Industrial Society: Whickham 1560–1765.* Oxford: Clarendon Press.

MacDonald, E. K. (1956). Follow-up of Illegitimate Children. *The Medical Officer* 361.

Macfarlane, A. (1980). Illegitimacy and Illegitimates in English history. In *Bastardy and its Comparative History* (ed. P. Laslett, K. Oosterveen and R. Smith), pp. 71–85 London: Edward Arnold..

Office for National Statistics (2009). Who is Having babies?. http://www.statistics.gov.uk/pdfdir/births1209.pdf.

Penn, M. (1979). *Manchester Fourteen Miles.* Firle: Caliban Books.

Peyton, S. A. (1928). *The Churchwardens' Presentments in the Oxfordshire Peculiars of Dorchester, Thame and Banbury.* Oxfordshire Record Society, Vol X.

Probert, R. (2009). *Marriage Law and Practice in the Long Eighteenth Century: A Reassessment.* Cambridge: Cambridge University Press.

Registrar-General of Births, Deaths and Marriages (1877). *Thirty-eighth Annual Report.*

—— (1919). *Eightieth Annual Report.*

Robin, J. (1987). Illegitimacy in Colyton, 1851–1881. *Continuity and Change* 2, 307.

Rogers, N. (1989). Carnal Knowledge: Illegitimacy in Eighteenth-Century Westminster. *Journal of Social History* 23, 355.

Roiphe, K. (2008). *Uncommon Arrangements: Seven Portraits of married life in London literary circles 1910–1939.* London: Virago.

Rose, L. (1986). *The Massacre of the Innocents: Infanticide in Britain 1800–1939.* London: Routledge & Kegan Paul.

Sheldon, S. (2009). From 'Absent Objects of Blame' to 'Fathers who Want to Take Responsibility': Reforming Birth Registration Law. *Journal of Social Welfare and Family Law* 31, 373–389.

Slack, M. (1987). Non-conformist and Anglican Registration in the Halifax Area 1740–99, *Local Population Studies* 38, 44–56.

Smallwood, S. (2004). Characteristics of Sole Registered Births and the Mothers who Register them. *Population Trends* 117, 20.

Smart, C. and Stevens, P. (2000). *Cohabitation Breakdown.* London: FPSC/JRF.

Spence, J., Walton, W., Miller, F. and Court, S. (1954). *A Thousand Families in Newcastle upon Tyne.* Oxford: Oxford University Press.

Szreter, S. (2007). The Right of Registration: Development, Identity Registration, and Social Security – A Historical Perspective. *World Development* 35, 67–86.

Wrightson, K. (1980). The Nadir of English Illegitimacy in the Seventeenth Century. In *Bastardy and its Comparative History* (ed. P. Laslett, K. Oosterveen and R. Smith), pp. 176–191 London: Edward Arnold.

10

The Changing Form of Birth Registration?

I. INTRODUCTION

THE HUMAN FERTILISATION and Embryology (HFE) Act 2008 and
the Welfare Reform Act (WRA) 2009 have recently instigated a number of
changes to legal parenthood and birth registration. The former extends
the status of legal parent (and the right to be registered as such on a child's initial
birth certificate) to a legal mother's female partner when certain conditions have
been met, while the latter makes joint birth registration compulsory save in a very
narrow set of exemptions. Academic commentary has inevitably begun to analyse
these legal changes and in doing so has started to consider the purpose of birth
registration more generally and its connection to parenthood law (eg Bainham,
2008; Blyth et al, 2009; Fortin, 2009; Lind and Hewitt, 2009; McCandless and
Sheldon, 2010a; Probert, this volume; Sheldon, 2009; Wallbank, 2009). In this
commentary the issue of a child's so-called 'right' to information about their
parentage – especially genetic parentage – and the role of law in either promoting
or securing this looms large. Despite the increasing attention excited by this
discourse, the idea that a child should have knowledge of their parentage is far
from a new phenomenon (see discussions in Archbishop's Commission, 1948;
Feversham Committee, 1960; Freeman, 1996). Likewise, the proposition that law
should somehow manage or organise this information has been in vogue for a
considerably longer period of time (Freeman 1996).

While it is beyond the scope of this chapter to delve fully into the history
of knowledge about parentage, the chapter does offer a consideration of the

[1] I am grateful to my colleagues at Oxford Brookes University, Ben Hunter and the participants of
the 2010 Cambridge Socio-legal Group Seminar, particularly Jonathan Herring and Sally Sheldon,
for helpful comments on earlier drafts of this chapter.

issue in the context of the legal regulation of assisted reproduction through the HFE Acts 1990 and 2008. The chapter begins by outlining a number of historical changes to birth registration in order to unpack how the purpose of birth registration has been understood over time, to include the question of whether the birth register has ever really been supposed 'as a true genetic record', as suggested by the *Committee of Inquiry into Human Fertilisation and Embryology* which preceded the HFE Act 1990 (Warnock, 1984, para. 4.21). This brief historical tracing will set the scene for the discussion of the first HFE Act. A controversial theme to emerge in the passage of this legislation was a concern with the state's role in deceiving a child about their parentage; a concern that was revisited both in the process leading to the removal of donor anonymity in 2004 (Human Fertilisation and Embryology Authority (Disclosure of Donor Information) Regulations, 2004) and in the recent passage of the HFE Act 2008. These two events are addressed in turn before a concluding discussion is offered.

Specifically, the analysis will examine debates about whether persons conceived though the use of donated gametes should be able to identify their genetic parents from their birth certificate and how these debates relate to notions of family privacy and the management of personal 'secrets' (Smart, 2007; 2009). The chapter questions whether using law to identify a gamete donor is a prioritisation of 'genetic truth' and considers whether doing so would instead help to reconceptualise the associations between bio-genetic and social parenthood. The chapter further questions whether birth registration is the most appropriate means of realising this legal reform.

II. HISTORICAL CHANGES TO BIRTH REGISTRATION

There has been a system of civil registration of births in this country since 1837, following the Births and Deaths Registration Act 1836. In her chapter in this volume, Rebecca Probert has provided a rich historical perspective to the inception of this system, relating it to the religious rite of baptism as well as the growing need to gather population statistics in an increasingly industrialised nation. I will not provide an historical overview here, but I want to say a brief word on what we can surmise about historical understandings of a child's 'right' to information about their genetic make-up through this tracing of changes to the provision and configuration of civil birth registration.

First, it is clear that the motivations for a comprehensive system of civil birth registration were multiple and did not straightforwardly relate to keeping some sort of historical or accurate record of bio-genetic parentage. For example, there is little coincidence in the fact that registration of births and deaths were, and continue to be, governed by the same statute, given the significance of fertility and morbidity data in analysing various signifiers of a country's population. Likewise, while the methods of generating population data since 1837 have become increasingly sophisticated and the range of issues ever expanding, all the major social research surveys of today such as the General Household Survey, as well as central registers such as the NHS Central Register, were necessarily preceded by a centralised system of birth (and death) registration.

Second, although birth registration certainly provided evidence of the legitimisation of children for the purposes of succession and inheritance, we do also have to acknowledge the socially constructed nature of 'legitimate'. The history of marriage law demonstrates that although notions of legitimacy were premised on the bio-genetic ties resulting from sexual intercourse, this was governed by *presumptions* in law as mediated through marriage, as opposed to *actual* 'blood ties' (Collier, 1995; Smart, 1987).

Third, there seems to be very little sense historically that a child had a 'right' to information about their genetic make-up for psychological or identity-based reasons, with birth registration being understood more as a process which could confer material entitlements relating to status, succession and inheritance, possibly also maintenance. With the shift in location of the civil birth registration system from the singular General Register Office (GRO), to the combined Office of Population Censuses along with the Government Social Survey in 1970, to form part of the Identity and Passport Service (IPS) in the Home Office in 2009, we can arguably trace a shift in the perceived purpose and role of civil registration towards identity, as population statistics come to be collected in ever more sophisticated and detailed ways. It is clearly difficult here to make direct comparisons in relation to historical and contemporary ideas about identity, given not least the very changing notions of childhood from the inception of civil birth registration (see Smart et al, 2001, Ch. 1). However, what can be traced is that birth registration and certificates have been periodically reconfigured in response to changing social ideas about parenthood, relating particularly to notions of illegitimacy, adoption practices and more recently, assisted reproduction practices. In these changes, there is no consistent or pervasive evidence that birth registration should guarantee a 'right' to information about one's genetic make-up.

III. REGULATING AND RECORDING DONOR-CONCEIVED BIRTHS

(a) Before the HFE Acts

The legal position on donor insemination up until 1987 was that the sperm donor was the child's putative father. For the mother's husband (clinically, access tended to be restricted to married couples) to be registered on the birth certificate was an act of perjury (Perjury Act 1911, section 4). Discretion from the various clinical actors involved as well as the stealth with which people typically presented themselves for donor insemination (if they didn't arrange it themselves in private) meant that in most cases, surreptitious birth registration secured the mother's husband's name as the child's father on the birth certificate

(Snowden and Mitchell, 1981). I can find no prosecutions for perjury in this context, indicating that this was a low priority for law enforcers and/or Registrars, despite the government commissioned Feversham Committee's grave warning that 'knowledge that there is uncertainty about the fatherhood of some is a potential threat to the security of all' (1960: para. 215).

With the increasing legal moves to remove the status of illegitimacy, section 27 of the Family Law Reform Act (FLRA) 1987 provided that a woman's husband could be registered as the father of a child born to her through donor insemination, providing that he consented to the procedure. Although the presumption of paternity has clearly always been based on the *presumed* genetic tie, as opposed to the *actual* genetic tie, in the FLRA we have the first explicit legal provision which allows for a man who is known *not* to be genetically related to the child to be recorded as the child's father on the initial birth entry. This demonstrates that even before the HFE Act 1990, birth registration was *explicitly* understood as recording something other than bio-genetic 'fact'. While this 'other' was certainly premised on dyadic understandings of parenthood and the significance of the bio-genetic ties resulting from heterosexual partnership (see further McCandless, 2009, Ch. 3), we see something much more socially constructed and complex being recorded; namely the notion that a child has two 'real' parents, which at this historical juncture meant a mother and a father who were in some sort of partnership with each other.

(b) The HFE Act 1990

(i) The Parenthood Provisions

The effect of the HFE Act 1990 with respect to birth registration was that it carried forward the common law presumption that a woman who gives birth to the child is its legal mother (The Ampthill Peerage, 1977) whether or not she is also the genetic mother (section 27) and extended the presumption of paternity in the context of donor insemination both to other techniques that used donor sperm and to the unmarried male partner of the mother if he was regarded as having 'treatment together' with the legal mother (section 28). Gamete donors were to remain anonymous, in line with most previous clinical practice (Pfeffer, 1993). If gametes were donated under the consent provisions of the legislation (see schedule 3) the gamete provider had their parental connections waived. Determining motherhood by the act of giving birth was regarded as a clear statement to this effect, while a specific provision excluding the sperm donor's parental status was inserted into section 28 (subsection 5). Clinical treatments with donated embryos were likewise regulated.

In cases of self-arranged donor insemination, where the insemination occurred through means other than sexual intercourse (described in section 28(2) as 'artificial'), the mother's husband would be the presumed father. However, what information a Registrar might realistically request should, for example, a genetic father seek to disrupt the presumption that the conception took place through sexual intercourse is questionable. Finally, if the woman was not married, the sperm donor would be considered the putative father in the context of self-arranged donor insemination. Evidently this is more straightforward for a Registrar if all the facts are presented, but we can surmise that in many instances of self-arranged donor insemination, a woman's male partner was surreptitiously registered as the father.

In cases of a surrogacy arrangement which availed of clinical treatment, the surrogate mother would initially be registered as the legal mother and her husband (or possibly unmarried partner) as the legal father (see Jackson, 2001, Ch. 6). With the legal parent(s)'s consent, parenthood could be *transferred* to the commissioning couple, who had to be married and have a partial genetic link to the child to be eligible to apply for a parental order under the HFE Act 1990 (section 30); effectively a fast-track adoption order. In all other cases, a full adoption order would have to be applied for. As with adopted children, children born through surrogacy have always had some sort of paper trail to their birth parent(s) (Morgan and Lee, 2001, Ch. 8). However, given techniques such as donor insemination and IVF, birth parent(s) here should not be conflated with genetic parents; rather it is only the bodily contribution of the gestational mother that can be traced.

What we see then is an attempt in the HFE Act 1990 to contain the 'confusing' effects of combining genetic material in contexts other than sexual partnership and as between people who have no intent of raising children together; indeed, they may not even have known the identity of each other. The HFE Act 2008, in many ways remains true to the spirit of the HFE Act 1990 with respect to the parenthood provisions (McCandless and Sheldon, 2010a). The legal presumption remains for husbands (section 35), while the 'treatment together' provision for an unmarried male partner is replaced with a series of 'agreed fatherhood conditions' (sections 36–37). More significantly, these provisions are extended to female civil partners and female partners respectively (sectionss 42–44). Likewise, eligibility for parental orders is extended to unmarried and same-sex couples with a partial genetic connection to the child (section 54).

In relation to birth registration, what we see in both Acts is a consolidation of the birth certificate as a record of *two legal parents* for the child, who may or may not be the genetic parents (although the legal mother at birth clearly remains the gestational mother) and following the HFE Act 2008, may be of the same gender. There is no requirement that the couple be in a 'marriage-like' or cohabiting relationship, but they must not be within prohibited degrees of relationship (sections 37(1)(e), 44(1)(e), 54(2)(c)). However, for parental order applications, the couple must also be 'an enduring family relationship' (section 54(2)(c)). Gamete donors remain anonymous and the birth certificate gives no indication that the child was donor-conceived. Nor has the child any paper trail to this, unlike the adopted or surrogate child who has a paper trail to their *birth* – as opposed to genetic – parent(s) (Adoption Act, 1976).

(ii) Concern with state deception

Despite the reality that birth registration was never really an infallible record of genetic parenthood, we see in the process leading up to the HFE Act 1990 a heightened concern with the role of the state in perpetuating a 'deception' with respect to a child's information about their genetic origins. While previous formal reports rebuked the practice of donor insemination as immoral (Archbishop's Commission, 1948; Feversham Commission, 1960) the Warnock Report (1984) was essentially supportive of donor conception, whether by the use of eggs, sperm or embryos. However, as Blyth et al. have noted, the Warnock Report also marked the first formal departure in the UK from the accepted wisdom that donor conception was best conducted in secret (2009). What can arguably be traced is a shift in concern from how donor insemination might cause problems between the adult partners involved to how donor conception might cause problems between the adults and children concerned, or what some authors have described as a shift in focus between *horizontal* to *vertical* relationships in the context of family law and policy (Collier and Sheldon, 2008).[2]

In the context of donor insemination, the Warnock Report recommended that a donor-conceived person should be informed about his or her conception (4.12); be able to obtain *non*-identifying information about their donor at the age of 18 (4.21); and suggested that birth certificates could be annotated with the words, 'by donation' (4.25). Similar recommendations were made in relation to egg and embryo donation (6.6, 6.8, 7.4, 7.6 and 7.7). In arguable conflict with this concern, however, the Warnock Report endorsed the practice of donor anonymity (4.22) and recommended that a woman's husband should be registered as the legal father of a child born with his consent from donor insemination, in recognition of his intention to assume full parental rights and responsibilities (4.17). It was acknowledged that this latter recommendation could be seen as 'legislating for a fiction' and compromising the register of births 'as a true genetic record' (4.25).

We can reconcile these seemingly conflicting recommendations by concluding that the Warnock Committee felt that a child should *not be deceived* about their genetic origins as opposed to a child having a 'right' to know the identity of, or be raised by their genetic parents. While they recommended that a donor-conceived person should be able to obtain non-identifying information at the age of 18, they were cautious about introducing the donor into the familial equation as an identifiable person, especially the sperm donor who they regarded as posing a particular threat to the nuclear family unit and the social father's sense of security within that unit (4.19–4.22; see further Thomson, 2008, Ch. 5).

---

[2] I am grateful to Sally Sheldon for highlighting this point to me.

Although the Warnock Report's suggestion to include 'by donation' was not inserted into the HFE Bill 1989, their concern about deceiving a child was clearly shared by some Parliamentarians and amendments to include such annotations were tabled in the House of Lords (HL Debs, cols 1306–1322, 13 February 1990). As Blyth et al note, these amendments were met with spirited resistance, with Lord Mackay characterising it as a 'discriminatory label' along the lines of illegitimacy, which had of course only recently been removed (2009: 209). This concern is still of significance to Lord Mackay, who in the debates leading up to the HFE Act 2008 queried how the registration of two women on a birth certificate was any different to annotating a birth certificate to signal donor conception and thus 'labelling' a child as donor-conceived (HL Debs, col 867, 4 February 2008). Before coming to address how the issue of birth registration was further discussed in these debates, I want first to discuss some developments in relation to the removal of anonymity for gamete donors.

(c) Removal of Gamete Donor Anonymity

Although the principle of donor anonymity was incorporated into the HFE Act 1990, the possibility of changed attitudes in the future towards anonymity was anticipated. A new regulatory body set up by the legislation, the Human Fertilisation and Embryology Authority (HFEA) was charged with maintaining a Register of Information about donors, recipients of donated gametes and embryos and children born as a result of all donor procedures provided by licensed clinics (section 31). Also, the legislation provided that a person intending to marry could enquire whether they were genetically related to their intended spouse (section 31) and for persons to obtain non-identifying information about their donor upon reaching the age of 18 (section 31). While these latter two provisions clearly relate to the benefit of knowing one's genetic history for medical reasons, their impact is surely limited given that one could just as easily have a non-marital sexual relationship or have the need to know about one's genetic make-up for medical purposes long before the age of 18 (see further Freeman, 1996). What we see instead is the debut of what has persisted as a sequence of rather uneven, socially mediated and pragmatic responses to the issue of when a person should be able to obtain information about their genetic origins when they have been donor-conceived. Indeed, even in the HFE Act 2008 which follows the removal of donor anonymity in 2004 (Human Fertilisation and Embryology Authority (Disclosure of Donor Information) Regulations, 2004), inconsistencies can be traced as to when someone is entitled to information (to include identifying information) about genetic make-up and genetic kin (Jones, 2010).

Given this unevenness, what then prompted the removal of donor anonymity in 2004? One important factor as acknowledged by Jane Fortin, is that the claim that children have a 'right' to information about their genetic make-up has been substantially reinforced by international human rights laws, to include the United Nations Convention on the Rights of the Child (UNCRC) and Strasbourg jurisprudence interpreting article 8 of the European Convention of Human Rights (ECHR) (Fortin, 2009). Direct legal challenges to the UK's position on donor anonymity based on these international provisions were made (Rose and Another v Secretary of State for Health and Human Fertilisation and Embryology Authority, 2002; UN Committee on the Rights of the Child, 2002). However, Fortin observes the contexts in which the relevant articles of the UNCRC were devised in response to – namely statelessness and the removal of children from their birth parents by totalitarian regimes – and criticises the UN Committee on the Rights of the Child for interpreting these articles in a way that promotes the idea that a child has a 'right' to knowledge of genetic origins, and even more crucially, to be *raised* by their genetic parents (which is clearly qualified by the words 'as far as it is possible'). In relation to the ECHR, although Fortin notes the increased willingness of the Strasbourg court to scrutinise claims involving a child's 'right' to know the identity of their genetic parents, she makes clear that the existing jurisprudence does not establish an absolute right and that the Strasbourg court remains concerned to finely balance other competing 'rights' under Article 8 (2009, 327).

What can be added to this acknowledgement of the influence of international human rights law, is the growing currency of 'rights' discourses for fatherhood and the reversion to genetic links in these discourses in the face of proliferating family forms (Collier and Sheldon, 2008; McCandless, 2009, Ch. 5; Smart, 2006; 2007). While the 2004 Regulations removed donor anonymity for both egg and sperm donors, they were discussed primarily in the context of sperm donors (see further Thomson, 2008, Ch. 5) and the issue of identifying a child's genetic parents continues to be framed as an issue of paternity. For example, the muted significance of the maternal genetic connection is clearly reinforced by the newly inserted provision in the HFE Act 2008 which explicitly debars a legal connection – either as the child's legal mother or female parent – on the basis of 'mere egg donation' (section 47; McCandless and Sheldon, 2010a).

Finally, as is usually the case with legislation in controversial areas, the originally implemented statute was not regarded to be the final word on the issue. Studies continued to investigate whether the information held on the Register by the HFEA would prove sufficient for donor-conceived persons (eg Blyth and Hunt, 1998; Blyth and Speirs, 2004) and even the first edition of the HFEA (1991) Code of Practice guidance to clinicians required that treatment centres should take into account a donor-conceived child's 'potential need to know about his or her origins' (para. 3.12) and invite patients to consider through counselling 'the advantages and disadvantages of openness about the procedure' (para. 6.10). In 2001, the Department of Health launched a public consultation on the issue of donor anonymity, introducing the new Regulations on the basis of this consultation and further deliberations (Department of Health, 2001; Frith et al., 2007).

However, in setting out the terms of the consultation and plans for reform, it was made clear that there was no plan to impose a statutory obligation on the legal parents of donor-conceived children to tell their children of the circumstances of their conception and genetic origins (Department of Health, 2001: para. 1.10). As such, notwithstanding the removal of donor anonymity, birth certificates would remain as they were and the identification of gamete donors would not entail the change or reconfiguration of any legal rights or responsibilities.

(d) The HFE Act 2008

(i) Public consultations, the Joint Committee and the proposed legislation

Despite the abovementioned determined position of the government, they reopened the issue by inviting comment on 'what measures would be appropriate, if any, to ensure that parents tell children conceived through gamete or embryo donation that they are donor-conceived?' in their public consultation on the reform of the HFE Act 1990 (Department of Health, 2005, 6.31). Although some respondents did suggest the implementation of a full legal obligation and/or annotation on a birth certificate, many were critical of the use of birth certificates to indicate that a person was donor-conceived (Department of Health, 2006: 6.7; People, Science and Policy, 2006, pp. 48–49).

Neither a legal parental obligation nor the annotation of birth certificates was provided for in the initially proposed legislation (Human Tissues and Embryos (Draft) Bill 2007). However, the issue of the perceived role of the state in sanctioning a deception through birth registration was to considerably vex the Joint Committee of the House of Lords and House of Commons whose job it was to scrutinise the legislation. However, despite extensive discussion, they came to no firm recommendation other than 'as a matter of urgency, the Government should give this matter further consideration' (Joint Committee, 2007, Vol. 1, para. 276). In response, the government stated a preference for educational rather than legislative measures to promote parental disclosure (Department of Health, 2007: p. 69) and no specific measures were incorporated into the HFE Bill 2007.

(ii) The Parliamentary Debates

The Bill was introduced into the House of Lords in November 2007 and the initial readings made clear that the issue of donor-conceived children and their genetic origins was far from closed. The scene was set with speeches by Lord Jenkin and Lord Hastings, who respectively queried whether the Bill needed a provision requiring parents to tell children they were donor-conceived and whether the Bill stood up to commitments under the UNCRC (HL Debs, cols 865; 689–90, 19

November 2007). It did not take long, however, for the issue of knowledge about genetic identity to become conflated with the proposed removal of 'the need for a father' provision from the welfare clause (eg per Lord Hastings, HL Debs, col 690, 19 November 2007; Lord Ahemd, HL Debs, col 841, 21 November 2007; Baroness Deech, HL Debs, col 22–3, 10 December 2007; Baroness O'Cathain, HL Debs, col 24–8, 10 December 2007; see further McCandless and Sheldon, 2010b) and for genetic identity to come to be spoken about almost exclusively in terms of paternity, to include the need for information about the paternal genetic history for medical purposes (Lord Alton, HL Debs, col 43–5, 10 December 2007).

There were others who raised concerns about how the legislation failed to encourage the rights and responsibilities of the sperm and egg donor, fostering a sense of 'rampant indifference' with respect to children (Archbishop of York, HL Debs, col 706–7, 19 November; Lord Patten, HL Debs, col 30, 10 December 2007; Claire Curtis-Thomas MP, HC Debs, col 1134, 12 May 2008). Others still – though perhaps for different motivations – picked up on the previously mentioned observation of Lord Mackay, that naming two women on a birth certificate was effectively the same as annotating it with 'by donation' (Lord Bishop of Newcastle, HL Debs, col 841, 21 November 2007; Baroness Deech, HL Debs, col 291, 12 December 2007; Baroness Williams of Crosby, HL Debs, col 299, 12 December 2007; Mark Simmonds MP, HC Debs, col 277, 12 June 2008).

What we see playing out in these discussions are a number of tensions, not only in relation to the purpose of birth registration and what information should be recorded on a birth certificate, but also in the conflation of several issues connected to parenthood in the Bill; namely the removal of the 'need for a father' provision, the extension of the parenthood provisions to a legal mother's female partner and the conflict between parenthood as a primarily genetic or primarily social construct. To elaborate on the latter and the lack of consensus on the role of birth registration, what we had in the Parliamentary debates was a range of opinions, from birth registration being regarded as an accurate 'genetic' record (eg Baroness Deech, HL Debs, col 291, 12 December 2007) to birth registration being 'a record of who a child's social parents are at any time' (Baroness Barker, HL Debs, col 860, 12 December 2007); neither of which are surely correct given that family law has long operated on presumptions and that a child's social situation may inevitably change over their life-span. Between these two poles were those who perhaps more realistically saw birth registration as about legal status (Dr Pugh MP, HC Debs, col 221–2, 12 May 2008; Dr Harris MP, HL Debs, col 256, 12 May 2008) and those who recognised the reality that the birth register was never a perfect record of biological or social fact, given the frailty of human nature (Viscount Craigavon, HL Debs, col 100, 10 December; Baroness Barker, HL Debs, col 860, 27 November 2007 and col 292, 12 December 2007).

Despite this lack of consensus on the purpose of birth registration (and in understandings of parenthood itself – see further McCandless and Sheldon, 2010a) what did seem to be agreed on was the perceived harm that deceiving a child about their origins might bring. The following speech extract from Earl Howe captured this sentiment well:

> In recent years the donation of sperm or ova may have become common place – we may take it for granted – but we should never let ourselves forget that to bring a child into the world in circumstances where one or more of his genetic parents is kept deliberately secret and anonymous is to saddle that child with a grave psychological handicap from the moment when later in life he becomes aware of his origins. Parents of children conceived by donation need to be made aware of the vital importance of being absolutely honest with those children about the circumstances of their conception, the way in which the breaking of this news is best done and the most propitious timing for doing so. They need to be aware that, for many children, the trauma and hurt of this knowledge never leaves them. Some children spend the rest of their lives recovering from the blow to their sense of identity and agonising over the injustice of their circumstances compared with those of children who grew up with their true parents (HL Debs, col 69, 10 December 2007).

As such, the issue of knowledge about genetic origins was cast as something psycho-social, to be considered in the context of a child's welfare, with much less being said with respect to, for example, inheritance and succession rights and incest than in years previous (see Brazier, 1998). But again, as with the Warnock Committee in 1984, the concern expressed here relates primarily to the act of *deception* and the potential harm that may be done to a child should they find out that their parents are not also their bio-genetic parents. It does not relate necessarily to a genetic understanding of parenthood, or the idea that parental rights and responsibilities should be automatically premised on the genetic link.

However, as with the Joint Committee, no agreement could be reached on the best way to move forward with the issue. Despite the acceptance from most that to name two women on a birth certificate would send a clear signal that a child was donor-conceived, it was thought that to annotate other birth certificates (ie those in the heterosexual context) would be too great an invasion of parental and family privacy. Proposals to leave the review of the question of parental disclosure and configuration of birth certificates of donor-conceived persons to the HFEA and secondary legislation (see amendment no. 146 tabled by Lord Jenkin, HL Debs, col 502, 28 January 2008) were rejected on the basis that the lack of consensus on the issue or how to move forward demanded primary legislation (Baroness Royall, HL Debs, col 509–10, 28 January 2008). Although no statutory obligation to review the question was inserted into the HFE Act 2008, a commitment was made by the (then Labour) government to review the issue in four years time (Baroness Royall, HL Debs, col 904, 4 February 2008; Dawn Primarolo MP, HC Debs, col 1160 12 May 2008).

IV. CONCLUDING DISCUSSION

Whether this review now happens given the recent change in government remains to be seen. What I would like to do in this closing discussion is to offer a perspective that seeks to connect these debates on donor conception and birth registration to the reforms relating to compulsory birth registration in the Welfare Reform Act.

Drawing on John Eekelaar's argument for a complete alignment between 'legal' and 'physical' truth in order to set about challenging the shame associated with illegitimacy, adoption and (male) infertility, as well as the generational power relations between adults and children (2006), Carol Smart seeks to bring to our attention the gendered power dynamics that are often inherent in family and reproductive secrets, as well as the danger of creating a hierarchy of 'truths' (2007; 2009). I find myself at once agreeing and disagreeing with both their analyses when I consider them in the context of donor conception. Eekelaar suggests that '[t]he modern quest for authenticity is associated with openness about the physical facts of one's birth rather than constructed legal truths' (2006, pp. 70–71). However, he does not elaborate on this statement or on how 'authenticity' or ontological security is constructed in the modern world, which as anthropological work on kinship has demonstrated, is a complex and at times contradictory process (eg Thompson, 2005). As with most work on genetic truth, Eekelaar's analysis refers exclusively to the paternal genetic link, his nod to maternity manifest with a much briefer mention of the French practice of allowing mothers to give birth anonymously (2006, pp. 71–72).

In agreement with Smart, I remain unsure how aligning physical and legal truth would categorically be more just towards children, or even how this would be done, given that physical truth is constructed in complex ways. Nor do I regard the keeping of reproductive secrets as inevitably manipulative or disingenuous (2009, p. 557). Finally, Eekelaar offers no satisfactory suggestion as to how or the extent to which the law should be used to 'align' this information in the many circumstances to which is might apply (for a problematic example, see Smart, 2009, p. 561). However, I make three points which set about challenging Smart's analysis, for the particular context of donor conception.

First, unlike Smart I do not think that Eekelaar's analysis is as reductive as she seems to suggest, in the sense that it does not necessarily prioritise a genetic or scientific 'truth' over other 'truths' in the context of family relationships (2009, pp. 553–554, 563, 565). While Eekelaar's discussion of parenthood does tend to slip into a dyadic and bio-genetic conceptual framework, he does clearly assert that 'a genetic link in itself does not establish an interest sufficient to warrant any legal entitlement to begin a relationship' (2006, pp. 69–70). Instead, he suggests that it does no more than render the genetic progenitor as a *potential* resource for the child (2006, p. 70). It seems then that under Eekelaar's analysis, knowledge of genetic origins through some sort of legal provision would not be to prioritise the genetic progenitors as the 'real' parents *per se*, and that while legal recognition may be given to their contribution, it does not necessarily have to be parental status and/or parental responsibility for the child.

Second, I suggest that while Smart's rich historical and cultural analysis sits well with retrospective reproductive secrets, we do perhaps have to question whether it holds the same currency for future assisted reproductive practices and the legal regulation thereof. Smart herself urges us to consider why some reproductive secrets are condoned while others are disapproved (2009, p. 561). If we return to the Parliamentary debates of the HFE Act 2008, we will remember that the concern with family privacy related primarily to donor insemination in the heterosexual context. In other words, a man's infertility was deemed a reproductive secret that legal documentation should keep. The power relations that this protects are arguably very different to some of the examples that Smart cites in relation to illegitimacy and extra-marital affairs (2007, Ch. 5; 2009, pp. 555–562). It is also worth noting that while egg donation came to be regulated in a similar way to sperm donation, surrogacy was never a 'condoned' reproductive secret and as previously mentioned, children born following such arrangements could trace their birth parent(s). In addition, it is questionable whether legally regulating parenthood in the context of assisted reproduction to mirror that of sexual reproduction has helped to lessen the sense of insecurity associated with male infertility. This leads me to my third point.

I would like to suggest that an alignment of legal and physical 'truth' in the limited context of donor conception, may well go some way to challenging the stigma of assisted reproduction and the associated (heterosexual) power relations that play out in legal constructions of parenthood. I want here to draw attention to Smart's assertion that certain practices *may* lose some of their stigma when the law changes (2009, p. 558). This is to some extent true, but as Smart has also acknowledged, we must be careful to critically examine such claims with respect to progressive social change (1989). In relation to donor insemination, it is interesting to note that despite a very secure position for the male partner of a woman availing of such treatment following the FLRA and the HFE Acts, the rates of donor insemination in the heterosexual context have decreased significantly and that reproductive technology has developed in such a way as to allow more men to become genetic fathers. Procedures such as ICSI (intra-cytoplasmic sperm injection) have become much more common-place for heterosexual couples (HFEA, 2007), despite the additional burden of IVF for the woman. I have elsewhere suggested that by assimilating donor insemination families into the normative legal framework, the HFE Act 1990 (and its successor) failed to substantively renegotiate the basis of fatherhood on anything other than the genetic link, to include intent (McCandless, 2009, Ch. 4 and 5). While fatherhood may currently be seen to be 'fragmenting' (Collier and Sheldon, 2008), this fragmentation remains closely aligned to genetic ideas about fatherhood. As a consequence, fatherhood as a care-giving and/or or social concept, for example, has never really been given sufficient legal authority and reversions to biology and associated patriarchal constructs continue.

Given this, there is surely scope for the argument that to legally acknowledge the fact of donor conception could potentially give clearer authority to the reality that parenthood (both motherhood and fatherhood) is sometimes complex and fragmented. The next question to be asked, however, is whether a person's birth certificate is the most appropriate place for that information to be recorded?

This is not a question with an easy answer as it is one that demands a much more substantive consideration of the purpose of birth registration (Bainham, 2008). Other academics have offered frameworks which seek to be sensitive to all those involved (Blyth et al, 2009) but which do not address birth registration in its general sense. Others still have looked at cognate issues, such as the difficulties that arise in relation to the need to record the sex of a child when this does not neatly fit within the state's dichotomised model (see Matambanadzo, 2005). Likewise, we could postulate that just as some people are keen to know their genetic make-up and regard it as a 'right', others will consider it a right *not* to know such information; just as people often reject information about genetic diagnostics relating to various illnesses (see further Laurie, 1999). I have already questioned the synthesis between debates surrounding genetic identity and the need to know about our genetic make-up for medical reasons. This could be refuted further given medical advancements which arguably do or will make this information less necessary. We also have to question and distinguish what personal information the state needs, and what personal information the state needs to make public, as these are not necessarily the same. What about those births which are not registered, or where a child is registered without a name? While precise numbers here are hard to estimate, between 1 April 2007 and 31 March 2008 there were 66 births registered in England more than 365 days after the child's date-of-birth, while a small number of children – approximately 6 – were registered without a name, signaling that birth registration may not always be a straightforward administrative process (General Record Office, 2008). How do those persons then relate to the modern administrative state? Finally, do people have a right *not* to be registered, or to be de-registered?

Fully addressing these questions is clearly beyond the scope of this chapter. However, by raising them I hope to have demonstrated that birth registration warrants a much broader review than how the birth certificates of donor-conceived persons should be configured. While I disagreed with some of Smart's arguments in relation to the role of law in managing reproductive and genetic secrets, her argument that law and policy must be considered in its broader historical, social and political context is clearly an important one (2009). To this, I would add that the reform of one legal area must not be considered in isolation to other legal issues and developments.

As such, there is the need to connect these debates surrounding genetic identity in the context of donor-conception with the use of birth registration in the Welfare Reform Act as a social policy tool to encourage joint responsibility for a child. Probert's close analysis in this volume demonstrates that the actual aims of compulsory joint birth registration are far from clear. However, given that the reforms relate not only to parental status but also to the conferment of parental responsibility (schedule 6, section 21), what we arguably see is an example of legal documentation and the associated notions of parental 'rights' being used as an incentive for 'responsible' parenting by unmarried fathers (see further, Collier, this volume; Ives, 2007). While section 111, Adoption and Children Act 2002 changed the law so that *voluntary* joint birth registration conferred automatic parental responsibility to unmarried fathers, it remains questionable whether *compulsory* joint birth registration will make certain unmarried fathers any more involved in their children's lives than they might otherwise have been (Wallbank, 2009). The birth certificate then comes to represent something much more than a legal record, or evidence, of who the child's parents were at the moment of birth; it comes instead to be seen more acutely as something that *facilitates* a relationship with a child.

This then is the key caveat to my discussion above and the argument that the law may usefully be used to facilitate information about genetic identity in the context of donor conception; that such measures can only if be progressive if they accept that parenthood can be fragmented and that it is not always appropriate to conflate legal recognition with legal status and/or other entitlements (Lind and Hewitt, 2009). Likewise, we must be careful of asking birth registration to do too much and consider whether there may be other more appropriately devised administrative processes for such legal moves.

REFERENCES

Archbishop's Commission (1948). *Artificial Human Insemination.* London: Society for the Propagation of Christian Knowledge.

Bainham, A. (2008). What Is the Point of Birth Registration?. *Child and Family Law Quarterly* 20, 449–474.

Blyth, E., Firth, L., Jones C. and Speirs, J. (2009). The Role of Birth Certificates in Relation to Access to Biographical and Genetic History in Donor Conception. *International Journal of Children's Rights* 17, 207–233.

Blyth, E. and Hunt, J. (1998). Sharing Genetic Origins Information in Donor Assisted Conception: Views from Licensed Centres on HFEA Donor Information Form 91(4). *Human Reproduction* 13, 3274–3277.

Blyth, E. and Speirs, J. (2004). Meeting the Rights and Needs of Donor-conceived People: The Contribution of a Voluntary Contact Register. *Nordisk Socialt Arbeid* 24, 318–330

Brazier, M. (1998). Reproductive Rights: Feminism or Patriarchy. In *The Future of Human Reproduction* (ed. J. Harris and S. Holm), pp. 66–76. Oxford: Clarendon Press.

Collier, R. (1995). *Masculinity, Law and the Family.* London: Routledge.

Collier, R. and Sheldon, S. (2008). *Fragmenting Fatherhood: A Socio-Legal Study*. Oxford: Hart.

Department of Health (2007). *Government Response to the Report from the Joint Committee on the Human Tissue and Embryos (Draft) Bill*, Cm 7209. London: HMSO.

Department of Health (2006). *Responses to the Consultation on the Review of the Human Fertilisation and Embryology Act*. London: HMSO.

—— (2005). *Review of the Human Fertilisation and Embryology Act: A Public Consultation*. London: HMSO.

—— (2001). *Donor Information Consultation: Providing Information About Gamete or Embryo Donors*. London: HMSO.

Eekelaar J. (2006). *Family Law and Personal Life*. Oxford: Oxford University Press.

Feversham, The Earl of (1960). *Report of the Departmental Committee on Human Artificial Insemination*, Cm 1105. London: HMSO.

Freeman, M. (1996). The New Birth Right? Identity and the Child of the Reproductive Revolution. *International Journal of Children's Rights* 4, 273–297.

Frith, L., Blyth, E. and Farrand, A. (2007). 'UK Gamete Donors' Reflections on the Removal of Anonymity: Implications for Recruitment. *Human Reproduction* 22, 1675–1680.

Fortin, J. (2009). Children's Rights to Know their Origins – Too Far, Too Fast? *Child and Family Law Quarterly* 21, 336–355.

General Record Office (2008). Responses to Freedom of Information requests, dated 14 July 2008 and 18 November 2008.

HFEA (2007). *A Long Term Analysis of the HFEA Register Data 1991–2006*. London: HFEA, available at http://www.hfea.gov.uk/docs/Latest_long_term_data_analysis_report_91-06.pdf.pdf.

—— (1991). *Code of Practice*, 1st Edition. London: HFEA.

Ives, J. (2007). *Becoming a Father/Refusing Fatherhood: How Parental Responsibilities and Rights are Generated*. Thesis submitted for the degree of Doctor of Philosophy, University of Birmingham.

Jackson, E. (2001). *Regulating Reproduction*. Oxford: Hart.

Joint Committee (2007) *House of Lords, House of Commons Joint Committee on the Human Tissue and Embryos (Draft) Bill, Vol I: Report, Session 2006–7, HL Paper 169–I, HC Paper 630–I*. London: HMSO.

Jones, C. (2010). The Identification of 'Parents' and 'Siblings': New Possibilities Under the Reformed Human Fertilisation and Embryology Act. In *Rights, Gender and Family Law* (ed. J. Wallbank, S. Chouddry and J. Herring), pp. 219–238. London: Routledge Cavendish.

Lind, C. and Hewitt, T. (2009). Law and the Complexities of Parenting: Parental Status and Parental Function. *Journal of Social Welfare and Family Law* 31, 391–406.

Laurie, G. (1999). In Defence of Ignorance: Genetic Information and the Right not to Know. *European Journal of Health Law* 6, 119–132.

Mantambanadzo, S. (2005). Engendering Sex: Birth Certificates, Biology and the Body in Anglo-American Law. *Cardozo Journal of Law and Gender* 12, 213–246.

McCandless, J. (2009). *Reproducing the Sexual Family: Law, Gender and Parenthood in Assisted Reproduction.* Thesis submitted for the degree of Doctor in Philosophy, Keele University.

McCandless, J. and Sheldon, S. (2010a). Human Fertilisation and Embryology Act (2008) and the Tenacity of the Sexual Family. *Modern Law Review* 73, 175–207.

—— (2010b). 'No Father Required?' Rewriting the Family through the Welfare Clause of the HFE Act 2008? *Feminist Legal Studies* 18, 201–225.

Morgan, D. and Lee, R. (2001). *Human Fertilisation and Embryology: Regulating the Reproductive Revolution*, 2nd Edition. London: Blackstone Press.

Pfeffer, N. (1993). *The Stork and the Syringe: A Political History of Reproductive Medicine.* Cambridge: Polity Press.

People, Science and Policy (2006). *Report on the Consultation of the Review of the Human Fertilisation and Embryology Act 1990.* London: People, Science and Policy.

Sheldon, S. (2009). From 'Absent Object of Blame' to 'Fathers who Take Responsibility': Reforming Birth Registration Law. *Journal of Social Welfare and Family Law* 31, 373–389.

Smart, C. (2009). Family Secrets: Law and Understandings of Openness in Everyday Relationships. *Journal of Social Policy* 38, 551–567.

—— (2007). *Personal Life: New Directions in Sociological Thinking.* Cambridge: Polity Press.

——. (2006). The Ethics of Justice Strikes Back. In *Feminist Perspectives on Family Law* (ed. A. Diduck and K. O'Donovan), pp. 123–138. Abington: Routledge-Cavendish.

—— (1989). *Feminism and the Power of Law.* London: Routledge.

—— (1987). 'There is of Course the Distinction Dictated by Nature': Law and the Problem of Paternity. In *Reproductive Technologies: Gender, Motherhood and Medicine* (ed. M. Stanworth), pp. 98–117. Oxford: Basil Blackwell.

Smart, C. Neal, B. and Wade, A. (2001). *The Changing Experiences of Childhood: Family and Divorce.* Cambridge: Polity Press.

Snowden ,R. and Mitchell, G. (1981). *The Artificial Family.* London: George Allen and Unwin.

Thompson, C. (2005). *Making Parents: The Ontological Choreography of Reproductive Technologies.* Cambridge, MA: The MIT Press.

Thomson, M. (2008). *Endowed: Regulating the Male Sexed Body.* New York: Routledge.

UN Committee on the Rights of the Child (2002). *Concluding Observations of the Committee on the Rights of the Child: United Kingdom of Great Britain and Northern Ireland*, CRC/C/15/Add 188. Geneva: Centre for Human Rights.

Wallbank ,J. (2009). 'Bodies in the Shadows' Joint Birth Registration, Parental Responsibility and Social Class. *Child and Family Law Quarterly* 21, 1–18.

Warnock, M. (1984). *Report of the Committee of Inquiry into Human Fertilisation and Embryology*, Cm 9314. London: HMSO.

Legislation

Adoption Act 1976

Adoption and Children Act 2002

Births and Deaths Registration Act 1836

European Convention of Human Rights 1950

Family Law Reform Act 1987

Human Fertilisation and Embryology Act 1990

Human Fertilisation and Embryology Authority (Disclosure of Donor Information) Regulations 2004 (SI 1511/2004)

Human Fertilisation and Embryology Act 2008

Human Fertilisation and Embryology Bill 1989

Human Fertilisation and Embryology Bill 2007

Human Tissues and Embryos (Draft) Bill 2007

Perjury Act 1911

United Nations Convention on the Rights of the Child 1989

Welfare Reform Act 2009

Cases

The Ampthill Peerage [1977] AC 547

Rose and Another v Secretary of State for Health and Human Fertilisation and Embryology Authority [2002] EWHC [2003] 2 FLR 962

11

Birthright had Nothing to do with it; Royal Inheritance in the Middle Ages

FRANCIS WOODMAN

IN THIS CHAPTER, I explore the theory and practice of 'birthright' as an evolving quasi-legal concept in the Middle Ages. For most people in all societies in medieval Western Europe, 'natural laws' governed inherited birthright. Thus, gender at birth determined a whole set of unwritten rules. A male child set off on a path very different from a female, even if the boy was the youngest offspring of all. For a very few it was different. I place a particular focus on the roles played by gender and pragmatism in arriving at inheritance of throne, lands and goods or 'movables' in decision-making. These evolving ideas were important as, through custom and practice, they influenced the emergent legal frameworks that came with later parliamentary regulation of birthright (Probert, this volume).

From the earliest periods of the Middle Ages (c.600-1000ce), most Western European societies adopted a common approach to 'birthright' when it came to inheritance – legitimate sons were assumed to have a 'natural' right, daughters got what they could, often nothing. Complications arose when men thought they had birthright to something through the bloodline of their mothers and this was a particular problem when it came to succession to a throne. Increasingly, thrones were viewed not as territorial property but something less tangible and therefore not governed by the same 'natural' rules of birthright and inheritance. The concept of 'natural' inheritance derived from the so-called 'Salic Law' that severely curtailed the birthright of females as opposed to males. Traditionally named after the supposed original tribe of the Franks, the 'Salians', this 'law' by the sixth century held that only sons could inherit 'Salian' land, ie 'ancestral' territory and movables, while women could inherit only 'movables'. As kings ruled over the land, the throne must only go to a male. However, even before the end of that century, the Frankish king Childeric had amended the 'law' to allow women to inherit land but only if there was no surviving closely related male. Of course the Salic Law was not law as we would understand it today, passed by council or parliament, but simply a ruling from above, based upon custom and practice. Both would change as societies evolved. As the kingdoms of early medieval Europe developed, there needed to be clearer rules to avoid disputes and even chaos upon the death of rulers and several variants of the Law evolved, especially significant when linked with the development of Feudalism where mastery of land was tied to military duty.

When it came to succession to the throne, 'birthright' remained unclear and variable in different Kingdoms – even when only male heirs were considered. Some European societies ruled that 'agnatic' succession should be used, whereby a ruler's brothers inherited in turn rather than the first ruler's eldest son. Only when all brothers had been exhausted would the line return to the eldest son of the first and so on. Some systems even divided inheritance equally among all sons or brothers, though with kingdoms this usually proved impractical. Often called the 'Semi-Salic' law, a woman only entered the picture if she was the eldest daughter of the last in the male line, who might have been a brother, a cousin or a nephew of the deceased man. A daughter would be considered the next in bloodline by birth to the last of the male heirs even if the inheritance had moved a considerable distance sideways from the original inheritor. Equally, the female descendants of the first ruler had their son's birthright displaced by the sons of an inevitably younger female claimant of the last. Such systems became so complex as to be unworkable. But one thing remained clear – men had 'natural birthrights' while women's rights were treated on an entirely pragmatic basis – they had 'rights' only as and when thought necessary to men.

By the high Middle Ages (after c.1000ce) things seem more settled. Eldest sons inherited, women were only brought into the frame when there were no sons or brothers, but there was a sister or daughter who had a son to whom the inheritance might pass by his mother's 'regained' birthright. This is sometimes known as the 'Quasi-Salic' system as it accepted a woman's right to pass her birthright to a son. The so-called 'Salic Law' and its variations would continue to be adapted and changed in an entirely pragmatic way. The problems it raised are amply illustrated by the series of chaotic succession crises in late medieval England.

I. THE PROBLEM OF ENGLAND

The Lancastrian Dynasty that ruled England and much of France between 1399/1400 and 1461 (and again briefly in 1470) had a major problem when it came to making its mind up over the birthright of women and the Throne. It veered from one initial and rigidly held view – that under no circumstances could a woman either rule or pass any supposed 'birthright' to a male heir – to quite the opposite view by the mid fifteenth century – not only could a woman pass on her birthright but she might even rule in her own right. This headstand is but one of the examples of the lack of any agreed rules, earlier examples unfortunately having failed to establish solid precedents for the future.

(a) Henry I, Matilda and Stephen

William the Conqueror †1089 took something of a French attitude when it came to disposing of his considerable territories. His son William (William II, 'Rufus') would get England, his son Robert Curthose, Normandy but his other son Henry nothing but cash. William Rufus died in a hunting accident in 1100, leaving England clear for Henry to take the English throne as Henry I. In 1105 Henry invaded Normandy and thus reassembled his father's empire (Fleming and Pope, 2006; Green, 2006).

The king still faced lingering hostility as the son of an invading 'foreigner'. Henry's own mother could claim some 'birthright' from the Anglo-Saxon royal line but it was his marriage to Edith, daughter of Malcolm III of Scotland, niece of Edgar Atheling and great-granddaughter of the English king Edmund Ironside that he hoped would settle this long running dispute over his 'legality' and 'birthright'. Henry's expected children from Edith would carry the 'birthright' to both the Norman line via their father and an older pre-conquest line of English kings via their mother. Henry clearly recognised his wife's 'birthright' to at least pass on her claim. This marriage had been a shrewd political move to assuage the remaining hostility of the English towards their Norman conquerors and to establish a 'legitimate' Anglo-Norman line quite distinct from any line from William the Conqueror's other children. It did not go according to plan. Henry's first child was a girl, Matilda. Then came the hoped for boy, William Adelin. As a child, Matilda married Henry V, emperor of Germany but he soon died and there were no children. Moreover, William Adelin was drowned in the White Ship disaster of 1120. With the death of the Anglo-Scottish Queen, no further male heirs could combine the unique English and Norman 'birthright' leaving Matilda as the king's only legitimate heir.

Henry was determined that his daughter should inherit the throne in her own right, stressing the bloodline and birthright of both her parents. While this marked a radical departure from 'Custom and Practice' it was for the king to rule and that's what he did. Strengthened by support from the king of Scotland, Henry forced the barons to swear allegiance to Matilda as heir to the throne upon Henry's death. However, when Henry died in 1135, sufficient numbers foreswore their allegiance, supporting instead the male claim of Stephen of Blois, grandson of the Conqueror by his daughter Alise. Stephen had no greater claim to be English than Matilda, but this counted little to the Norman barons. As Count of Boulogne Stephen was extremely rich but what mattered most to the barons was that he was a man (Crouch, 2000, Davies, 1967).

When Matilda heard of her father's death she was in Anjou with her (much younger) second husband, Geoffrey Count of Anjou, whom she had married in 1128. Stephen acted quickly. He arrived in England and claimed the throne. Matilda immediately began military efforts to remove him, beginning with the conquest of Normandy, which she accomplished only in 1144.

What followed was a long and tedious civil war, in which neither side struck the fatal blow, leaving England to descend into anarchy and chaos. What matters here is the eventual settlement for there had to be one. By 1148 Matilda had still failed to be crowned in England but had restored her 'birthright' in Normandy, held now with the help of her young son Henry Plantagenet. There they both waited until the increasingly troubled reign of Stephen drew to a close. Eventually Henry Plantagenet arrived in England in force and demanded a settlement of the throne in his favour. During the protracted fighting around Wallingford, Stephen's own son Eustace died and the king was left little choice but to agree. Under the Treaty of Wallingford, 1153 and soon after confirmed at Winchester, Stephen would continue to reign till his death (in fact some months later) and the throne would then pass to Henry Plantagenet by right of his mother (Bradbury, 1969). The treaty in effect recognised the right of women to pass their birthright to the throne to their sons because, after all, Stephen's own claim depended upon his mother. Logically, as Matilda was the daughter of the previous legitimate king, Henry I, her son should have supplanted Stephen there and then but the *realpolitik* of the situation dictated the opposite. When Stephen died, Henry Plantagenet became Henry II, bypassing his mother who was never to be crowned queen in her own right. From 1153, no king of England, until 1399, would face the dilemma of being 'son-less' so the 'precedent' of Wallingford would not be put to the test. In 1399 it would be.

(b) The claim of Edward I to the throne of Scotland, 1291

The ancient line of Scottish kings ran out in 1291, leading the way for the claim by the English king, Edward I. Exactly how, is revealing in the changing and adaptable nature of female birthright and inheritance. He had to go back a long way, c.1100, and skip *twice* through the female line (Watson, 1998).

The Normans had had no blood or 'birthright' claim to the English throne, they had simply just taken it by force. The Anglo-Saxons themselves had only a loose idea of primogeniture when it came to the throne, often choosing a new king by the acclamation of the earls. Of course, a shrewd king could line up his chosen son without too much difficulty but Edward the Confessor †1065 had no children and the throne became vacant. Whatever may or may not have been promised or sworn, in these circumstances the English throne remained the gift of the earls. They chose Harold.

The Norman invasion and subsequent occupation left many unhappy and dispossessed Anglo-Saxons, including a number of 'heirs' of earlier kings. Among these was Margaret, daughter of Edward the Exile. Margaret, later to be canonised, was then married to the Scottish king, Malcolm III. To many, Margaret carried the closest bloodline by birth to the older royal houses of England, a birthright she could pass to her offspring.

Henry I of England, as detailed above, had shrewdly chosen to marry Margaret's daughter, Edith, in an attempt to buy off English dissatisfaction and provide a line of Norman heirs who would carry the bloodline of an Anglo-Saxon royal house. After the 'interruption' of the smooth succession by Stephen, the throne finally passed to Henry Plantagenet, Matilda's son, in 1153 in accordance with the terms of the Treaty of Wallingford. Edward I †1309, was the great grandson of Henry II, and therefore the great-great-great-great grandson of Malcolm III of Scotland by his marriage to yet another Matilda, daughter of St. Margaret. It was not the Anglo-Saxon element that exercised Edward I, it was the bloodline of Malcolm III, transmitted to Edward through two females. No wonder Edward restated the then extant 'rules' concerning the inheritance birthright of all his 19 children including his daughters. If he wanted to claim the Scottish throne in the absence of any other candidate he had no choice. The 'rules' such as there were had been redefined by Edward's father Henry III †1272. Eldest sons succeeded their fathers (or in the subsequent case of Richard II, his grandfather, as his own father pre-deceased his father by a year). Edward I further required the husbands of his many daughters to swear that they would respect the inheritance of the throne to the eldest son of his sons *in sequence of age*. Sons of his royal daughters could come into play but only if all the direct male-to-male lines failed. Women themselves were not considered suitable as rulers but a general assumption had developed in many parts of Europe that in certain circumstances a daughter, or sister, could 'pass' her royal birthright to a son if one was already living. In this way, Edward sought not to justify his position in England but his claim to Scotland. It failed, so Edward invaded instead.

(c) The heirs of Richard II

In 1399 England was in turmoil. There was a king, Richard II, and no one doubted his legal right to govern. As the only surviving son of Edward the Black Prince †1376, eldest son and heir to Edward III, it was his birthright. But King Richard remained childless through both his marriages, though his second wife was still under age (12) at the time of his eventual death in 1400.

Almost as soon as Richard succeeded his grandfather in 1377 at the age of 9, there was heated debate as to who was his heir 'presumptive'. Children often died young, especially if helped on their way by ambitious relatives. A throne was at stake, England plus the considerable empire remaining in France.

Richard II was significantly an only child with no surviving 'spares' of either sex. Thus Richard's heir should have been a simple matter – his father had had several younger brothers so the next uncle in line was the young king's heir. Well no, for the next uncle, Lionel Duke of Clarence was already dead but he did have a daughter Philippa who had married Roger Mortimer, Earl of March, and they had a son, also Roger. In a general understanding of the rules, Philippa's 'birthright' could be passed to her son Roger, who should therefore have been declared 'heir presumptive' (fig.1). He was and then he wasn't. Richard would not be drawn definitively on the subject and continued to prevaricate for the rest of his short life (Dunn, 2002).

The main challenge came from John of Gaunt, Duke of Lancaster, and the next living uncle in line. He argued that women could not pass on their birthright under any circumstances and that only males of a continuous male line had such rights. Thus *he* was the heir and upon his death the right would pass to *his* son Henry Bolingbroke. This was a particular reading of the ancient 'Salic Law'. John's attempts to 'alter' the rules as currently understood needed the consent of the king's council, Richard being still too young to rule alone. However, the king's council was controlled by Roger Mortimer, the heir 'presumptive' via his mother's 'birthright' under the existing 'interpretation'. Needless to say, Gaunt's suggestions fell on deaf ears (Armitage-Smith, 1904).

Apart from anything else, changing the rules, albeit ad hoc ones, would have made nonsense of England's current political and military stance against France. England had been at war with the French for almost 50 years in what would become known as the Hundred Years War. Why? The Capetian line in France had passed from father to son for centuries until the early fourteenth century. King Philip IV *'le Hardi'* had several male heirs so there was no reason to suppose that the male-to-male line would not continue. However, heir after heir came to the throne, each dying childless. The last, Charles IV †1328, left only a one-year old daughter and a pregnant wife. When in due course she gave birth, it was to another daughter (Taylor, 2001).

There remained Charles' sister Isabelle. She had married and had a son so her 'birthright' could have kicked in on her son's behalf. Unfortunately, Isabelle had married Edward II of England, had murdered him and placed her young son on the throne as Edward III. France would not accept the underage king of England as their king and that was final. A commission looked into the inheritance and decided that the Count of Valois was heir, being a direct male-to-male descendant as a grandson of Louis IX. They invoked a 1316 French 'revision' of the 'Salic Law' that had ruled not only against female succession but also against the right of females to pass on such title to a son. This was one of so many variations of the basic sixth century law across Europe that it was likely to be challenged. England challenged.

The point here is that by the reign of Richard II, England had already fought decades of a costly war against the French in order to uphold the female right to pass her birthright to her son in the absence of other closely related males. For Roger Mortimer, Earl of March, that could mean only one thing – he was Richard II's undisputed heir. Not to be so would render England's overseas efforts pointless and futile.

The issue was finally resolved after Gaunt's death which led to an invasion by his exiled son Henry Bolingbroke. This successful coup soon led to the 'abdication' of Richard II and the acclamation of Bolingbroke as King Henry IV by his father's 'birthright'. Such issues as 'women's birthright' were swept aside by violence and executions, the 'legitimate' claimants, the Mortimer offspring, being tidied away although, as it would prove, not sufficiently 'neutralised'. Once again, the issue of a woman's birthright regarding the throne was swamped by warfare and political expediency (Bennet, 1999; Mortimer, 2007; Wylie, 1884).

(d) Henry VI and the problem of succession

After fifty years of Lancastrian rule the then king, Bolingbroke's grandson Henry VI, remained childless despite being in his late twenties and after six years of marriage. Who was his heir? As the only child of Henry V there were no spares and even his uncles had died off without (legitimate) children. However, to many, Henry VI should not have been on the throne at all, the Lancastrians having usurped the throne of Richard II and denied the 'natural' birthright of his heir, Roger Mortimer (from his mother) and his children (Mortimer, 2006). To those people, the true king would be Richard, Duke of York, whose mother, Anne Mortimer, was the eldest heir of Roger to have a surviving son. At some stage the Lancastrian party produced a document claiming to be a copy of a lost agreement of 1376 made between John of Gaunt and the dying Edward III. This 'agreement' supposedly ruled that sons of daughters (ie Edward's great grandson by Phillipa) could not succeed, but that the line must pass male-to-male (Bennet, 1998). However, no actual original proof of this agreement was ever produced, merely a 'copy' dating from a later, more convenient moment. This was the 'male-to-male' line proposed unsuccessfully by Gaunt to the king's council in the reign of Richard II. While this 'deathbed agreement' might support the Lancastrian hold on the throne by the 'birthright' of Henry Bolingbroke and his son and heirs, it tied the hands of the subsequent king, Henry VI who had no male heirs close in blood. Even denying the claim of Richard, Duke of York, to be the legitimate king via the Mortimer claim, Richard was still probably the closest surviving male descendant of Edward III and therefore 'heir presumptive', being descended male-to-male through his father and grandfather from Edward III. But the Lancastrians were desperate to stop Richard. The extraordinary solution was a seven-year old little girl, Margaret Beaufort (Jones and Underwood, 1992).

The Lancastrian party had to stop thinking in terms of who by 'birthright' was the heir to Edward III but instead concentrate on the true 'heir by blood' of John of Gaunt. Committed firmly to the authenticity of the 'deathbed agreement' with Edward III giving the throne to Gaunt, it was therefore *his* heir that should be sought not Richard II's. Gaunt also had sons by his third wife Katherine Swynford though famously they were all born illegitimately. Bastard children could not inherit nor could they pass on property to their heirs unchallenged. Gaunt eventually married Katherine and set about legitimising the children. He approached the Pope, King Richard II and Parliament, all of whom agreed, surprisingly so on Richard's part as it created yet another potential male-to-male blood line to the throne. The legitimised children were the Beauforts, named after the French castle in which most were born. Having arrived in this world with no 'birthright' they suddenly found themselves not only legitimate but also royal. Great marriages ensued and most produced sons and daughters. Richard II apparently saw no danger in this secondary line of the offspring of John of Gaunt (actually third as he also had heirs from his intermediate Castilian marriage), but Gaunt's only legitimate son Henry IV thought otherwise. The Beauforts were his half siblings but he was clearly anxious that they should pose no future threat as rivals to the throne. When re-confirming their legitimisation his chancellor added 'saving a claim to the throne'. As with rulings on royal male and female inheritance it was generally acknowledged that the decisions of one king could not bind his successor but the whole justification of Lancastrian rule hinged upon male-to-male succession according to 'birthright' (fig.2).

By 1450, the Lancastrians were left standing on their heads. If Henry IV's male line had run out, then his eldest half-brother's legitimised line would have to step in, Gaunt's Iberian grandchildren being evidently dismissed as 'foreign'. The eldest Beaufort John, Earl of Somerset, had died in 1410 leaving a son, John as the second Earl and later Duke. He died in 1444 leaving only a one-year old daughter Margaret (Jones and Underwood, 1992). She was therefore the closest in blood to the previous 'heir' but unfortunately was a girl. Un-betrothed there was no husband-to-be waiting in the wings to claim all and in usual circumstances both her age and sex would have eliminated her from inheritance in favour of her adult, married uncle, Edmund Beaufort. But Henry VI intervened, granting the title of Duke of Somerset to Edmund but not the wealth. That would go to little Margaret Beaufort and whomsoever she eventually married. Margaret would be given the 'birthright' not only to the great Beaufort wealth but also to the throne itself. While it is not clear exactly when the idea came into Henry VI's increasingly muddled head, by 1450 the childless king clearly considered Margaret true heir by 'birth and blood' to John of Gaunt and therefore his heir presumptive to the throne. Gaunt's spurious 'male-to-male' agreement had to be quietly shelved. Margaret had been created the richest heiress of the era and Henry destined her to marry his half-brother Edmund Tudor – one of the sons of the king's mother by her subsequent marriage to Owen Tudor. Edmund Tudor had no 'birthright' to the English throne though he was, via his mother, a grandson of the French king, Charles VI. If Edmund Tudor married Margaret Beaufort with her 'birthright' to the 'Lancastrian' English throne, then he could reign alongside her as king by right of his wife and their son and heirs would continue the Lancastrian bloodline albeit with a hefty dose of French and Welsh.

All of this must have seemed insanity to the increasingly powerful opposition faction supporting the claims of the Yorkist duke Richard but by 1450 Margaret at seven could be betrothed and the clock for action had started ticking. Should they overthrow the king on the same grounds that the Lancastrians had used against Richard II – that the king had become unfit to govern? A small girl could easily be brushed aside and increasingly the adult, sane Richard, Duke of York looked preferable for much of English society.

Henry's thinking was clearly driven by the desire to advance the fortunes of his half-brother Edmund Tudor and not simply resolving the 'birthright' question of Gaunt's 'true' heir. If the king's party were now finally to reject Gaunt's demand of an only male-to-male inheritance and allow a claim to pass through female hands then there was a better candidate, one who did not have the hurdle of legitimisation to overcome. Gaunt's first marriage produced a number of daughters including Elizabeth, sister of the future Henry IV. She had married John Holland, Duke of Exeter, half-brother of Richard II and himself royal via his mother Joan, Countess of Kent. Elizabeth was indisputably legitimate as was her marriage and therefore her male heirs. In 1450 that heir was Henry Holland, 3rd. Duke of Exeter. Holland's hand was further strengthened by his mother's own 'birthright' being herself the great granddaughter of Edward III (fig.3). So why was his Lancastrian 'birthright' ignored in favour of a small girl whose own line had had to be legitimised? There were two possible reasons neither of which belongs in any 'rational' decision making process. Firstly, rejecting Holland would advance Tudor. Secondly, Holland was deeply disliked as a person. On such things the destiny of nations hung. 'Birthright' had nothing to do with it.

Things came to a head in 1453 when quite unexpectedly the queen, Margaret of Anjou, announced she was pregnant. The paternity was immediately questioned but not by the king, and especially not by him when the child was a boy. Suddenly Margaret Beaufort's 'birthright' as heir to the throne went on the back burner and the Yorkists had to galvanise into action.

The Yorkists spread the rumour, probably true, that the father of the young boy was in fact Edmund Beaufort, Duke of Somerset and that as the child was illegitimate he had no 'birthright' to the throne, Lancastrian or otherwise. But the Lancastrian cause rallied around the king and war became inevitable.

The Duke of York's son, Edward, finally seized the throne by his father's 'birthright' as descended from Roger Mortimer and after a few mishaps, founded a dynasty of kings that lasted until 1485.

When Richard III was overthrown and killed by Henry Tudor it was justified both as the removal of a usurper to the Lancastrian 'birthright' to the throne and of a ruler unfit to rule. Henry VII would reign by the 'birthright' of his mother Margaret Beaufort so from then on it would be all but impossible to ignore female 'birthright' to the most important inheritance of all – the throne – saving that the eldest son would always retain precedence. Henry VIII's justification for sustaining Tudor rule was through his Yorkist mother and 'Lancastrian' grandmother. Gender was no longer an issue of 'birthright' when it came to the throne. Hence Mary I and Elizabeth I ruled in their own right and James I succeeded by his mother's birthright (Mary Stuart, Queen of Scots).

Statute law came with the Glorious Revolution of 1688. The Act of Settlement finally removed gender discrimination of regal inheritance, though retaining a 'sons first' policy, and replaced it with discrimination by religion. Gender was an accident of birth, religion a matter of choice. Hence today, Elizabeth II occupies the throne by her 'birthright' and her decision to remain a Protestant.

All these issues highlight the unique problem of birthright and rule. For all but a very few, gender at birth determined a whole set of unwritten rules. Yet apparently these same 'natural laws' that governed all societies in medieval western Europe when it came to inherited birthright could be thrown out of the window when it came to the most important inheritance of all – power. Whereas all free people understood and generally respected the 'natural' laws of birthright and inheritance, no one, as far as we know, ever questioned the fact that this could be bent, manoeuvred and indeed stood on its head when it came to the single most important 'birthright' that affected everyone's life.

What is surely most remarkable is that the purely pragmatic and often 'illegal' decisions on such matters at the very top did not filter down through the rest of society and pose a challenge to the 'natural order' of such things. One law for some, another for the rest.

This history of this period has been well recorded and dissected, though rarely as a gender issue. Below are general and specific works covering most aspects of the history, including more recent works of reference.

REFERENCES

Armitage-Smith, S. (1904). *John of Gaunt* reprinted 1964. London: Garden City Press.
Bennett, M. (1997). *Richard II and the Revolution of 1399*. Stroud: Sutton Press.
—— (1998). Edward III's Entail and the Succession to the Crown. *English Historical Review (EHR)* 113, 580–609.
Bradbury, J. (1969). *Stephen and Matilda: the Civil War of 1139–1153*. Stroud: Sutton Press.
Crouch, D. (2000). *The Reign of King Stephen*. Harlow: Pearson Longman.
Davis, R H C. (1967). *King Stephen, 1135–1154*. Harlow: Longman.
Drew, K. F. (1991). *The Laws of the Salian Franks (Pactus legis Salicae)*. Philadelphia: University of Pennsylvania Press.
Dunn, A. (2002). Richard II and the Mortimer Inheritance, in *Fourteenth Century England* (ed. C. Given-Wilson). Woodbridge: Sutton.
Given-Wilson, C. (1993). *Chronicles of the Revolution 1397–1400*. Manchester: Manchester University Press.

Green, J. A. (2006). *Henry I: King of England and Duke of Normandy.* Cambridge: Cambridge University Press.

Fleming D. F., and Pope, J. M. (2006). Henry I and the Anglo-Norman World: *Studies in Memory of C. Warren Hollister.* (Haskins Society Journal, Special Volume17). Woodbridge: Boydell Press.

Jones, M. K. and Underwood, M. (1992). *The King's Mother.* Cambridge: Cambridge University Press.

Mortimer, I. Richard II and the Succession to the Crown (2006). *History* 303, 320–336.

—— (2007). *The Fears of Henry IV.* London: Vintage.

Prestwich, M. (1997). *Edward I* (updated ed.). New Haven: Yale University Press.

Taylor, C. (2001). The Salic Law and the Valois succession to the French crown. *French History* 15, 358–377.

Watson, F. J. (1998). *Under the Hammer: Edward I and the Throne of Scotland. 1286–1307.* East Linton: Tuckwell Press.

Wilkinson, B. (1939). The Deposition of Richard II and the Accession of Henry IV. *EHR* 54, 215–239.

Wylie, J. H. (1884–98). *A History of England under Henry the Fourth*, 4. vols. London: Longmans, Green & Co.

FIGURES

Figure 1: The sons of Edward III and their heirs.

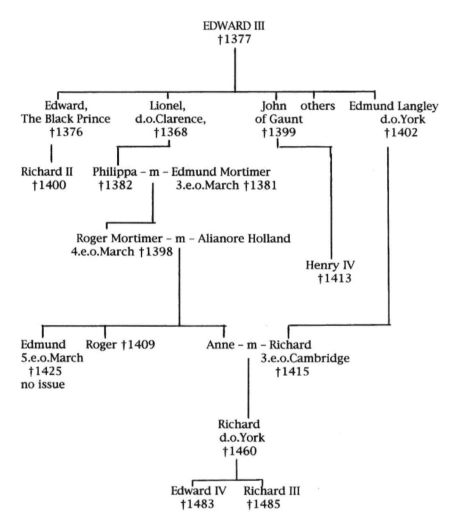

The Mortimer claim descended via Philippa, daughter of Lionel Duke of Clarence, second son of Edward III.

The Yorkist claim descended via Philippa and her granddaughter Anne. This was considerably enhanced by the marriage of Roger Mortimer, 4th. Earl of March to Alianore Holland, a granddaughter of Joan, Countess of Kent from her first marriage to Thomas Holland. Joan, subsequently the wife of Edward the Black Prince and mother of Richard II, was a granddaughter of Edward I from his second marriage to Margaret of France, a daughter of King Philip III of France. Furthermore, Anne Mortimer married

Richard, Earl of Cambridge, himself a grandson of Edward II from his youngest son, Edmund Langley.

Figure 2: The Beaufort line and Lady Margaret's 'birthright'.

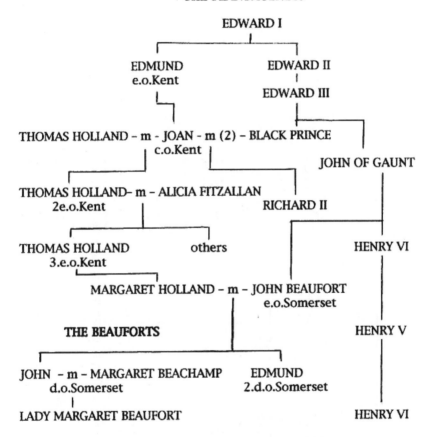

The Beaufort claim depended entirely upon the legitimisation of the Beaufort off-spring of John of Gaunt and the royal descent of Margaret Holland, granddaughter of Joan, Countess of Kent.

Figure 3: The 'legitimate birthright' of Henry Holland, 3rd. Duke of Exeter.

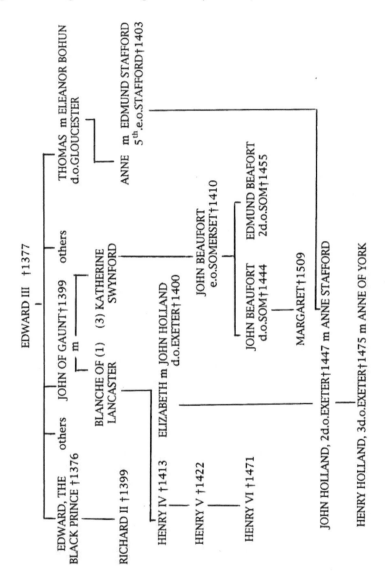

As the grandson of Elizabeth Plantagenet, legitimate daughter of John of Gaunt and sister of Henry IV, his claim was better than that of Margaret Beaufort whilst having the same Holland Anglo-French descent as the Beaufort sons, John and Edmund. If descent via the female 'birthright' was suddenly in vogue with the Lancastrians, then Henry Holland was by far the best candidate.

12

Infanticide and Insanity in 19th Century England

SHELLEY DAY SCLATER

I. INTRODUCTION

MANY OF THE chapters in this volume show that for many parents, childbirth is a positive and joyful experience. But equally there are situations, as Martin Richards suggests in the Introduction, where birth is linked with personal, medical or social problems or indeed casts a long shadow over the lives of those concerned. Psychiatric illness following childbirth is one such situation. The Royal College of Psychiatrists[1] suggests that between 10 to 15 women in every 100 may be affected by 'postnatal depression' in the weeks or months after the birth. Similar to depression at other times of life, post natal depression manifests itself as low mood, anxiety and difficulty in managing the baby. More serious is 'puerperal psychosis' which affects approximately 1 in every 1000 women. In both types of psychiatric illness, fears that the mother will harm her baby are not uncommon, though instances of actual harm are rare. There is no consensus on the causes of post natal depression, though a number of risk factors are known. The illness can also strike for no apparent reason.

Medical knowledge of what we now call post natal depression took shape in the 19th Century at which time it was referred to as 'puerperal insanity'. This chapter is concerned with the emergence of puerperal insanity as a discrete diagnostic category. The chapter examines the social conditions in which medical knowledge defined the condition and came to regard it as a specific 'disease of the mind' different from the range of other insanities of the time. In the mid 19th Century, infanticide – the killing of newborns and infants – was a widespread social problem that the criminal justice system struggled to contain.

---

[1] http://www.rcpsych.ac.uk/mentalhealthinfoforall/problems/postnatalmentalhealth/postnatalde pression.aspx, accessed on 20 September 2010.

The chapter argues that it was through its links with infanticide that puerperal insanity emerged as a discrete syndrome.

At the present time, the Infanticide Act 1938 effectively provides a partial defence to the killing of an infant by recognising that, where the balance of a woman's mind is disturbed as a consequence of giving birth, she should not be held to be guilty of murder (which has a mandatory life sentence) but will instead be guilty of manslaughter (which has a lesser penalty). Prior to 1803, cases of suspected infanticide were prosecuted according to a statute of 1624 under which, where the death was concealed, the mother was presumed guilty of infanticide unless she could prove that the baby had been born dead; unusually, the burden of proof of innocence was on the accused. Many women were however acquitted on evidence that they had prepared for the baby's arrival – the so-called 'benefit of linen' defence. In 1803 the Ellenborough Act (43 Geo 3 c.58) repealed the earlier statute and proof of murder became a requirement. It also permitted juries to convict on a lesser charge of 'concealment of birth' punishable by two years in prison. The 1938 Act remains in force, and it is thought that killing of neonates is some four times higher than murder in the population.[2]

On 10th March 1848 Martha Prior, 37, appeared before Lord Chief Justice Denman at the Lent assizes in Chelmsford, accused of the murder of her thirteen day old infant by cutting its throat with a razor. This was not an unusual type of case, but it turned out to be a singular one that resonated with a wide range of concerns – popular, legal and medical – and so had consequences well beyond the personal ones for Mrs Prior, and well beyond the limits of the legal system that sought to deal with her.

Mr Bell, giving medical evidence at Martha Prior's trial, testified that, at the time the prisoner destroyed her child, she was incapable of controlling her actions. When cross-examined, he stated that she had acted under the sudden and uncontrollable impulse of a mind previously diseased. In his summing up, the judge considered the opinion of the medical man to have been 'rashly formed', but nevertheless the jury went on to acquit Mrs Prior on grounds of insanity.

This seems to have been the first known case of a woman who was acquitted on a charge of infanticide on grounds of an insanity that was specifically 'puerperal' – namely a temporary derangement brought on by the birth itself. Martha Prior's case received particularly close coverage in the medical press. The *Journal of Psychological Medicine* reported on the case, and on the judge's remarks (Anon., 1848a, p. 479) as did *The Lancet*, the leading professional medical journal of the day (Anon., 1848b). The case was also discussed in medical texts and articles (for example, Bucknill, 1857, pp. 85–7).

---

[2] http://www.independent.co.uk/news/uk/crime/scrap-outdated-infanticide-law-say-judges-495016.html accessed on 20 September 2010.

It was, of course, not uncommon for juries at the time to acquit infanticidal women – it was almost always women who were charged with the offence – or for such women to be found guilty of the lesser charge of 'concealing the birth'. This, however, was regarded as lamentable by many medical men. Taylor (1865), for example, saw the tendency to acquit as epitomising the faulty workings of an antiquated legal system that was ill-equipped to take account of modern scientific facts. Greaves (1863) lamented the law's wilful ignorance of plain physiology and the unscientific nature of legal decision-making.

The presence of so-called mental derangement had become a possible line of defence for women accused of infanticide as early as the late 17th century. However, as Hoffer and Hull (1981) remind us, 'derangement' did not automatically secure an acquittal or a pardon. In 1688 Sinah Jones was convicted of murder despite evidence that she was mentally deranged when she suffocated her newborn 'bastard.' At common law, only 'idiots' and 'lunatics' could gain pardon for their acts, and then only after they had been convicted. Temporary derangement was not a reason for acquittal until the infanticide cases of the late 17th century (Walker, 1968). Even then, 'lunacy' alone was not sufficient to establish non-responsibility. 'Temporary fits', when women went 'out of their senses' might be successful only if coupled with another defence, such as 'benefit of linen' – where the accused could prove that she had made preparations for the baby's arrival (Radzinowicz, 1948). This suggests that the main concern of the law was to tackle the concealment of illegitimate birth and not the punishment of infanticidal women *per se*. The effect of this kind of defence was to sidestep the *mens rea* question of 'malice aforethought' – loosely meaning motive, intention and perhaps premeditation. It is perhaps because 18th century juries were already prepared to sidestep such issues that the insanity defence was able to succeed alone in the 19th century cases; a claim of insanity effectively overrode issues of intention, motivation and responsibility.

Whether the child had, in fact, even been born alive proved to be a stumbling block in proving that murder had taken place. By the 18th century, the validity of medical proofs of live birth was being questioned (Hunter, 1784). Antagonism between medicine and law was obvious in cases such as that of Mary Clifton in 1774, when the judge discounted the doctor's evidence that the bastard neonate had been born alive. These questions remained vexed ones well into the 19th century (Cummin, 1836) and issues related to infanticide occupied the attention of persons concerned with medical jurisprudence (e.g. Taylor, 1865). As Smith (1981) argues, such concerns revealed a deep-set opposition between medical and legal discourses.

Despite attempts to control infanticide by the operation of the criminal law, by the middle of the 19th century it was widely believed that numbers were on the increase. Infanticide acquired a new kind of social visibility as a problem that had to be stamped out. Against this background, Martha Prior's case was significant in that she was said to be suffering from a 'puerperal insanity' – a temporary derangement and a specific disease category, the diagnosis of which was alone sufficient to secure her acquittal.

This chapter examines the context in which Martha Prior's case took on such significance and offers a close analysis of the meshing of and the tensions among medical and legal discourses and practices that resulted in the emergence of 'puerperal insanity' as a discrete disease in the middle of the 19th century.

II. THE PROBLEM OF INFANTICIDE

There is ample evidence that infanticide was seen as a major problem which 19th century British society faced (Johnson, 1814; Hutchinson, 1820; Ryan, 1862; Langer, 1973; Sauer, 1978) and had to 'contain'. By the 1840s both the popular and the medical press were giving extended coverage to the general problem as well as to specific cases. It was seen as symptomatic of a callous attitude to infant life and, in the 1860s, was seen as a national stigma and a social evil.

> There can be little doubt, not withstanding our boasted civilisation, and the greatly increased facilities for the detection of offenders, the crime of infanticide is as prevalent now, or even more so, than at any previous period of our history. (Anon., in *Social Science Review*, 1864, p. 452).

Whilst it is not clear how closely tied were the concerns of observers to the realities of the crime – true numbers are probably impossible to estimate – the widespread scale of infant death, from both natural and unnatural causes, caused considerable alarm from the early part of the century.

> There is, pervading all ranks of society, far too low an estimate of the sanctity of foetal and infantile life. Until a better tone of public feeling prevails, we shall endeavour, by penal enactments, to prevent these crimes which disgrace humanity. (Greaves, 1863, p. 1).

Others saw it as something associated with the practices of the lower classes:

> [T]he crime of infanticide has spread to a fearful extent, and seems to be extending rapidly amongst the humbler classes of society ... (Ryan, 1862, p. 19).

Infanticide was not a new phenomenon – as long ago as medieval times ecclesiastical courts had prescribed severe penance for infanticidal parents – and concerns about the practice had, over the years, taken a variety of forms. But in the mid 19th century, infanticide appeared as a major social problem with which medicine men and lawyers grappled. I am concerned here, not with whether the concerns were realistic or grounded, but with the way that infanticide was formulated as a particular kind of problem at this time. My analysis of the accounts and cases of the time (Day, 1985) revealed that infanticide took shape at the intersection of a number of discourses – primarily medical and legal; puerperal insanity appeared as a discrete disease category, making possible individual diagnosis. Thus in the years after Martha Prior's case, the possibility of such an individual diagnosis would transform infanticide from a social problem to an individual one. The possibility of a diagnosis of puerperal insanity meant that infanticide became, not a social problem linked to widespread poverty, inadequate health care and oppressive gender relations but instead became an individual issue, a consequence of the deranged psychology of individual women.

Some appreciation of the broader social background, and the discursive frameworks and practices within which infanticide took shape in the 19th century is essential. One important dimension was the interpretive framework that infanticide shared with reproduction more generally, and stillbirth, abortion and miscarriage in particular.

(a) Reproduction

Infanticide demanded medical involvement for several reasons: first, as regards determining the cause of infant death; considerable controversy surrounded the validity and the acceptance of such evidence (Cummin, 1836; Hunter, 1784; Ryan, 1862; Taylor, 1865). Secondly, infanticide was located in the same medical discourse as broader reproductive issues and, as far as the law was concerned, the 1803 'Ellenborough Act' placed infanticide in the same legal framework as abortion and both were seen to undermine a general principle of the sanctity of life. Infanticide and abortion were both associated with ideas about 'the collapse of sexual restraint' and the consequence that 'the bonds which hold society together would be broken asunder', as one commentator in the *Legal Examiner* asserted (Anon., 1832, p. 11). It is likely that deeper anxieties about unfettered female sexuality underlay the attempts to regulate infanticide and abortion, but there was some ambivalence about proposals that purported to lessen the incidence of such crimes. For example, the establishment of a Foundling Hospital (Ryan, 1862, p. 51) was regarded as a possible encouragement for sexual immorality. Further, many argued that it was the severity of the 1803 law that led juries to be so reluctant to convict infanticidal women.

In broader medical discourse, a woman's reproductive capacities were seen as the source both of her strength and power, and of her weakness and vulnerability, physical and psychical. Ambivalence about women's power and vulnerability readily found expression in the infanticide debates. Johnson (1814, p. 394) for example said that:

> Proportioned to the value of woman's chastity and virtue, is the mischief that results from her vice and profligacy.

Ryan (1862, p. 31) argued that one of the means of preventing infanticide would be:

> [A] sincere and charitable attempt to make women more independent and therefore more self-reliant.

But he added the proviso that women must not become

> [U]nfeminine, for in that they would lose the chief charm of their sex. That dependence which they must ever have upon man as the stronger and more indomitable animal, ever ready to meet danger and prompt to avert it, is to be met, not by an emulation for which their weaker physical frame is unfitted, but by those fond and considerate kindnesses, and that trusting confidence which peculiarly belongs to their sex; and which makes them in their very weakness often more influential and more powerful than the opposite sex in all its boasted manhood. ...

Thus, ambivalence about the power and the vulnerability of women, with their assumed roots in the reproductive organs and functions, constituted an important element of the emotional undercurrents of the infanticide debates.

(b) Illegitimacy

The social visibility of infanticide had long involved single, poor women and women who violated norms of sexual propriety. Married women were much less likely to be accused and prosecuted and their claims of temporary insanity – as in Martha Prior's case – were more likely to be believed (Hoffer and Hull, 1981). It was popularly believed that it was abandoned women – usually young servant girls – who would have been most strongly motivated to rid themselves of unwanted children, either by abortion or infanticide. Ryan (1862, p. 43) commented on the supposed plight of such women when he said:

> She is, therefore, tied down neck and heels to attend to this child herself – all chances of future exertion is denied her – down, down she is chained to the muddiest banks of society ...

Hunter's treatise on infanticide (Hunter, 1784) had referred specifically to 'bastard' children and was often cited as the cause of leniency shown to mothers by the courts. As Cummin (1836, p. 5) puts it:

> ... [K]nowledge of women has enabled me to say ... that women who are   pregnant, without daring to avow their situation, are commonly objects of the greatest compassion; and generally are less criminal than the world imagine. In most of these cases the father of the child is really criminal, often cruelly so; the mother is weak, credulous and deluded ...

The belief that shame was an important motivation for infanticide seems to have been a major reason behind the restriction of admission to the Foundling Hospital to infants of single women of 'previously good character' who had no paternal support (King, 1865).

(c) Poverty and Perinatal Mortality

Perinatal mortality rates among illegitimate infants were high, even for their particular social group. And in 1879 Drysdale estimated that one in four working class infants could be expected to die within a year of birth, and for illegitimate infants the death rate was one in three. Ryan (1862) reported that, in one workhouse, the death rate for illegitimate infants stood at 46% at a time when the average mortality rate of infants was 14.6%. But, crucially, general infant mortality and infanticide were difficult to distinguish. Drysdale (1866) said that infanticide by omission was ten times more common than infanticide by commission. Ryan (1862), on the basis of data from the deaths of children under two, showed that infant deaths through starvation, suffocation, want and neglect, exposure, and natural disease shaded into infanticide by commission, and in individual cases it was not always possible to ascertain precisely how the child had died.

Deaths on so-called 'baby farms' were estimated to be as high as 90% (Greaves, 1863), and three times as likely for illegitimate children as for the babies of married mothers. Baby farms were regarded as something of a national scandal, and seen as populated by the children of women lacking in natural maternal affection. But, at another level, baby farms were crucial to the livelihoods of many working class mothers, enabling them to take up employment, including as wet nurses. Such employment must have been a lifeline for unmarried mothers who could have faced considerable obstacles in obtaining financial support owing to the ways the Poor Laws operated. Unmarried mothers were entitled only to a shilling a week from the Parish, whereas Ryan (1862) argued that to stem the tide of infanticide they would need at least seven shillings and six pence per week.

However, it is noteworthy that in the infanticide debates, poverty tended not to be regarded as a broader social problem to be tackled politically and in a widespread manner. Rather the focus was on the effects of poverty on the individual woman; poverty was seen as a powerful incentive for unmarried mothers to rid themselves of their babies. These women may be unfortunate but they were also culpable for allowing themselves to be driven to such desperate measures. Within the medical community there was ambivalence too. The sadness, desperation and dangers of poverty were recognised. For example, the *London Medical Gazette* of 1838, commenting on an amendment to the Poor Law, deplored

> This diligent series of attempts to make the poor live on less and less – to make those whose income is brought down ... to a minimum insufficient to procure food and raiment, provide for medical advice out of their slender means ... (Anon., 1838, p. 1017).

This writer obviously had an axe to grind, but he was not slow to link the issue of the personal poverty of individual women to the much broader issue of the maintenance of social order: 'A nation does not die, but its patience comes to an untimely end.' (Anon., 1838, p. 1017).

The concern of that editor with the plight of the poor was part and parcel of the medical profession's campaign relating to provisions for the payment of medical services under the Poor Laws. Another leading article reported:

> [T]he principle adopted by the [Poor Law] Commissioners for determining the value of the services of a medical man, was unjust to the profession and likely to be attended with injury to the poor. (Anon., 1845a, p. 1115)

Such 'injury to the poor' included unnecessary infant death, as well as problems with midwifery that I will discuss in a moment. In both areas, fundamental issues to do with the professionalisation of medicine were at stake. For example, in 1844, the Registrar for Births and Deaths in Manchester, reported on the 'increased mortality among children under the hands of *uneducated* practitioners' (my italics). He argued that:

> Nearly one third of all deaths of children that I register appear to have been from remediable diseases, and ... the deaths have occurred either under the necessarily improper treatment of uneducated persons, or, what is nearly as bad, from no treatment at all . (Leigh, 1844, p. 781)

(d) Quacks, Uneducated Practitioners and Ignorant Midwives

Medical practitioners were apt to see infant deaths as attributable to the workings of the Poor Law insofar as it provided for an unsatisfactory system of remuneration for doctors attending paupers. But the alarm generated by the reference to 'uneducated persons' must also be seen in the context of the debates over the forthcoming Medical Reform Bill that would seek to regulate the practices of apothecaries and chemists from whom medical practitioners were anxious to dissociate themselves.

> Dealers in medicines, therefore – very necessary men, we will grant them – we will never allow that the apothecary, as the worshipful company meets us in the mercantile world, is any part or parcel of the medical profession. We hold the conjunction between the practice of medicine and the trading company, effected in 1815, as one of the most unfortunate incidents that ever befell the profession of physic, and we do say emphatically that we rejoice most heartily in the prospect of a speedy separation between them. (Anon., 1844, p. 203)

In the years leading up to the Medical Reform Bill, the apothecaries and chemists found themselves associated with the horrors of infanticide. Denouncing the operation of 'burial clubs', a leading article in the *London Medical Gazette* for 1844–5 suggested that 'ignorant chemists and druggists' were 'the parties under cover of whom the present system of child murder is especially carried on' (Anon., 1844–5, p. 209).

Similarly, medical concerns with poverty, the poor remuneration of medical men under the Poor Laws, and issues of professionalism, education and licensing also came together in the case of midwifery. To a leader writer in the *Medical Gazette* of 1845 it seemed probable that

> [F]emale midwives are chiefly selected by the poor, not from any feelings of delicacy, but from the lowness of their charges: and this objection to any restriction on female practice could not be met unless the charges of medical practitioners were regulated ... by a Government tariff. To any interference of this kind, there would undoubtedly be strong opposition on the part of the profession. (Anon., 1845b, p. 781)

The 'objection' referred to here was the licensing of midwives and the restriction on female practice among the poor. Another Leader in the same volume expressed satisfaction with the proposals of the Medical Reform Bill to make provision for an examination in midwifery and the subsequent registration of those who passed the exam (Anon., 1845c). The concern with infanticide was an important lever used by the medical general practitioners in their professional rivalry with the midwives. During the 1840s it was common explicitly to associate midwives with the crime. For example, in *The Lancet*, the medical journal that was read widely by general practitioners (and edited by Wakley who was also a coroner and who therefore saw many cases of infant deaths), references to the involvement of midwives in infanticide are many. The alleged culpability arose from their 'drunkenness and ignorance' (Anon., 1848c, pp. 345–6) or because they performed their duties in a 'coarse and brutal manner'. The doctors proposed that if the incidence of infanticide was to be reduced, it would require a law that enabled women to get proper medical assistance at the time of delivery. But such assistance was not defied in purely medical terms. It also meant proper financial remuneration for the doctor and a certain autonomy for him from the confines and strictures of the Poor Law and its authorities. Paradoxically, an incident in which a doctor had been responsible for the deaths of a mother and her child was used to support the doctors' case against the midwives.

In this 'Croydon Case' in 1848 a doctor had been called to a labouring woman. He had visited her several times but, on realising that she did not have the necessary document that would ensure he was paid by the Poor Law Authorities, the doctor did not return. The woman was left to labour on her own, and both she and the infant died. There was a public outcry against the doctor, but his professional colleagues supported him and used the case to argue for professional autonomy for doctors in their struggle against the midwives. Midwives were often blamed for the fact that doctors were not present at confinements which had fatal results. A leading article in the *London Medical Gazette* of 1845 argued that many maternal deaths could be attributed to

> [T]he unskilful treatment on the part of midwives, who only call in a medical practitioner when it is too late to render effectual assistance . (Anon., 1845b, p. 782)

It remained common practice for local midwives to attend labouring women until well into the 19th century. But as the century progressed, midwives were increasingly accused of collusion in infanticide. Greaves (1863, p. 11) commented on a legal loophole which he believed midwives exploited in an organised way:

> It is said that a certain number of female practitioners, when engaged by a pregnant woman to attend her, inquire whether she wishes for a living child, or not, adding that their fee for a living child is so-and-so, for one still-born, so much more. If an instance of the practice thus indicated were detected, it would ... be impossible to punish the offender, provided she did her work effectively.

Thus if the midwife did not merely injure the child but ensured its death before it was fully born, she could avail herself of a legal loophole. A child who was not fully born was not considered to be legally alive, and therefore it could not be the victim of murder (Hunter, 1784; Ryan, 1862; Taylor, 1865)

> ... [A]ccording to the law of England, a child only partially born is not regarded as a living being, and hence it is no crime to inflict upon it wilfully any amount of injury, provided that the injury be sufficient to prevent its being born alive. Here lies the great difficulty of obtaining a verdict of child murder. Real life and legal life are nice distinctions, which are not always fully realised by jury men (Anon., 1864, p. 454)

(e) Medical Jurisprudence

The fact that an infant could be killed before it was fully born, even though it may have been shown to have breathed before its death (Hunter, 1784) was a source of great controversy over forensic evidence (Cummin, 1836). It was not uncommon for courts to discount medical 'proof' of live birth and for the accused to be acquitted or indicted on the lesser charge of concealment of the birth.

Thus the medical struggles with the midwives, as well as being linked to doctors' own professional issues, became embroiled within broader on-going medico-legal debates about the distinction between medical and legal life. Through the linking with midwifery, infanticide found another route into the medical discourse of reproduction. The culpability for a range of reproductive misfortunes and misdemeanours – stillbirth, abortion, infanticide, and the excesses of female sexuality – was shared among women, as mothers and as midwives. Medical science – both obstetric and forensic – presented itself as the only salvation for the unfortunate infants who were otherwise destined to be the victims of such female practices. And following Martha Prior's case, the newly emerging specialism of psychiatry (or 'alienism' as it was then called) would be added to that list.

(f) Mad, Bad, or Badly-Done-To?

If women – both mothers and midwives – were capable of mistreating or killing infants, then the question arose as to whether they should be pitied – as Hunter had long ago argued (Hunter, 1784) – or whether they ought to be punished. Cummin (1836) had stressed the necessity of bringing the guilty to punishment, but most commentators of the time saw the difficulty of achieving such an outcome and the problems inherent in it. Ryan (1831, p. 179), for example, in his influential *Manual of Medical Jurisprudence,* said

> Enough has been said to warn the practitioner against committing errors, which have but too often led to the execution of innocent women..

And similarly Sewell (1846, p. 808) argued that because of the numerous accidents associated with childbirth

> [A] jury should be extremely cautious how they return a verdict of wilful murder against the unfortunate mother ...

The problem with the midwives was debated in Parliament in the 1840s. Lord Ashley had proposed some resolutions that would give medical men independent authority over midwives in childbirth cases, as well as autonomy from the confines of the Poor Law. His proposals were reported at length in *The Lancet.*

> His first resolution would prevent the recurrence of those dreadful scenes ... whereby pregnant women, in consequence of the delay purposefully thrown in their way by the [Poor Law] relieving officers, had been compelled to send for ignorant midwives, who performed their duty in such a coarse and brutal manner, as led very frequently to mutilation, and even to death. He showed at some length that the present mode of relief [under the Poor Law] had operated in a most dreadful manner on young women, both married and unmarried, by leading to a great increase in the crime of infanticide. If the House was anxious to reduce a crime now so rife, it must enable the women to apply to the Medical Officer, and obtain relief at once (Anon., 1848c, p. 346).

Doctors argued that in the name of health and safety, they alone ought to control childbirth. To further their case, the doctors aligned themselves with the best interests of the poor, but in doing so some of the social problems of widespread poverty were recast as medical issues – one manifestation of a wider drive to bring the apparent certainty and authority of science to bear on problems that hitherto had proved to be insoluble.

But the courts would not easily accept the authority of science. Indeed, as Smith (1981) has shown, there were often clashes between medical and legal discourses, and particularly so when issues – such as infanticide – drew divided opinions between traditional versus scientific ways of ordering the world.

As far as the law was concerned, infanticide was a criminal offence, to be dealt with by the criminal justice system. Taylor (1965) was not alone in drawing attention to the anomalous situation whereby coroners' inquests readily returned verdicts of wilful murder and yet when the women were brought for trial at the assizes, they were commonly acquitted. For every alleged infanticide that resulted in acquittal, the problem of infant deaths shifted away from the discourse of individual crime and instead seemed an instance of the more general problem of high infant mortality. The criminal justice system strained to contain infanticide within the boundaries of its discourses and practices.

The unwillingness to convict on the part of juries was referred to by Ryan (1862, p. 26) as giving 'a silent sanction to the detestable practice' and yet the fact remained that it was difficult to establish the cause of death with sufficient certainty to sustain a murder charge. The alleged victims would have met their fate in a variety of ways. 'Overlaying' was said to be a common cause of death, yet few smothered victims could be proved to have been murdered. Poisoning by opium also occurred, but since it was common practice to quieten infants with small doses of narcotics, it was difficult to establish the necessary *mens rea* for murder (Severn, 1832). The issue of narcotics was a significant one in the denouncement of the apothecaries by the medical profession.

> If the druggist is sometimes applied to for the medicine which, with greater propriety and safety would be prescribed by a medical man, he is too often asked for compounds which no medical man would prescribe; such as ... 'soothing syrup', 'mothers' blessing'. (Anon., 1844–5, p. 209)

By far the most common causes of infant death appear to have been 'neglect' and other 'harmful' treatments such as the feeding of indigestible food. 'Neglect' ranged from starvation to more subtle practices and omissions, such as not calling a doctor when an infant was ill (Hutchinson, 1820). Mahon (1813) had argued that infanticide differed from homicide proper in that

> [I]ndependent of the means in which unnatural or wicked mothers may employ to deprive these helpless beings of life, the mere omission or negligence of necessary succour may equally prove the cause of death.

The treatises on medical jurisprudence published in the 19th century consistently included an extended discussion of infanticide, devoting attention to the possible causes of death and the sorts of medical evidence needed as proof of murder. References to the insanity of the mother became increasingly common towards the middle of the century. Sometimes when infants died at birth it was attributed to the mother's failure to obtain proper medical assistance with the birth (which physicians argued was the fault of the Poor Law officers). Whilst by no means necessarily murderous in intent, 'neglect' was more often spoken of in terms of wilful infanticide than it was in terms of poverty, ignorance or accident.

It was widely believed that the law had failed to check infanticide (Greaves, 1863; Mahon, 1813; Martin, 1826; Ryan, 1862; Scott, 1826)). But it was not the law that was seen to be at fault, rather its interpretation. As Greaves (1863) remarked:

> [T]he law, as interpreted by those who administer it, has practically for many years, tended but little to check the commission of this crime.

The interpretation depended in part on the court's interpretation of the expert evidence of the medical witnesses. As Taylor (1865, p. xiii) remarked in the preface to his major text on medical jurisprudence,

The chapters on infanticide will furnish numerous illustrations of the measure which counsel take of the intellectual capacities of common juries. The defences made are frequently such as no man would venture to place before a jury of educated men. These 'powerful' or 'forcible' addresses, as they are termed by the press, full of burning eloquence and impassioned logic, have frequently withdrawn the attention of the jury from the real facts, and have procured verdicts of acquittal contrary to the evidence and all the medical circumstances of the case.

To Taylor's mind, the tendency to acquit epitomised the workings of an antiquated legal system ill-equipped to take proper account of scientific fact. It must have seemed to the campaigning medical men that convictions could only be secured when the evidence accorded with common sense judgements of murder. As Martin (1826, p. 36) put it:

Prosecution takes no pains to convict, and judges and juries are determined not to believe that a child has been murdered; unless they find it with its throat cut or its brains dashed out upon the pavement.

Greaves (1863) attributed the reluctance to convict to the wilful ignorance of the 'plainest physiological facts' that 'set at defiance the rules of logic.' He lamented the 'unscientific' nature of legal decisions in infanticide cases. It was almost certainly the case that the legal system had difficulty with the whole notion of scientific 'facts' and their relation to legal facts with which the courts were more familiar. But there were wider issues involved too; an awareness that, in many cases, the mother's seducer was in some degree to blame for the whole sorry situation. Ryan (1862, pp. 81–2) argued that poor vulnerable girls who were seduced by wealthy men and then cast aside were

[I]n such a miserable plight …. [they are] much to be pitied, and their case well deserves to be taken up by the philanthropic and the charitable .

Taylor (1865, p. 986) reported, quoting the Annual Report for the Coroner of Middlesex, that the judge and jury were anxious to avoid a verdict that consigned a woman to death when she was 'more sinned against than sinning.' One can imagine why juries might have been circumspect, especially given the difficulty in proving that the child had not been still-born.

The medical witness may prove most clearly that the child was alive when the alleged injuries were inflicted; he may show beyond question that these injuries caused its death, and this, to minds versed in legal niceties, would be sufficient to ensure a verdict of murder. But counsel for the defence then asks the witness whether he can swear the child was born alive, and as must occur in a very large proportion of cases, the medical witness replies that he cannot so swear. (Anon., 1864, p. 454)

Even in cases where it could be established that the child had not been still-born, there were difficulties in proving that it had been killed intentionally and that there was the necessary *mens rea* for murder. Taylor (1865) observed that in cases where the mother could not be discovered, coroners' juries seemed to have no problem in passing verdicts of wilful murder. But where there was a woman who could be sent to trial, there was much more hesitation at the inquest. The Coroner for Middlesex stated in his Annual Report for 1865 that there had been 69 inquests on newborns, of which 56 had occasioned verdicts of wilful murder. But all persons charged were acquitted (Taylor, 1865, p. 986).

Smith (1981) argues that juries' failure to convict reveals the working of a discourse within which women were characterised as inherently irresponsible and therefore unpunishable for their misdeeds. Irresponsibility, it seems, was in the nature of femininity. It would then be but a small step to attribute the killing of infants by their mothers to mental aberration.

The disease puerperal insanity took shape as a discrete diagnostic category against this background. Crucially, a diagnosis of insanity served to sidestep the whole issue of *mens rea*, of intent and, as one of the defining symptoms of the disease was said to be violent – even murderous – impulses towards the infant, the vexed question of motives and intentions were effectively disposed of.

(g) Infanticide and the Insanity Plea

Whatever the reasons for the large numbers of acquittals in infanticide cases, they were important in the context of the insanity plea that developed in the 19th century courts as a mitigating defence for murder charges. These acquittals had a significance that penetrated deep into the underlying philosophies of both medicine and the law. They highlighted the difficulties in drawing a clear distinction between responsible and irresponsible conduct, between blameworthiness and innocence. Infanticide was a central issue in the medico-legal disputes over the insanity plea. The main area of controversy centred round the legal 'right-wrong' test before 1843, and the M'Naghten (sometimes called McNaughton) Rules after that (the Rules codified a principle that insane people could not be held criminally responsible for their acts and were supposed to clarify the criteria for acceptance of a plea of insanity) (West and Walk, 1977).

Daniel M'Naghten, apparently acting under delusions of persecution, and aiming for the Prime Minister Sir Robert Peel, fired at and mortally wounded his private secretary. At his trial, medical evidence of insanity was presented and the jury found M'Naghten not guilty on grounds of insanity. But the trial, and the medical evidence, caused such controversy that the House of Lords instructed a panel of judges to give their opinions on several points of law that arose. The result was the M'Naghten Rules (which remained unreformed until 1957). The newly emerging professional 'alienists' – as the early psychiatrists were called – were unhappy with the Rules, partly because of the limitations of the role assigned to the medical witness, but also because of the pre-eminence accorded to the cognitive faculties – the focus on whether the accused 'knew' what s/he was doing was wrong – and the consequent neglect of the role of emotion in insanity. As the alienists saw it, this prioritising of cognition and neglect of emotion flew in the face of the most recent medical facts established scientifically. As Dr. Davey, speaking at the Annual Meeting of the Association of Medical Officers of Asylums and Hospitals for the Insane said:

> Consciousness, or the ability to distinguish right from wrong, is no criterion either of a sound mind or of responsibility; ... in fact, nine-tenths of those insane persons who possess the physical power necessary to the commission of violence, know full well what is going on about them; and that, moreover, they will commonly manifest, during even the greatest excitement, an acute intelligence,   and   not   unfrequently surprise one by the force and brilliancy of their reasoning powers . (Davey, 1859, p. 32).

The significance of M'Naghten's trial and the subsequent formulation of the 'Rules' extended beyond the law regarding the criminally insane, and beyond any implications for infanticide cases, and penetrated into the heart of society. Daniel M'Naghten's subversive act, and its outcome, has to be seen against a background of fear of national unrest: the activities of the Chartists and the Unions, the Anti-Corn Law League, and agitation for extended suffrage, demands for child labour reforms, as well as widespread social deprivation undoubtedly provoked fears that things could potentially get right out of control. The dangers of radicalism must have seemed ever-present.

In this context, it is somewhat paradoxical that it was over the M'Naghten Rules that alienism and the law locked horns with each other. The law and medicine had similar aims: both were ways of dealing with social problems and maintaining order. Alienists believed that the only way to ensure a rational ordering of society was to found it upon the truths of science. The law, conversely, seemed determined to rely on its more traditional methods. In the context of infanticide, the old and the new forms of power came into conflict with each other. The power of law was traditional, visible, punitive, while that of medicine was new, hidden, scientific and treatment-oriented (Donzelot, 1981; Foucault, 1973, 1977).

(h) Puerperal Insanity

It was in this context that in 1848 Martha Prior was acquitted on a charge of infanticide on grounds of an insanity that was specifically called puerperal. Whilst puerperal insanity – insanity consequent upon the birth of a child – shared characteristics with mania and melancholia as the more general forms of insanity, it had a number of what were frequently referred to as 'striking' or 'peculiar' features, ones that pointed to its uniqueness as a disease, and which were pivotal in diagnosis. First, as was true for no other insanity, the event that precipitated it – birth – was known, even if the precise nature of the causation could not clearly be specified. Secondly, its prognosis was good; authorities of the time unanimously agreed that in most cases it was a disease of limited duration. Thirdly, although the precise relationship between puerperal insanity and reproductive physiology could not be specified, the long-accepted notion of 'sympathy' – in this case, between the womb and the brain – accorded the relationship sufficient 'certainty' that was not available to other types of insanity that might be invoked by the defence in murder trials. At the same time, the notion of 'sympathy' provided a framework within which the possibility of a more detailed elucidation of the connections between the physical and the mental could be provided by science. Dr Reid, writing on puerperal insanity (Reid, 1848, p. 129) said, 'Any serious disturbance in the uterine functions speedily affects the brain.' For him, puerperal insanity was directly linked to the exertions of parturition.

As well as these features of the disease that were to mark it out from other forms of insanity, there were a number of symptoms that were considered to be characteristic. By the late 1840s, following Martha Prior's acquittal, tendencies to violence, homicidal impulses, and a propensity to obscenity had become stable 'striking' aspects of the symptomatology. While such symptoms were also mentioned in relation to more general forms of mania, writers of the time considered them to be characteristic of puerperal insanity. A further feature of puerperal insanity, occasionally cited as 'characteristic' but which was also evident in some other insanities was the 'consciousness' that was said to accompany the insane impulses: puerperal women were sometimes cited as unique in that a knowledge of the wrongness of their desires to destroy their infants accompanied those desires.

The significance of puerperal insanity in Martha Prior's case lay in the fact that it was the same, but also crucially different from other insanities. Both the general and the particular features of puerperal insanity articulated with a wide range of legal, medical and medico-legal concerns about both infanticide and the insanity defence. The uniqueness of puerperal insanity, as a disease, was something that lent considerable weight to the rather more vague and less definable insanities that might be invoked as legal defences. When invoked to 'explain' cases of infanticide, puerperal insanity also lent weight to the doctors' insistence that law be based on verifiable scientific facts; it played its part in the rise to dominance of a medical discourse and so had an influence beyond its immediate invocation as a defence in the 19th century criminal courts.

ACKNOWLEDGEMENT

This chapter is based on extensive primary research carried out for my PhD thesis in the early 1980s. I am grateful to the ESRC for financial support, and to my then supervisor Martin Richards, and my examiners Ann Oakley and the late Roy Porter for their support and feedback. Karl Figlio, Bob Young and Les Levidow, then of the *Radical Science Journal* collective, also assisted. The editors and other contributors to this volume provided insightful and supportive feedback, for which I am also grateful. Responsibility for errors and omissions remains my own.

REFERENCES

Anon. (1832). Trial of William Russell at the Essex Assizes. *Legal Examiner* **2**, 10–13.

—— (1838). (Leading article). *London Medical Gazette, N.S.* **ii,** 1017–1020.

—— (1844). (Leading article). *London Medical Gazette, N.S.* **ii,** 200–203.

—— (1844–45). (Leading article). *London Medical Gazette, N.S.* **i,** 209–214.

—— (1845a). (Leading article). *London Medical Gazette, N.S.* **i,** 1115–1117.

—— (1845b). (Leading article). *London Medical Gazette, N.S.* **i,** 779–782.

—— (1845c). (Leading article). *London Medical Gazette, N.S.* **i,** 73–75.

—— (1848a). Chelmsford – Charge of Murder – Acquittal on ground of puerperal insanity, *Journal of Psychological Medicine and Mental Pathology*, **1,** 478–480.

—— (1848b). [Martha Prior's case] *Lancet* **I,** 318–9.

—— (1848c). Lord Ashley's Poor Law Medical Resolutions. *Lancet* **i,** 345–346.

—— (1864). Child murder and its punishment. *Social Science Review, N.S.* **2,** 452–459.

Bucknill, J.C. (1857). *Unsoundness of Mind in Relation to Criminal Acts.* Second edition. London: Longman, Brown, Green and Longmans.

Cummin, W. (1836). *The Proofs of Infanticide Considered, including Dr Hunter's Tract on Child Murder.* London: Longman, Rees, Orme, Brown, Green and Longman.

Davey, J.G. (1869). Insanity and Crime: Communication by Dr. Davey. *Journal of Mental Science* **6,** 31–38.

Day, S. (1985) *Puerperal Insanity: The Historical Sociology of a Disease.* Unpublished PhD Thesis, University of Cambridge.

Donzelot, J. (1981). *The Policing of Families.* Trans. R. Hurley. London: Hutchinson.

Drysdale, C.R. (ed) (1866) *Debate on Infanticide in the Harvein Medical Society of London.* London: Longmans.

—— (1879). *The Mortality of the Rich and Poor.* London: Longmans.

Foucault, M. (1973). *The Birth of the Clinic.* Trans. A.M. Sheridan Smith. London: Tavistock.

—— (1977). *Discipline and Punish.* Trans. A. Sheridan. London: Allen Lane.

Greaves, G. (1863). Observations on some of the Causes of Infanticide. *Transactions of the Manchester Statistical Society* 1–24.

Hoffer P.C. and Hull N.E.H. (1981). *Murdering Mothers: Infanticide in England and New England 1558–1803.* New York: University Press.

Hunter, W. (1784). On the Uncertainty of Signs of Murder in the Case of Bastard Children. *Medical Observations and Inquiries* **6.**

Hutchinon, W. (1820). *A Dissertation on Infanticide and its Relations to Physiology and Jurisprudence.* London: John Souter.

Johnson, C. (1814). An Essay on the Signs of Child Murder in New Born Children. *Edinburgh Medical and Surgical Journal* **10,** 394–412.

King, H. (1865) Foundlings and Infanticide. *Once a Week* **13**, 332–336.

Langer, W.L. (1973). Infanticide: A Historical Survey. *History of Childhood Quarterly* **1**, 353–365.

Leigh, J. (1844). Increased Mortality among Children under the Hands of Uneducated Practitioners. *London Medical Gazette N.S.* **ii**, 781–783.

Mahon, P.A.O. (1813). *An Essay of the Signs of Child Murder*. Trans C. Johnson. London: Longman and Co.

Martin, P.J. (1826). Observations on some of the Accidents of Infanticide. *Edinburgh Medical and Surgical Journal* **26**, 36–40.

Radzinowicz, L. (1948). *A History of the English Criminal Law and its Administration from 1750, Vol. 1*. London: Stevens.

Reid, J. (1848) On the Causes, Symptoms and Treatment of Puerperal Insanity. *Journal of Psychological Medicine and Mental Pathology* **1**, 128–147 and 284–289.

Ryan, M. (1831). *A Manual of Medical Jurisprudence*. London: Renshaw and Rush.

Ryan, W.B. (1862). *Infanticide: Its Law, Prevalence, Prevention, and History*. London: Churchill.

Sauer, R. (1978). Infanticide and Abortion in 19th Century England. *Population Studies* **32**, 81–93.

Scott, D. (1826). Case of Infanticide, with Remarks. *Edinburgh Medical and Surgical Journal* **26**, 62–64.

Severn, C. (1832). *First Lines to the Practice of Midwifery: To which Are Added Remarks on the Forensic Evidence Requisite in Cases of Foeticide and Infanticide*. London: S. Highley.

Sewell, Dr. (1846). On a Source of Error in Supposed Infanticide. *London Medical Gazette N.S.* **ii**, 808.

Smith, R. (1981). *Trial by Medicine: Insanity and Responsibility in Victorian Trials*. Edinburgh: Edinburgh University Press.

Taylor, A.S. (1865). *The Principles and Practice of Medical Jurisprudence*. London: Churchill.

Walker, N. (1968). *Crime and Insanity in England, Vol. 1*. Edinburgh: Edinburgh University Press.

West, D.J. and Walk, A. (eds). (1977). *Daniel McNaughton: His Trial and Aftermath*. Kent: Gaskell Books.

Part 4:

Timing of Birth

13

Explaining the Trend Towards Older First Time Mothers – A Life Course Perspective

IRENEE DALY

I. INTRODUCTION

NEVER BEFORE HAVE women started their reproductive careers so late in life. This is not just a trend in the UK, but it is also seen across Europe and other Western nations. In the UK, the number of women having their first child after the age of 30 has risen from 64.1 births per 1,000 women in 1978, to 113.1 per 1,000 in 2008. More specifically, while 25% are born to women under 25 and 54% of babies continue to be born to women aged between 25–34, 20% are born to women aged 35 or older (Office of National Statistics, 2008; 2009). This shift towards older motherhood, especially in the 35+ age bracket, is of great concern to the medical community given that the capacity of the female reproductive system to bear children does not last the entirety of a woman's lifetime (Hansen et al., 2008). Menopause, the permanent cessation of ovarian function, usually happens in midlife and signals the end of a woman's fertile phase. However, the reproductive system begins ageing many years prior to this event (Peters et al., 2007). So much so, that a woman's age is now acknowledged as the single most important determinant of women's fertility (Dunson et al., 2002) with 35 considered to be a watershed. In simple terms, the longer a woman waits to try to conceive, the greater the probability that age-related factors will reduce her chances of getting pregnant.

In 2005 the BMJ published an article 'Which career first? The most secure age for childbearing remains 20–35'. The express aim of this article was to reiterate that 'age-related fertility problems increase after 35 and dramatically after 40'. They also remarked that '…deferring [child bearing] defies nature and risks heartbreak…if women want room for manoeuvre they are unwise to wait till their 30s' (Bewley et al., 2005, pp. 588–589). They also suggested that the very availability of infertility treatment such as in vitro fertilisation (IVF) could 'lull women into infertility while they wait for a suitable partner and concentrate on their careers and achieving security and a comfortable living standard... but these expensive invasive treatments have high failure rates.' (Bewley et al., 2005, p. 588). This article caused a media maelstrom, with pundits denying that women were trying to have it all, (as the article inadvertently suggested) but that life circumstances forced women into deferral (Mangan, 2006; Walter, 2005; Williams, 2005; 2008; 2009). This chapter addresses three questions arising from these exchanges:

1. Would women actually prefer to have children earlier but feel obliged to postpone?
2. Do women understand the risk factors involved in later motherhood, especially age-related fertility decline?
3. Do women consider assisted reproductive technologies (ARTs) as a reliable way to extend the window of natural fertility?

(a) Concerns for Older Mothers

Medically there are a number of concerns for older mothers. Even if a pregnancy is achieved there are significant age-related concerns for both the woman and child. For the mother some of these include higher incidence of haemorrhage from placenta praevia, high blood pressure, gestational diabetes and abnormal labour patterns. For the child, there is the increased risk of pre-term delivery, a higher risk of births by Caesarean section, low birth weight, and more admissions to special care units (Khanapure and Bewley, 2007).

The most well-known age-related risk is the chance of having a child with an autosomal disorder. As a woman ages, so do her eggs. Older eggs have more fetal and chromosomal abnormalities. This can result in an abnormal embryo which is destined to miscarry or can increase the risk of an autosomal disorder such as Down's Syndrome (Forbus, 2005).

Therefore, women over 35 trying to have their first child can be classified into two groups: those who have a successful live birth – who may or may not encounter the medical problems outlined above, and those who desire to have children but discover that they cannot. Such involuntary childlessness can occur for a number of reasons, such as a pre-existing medical problem or, as already outlined, because of age-related fertility decline. For those without medical problems, commentators have suggested extended time in education or the desire to prioritise their career as the reasons why women are having children later in life. While these trends have undeniable impact, Simpson (2007, p. 1) notes there are many factors that have been implicated in this trend that are often 'mutually-interrelated with their relative impact often difficult to quantify', a sentiment which is palpable when one talks to this generation of women. A foundation stone of this chapter is that social and academic commentators have overlooked the degree to which women understand just how soon age-related problems comes into effect and the magnitude of the effect. While there is a paucity of social science research addressing this issue in particular, the little there is suggests that women do lack relevant reproductive knowledge (Bunting and Boivin, 2008; Friese et al., 2006; Lampi, 2006; Lampic et al., 2006; Maheshwari et al., 2008).

II. METHODS

The research and subsequent findings discussed in this chapter are based on in-depth qualitative interviews with professional women (N=32), which took place over a nine-month period between April 2009–January 2010. Criteria for inclusion in the study were that all women had to be between 28–32 years of age, childless, and living in London or Cambridge. They also had to have at least one university degree. Women were interviewed once, at a location of their convenience. As a result interviews took place in coffee shops, their homes, work places and university interview rooms. The interviews lasted about one hour. Women were recruited using a snowballing technique whereby initial contact was made with a group of women, who then recruited other women they knew or worked with.

The interview schedule was designed in such a way that the women gave their general views on becoming a mother, such as what they considered to be a good time, or a good age to have children, and how they would feel if they were only able to start their family later than this. As the interview progressed, the questions became more specific. During this stage women were given figures from the HFEA relating to natural fertility decline and also the current success rates for IVF. This interview structure allowed women to reflect on what they had said earlier in the interview, in light of the statistics they were presented towards the end.

Although this research concerns itself with women's understanding of age-related fertility decline, an issue of most concern for those over 35, it was decided that it was ethically dubious to recruit childless women in this older age group. Discussing age-related fertility decline with a group of older women would have been immediately pertinent to such women and thus (if they were unaware of fertility decline) possibly upsetting. Therefore the decision was made to interview younger women.

III. THE LIFE COURSE PERSPECTIVE

While issues to do with education and career explain in part why women are waiting until they are reproductively older before starting a family, a comprehensive explanation has remained elusive. In this chapter principles of the life course perspective are used in an attempt to address this gap. Using this lens, the chapter demonstrates that there is a misalignment in today's society between what is socially considered old and what is reproductively old. This issue is discussed and characterised in terms of the lack of synchronisation between social and biological clocks. The research discussed in this chapter demonstrates that women in their late 20s and early 30s very much consider children as being part of their future. However, the women I interviewed also showed themselves to be only vaguely aware that feeling and acting young does not keep them reproductively young. How both the misalignment and lack of reproductive understanding have evolved, will be discussed in the context of two main tenets of the life course perspective; historical time and the timing in lives. In the process of outlining this framework, the three earlier questions regarding postponement, risk factors and reliance on reproductive technologies will be addressed. Examples will be given to demonstrate that shifting social clocks and a misunderstanding of what is fact and what is fiction in both natural and assisted reproduction, accounts for the shift towards older first time mothers.

(a) Development in the Adult Years

Life course theory has arisen out of a desire to understand 'development' during the adult years, a construct usually reserved for the discussion of childhood and adolescence. Kimmel (1974, p. 55) suggests that adult development can be conceptualised as 'regulated and timed by an individual's subjective sense of himself as he actively assimilates and integrates the age-related biological and social events' and that 'such timing of events are related to age largely because the events themselves are related to age in our society.'

The life course perspective argues that adult development is best understood as being a complex interaction between time and culture that creates the major punctuation marks, or milestones, across the lifecycle (Elder Jnr, 1975; 1997).

In comparison to other theories of adult development (most notably Erikson (1950) and Levinson (1996)), the life course perspective is more flexible as it allows for development to proceed even if an adult does not reach each of life's possible developmental milestones. We can talk about certain events such as leaving school, starting university, leaving university, getting a first job, getting married, and having children as being socially prescribed points of development in adulthood. However, the life course approach allows for any of these milestones to be skipped entirely or to happen in a different sequence. So while having children is considered to be one of the most universal and relevant developmental milestones that a woman can expect to encounter in adulthood (Letherby, 1994; Purewal and Van Der Akker, 2007), she is not considered less developed if she remains childless. These developmental milestones are therefore achieved rather than ascribed.

(b) The Language of Later Motherhood

In the absence of an integrated framework through which to discuss the issue of older motherhood, it has become customary to refer to women who are waiting until their 30s to start their family as *postponing or deferring* motherhood (Bewley et al., 2005; Maheshwari et al., 2008; Simpson, 2007; Sobotka, 2004; Welles-Nystrom, 1997). The use of this terminology implies two things. Firstly, that women are making conscious decisions not to have children, until some unspecified point in their future. Secondly, it suggests that women desire to have children at a younger age, but for reasons beyond their control, they have had to wait. While there is no denying that an increasing number of women are waiting until their 30s to have their first child, the women interviewed in this research gave no indication that they would have liked children at a younger age, or that there were external factors that were forcing them to wait. In fact, and as will be illustrated, many of these women struggled with the idea of having to be ready to have children in their early 30s. Rather than it being an intentional deferral, the findings show that it simply hadn't occurred to them that there might be a biological reason why they should reconsider the timelines that they have drawn for themselves. In the following section it will become apparent that these issues can be traced to the changing social understanding of age, which is impacting upon women's ideas about the right time to have children.

IV. THE TIMING IN LIVES

The life course principle of timing in lives considers that the 'developmental impact of a succession of life transitions or events is contingent on when they occur in a person's life' (Elder, 1998 p. 3). The age when individuals experience transitions is likely to affect how they behave, think and feel. According to Neugarten and Datan (1973), individuals develop a mental map of the life course and they anticipate that certain events will occur at certain times and at certain ages. Neugarten et al. (1965) coined the term 'social clocks' to capture this idea, which they defined as internal indicators to the person that they are 'on time' or 'off time'. Using the concept of social clocks we can investigate whether women desire to have children at a younger age but are intentionally postponing them. Firstly, we must address what it means to be on or off time. Neugarten contends that we have awareness of what a normative life timetable looks like, with milestones positioned across this timetable, and when we should reach each of them. Thus, as individuals, there is a time when we can expect to go to work, to marry, raise children, retire and grow old.

Neugarten (1979, p. 887) argues that the existence of social clocks can be seen in the fact that 'men and women compare themselves with their friends, siblings, work colleagues or parents in deciding whether they have made good' and that this social comparison is done 'always with a time line in mind.' The current research found compelling evidence of the continued existence of social clocks, and how people look to their peers to judge where they are in their own life course:

> My two best friends got married last summer, then in the States, of my good friends from university, only one has gotten married...we were 26 and all her other bridesmaids were from [mid-west city in the US] were like 'woah, you guys aren't married?' and we were like 'yeah yeah, we're from the East Coast' and they were like 'weird'. (29-year-old Consultant, London)

> Probably I cared about the fact that I wasn't married, I certainly didn't care about the fact that I didn't have children-none of my peers had children – my peers still have none. My friends who I went to university with don't have children... (30-year-old Lawyer, London)

> I guess it might just be odd if you're out of sync with your friends and they've all done it [have children], you just make some new friends and go find the ones without some babies. (30-year-old Publisher, Cambridge)

> No not quite yet...I think maybe in a couple of years' time we might be hitting that [having children] like friends have just started to get married now. (29-year-old Engineer, London)

> I think there's a lot of women that are about my age, that are planning on having kids, that talk about wanting to have kids, but it's so far in the future. I guess if everyone is waiting quite a long time... (29 year old Antiques dealer, London)

Neugarten et al., (1965; 1979) identify highly consensual conceptions about the ideal timing of life course milestones such as the age range when someone should expect to get married (age range 19–25 for men, 19–24 for women), start a career (20–22 years) and retirement (60–65 years of age), with over 80% of those sampled agreeing with these age ranges. These studies, dated as they are, present a frame of reference with which to compare the current generation of women. From the interview extracts above, two things are immediately apparent. Firstly, for the women that are the focus of this chapter, it was considered a personal preference to be married before starting a family. Secondly, almost all women considered it desirable to have children – but just not yet. Indicating that what women themselves consider to be an appropriate time to have children has changed.

How can we account for the shift in childbearing from a woman's 20s to her 30s? How social clocks exert their influence is central to answering this question. According to Neugarten and Moore (1968), age norms and expectations operate as prods and brakes upon behaviours, in some instances hastening an event, in others delaying it. Keeping the construct of social clocks in mind, one can see how a childless woman at the end of her 20s could look to her peers to determine if she herself is on or off time. When she sees that her peers are not yet married, or are still to have children, she can reflect that she is on time, and comfort herself that there is no reason to be concerned. In the above quotations, and in these interviews in general, children were very much mentioned as being part of these women's life plan. There was no sense that they felt it necessary to postpone having children because of their careers, nor was there a sense of panic about waiting. What was clear was that in their minds there was a sequence to life's milestones, and that children were a milestone that belonged to their future, rather than their present. This is a sentiment that can be inferred from many of quotations in this chapter.

V. HISTORICAL TIME

The second life course principle, historical time, proposes firstly that different birth cohorts are exposed to different historical experiences, which are associated with different restrictions and possibilities and secondly, that you cannot separate a person's development from the specific historical time and place (Elder Jnr et al., 1996; Elder Jnr, 2002). It is easy in retrospect to see the impact of an historical event on those that have lived through it. But, how do we capture the current social and cultural milieu? In other words, what are the contemporary historical influences on these young women, which can contribute to our understanding of why certain women are having children later? There are numerous contemporary historical events and issues that could be discussed, including the influence of contraceptives, women's increased presence both in education and the professional workforce or even a desire not to be vilified by a society that associates younger teenage motherhood with disadvantage and lack of ambition. However, in this chapter the focus is on two events that are particular relevant to this cohort of women:

1) The increased role of science and technology in everyday life;
2) Delayed entry into adulthood.

(a) The Decade of Science

It is widely understood that we are living in an era of rapid scientific advancement. The ten years between 1999–2009 are already being referred to as the decade of science. From neuroscience to nanotechnology, stem cell research to space technology and the omnipotence of the internet, it is immediately apparent how science and technology have very much become part of our daily lives. This is particularly true in the field of health and medicine. The ubiquity of, and now widespread reliance on, comparatively recent diagnostic technology, such as CT scanners (invented in 1972) or MRIs (first scan in 1977) illustrates the increased involvement of technology on our lives, which for the most part we have welcomed (Ragone and Sharlak, 2000). We rely on science because we consider it to be precise, predictive and reliable. So much so, it is now commonplace, and even expected of us, to turn to the world of science to identify, assess, and solve emerging global challenges such as climate change, disease pandemics, and food security.

In an era of 24-hour news, there is a steady stream of stories related to new scientific breakthroughs and discoveries. However, all too often such advances are reported as certainties rather than tentative but promising findings. Peters et al., (2007) argue that societal expectations are shaped by the media, who are prone to calling attention to the positive outcomes and playing down the negative ones. This is a very important point when it comes to discussing and understanding the science and technologies that can be used to help women get pregnant.

A key concept in this chapter is whether women have come to believe that assisted reproductive technologies (ARTs) are more reliable than they actually are, as was originally suggested by Bewley et al. (2005). Peters et al. (2007) argue that a tension exists between our impressions of science as being exact and dependable, and the current realities offered by ARTs, where the realities are much more ambiguous (Tjørnhøj-Thomsen, 2005). While some in the medical community and private fertility clinics in particular may overstate the reliability of ARTs, the way in which these technologies are portrayed by the media also needs to be considered.

Farquhar (1996) points out that unlike other areas of medical science, ARTs produce both popular and professional-medical narratives. Narratives about ARTs appear everywhere in popular culture: films, radio, television (talk shows, soap-operas, and dramas) as well as being written about both from a science and popular culture angle in many Western newspapers and popular magazines. However, as both Farquhar (1996) and Peters et al. (2007) suggest, such discourses do not just produce unbiased textual accounts of the facts, they also produce subjective positions. These representations construct understandings of such technologies, their possible uses, their availability and how they are comprehended.

Since the birth of Louise Brown in 1978, the first child conceived through IVF, the hopes of all infertile couples of achieving biological parenthood have been heightened. While such methods may be increasingly available, over 30 years later they still provide no guarantee that all couples using them will be able to achieve parenthood. The latest Human Fertilisation and Embryology Authority (HFEA) success rates (2007) starkly illustrate this, with only 23.7% of all IVF treatments resulting in a live birth, with 32.3% for women under 35 and 27.7% for women aged 35–37.

While ARTs may well be in the popular consciousness, it is clear that how they work and their success rates are not well understood. Many of the women interviewed in this research, when asked how well IVF worked, were aware that it was not a perfect science, and were often very well versed about specific issues such as the expense and stress involved. However, there were also some that appeared confused about different aspects of reproductive technologies, such as the need for egg donation in the case of much older women. Some women therefore appeared to be over-optimistic as a result of some of the images they had seen in the media:

> I guess that if it [IVF] can make a 70 year old pregnant, it must be fairly successful. I think it costs a lot of money and I think it puts a lot of stress on the couple as well. (32-year-old Computer Scientist, London)

As each interview progressed the questions became more specific, culminating in the women being given a table of HFEA IVF success rates (such as those cited above) broken down by age. It was only at this point that the bleak reality became apparent to all the women interviewed – ie this technology is not as predictable, reliable or advancing as rapidly as other avenues of medical science; and most importantly, that it does not compensate for the natural decline of fertility with age. This was true even for the women who had previously demonstrated a good rudimentary understanding of how IVF works:

> I guess I've had that a little bit in my head myself, like not that much you know, I'm still hoping that I'm going to be doing it young. But if I knew I wasn't going to for a bit I would have that in my head, that I will always be able to go to IVF if I really wanted. (31-year-old Investment Banker, London)

> I don't know, I guess maybe not so much explicitly IVF, but more and more people think 'oh you can do something', so I haven't really thought what it might be but there is always something that can fix it, so yeah, it's kind of odd to think that there isn't. (30-year-old Publisher, Cambridge)

> I think people would think the main obstacle was the money because I think it's meant to be quite expensive. Where if you had enough time and money you would be able to do it, I think it's kind of what people would think. (31-year-old Solicitor, London)

(b) Delayed Adulthood

A second feature common to this historical cohort is their delayed entry to adulthood, which is now more complex and less uniform than in the past (Arnett, 2007). As a result of sweeping demographic shifts, the increased uptake of both tertiary and graduate level education, and the changing patterns of marriage and parenthood, there are increasing calls for the inclusion of a life stage called 'emerging adulthood', between adolescence and adulthood (Arnett, 2000; 2001). In the United States, the Brooking Institute has investigated these trends and found that the current generation of young people are not always able to achieve the milestones that their parents would have traditionally associated with entry into adulthood. These include moving away from home, financial independence, getting married and starting a family. Specifically, they found that in 1960, 70% of 30 year olds had achieved these milestones, but by 2000 only 40% of 30 year olds could claim these as accomplishments (Galston, 2004).

It is evident that a similar trend is taking place in the UK. One of the key markers of the transition to adulthood is moving out of the parental home.

Britain has twice as many adult children moving back to the family home after a time away (usually university) as anywhere else in Europe. Berrington et al. (2009) found that in 2006/07, 25% of 25–29 year-old men and 13% of 25–29 year-old women were living with their parents. In the 30–34 age bracket 10% of men and 4% of women continue to live in the parental home. When questioned about these living arrangements, two specific reasons predominated for the 25–29 year olds: 36% said that they considered it to be their home and that they had no plans to move (39% of men and 29% of women gave this reason) while 35% of both men and women expressed a desire to buy or rent but said they couldn't currently afford it. Other reasons included precarious careers, and the growing gap between capital costs and incomes (ONS 2009). All of these factors make some young people feel like they are in a state of suspended animation, which prevents them from feeling like they are truly adults. A sentiment that was expressed by some women interviewed:

> I started with this really long internship style introduction, you work for free and then you work on a contract basis and work part-time and then you have been working for 3–4 years before you have the first real position and then it is obviously a junior position… so I have been working in this particular job for 5 years and it was probably 2 years ago that I became the senior science person but it took 3 years prior to that of working for free so that it is only now that I have a salary that I can actually survive on. And that sense of seniority – as long as you are a junior staff member or a newbie you're not afforded a responsibility fitting your age, so you don't live up to it so you continue to act like a child because you don't have that responsibility… so the second you get a senior job…it manifests itself as a slightly more serious attitude to things…. it doesn't necessarily make it conducive to having children because you are working too hard but at least you have this sense that you are validated, finally an adult and respected and given that credibility almost to start acting in an adult way. … Technically we become adults at 18, my perception is that it has shifted, so technically we are adult but because of these other things our generation don't kind of consider ourselves adults (32-year-old NGO employee, Cambridge)

Interestingly, a Swedish study found that young people continue to look to traditional milestones such as marriage, homeownership and job security as being indicative of having achieved grown-up status. Moreover, it was also considered desirable to have achieved these milestones before one embarked on starting a family (Lampic et al., 2006). Unfortunately however, it seems that these achievements were more easily accomplished by their parents' generation.

VI. UNDERSTANDING BIOLOGICAL CLOCKS

When asked what the right age was for a woman to have a baby, the women interviewed for this chapter, tended to talk not about biological deadlines, but about needing to feel 'ready' to have children. As each of these interviews unfurled, there was a dawning realisation for many of these women that there were age-related biological reasons why it would be better for them to have children in their early rather than late 30s. This led to a palpable tension between conflicting social and biological clocks, between feeling young in their heads, but an emerging understanding that they were ageing reproductively:

> [I]t's just totally odd such a funny conflict… and…there's this one thing you've got to change your life for – you have to do it [by]…35..! (28-year-old Academic, Cambridge)

> I think it's really hilarious about how the optimum age [to have children] is more like 17 which I think is a whole lot of madness, and I just think how wrong nature can be sometimes because maybe it's these days whether women mature later… I would say the average 17 year old doesn't have a hope in hell's chance of being mature enough to deal with a baby, for god's sake I'm rocking 31 and the thought [of having children] scares me. (30-year-old Manager, London)

> Back to my first point about having your first kid before 30 and the sort of time lining everyone sort of has in their head, for example if you think, 'OK if I want to have my first kid before I'm 30 then I have to get married you know let's say a year before at least and then I've got to know the guy two years before' so you sort of work backwards and then you're like 's**t I've completely overshot' um, it's never going to happen. But for me it's mostly about getting married um and so obviously now that I'm engaged you know, phew, pressure off!.. I mean I was just literally in my room listening to the radio and it was that advert for like 'if you can't get pregnant, you know, you come to this clinic' and then they said you can donate eggs and then they gave an age so if you're between I don't know 28 and 35 I was like 'what the hell, how's that supposed to make me feel' if I'm just listening, you know, they're saying basically you're past the age of donating eggs if you're past 35. (28-year-old Consultant, London)

This obviously begs the question: how has the conflict between these two clocks developed? The previous section outlined how science and technology have been internalised in the popular consciousness as being dependent and reliable. If the media are the main conduit by which women learn about science and technology, particularly ARTs, and are constantly presented with headlines such as: *With eggs in the freezer, who needs Mr. Right?* (The Times, Oct, 2006), *For women worried about fertility, egg bank is a new option* (The New York Times, Sept, 2004), *Egg-freezing techniques will change the face of motherhood* (The London Times, Oct, 2006), *The new revolution in making babies* (Time magazine, Jun, 2001), women could be forgiven for believing that science has defeated nature (Pfeffer, 1993).

However, inaccuracies in the media, while pertinent, are not the only issue. Over the course of the interview, many of these otherwise well-educated women demonstrated a rudimentary and shaky understanding of human reproduction in general. This was especially apparent as regards their understanding of how natural fertility has been affected by scientific advancement and what is now possible with the help of technology. For example, when the interviewees were shown pictures of postmenopausal mothers and were asked to think about how these women got pregnant, the following answers were elicited:

Well, maybe this...the 62 year old, well, she maybe...she is still naturally able to have kids but I would have thought that there was some sort of assisting pregnancy that assisted treatments for the older ones...I am...I am making a presumption, yeah...So probably she would have to stay on some sort of pill or whatever for a long time. Yeah, to extend her fertility and then use whatever treatments were available to get pregnant, I don't know. I don't know why people would want to do that because then you would obviously think that you know, when you get to a certain age, you do start thinking about well, I am going to...I am going to go through menopause sometime soon...so I just keep taking my you know, my pill because maybe when I am 70, I want to have kids. It just seems a bit weird (32-year-old Computer Scientist, London)

No, I think as far as natural fertility is concerned people do have this notion that there's a ... there's a window in which you have children, you know, as you get older your fertility naturally decreases so I think in terms of natural fertility we sort of know that already.
(Interviewer): Okay. And what ... what do you imagine that window to be?
Oh, natural fertility? Well, biologically I would say it's up to menopause, it's up to, you know 50, that age, thereabouts. Well, again, you know talk about social factors too and even if you can actually physically have a child at age 45 is that such a good idea? You know, can you actually provide that child with the right kind of, you know, good upbringing and are you compromising things along the way by having a child so late (32-year-old Recruiter, London)

As the above extracts illustrate, the women interviewed in this research exhibited a worrisome confusion about how natural reproduction has been affected by reproductive technologies. Women seem prone to thinking that their biological clocks have been extended, that they can be slowed down by means of technology, a point also noted by Bewley and Foo (this volume). In the quotations, above there is clear confusion as to whether the postmenopausal mothers could have children naturally at 62, whether they had frozen their eggs when they were younger, whether staying on the pill had extended their fertility and an assumption that getting pregnant at 45+ was relatively straight forward. The only concern about having children at 45 or 50 years of age was deemed to be the ability to provide for the child. Strikingly, there was no articulated understanding that postmenopausal women need donor eggs in order to achieve pregnancy, which as Braude and El-Toukhy (this volume) point out, is an issue of great concern. Given this confusion, it is no wonder that many women find out for the first time about the extent of age-related fertility decline and the limited capabilities of ARTs from their doctors when it is already too late, a situation that is often bemoaned by the medical community.

VII. CONCLUSION

Increasingly women expect to be able to control their reproductive life course. As Friese et al. (2006, p. 1555) point out, this generation of women are a group 'that had high degree of access to, and confidence in, birth control technology and grew up believing that the human reproductive process is readily subject to human control'. This increased control of both conception and pregnancy has been steadily progressing and has allowed women to continue making active choices for themselves and so women today belong to a very different reproductive world. On the surface, ARTs appear to offer women this greater reproductive choice and control. What was once mainly offered as a solution for women who could not conceive due to blocked fallopian tubes can now help women without uteruses and women without eggs. Infertile or sub-fertile men can now also have their own biological children. Such advances are no doubt remarkable, especially for those who have successfully used ARTs. However, as reproductive medicine continues to develop, no palpable effort has been made to explain the real meaning of these advancements to women. It seems that it has fallen to the media to fill this educational gap. This is especially true in terms of the difference between what they can currently deliver and what their promise in the future may be.

In conclusion, this chapter aims to show that the life course paradigm is a useful and compelling lens through which to understand the phenomenon of later motherhood. The cultural milieu of later entry into adulthood has resulted in this developmental milestone being met at a later age. However, what is also clear is that many women don't appear to think in great depth about their future milestones. Like many other aspects of life, they deal with it when they get there and this makes it difficult to educate them about risk factors such as age-related infertility. These women's own acknowledgement that they 'just haven't got there yet' combined with a culture of faith in science and technology has resulted in the misconception that biological clocks can be slowed down through the use of ARTs. This may indeed be the future; it is certainly not the present.

REFERENCES

Arnett, J. J. (2000). Emerging Adulthood: A Theory of Development from the Late Teens through the Twenties. *Amer. Psych.* 55, 469–480.

—— (2001). Conceptions of the Transition to Adulthood: Perspectives from Adolescence through Midlife. *J Adult Dev.* 8, 133–143.

—— (2007). The Long and Leisurely Route: Coming of Age in Europe Today. *Current History* 106, 130–136.

Barnett, R. C. and Baruch, G. K. (1978). Women in the Middle Years: A Critique of Research and Theory. *Psychol Women Quart.* 3, 187–197.

Berrington, A., Stone, J. and Falkingham, J. (2009). The Changing Living Arrangements of Young Adults in the UK. *Pop Trends*, 138, 27–37. On-line article (see http://www.statistics.gov.uk/downloads/theme_population/Pop-trends-winter09.pdf)

Bewley, S., Davies, M. and Braude, P. (2005). Which Career First? *BMJ.* 331, 588–589.

Bunting, L. and Boivin, J. (2008). Knowledge about Infertility Risk Factors, Fertility Myths and Illusory Benefits of Healthy Habits in Young People. *Hum Reprod.* 23, 1858–1864.

Dunson, D. B., Colombo, B. and Baird, D. D. (2002). Changes with Age in the Level and Duration of Fertility in the Menstrual Cycle. *Hum Reprod.* 17, 1399–403.

Elder Jnr, G. H. (1975). Age Differentiation and the Life Course. *Annu Rev Sociol.* 1, 165–190.

—— (1997). The Life Course as Developmental Theory. Society for Research in Child Development. 5th April 1997, Washington, DC.

——(1998). The Life Course as Developmental Theory. *Child Devel.* 69, 1–12.

—— (2002). The Life Course and Aging: Some Accomplishments, Unfinished Tasks and New Directions. In: Gerontological Society of America, 11th November 2002, Boston, Massachusetts.

Elder Jnr, G. H., George, L. K. and Shanahan, M. J. (1996). Psychosocial Stress over the Life Course. In *Psychosocial Stress. Perspectives on Structure, Theory Life-Course and Methods* (ed. H. B. Kaplan), pp 247–292. London: Academic Press.

Erikson, E. H. (1950/1995). *Childhood and Society.* New York: Vintage Press.

Farquhar, D. (1996). *The Other Machine. Discourse and Reproductive Technologies.* London: Routledge.

Forbus, S. B. (2005). Age-related Infertility. Tuning into the 'Ticking Clock'. *AWHONN Lifelines.* 9, 126–132.

Friese, C., Becker, G. and Nachtigall, R. D. (2006). Rethinking the Biological Clock: Eleventh-Hour Moms, Miracle Moms and Meanings of Age-Related Infertility. *Soc Sci Med.* 63, 1550–1560.

Galston. W. (2004). The Changing 20's [Online]. Available: http://www.brookings.edu/speeches/2007/1004useconomics_galston.aspx. [Accessed 7th March 2008].

Hansen, K., Knowlton, N., Thyer, A., Charleston, J., Soules, M. and Klein, N. (2008). A New Model of Reproductive Ageing: The Decline in Ovarian Non-Growing Follicle Number from Birth to Menopause. *Hum Reprod.* 23, 699–708.

H. F. E. A. (2009). Latest UK IVF figures – 2007 [Online]. Available: http://www.hfea.gov.uk/ivf-figures-2006.html#1276 [Accessed 15th February 2010].

Inhorn, M. C. (2008). Assisted Reproductive Technologies and Culture Change. Annu Rev *Anthropol*. 37, 177–196.

Khanapure, A. and Bewley, S. (2007). Ageing Motherhood: Private Grief and Public Health Concern. *South African Journal of Obstetrics and Gynaecology*. 13, 20–22.

Kimmell, D.C. (1974). *From Adulthood to Ageing: An Interdisciplinary Developmental View*. New York:Wiley.

Lampi, E. (2006). The Personal and General Risks of Age-Related Female Infertility: Is there an Optimistic Bias or Not? *Working Papers in Economics* 231.

Lampic, C., Svanberg, A. S., Karlström, P. and Tydén, T. (2006). Fertility Awareness, Intentions Concerning Childbearing, and Attitudes towards Parenthood among Female and Male Academics. *Hum Reprod*. 21, 558–64.

Letherby, G. (1994). Mother or Not, Mother or What? Problems of Definition and Identity. *Women Stud Int Forum*. 17, 525–532

Levinson, D. J. (1996). *The Seasons of a Woman's Life*. New York: Alfred A. Knopf.

Maheshwari, A., Porter, M., Shetty, A. and Bhattacharya, S. (2008). Women's Awareness and Perceptions of Delay in Childbearing. *Fertil Steril*. 90, 1036–42.

Mangan, L. (2006). Enough of the Advice for 'Middle-aged' Mums. The Guardian, 16 August 2006.

Neugarten, B. L. (1979). Time, Age, and the Life Cycle. *Am J Psychiat*. 136, 887–894.

Neugarten, B. L., Moore, J. W. and Lowe, J. C. (1965). Age Norms, Age Constraints and Adult Socialization. *Am J of Soc*. 70, 710–717.

Neugarten, B. L. and Moore, J. (1968). The Changing Age-status System. In *Middle Age and Aging* (ed. B. Neugarten), pp. 5–21. Chicago: University of Chicago Press.

Neugarten, B. L. and Datan, N. (1973). Sociological Perspectives on the Life Cycle. In *Life Span Developmental Psychology. Personality and Socialisation* (ed. P. B. Baltes and K. W. Schaie), pp. 180–204. New York: Academic Press.

The Office of National Statistics (2008). *Population Trends*. London: Palgrave Macmillan.

—— (2009). [Online] available: http://www.statistics.gov.uk/StatBase/Product.asp?vlnk=6303. [Accessed 23rd January 2010].

Peters, K., Jackson, D. and Rudge, T. (2007). Failures of Reproduction: Problematising 'Success' in Assisted Reproductive Technology. *Nursing Inquiry*, 14, 125–31.

Pfeffer, N. (1993). *The Stork and the Syringe: A Political History of Reproductive Medicine*. Cambridge: Polity Press.

Purewal, S. and Van Der Akker, O. (2007). The Socio-cultural and Biological Meaning of Parenthood. *J Psychosom. Obstet Gynaecol. Categories* 28, 79–86.

Ragone, H. and Sharlak, W. K. (2000). Reproductive and Assisted Reproductive Technologies. In *The Handbook of Social Studies in Health and Medicine* (ed. G. L. Albrecht, R. Fitzpatrick, and S. C. Serimshaw), pp. 308–322. London: Sage.

Settersten, R. A. (1997). The Salience of Age in the Life Course. *Human Development* 40, 257–281.

Simpson, R. (2007). Defying Nature?: Contemporary Discourses around Delayed Childbearing and Childlessness in Britain. GeNet Seminar: Low Fertility in Industrialised Countries. May 2007. London School of Economics.

Sobotka, T. (2004). Is Lowest-low fertility in Europe Explained by the Postponement of Childbearing? *Popul. Dev Rev*. 30, 195–220.

Tjørnhøj-Thomsen, T. (2005). Close Encounters with Infertility and Procreative Technology. In *Managing uncertainly. Ethnographic studies in illness, risk and the struggle for control*: (ed. M. Steffen, R. Jenkins, and H. Jessen), pp. 21–92 Copenhagen: Museum Tusculnum Press, University of Copenhagen.

Walter, N. (2005). *Must Biology Punish those Women who Dare to be Free?* The Guardian, 12 October 2005.

Welles-Nystrom, B. (1997). The Meaning of Postponed Motherhood for Women in the United States and Sweden: Aspects of Feminism and Radical Timing Strategies. *Health Care Women Int*. 18, 279–299.

Williams, Z. (2005). *A Fertile Gesture*. The Guardian, 1 October 2005.

—— (2008). *The Fertility Panic*. The Guardian, 2 January 2008.

—— (2009). *The Fertility Time Bomb is Just as Much about Men*. The Guardian, 17 June 2009.

14

Too Late or Too Many – Dilemmas Facing the Modern Woman Seeking Help with Fertility

PETER BRAUDE AND TAREK EL-TOUKHY

THERE IS INCONTROVERTIBLE evidence of a shift in the age at which women are giving birth to their first babies (Botting and Dunnell, 2000). According to the UK Office for National Statistics, there are now more first-time births from mothers in the 30–34 year old group than in those aged 25–29, and 50% more women aged 40 to 44 are having babies than 10 years ago. The USA has shown a similar trend. Between 1991 and 2001 the number of first births per 1000 women increased by 36% for the 35 to 39 year old group, and by 70% for those aged 40 to 44. With an increasing number of news reports of women giving birth in their late forties and early fifties, it may be understandable that some older women might feel that modern assisted conception techniques, such as IVF, will come to their rescue and allow them to have their own children (Heffner, 2004). It is sad that in so few of these reports is the use of donated eggs ever mentioned, thus perpetuating the myth that medical science can beat the 'biological clock'.

I. LEAVING IT TOO LATE

The natural history of the oocyte, from embryo to menopause is often ill understood even by professionals who offer advice to those who consult them (Bewley et al., 2005). During embryonic life, early germ cells and their progeny (primary oocytes) undergo replication (mitosis), resulting in the presence of around 7 million eggs within the fetal ovary by the 6th month of pregnancy. However, from the meticulous work done on fetal ovaries by Baker in the early 1960s (Baker, 1963) it became apparent that there was a massive spontaneous regression by the 8th month of intrauterine life resulting in there being only around 1 million eggs at the time of birth. Further reductions occur due to spontaneous degeneration during prepubertal life, leaving around ½ million remaining at puberty, and then further losses in cohorts with each menstrual cycle. Only 400–500 oocytes are released for fertilisation during an entire female reproductive life (Figure 1).

Figure 1
(a) **Histological sections of the ovary demonstrating the change in number of primary oocytes in ovary at birth, 25y and 50y.**

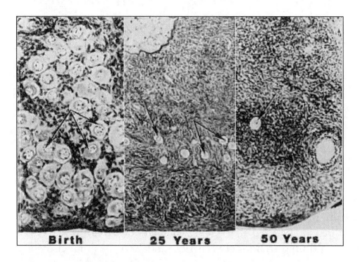

(b) **Rise and fall in the number of oocytes in the human ovary with age (from Baker 1963)**

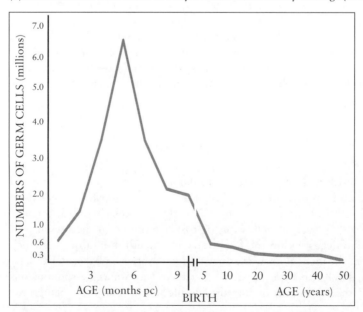

Although only one egg is generally ovulated each month, many (around 40) start on their maturation journey but fail to complete the process, undergoing the degenerative process called atresia (Gougeon, 1986; Gougeon and Testart, 1986). This natural loss may be accelerated by acute or chronic illness, autoimmune disease, inflammatory responses to sexually transmitted infections, surgery to the pelvis and ovaries, or the use of gonadotoxic therapies for cancer. This natural decline in egg number during the reproductive years is not uniform. Faddy and colleagues (Faddy et al., 1992) postulated an accelerated decline from around the age of 38, with a further acceleration in the early forties. The period of this reproductive decline, the climacteric, may be accompanied by irregular menstrual cycles as well as mood swings and body changes, such as dry hair and skin, and decrease in vaginal moisture. When there are too few (around 1000), competent oocytes remaining able to respond appropriately to rising follicle stimulating hormone (FSH), cycling becomes irregular and eventually ceases and the last period occurs – the menopause. There is no credible evidence that laying down of new ovarian eggs from endogenous stem cells can slow or reverse this progressive loss despite several popular claims to the contrary. Since the pool of oocytes is determined at birth and cannot be added to thereafter, the age-related fertility decline cannot be prevented or enhanced (Faddy and Gosden, 2007).

(a) The Bad News

These stark figures in the decline of egg numbers with age lead to particular consequences. First, natural conception declines with age (Baird et al., 2005; Figure 2). Second, this decline in fertility is not overcome by assisted conception technology since live-birth rates per cycle mirror this decline from about the age of 35 (Figure 3). Third, besides the reduction in residual oocyte numbers (called the 'ovarian reserve'), there is an accompanying reduction in the quality and normality of those eggs surviving until this time. This manifests overtly by an age-related rise in the occurrence of survivable aneuploidies (errors in chromosome number) such as Down and other syndromes associated with mental and physical disability, as well as an increase in lethal abnormalities which result in early or later miscarriage (Figure 4). By the time a woman is 40, her risk of having a Down syndrome pregnancy is around 1 in 100 and of any chromosomal abnormality around 1 in 66. Comparable numbers are 1 in 30 and 1 in 20 by the time of reaching 45. The fact that the age related decline in successful use of ART can be overcome, irrespective of age, by the use of eggs donated by young women, tends to confirm that the decline has more to do with oocyte quality than with changes in uterine receptivity or in pregnancy carrying capacity (Figure 5). Thus it is the physiology of oocyte development that precludes any concept of maintaining or postponing fertility into later years since the decline cannot be arrested or postponed.

Figure 2: Marital fertility rates in different societies based on historic data. Redrawn from ESHRE Capri workshop; (Baird et al., 2005).

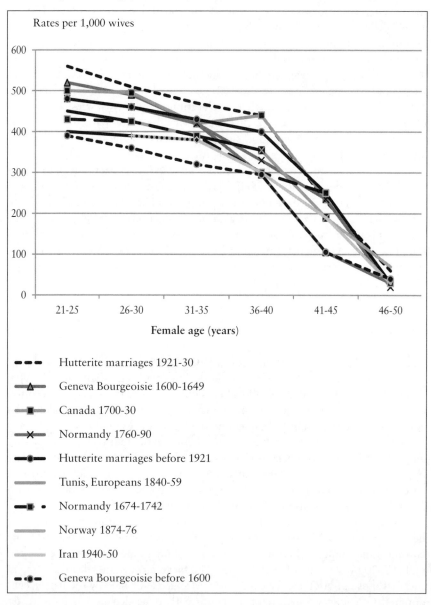

Figure 3: Graph demonstrating consistency of reduction in live-birth rates after ART with woman's age which mirrors that of natural loss of fecundity in fig 2 (HFEA, 2007).

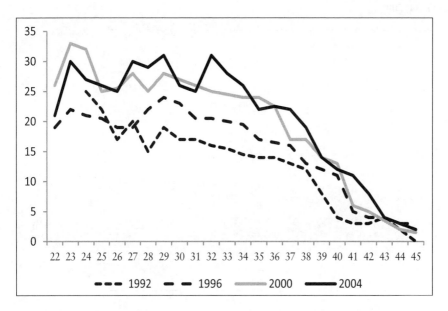

Figure 4: Change in fertility and miscarriage rates with age (modified from Heffner, 2004).

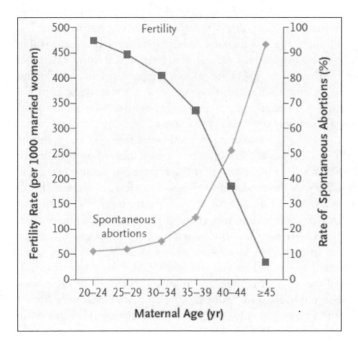

Figure 5: Percentage of embryo transfers that resulted in live births after ART cycles in women of increasing age using their own embryos (-l-) or donated eggs (-n-) (From SART, 2008).

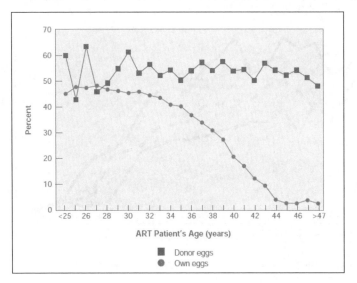

(b) **Finding Out**

For those who are not yet in relationships committed to childrearing, there is a growing market in tests which purport to predict fertility potential with age, and, for those sufficiently anxious, offers to cryopreserve oocytes to 'suspend' the decline in egg numbers. Each of these has inherent dangers. It is not possible to predict precisely when a significant reduction in ovarian reserve will occur in order to take pre-emptive action. There are seldom symptoms of this continuing natural prodigious loss, and when there are symptoms – shorter cycles, or mood changes or hot flushes – it already indicates that the loss has been so profound that the woman is manifesting signs and symptoms of entering the climacteric. Although it is easy enough to demonstrate by ultrasound scanning and count of antral follicles (AFC) (Khairy et al., 2008), or by measurement of anti-mullerian hormone (AMH) (Lambalk et al., 2009) that the reserve has dropped, there is currently no reliable means of predicting for how long fertility potential will be maintained (Maheshwari et al., 2006). So, despite contrary information in the press, by the time any test reveals that there might be a decreasing ovarian reserve, it is usually too late even to store their oocytes. The key to successful cryopreservation lies in recruiting large numbers of oocytes, such that many good eggs are obtained which will survive the freezing and thawing process, in order to be fertilised in sufficient numbers to allow a real chance of pregnancy when they are transferred back to the woman. One estimate is that only 1 in 50 frozen eggs will result in a pregnancy – and by the time a woman is sufficiently concerned about her dwindling ovarian reserve there are usually too few competent oocytes to respond.

(c) The Good News

This is not to say that childbearing cannot be undertaken post-menopausally; competent oocytes can be obtained from an alternative source. It has been understood both in concept and in practice since 1983 (Lutjen et al., 1984) that pregnancy can be initiated using embryos in an artificially primed uterus maintained on sequential estrogen and progesterone medication. Oocytes can be donated by a younger woman responsive to hormonal stimulation and fertilised with the sperm from the recipient's partner. Alternatively, embryos can be donated by another couple. The source of such conceptions is often not revealed in press articles, creating the erroneous impression that the pregnancy which was initiated in an IVF unit developed from the woman's own eggs despite her advancing years.

It may be too simplistic to assert that the observed change in the time of childbearing or of seeking help to conceive is deliberate or planned (see Daly, this volume). What is incontrovertible is that it is happening, and many women will find, despite assurances in the press or by their health professionals, that by the time they get around to seek help, it may already be too late. If indeed social change is fuelling such delay, then perhaps there may be good reason for women to contemplate egg preservation at younger age to ensure that the vicissitudes of declining ovarian reserve can be overcome (Lockwood, 2006).

II. CONCEIVING TOO MANY

Our reliance on ART to overcome reduced or declining fertility, has resulted also in an epidemic of multiple pregnancies and births. In part this is historical, and in part the result of the uncertainty of success when facing unfavourable odds of conception.

In contrast to the egg retrieval in a natural cycle, by which means the first IVF birth in 1978 was conceived (Steptoe and Edwards, 1978), the use of hormones and drugs to stimulate multiple follicular development (superovulation) in the ovary was (Wood et al., 1981), and is, more usual. Naturally occurring ovarian stimulating hormones, follicle stimulating hormone (FSH) and luteinizing hormone (LH) are excreted in the urine of post-menopausal women, from where they have been extracted for pharmacological purification and preparation to treat women who were not ovulating spontaneously and hence were infertile (Homburg and Howles, 1999). From the early days of IVF, rather than rely on trying to retrieve the single egg naturally matured in the ovarian cycle, supra-physiological doses of these hormones were administered to try and increase the number of oocytes that could be obtained surgically in an attempt to improve the number of potentially viable cleaving embryos available (Trounson et al., 1981). Then as now, there were few criteria on which to base an estimate of the implantation potential of *in vitro* derived embryos. Hence with a low pregnancy success following embryo transfer, it was noted that placement into the woman of more embryos could raise the overall chances of pregnancy. It thus became the norm to replace three or even four embryos in the hope that at least one might implant and generate a pregnancy. Not surprisingly in some cases two, three or more embryos would implant resulting in high order multiple pregnancies, then considered to be an inevitable consequence of the drive to improve the successful outcome of IVF.

As techniques of egg retrieval simplified, regimes for stimulation improved, and culture conditions became more physiological, pregnancy rates increased; however, the concept of multiple embryo replacement was not modified accordingly. Thus all countries practising ART noted a significant and inexorable rise in the rate of triplet and twin pregnancy. In the USA the multiple birth rate for IVF cycles is over 39%, and over 50% of the 15,000 ART babies born annually are within multiple deliveries (SART, 2008). Within Europe, although the rate is still high, there has been a fall in reported multiple births from 27% in 2000, to 21.8% in 2005 (Nyboe Andersen et al., 2009).

The significant mortality and morbidity of triplet pregnancy was probably the single biggest driver toward change (El-Toukhy et al., 2006). Despite the undeniable difficulties and morbidity posed by a triplet pregnancy for the mother – the abdominal discomfort and size, the increased antenatal and postnatal complications of higher order multiple pregnancy – the greatest risk was to the babies themselves due mainly to the frequent and often very early preterm labour which resulted in significant complications of prematurity such as neonatal death or cerebral palsy. The cost of care for children born in multiple births is profound. Henderson and colleagues (Henderson et al., 2004) estimated that obstetric care costs for a twin pregnancy are twice that for singletons, and 4.5 times for triplets. It is also clear that preterm birth is a major predictor of how much an individual will cost the community during its first five years of life (Petrou et al., 2003). In the USA the equivalent costs for low birth weight (LBW) babies born weighing under 1000g was £39,483 and around £22,541 for LBW babies between 1000–1499g, whilst outside of the USA the costs are £29,757 and £14,986 respectively. The burden on the health care budget continues after the neonatal period, as premature and/or low birth-weight babies are more likely to have special needs, ongoing paediatric care and other therapies, as well as special education compared with normal birth-weight children (Stevenson et al., 1996a, 1996b).

(a) Effecting Change

In response to the escalating number of triplet births in the UK, the Human Fertilisation and Embryology Authority (HFEA) introduced a recommendation that no more than two embryos should be replaced in women under the age of 40, unless in exceptional circumstances. Although there was some decrease in the numbers of triplets, a few clinics continued to replace three embryos in young women, declaring all their cases to be exceptional. It was only when the replacement of two embryos became enshrined in the HFEA Code of Practice, and thus enforceable by the regulator, did the triplet rate decline. However the rate of twins continued to rise (Figure 6).

Figure 6: Change in number of triplet and twin birth in the UK between 1974 and 2004 (Office of National Statistics UK, 2007).

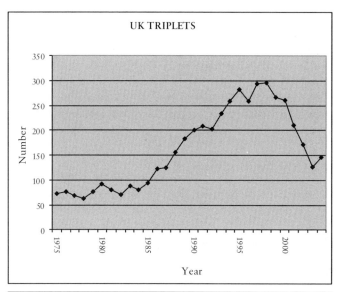

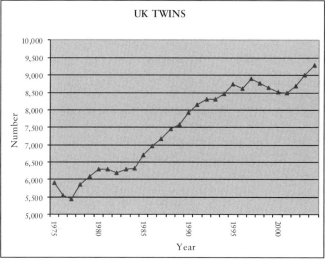

The reasons for this are understandable. There was, and still is, debate among fertility practitioners as to whether twins are really an adverse outcome of ART, especially when measured against an alternative of failure to conceive (Gleicher and Barad, 2009). In 2004 the middle ground of a planned singleton birth following IVF seemed unattainable, or certainly not worth the risk. Significant steps were taken by a number of countries, either through professional cooperation or by legislation, to try and reduce their multiple pregnancy and birth rates. Part of the difficulty in moving to single embryo transfer is the lack of reliable criteria on which to base the assessment of embryos at cleavage stages by which a reliable indication of likely implantation potential can be made, thereby to allow elective single embryo transfer. Jan Gerris and colleagues (Van Royen et al., 1999) developed a scheme for identifying 'top grade' embryos, increasing the likelihood of selecting a progressive embryo for transfer, and with additional patient criteria, provided a way of moving towards single embryo transfer. Their application to controlled but non-randomised studies, suggested that single embryo transfer (SET) in selected patients with carefully graded embryos at cleavage stages may be able to achieve similar pregnancy rates to double embryo transfer (DET) but cut the proportion of twin pregnancies dramatically (31% to 1.4%) (Bergh, 2005).

In Sweden, there was agreement among health professionals who accepted that with careful grading of embryos and selection of patients, some reduction could be achieved by single embryo transfer. Over a 5-year period they achieved a steady increase in the number of centres practising elective single embryo transfer, and demonstrated that an acceptable level of pregnancy following ART could be maintained without parents and their offspring having to risk multiple pregnancy (Figure 7). However, universal application of compulsory single embryo transfer in randomised trials seems to suggest that, although multiple pregnancy rates can be reduced, it might come at the expense of some pregnancies in the fresh stimulated cycle. Some or all of this loss might be clawed back using the additional embryos which had been frozen, giving a highly acceptable cumulative pregnancy rate (Gerris, 2005). Due to enormous cost to the state of the consequences of multiple birth, including the increased care for mothers during pregnancy, their intrapartum care, the neonatal care of premature infants, and the lifelong care of damaged children, the Belgian government was the first to accept the costs of repeated IVF cycles (up to 6 in a lifetime) if only one embryo was replaced in the first two cycles of treatment in women under the age of 36, with a maximum of two embryos in further attempts, or if the woman was between 36 and 40. The estimated short-term gain from this strategy in terms of reduced maternity and neonatal care was €7.2million, and long-term cost gain accrued from the prevention of 35 handicapped children of between €50m and €70m based on €1.5m–€2m lifetime cost for each event saved (Ombelet et al., 2005). The first year results of this strategy reported in 2005, revealed the multiple pregnancy rate had reduced from 24% (2002) to 8.5% without any reduction in the conception and live-birth rate.

Figure 7: Change in multiple births following a change in policy to selective single embryo transfer (SET). Despite the reduction in multiple pregnancy, overall pregnancy rates following IVF remain steady. (Adapted from Karlstrom and Bergh, 2007)

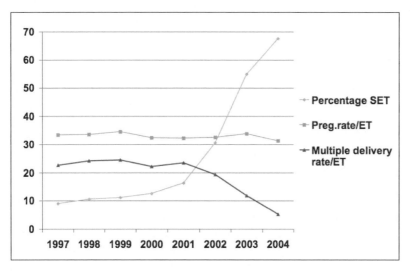

(b) Blastocyst Transfer

As an alternative to selection of embryos at cleavage stages, improved understanding of embryo requirements in vitro, and improvement of culture conditions, has allowed laboratories to culture cleavage stage embryos to the blastocyst stage more reliably. This extended period of culture for two or three days allows the embryos to manifest a degree of 'self-selection' of developmental potential, ie only the best or most developmentally competent will form morphologically normal blastocysts on time, thus allowing a single developmentally appropriate embryo to be selected more easily for transfer. Randomised trials comparing single blastocyst transfer with single cleavage stage transfer confirmed the increased chances of clinical pregnancy with blastocyst stage embryos, and confirmed the enormous reduction in multiple pregnancy that could be achieved by so doing (Papanikolaou et al., 2006). Where two blastocysts are transferred, there was only a modest increase in pregnancy rates, but multiple rates become unacceptable (Criniti et al., 2005).

What is clear is that the chance of multiple pregnancy – like that of any pregnancy – is likely to be age related, and related also to the receptivity of the uterus to initiating and maintaining a pregnancy. Those most likely to conceive twins after the transfer of two embryos, will be those most likely to conceive a singleton should only one embryo be replaced. Thus the first cohort, in which a reduction in the incidence of multiple pregnancy is most likely to be achieved, comprises women 35 years or younger in their first cycle of treatment, especially when they have a number of good quality embryos allowing for both fresh transfer and additional embryos for cryopreservation. Where this has been practised the effect on multiple birth rates has been remarkable (Khalaf et al., 2008).

(c) Theory to Reality – One Child at a Time

Acting on the findings of the expert committee they engaged (One child at a time – http://www.hfea.gov.uk/docs/MBSET_report_Final_Dec_06.pdf), the HFEA has set as a target the reduction of twin pregnancy to 10%, which they hope will be achieved in a stepwise fashion over three years (http://www.oneatatime. org.uk/). This will be accomplished by focussing on output (twins), rather than simply input (a mandatory restriction on the number of embryos replaced), thus allowing clinics to use their clinical judgement to decide how they will achieve the set maximum twin rate which will be adjusted downward each year until the national target is achieved. The premise of such an approach is that each clinic, its population and its practice may differ, and it will be up to each clinic to develop a *multiple pregnancy reduction strategy* whereby they will decide in whom, at what developmental stage, and what proportion of patients need to have single embryo transfer to reach their goal. Although the first target was modest – a reduction in each clinic to the average national multiple pregnancy rate achieved by UK clinics prior to the twin reduction policy being adopted (24%) – the range of multiple pregnancies varied considerably between clinics, and some had a significant way to go. The results of the first year have shown that although the set target of 24% was achieved, ostensibly there had been no change on previous years. However closer inspection of clinic data suggests that whilst some compliant clinics (47) had made significant changes to achieve the 24% target – their mean multiple birth rate was 17.5% with a range of from 5.6%–24%, 22 others had not achieved target with a range of multiple pregnancy from 24.7% to 36.2% which elevated the mean result. The possible reasons for this reluctance to move, are discussed in the chapter by Jackson and Abdalla (this volume).

(d) Next Steps

Although there has been a demonstrable increase in single embryo transfer in the under 35-year-old group, the rate of twin births in the 35–37 year old group continues to climb. Perhaps now that individual clinics have developed a methodology and have seen that twin reduction is feasible without a concerning reduction in pregnancy rate in the under 35 year old group, clinics might develop the confidence to apply their methods to the 35 to 37 year old group, the age range in which multiple pregnancy seems as likely, but where the effects of multiple pregnancy might be more serious due to the increased age of the mother. Clinics may also become more confident about applying their developed rules more rigorously to the under 35 year olds.

There is however also no doubt that part of the concern expressed by patients in the UK about signing up to single embryo transfer is to do with funding of IVF (Leese and Denton, 2010). Single embryo transfer could be applied more readily in Belgium, and implemented by statute in order to receive state funding, because it came with the promise of 6 cycles of treatment. The variation in provision in the UK (from 0–3 cycles, and with or without freezing cycles), and with a wide range of arbitrary rules about who is and is not eligible to receive that funding, makes acceptance of single embryo transfer more difficult. On one hand we have a non-governmental statutory regulator (HFEA) setting binding rules on multiple pregnancy reduction, and on the other hand, paltry and arbitrary National Health Service funding. Appropriate financial provision with equitable national rules is the one stimulus that could achieve significant compliance. The sadness is that Primary Care Trust decisions are parochial by nature, and seldom far-sighted enough to appreciate the potential gains to overall health provision and the national economic advantage of reducing multiple pregnancies. We can but hope that there will come the day when a Health Secretary appears who has the wit and courage to make the change.

REFERENCES

Baird, D. T., Collins, J., Egozcue, J., Evers, L. H., Gianaroli, L., Leridon, H., Sunde, A., Templeton, A., Van Steirteghem, A., Cohen, J. et al. (2005). Fertility and Ageing. *Hum Reprod Update* **11**, 261–76.

Baker, T. G. (1963). A Quantitative and Cytological Study of Germ Cells in Human Ovaries. *Proc R Soc Lond B Biol Sci* **158**, 417–33.

Bergh, C. (2005). Single Embryo Transfer: A Mini-review. *Hum Reprod* **20**, 323–7.

Bewley, S., Davies, M. and Braude, P. (2005). Which Career First? *Bmj* **331**, 588–9.

Botting, B. and Dunnell, K. (2000). Trends in Fertility and Contraception in the Last Quarter of the 20th Century. *Popul Trends*, 32–9.

Criniti, A., Thyer, A., Chow, G., Lin, P., Klein, N. and Soules, M. (2005). Elective Single Blastocyst Transfer Reduces Twin Rates without Compromising Pregnancy Rates. *Fertil Steril* **84**, 1613–9.

El-Toukhy, T., Khalaf, Y., Braude, P. (2006). IVF Results: Optimize not Maximize. *Am. J. Obstet. Gynecol.* **194**, 322–331

Faddy, M. and Gosden, R. (2007). Numbers pf Ovarian Follicles and Testing Germ Line Renewal in the Postnatal Ovary: Facts and Fallacies. *Cell Cycle* **6**, 1951–2.

Faddy, M. J., Gosden, R. G., Gougeon, A., Richardson, S. J. and Nelson, J. F. (1992). Accelerated Disappearance of Ovarian Follicles in Mid-Life: Implications for Forecasting Menopause. *Hum Reprod* 7, 1342–6.

Gerris, J. M. (2005). Single Embryo Transfer and IVF/ICSI Outcome: A Balanced Appraisal. *Hum Reprod Update* 11, 105–21.

Gleicher, N. and Barad, D. (2009). Twin Pregnancy, Contrary to Consensus, is a Desirable Outcome in Infertility. *Fertil Steril* 91, 2426–31.

Gougeon, A. (1986). Dynamics of Follicular Growth in the Human: A Model from Preliminary Results. *Hum Reprod* 1, 81–7.

Gougeon, A. and Testart, J. (1986). Germinal Vesicle Breakdown in Oocytes of Human Atretic Follicles during the Menstrual Cycle. *J Reprod Fertil* 78, 389–401.

Heffner, L. J. (2004). Advanced Maternal Age – How Old is too Old? *N Engl J Med* 351, 1927–9.

Henderson, J., Hockley, C., Petrou, S., Goldacre, M. and Davidson, L. (2004). Economic Implications of Multiple Births: Inpatient Hospital Costs in the First 5 Years of Life. *Arch Dis Child Fetal Neonatal Ed* 89, 542–545.

HFEA. (2007). A Long Term Analysis of the HFEA Register Data (1991–2006). Human Fertilisation and Embryology Authority, London.

Homburg, R. and Howles, C. M. (1999). Low-dose FSH Therapy for Anovulatory Infertility Associated with Polycystic Ovary Syndrome: Rationale, Results, Reflections and Refinements. *Hum Reprod Update* 5, 493–9.

Karlstrom, P. O. and Bergh, C. (2007). Reducing the Number of Embryos Transferred in Sweden – Impact on Delivery and Multiple Birth Rates. *Hum Reprod* 22, 2202–7.

Khairy, M., Clough, A., El-Toukhy, T., Coomarasamy, A. and Khalaf, Y. (2008). Antral Follicle Count at Down-Regulation and Prediction of poor Ovarian Response. *Reprod Biomed Online* 17, 508–14.

Khalaf, Y., El-Toukhy, T., Coomarasamy, A., Kamal, A., Bolton, V. and Braude, P. (2008). Selective Single Blastocyst Transfer Reduces the Multiple Pregnancy Rate and Increases Pregnancy Rates: A Pre- And Postintervention Study. *Bjog* 115, 385–90.

Lambalk, C. B., van Disseldorp, J., de Koning, C. H. and Broekmans, F. J. (2009). Testing Ovarian Reserve to Predict Age at Menopause. *Maturitas* 63, 280–91.

Leese, B. and Denton, J. (2010). Attitudes towards Single Embryo Transfer, Twin and Higher Order Pregnancies in Patients Undergoing Infertility Treatment: A Review. *Hum Fertil (Camb)* 13, 28–34.

Lockwood, G. (2006). Oocyte Cryopreservation: Time to Come in out of the Cold. *Women's Health Medicine* 3, 128–129.

Lutjen, P., Trounson, A., Leeton, J., Findlay, J., Wood, C. and Renou, P. (1984). The Establishment and Maintenance of Pregnancy Using in Vitro Fertilization and Embryo Donation in a Patient with Primary Ovarian Failure. *Nature* 307, 174–5.

Maheshwari, A., Fowler, P. and Bhattacharya, S. (2006). Assessment of Ovarian Reserve – Should we Perform Tests of Ovarian Reserve Routinely? *Hum Reprod* 21, 2729–35.

Nyboe Andersen, A., Goossens, V., Bhattacharya, S., Ferraretti, A. P., Kupka, M. S., de Mouzon, J. and Nygren, K. G. (2009). Assisted Reproductive Technology and Intrauterine Inseminations in Europe, 2005: Results Generated from European Registers by ESHRE: ESHRE. The European IVF Monitoring Programme (EIM), for the European Society of Human Reproduction and Embryology (ESHRE). *Hum Reprod* 24, 1267–87.

Ombelet, W., De Sutter, P., Van der Elst, J. and Martens, G. (2005). Multiple Gestation and Infertility Treatment: Registration, Reflection and Reaction – The Belgian Project. *Hum Reprod Update* 11, 3–14.

Papanikolaou, E. G., Camus, M., Kolibianakis, E. M., Van Landuyt, L., Van Steirteghem, A. and Devroey, P. (2006). In Vitro Fertilization with Single Blastocyst-Stage versus Single Cleavage-Stage Embryos. *N Engl J Med* 354, 1139–46.

Petrou, S., Mehta, Z., Hockley, C., Cook-Mozaffari, P., Henderson, J. and Goldacre, M. (2003). The Impact of Preterm Birth on Hospital Inpatient Admissions and Costs during the First 5 Years of Life. *Pediatrics* 112, 1290–7.

SART. (2008). Assisted Reproductive Technology Success Rates: National Summary and Fertility Clinic Reports 2006. US Department of Health and Human Services, Centers for Disease Control and Prevention, Atlanta, Georgia, USA.

Steptoe, P. C. and Edwards, R. G. (1978). Birth after the Reimplantation of a Human Embryo. *Lancet* 2, 366.

Stevenson, R. C., McCabe, C. J., Pharoah, P. O. and Cooke, R. W. (1996a). Cost of Care for a Geographically Determined Population of Low Birthweight Infants to Age 8–9 Years. I. Children without Disability. *Arch Dis Child Fetal Neonatal Ed* 74, 114–117.

Stevenson, R. C., Pharoah, P. O., Stevenson, C. J., McCabe, C. J. and Cooke, R. W. (1996b). Cost of Care for a Geographically Determined Population of Low Birthweight Infants to Age 8–9 Years. II. Children with Disability. *Arch Dis Child Fetal Neonatal Ed* 74, 118–121.

Trounson, A. O., Leeton, J. F., Wood, C., Webb, J. and Wood, J. (1981). Pregnancies in Humans by Fertilization in Vitro and Embryo Transfer in the Controlled Ovulatory cycle. *Science* 212, 681–2.

Van Royen, E., Mangelschots, K., De Neubourg, D., Valkenburg, M., Van de Meerssche, M., Ryckaert, G., Eestermans, W. and Gerris, J. (1999). Characterization of a Top Quality Embryo, a Step Towards Single-embryo Transfer. *Hum Reprod* 14, 2345–9.

Wood, C., Trounson, A., Leeton, J., Talbot, J. M., Buttery, B., Webb, J., Wood, J. and Jessup, D. (1981). A Clinical Assessment of Nine Pregnancies Obtained by in Vitro Fertilization and Embryo Transfer. *Fertil Steril* 35, 502–8.

15

IVF Birth Data Presentation: Its Impact on Clinical Practice and Patient Choice

EMILY JACKSON AND HOSSAM ABDALLA

I. INTRODUCTION

IN THE UK, the Human Fertilisation and Embryology Authority (HFEA) is under a legal duty both to collect certain information from clinics (Human Fertilisation and Embryology Act, section 13(2)), and to provide 'to such extent as it considers appropriate' advice and information for 'persons who are receiving treatment services' (Human Fertilisation and Embryology Act 1990, section 8(c)). Data collection and dissemination is then a central part of the HFEA's remit, and it takes this aspect of its duties seriously. In order to minimise human error, Electronic Data Interchange (EDI) and 'intention to treat' forms were rolled out across the sector in 2007. This system should, in theory at least, mean that *all* of the information that clinics record themselves about the treatments they provide, or start to provide, is automatically relayed to the Authority's secure servers. Having collected a vast data set, the HFEA has committed itself to publishing clinic-specific 'success rates', and other information about licensed centres, in its patients' guide to fertility services, now called *Choose a Fertility Clinic* (HFEA website at http://guide.hfea.gov. uk/).

Of course there are multiple reasons for the HFEA's duties in relation to data collection and dissemination. It is, for example, bound to maintain a Register which can be consulted by those conceived as a result of fertility treatment, principally treatment involving donated gametes, in order to find out information about their origins. Since the 2008 reforms to the Act came into force, data from the register can, in certain circumstances, be released to researchers (HFE Act 1990, section 33D). It is not our purpose in this chapter to consider all of the different types of information which the Authority collects, and its uses. Our focus is on the narrower question of the publication of clinic-specific outcome data as a facilitator of informed patient choice.

It will be our contention that there are grounds for scepticism about whether the publication of so-called 'success rates', in practice, enables patients to make informed choices about their treatment. More importantly, the publication of clinic-by-clinic outcome data, and the 'league tables' that result, present clinicians with a series of incentives towards clinical practices which may not be in patients' best interests. If they do not provide meaningful information, and at the same time may be drivers for less than ideal patient care, there is, perhaps, reason to think about whether other uses of the HFEA's extraordinary data set might be more useful to patients and to people contemplating undergoing fertility treatment.

II. THE USERS OF SUCCESS RATE DATA

There are a number of possible 'consumers' of the information the HFEA publishes about the outcomes of treatment in individual clinics. The first and most obvious constituency is patients, or potential patients, who are considering where they should go to have their next or their first cycle of fertility treatment. While access to NHS-funded fertility treatment varies considerably across the UK, the majority of cycles (around 80%) are privately funded, and while all people undergoing fertility treatment, by definition, want to become pregnant as quickly as possible, where a patient's funds are limited, there is an additional reason to seek out the clinic where one has the best chance of successful pregnancy on the first or second attempt. As is clear from Peter Braude's chapter (this volume), many women are not starting a family until their mid to late thirties, and once they realise that they may need medical assistance with conception, these are patients 'in a hurry', aware of the rapid decline in a woman's fertility which takes place in her late thirties and early forties.

Where treatment is provided within the NHS, outcome data are also important for PCT commissioners, who are under increasing pressure to prove that they are getting value for money. Crudely put, the more babies that are born per £ (or more likely, £5000) spent, the better. The need to prove value for money is especially important in the fertility sector given the not uncommon view that cancer medicine, or other life-saving or acute services, should take priority over attempting to provide babies to infertile couples.

Within the NHS too, the so-called 'choice agenda' means that NHS-funded patients are no longer simply told where their treatment must take place. Rather, NHS patients may be given a choice of a number of local clinics. For obvious reasons, patients want to maximise the likelihood of having at least one baby as a result of NHS-funded treatment. No PCT will pay for unlimited access to IVF, and so NHS patients are especially keen to make sure that they are able to start a family before their eligibility for NHS funding runs out. Given that NHS funding will follow the patient, clinics which offer NHS services want to ensure that they are an attractive destination for NHS patients.

Finally, the media, and especially the printed newsmedia in the UK, are intensely interested in the fertility sector. Of course, media interest tends to be concentrated on controversial cases or complex ethical dilemmas – older mothers, for example, or whether it is acceptable to use preimplanation genetic diagnosis (PGD) for susceptibility genes. Nevertheless, publication of the HFEA's clinic-specific outcome rates has commonly been followed by a rash of stories in the press about 'IVF league tables'. Regardless of whether the average man or woman in the street is interested in whether more babies are born in one clinic than another, it is evident that these stories represent invaluable and free publicity for clinics which appear to perform better than the others. If I am a woman about to undergo my first IVF cycle, of course I want to be treated in a centre which my daily newspaper tells me is more successful at achieving pregnancies following IVF.

The appetite for the publication of clinic-specific outcome data is therefore considerable, and evidently one of the most important reasons why this information seems useful is that it appears to assist people contemplating fertility treatment to make informed choices about where to be treated, and, in particular, to select a clinic where they may have the best chance of becoming pregnant. In what follows, we question whether this is in fact the case. First, we highlight a number of ways in which clinics might adapt clinical practice in order to ensure that they perform well in the resulting league tables, not all of which are necessarily compatible with clinical best practice. Secondly, we query the usefulness of clinic-specific data publication. Drawing upon the experience of Australia and New Zealand (ANZ), where national data are published but the results for individual clinics are not, we maintain that it is nationwide statistics that may, in fact, provide more useful predictive information to patients who understandably have a keen interest in their chance of achieving pregnancy.

III. DATA PUBLICATION AND CLINICAL PRACTICE

Every clinic in the UK has a vested interest in appearing to be a high-performing centre when outcome data are published. For private clinics, considerable profits can be made if potential patients regard the clinic as an attractive place to receive treatment, and in NHS clinics, PCT commissioning will be led by the need to divert funds where they are likely to 'do most good'. But how are the 'success rates' which are scrutinised intensely by patients and PCT commissioners calculated? There are a number of different options, but in the UK, this has historically been done through counting 'live births per cycle started' (HFEA, 2009). It could be argued this is exactly the information that matters most to patients. They want to know what their chance is – once they have embarked on a cycle of treatment, by taking drugs, having regular scans and, in the majority of cases, handing over a not inconsiderable sum of money – of ending up with a live baby. Yet for a number of reasons, as we explain in the following section, this measure of a clinic's success may be problematic.

(a) Incentives to Poor Practice

The first and most obvious consequence of relying on 'live births per cycle started' as a measure of success is that it provides an incentive to transfer more embryos in each treatment cycle. A clinic that routinely puts back two embryos in good prognosis patients, under the age of 35, is likely to have a high live birth rate per cycle started. It is also likely to have an unacceptably high rate of twin pregnancies. As Peter Braude (this volume) makes clear, multiple pregnancies represent the most serious health risk of fertility treatment, with significantly higher rates of prematurity and disability among offspring (Bryan, 2003). Multiple pregnancies also pose a greater risk to the health of the pregnant woman – rates of hypertension, pre-eclampsia and gestational diabetes are higher – and mothers of twins are twice as likely to die during pregnancy or birth (Elster, 2000). The physical and psychological strain of caring for twins, especially in the first years of life, is considerable (Strauss et al., 2008).

The impact of multiple births extends beyond the individual family to impose additional costs on the NHS, both immediately after birth, when twins are more likely than singletons to spend their first days or weeks in a neonatal intensive care unit, and through the increased ongoing health and social care costs associated with disability. As well as being a better outcome for mothers and babies, IVF treatment that results in one baby at a time is therefore more cost-effective for the NHS, and for society as a whole (Veleva et al., 2009; Wolner-Hanssen and Rydhstroem, 1998).

In patients under the age of 35, and perhaps even under the age of 38, on their first or second cycle of IVF, where there are good quality embryos to choose from, best clinical practice would be to replace only one embryo – called 'elective single embryo transfer' or eSET. The HFEA now requires clinics to have a 'multiple birth reduction strategy', and this should set out the criteria used to determine which patients should be encouraged or persuaded to have eSET. In its first year of operation, there was evidence that clinics were successful in reducing the number of twin pregnancies in women under the age of 35, but ironically, twin pregnancies in women aged 36–38 actually increased, suggesting that for this age group too, good prognosis patients should not have two good quality embryos transferred.

In tension with the move towards encouraging eSET, the publication of 'live birth per cycle started' might appear to penalise clinics who are successfully implementing an effective eSET policy, because regardless of how many healthy singleton babies born at full term, they are producing – which Min et al. (2004) propose should be regarded as the ideal outcome of IVF treatment – their 'success rates' will appear to be lower. Nevertheless, these clinics are, in fact, providing healthier outcomes for their patients and if the results of subsequent frozen embryo transfers were to be added they would achieve *identical* delivery rates, *with almost no multiple births*. Results from frozen cycles are, however, not counted in the headline figures of any clinic. This in turn leads some clinics to discourage embryo freezing: those patients who have enough embryos to freeze will be those with the highest chance of becoming pregnant on a subsequent fresh cycle, as they will tend to be patients who produce a high number of eggs. Overall this means that women may undergo more ovarian stimulation than is necessary, and treatment will cost more (a fresh cycle is more expensive than a frozen one). Given that most patients pay for their own treatment and, where treatment is provided in the NHS, resources are scarce, it is self-evidently undesirable to provide a disincentive towards performing cheaper frozen cycles (Lieberman et al., 2005). Again, a comparison between Australia and New Zealand – where clinic-specific success rates are not available – and the USA and the UK, where they are, is instructive. The ratio of frozen embryo transfer cycles to fresh embryo transfer cycles, where women are using their own eggs, is 68.7 per cent in ANZ, compared to 24 per cent in the UK and 22 per cent in the USA.

Another problem with 'live birth per cycle started' as a measure of success is that clinics have an incentive only to report the starting of cycles where there is a good chance that a baby might result. EDI is meant to capture *all* cycles started in the UK through the electronic transmission of the 'intention to treat' form. Yet there are grounds for suspicion as to whether it in fact does so, given that a growing number of clinics report *no* abandoned cycles. In 2002, only one clinic claimed to have had no cancelled cycles, rising to five clinics in 2005 and 14 in 2007 (Abdalla et al., 2009). This cannot be an accurate statistic. More clinics still – approximately half of all centres in the UK – report cancellation rates of less than three per cent, which is also implausible. Proper careful monitoring for ovarian hyper-stimulation syndrome (OHSS) will inevitably mean that cycles have to be abandoned on health grounds. Furthermore in five to 20 per cent of cycles, women will either respond poorly or not at all to ovarian stimulation medication, and will not proceed to egg collection. More cycles will have to be cancelled because the male partner was unable to attend or produce sperm, or because no sperm were recovered following attempted surgical sperm retrieval, which may be needed for men who have no sperm in their ejaculate. In clinical terms, having abandoned cycles is an inevitable consequence of IVF. Yet abandoned cycles appear to bring down 'success rates', when these are calculated as 'live births per cycle started'. Patients, and indeed the HFEA, are therefore misled about the frequency of abandoned cycles. The measure of 'success' reported by those clinics, which report never stopping a cycle before embryo transfer, is thereby distorted.

On this particular issue, it could be argued that the HFEA should ensure that the data it receives from clinics are not skewed in this way by the under-reporting of cycles started. Clinics who report no or few abandoned cycles should have their patient records scrutinised especially closely upon inspection so that misreporting can be detected and steps taken to ensure it is not repeated. It should also be possible to design the electronic delivery system so that clinics are not able to decide whether or not to report starting a cycle after they know whether it is likely to proceed to embryo transfer (and hence perhaps enhance the success measure), or whether it has had to be abandoned (and hence will diminish the 'live birth rate' figure).

More concerning for patients is that this particular measure of success provides clinics with an incentive never even to start treating a poor prognosis patient whose chance of a live birth is low. If a woman has poor ovarian reserve – measured by Follicle Stimulating Hormone (FSH) and/or Anti Mullerian Hormone (AMH) levels or by counting the antral follicles in each ovary using ultrasound – the chance of achieving a live birth, while still reasonable, will be significantly lower than women who have good ovarian reserve. By refusing to treat such women, or diverting them to other types of treatment which do not contribute to the headline measure of success – gamete intra-fallopian transfer (GIFT) or intra-uterine insemination (IUI) rather than IVF, for example – poor prognosis patients are not allowed to lower the clinic's success rates.

In the US, where the evidence is overwhelming that the publication of 'success rates' – calculated as live birth per cycle started – is a driver for multiple embryo transfer, there also appears to be evidence that women are diverted to egg donation programmes earlier than is necessary. In the US, 11.1 per cent of IVF cycles involve oocyte donation, compared to 2.8 per cent in ANZ and 3.9 per cent in the UK. Since there are no grounds for believing that women in the US are more likely to suffer from ovarian failure, it is evident that a significant number of American women, who would be treated with their own eggs in ANZ or the UK, are being advised to use donated eggs instead. If the chance of a live birth using a woman's own eggs is in the region of 20 per cent, whereas the chance if donor eggs are used is 50 per cent, women in the US may be persuaded that egg donation is the better option for them *ab initio*. In practice, however, most women prefer to try to conceive with their own eggs – both because they would like a baby that is genetically related to them, and because treatment with their own eggs will be cheaper – and regard egg donation as a last resort if this is not feasible, rather than a 'first resort' in order to boost their clinic's live birth rate. Apparently higher IVF success rates in the US may then be explained by the fact that the only patients included in standard IVF programmes – used to calculate the headline success rates – are women with good ovarian reserve, undergoing fresh rather than frozen cycles.

As well as trying to avoid poor prognosis patients lowering their live birth rates, some US clinics have devised techniques to entice good prognosis patients, who are capable of enhancing rather than detracting from 'success rates', into their programmes. One, at first sight patient-friendly policy, is to offer a money-back 'guarantee' of pregnancy to qualifying patients. A patient who has a good ovarian reserve and no previous failed cycles might be invited to pay for two cycles 'up front', with a money back guarantee if she is not pregnant following those two cycles. Because it can be predicted that a good proportion of these patients will be pregnant after one cycle, the scheme more than pays for itself, and has the added bonus, for clinics, of offering an attractive 'carrot' to patients who are likely to increase the number of 'live births per cycle started'.

(b) An Alternative Measures of Success?

So if 'live birth per cycle started' may create a number of perverse incentives in the clinic, is there an alternative measure of success which could avoid these pitfalls? One possibility is the use of live birth per embryo transferred. This assesses the capacity of what IVF clinics produce (an embryo) to achieve their objective (live birth event). So – on this measure of success – if one embryo is put back in ten patients, leading to five singleton births, the 'success rate' is 50 per cent, with a multiple birth rate of zero. On the other hand if two embryos are put back in ten patients, leading to three twin births and two singletons (which would also have a 50 per cent 'success rate' on 'live birth per cycle started'), where 'live birth per embryo transferred' is used, the 'success rate' is instead 25 per cent, with a multiple rate of 30 per cent. This measure of success – in direct contrast to the 'live birth per cycle started' measure – provides an incentive towards *good* clinical practice, by encouraging clinics to transfer fewer embryos. Clinics which have a high elective single embryo transfer rate will appear to do especially well on this measure of success because in eSET, the best single embryo is transferred.

The HFEA does now publish 'live birth event per embryo transferred' as an alternative measure of success, and it is clear that it changes the picture considerably. An apparently high-performing clinic, let's call it X, which has a predicted chance of pregnancy of between 42.9 and 67.0 per cent, most likely around 55 per cent, for IVF in women under 35, when 'live birth per cycle started' is the measure, seems to have a significantly higher chance of success when compared to clinic Y, which has a predicted chance of between 37 and 51.5 per cent, most likely around 44 per cent, in the same patient group. When 'live birth per embryo transferred' is used instead to compare these two clinics, clinic X will have a predicted chance of between 22.5 and 39.3 per cent, most likely around 30.2 per cent, which is not different at all from clinic Y which, on this measure, has a predicted chance of between 25.8 and 36.9 per cent, most likely around 31.1 per cent. Furthermore, Clinic X's multiple pregnancy rate in this patient group was 38.1 per cent, which is significantly higher than clinic Y, where the multiple rate was 22 per cent. Any apparent advantage of clinic X over clinic Y, on the 'live birth per cycle started' measure, is then wholly explained by the fact that it transfers a higher number of embryos (with a consequential higher multiple rate), rather than because it is more competent. Yet patients who consult the 'live birth per cycle started' outcome data, (which remains the main indicator, even on the HFEA's website) will undoubtedly be led to believe that clinic X is 'better' at IVF than clinic Y.

(c) Data Publication in Australia and New Zealand

In Australia and New Zealand, where clinic-specific data are not published, nationwide information helps to explain the variation in different numbers.

Outcomes of autologous fresh cycles by women's age group, Australia and New Zealand, 2007 (Wang et al., 2009)

Stage/outcome of treatment	≤30	30–34	35–39	40–44	≥45	All
Initiated cycles	3717	8945	12,798	7528	586	33,575
Embryo transfers	2974	7307	10,193	5514	349	30,483
Clinical pregnancies	1322	2789	3084	876	10	8081
Live deliveries	1120	2281	2352	546	6	6305
Live deliveries per initiated cycle (%)	30.1	25.5	18.4	7.3	1.0	18.8
Live deliveries per transfer cycle (%)	37.7	31.2	23.1	9.9	1.7	23.9
Live deliveries per clinical pregnancy (%)	84.7	81.8	76.3	62.3	60.0	78.0

As is evident from the above table, we can see that for a woman of 33, nationally 25.5 per cent of initiated cycles lead to a live delivery; this figure goes up to 31.2 per cent for women who get as far as embryo transfer (ie the ANZ data is explicit about the number of cycles which have to be abandoned between starting the drug regime and embryo transfer), and if a clinical pregnancy is achieved (ie a positive fetal heart on ultrasound scan), 84.7 per cent of women will go on to deliver a live baby.

At first sight, these statistics might not look as promising as the rates achieved above by clinic X in the UK. Does this mean that Australian and New Zealand fertility doctors lack the skill of their counterparts in the UK and the US? In fact, nothing could be further from the truth. Pregnancy rates in Australia and New Zealand are comparable with those in the UK and the US, but their rates of eSET are high and their multiple birth rate is low (12%). In short, Australian doctors are *better* at achieving the goal of healthy, live singleton births in IVF patients. Comparing national data for women undergoing IVF treatment in the US, an average of 2.6 embryos are replaced; in the UK this figure is 1.9 and Australia/ New Zealand it is 1.4. On the 'live birth per embryo transferred' measure, both the US and UK clinics have a success rate of 13.8 per cent; while ANZ clinics, on the other hand, have a success rate of 18.2 per cent (Abdalla, 2010).

What is undoubtedly evident in Australia and New Zealand is that the incentive for individual clinics to exclude poor-responders is absent. There might be good clinical reasons to give a woman who has a low chance of success frank information so that she is able to decide whether it is worth her undergoing IVF, but to completely rule out treating someone because she might distort one's success rates is a different matter. Because clinics in Australia and New Zealand are not in competition with each other in the same way as in the UK and the US, there is nothing to be gained by discouraging, or even turning away 'bad' patients and trying to entice 'good' ones.

IV. ARE CLINIC-SPECIFIC SUCCESS RATES USEFUL FOR PATIENTS?

In the previous sections we showed how publishing clinic-specific 'success rates' may unintentionally serve to encourage practices like patient exclusion policies, multiple embryo transfer and the misreporting of abandoned cycles. If it was nevertheless useful for patients to have access to high-quality data comparing outcomes in different clinics, the important question would be: can a measure of success be devised that removes the perverse incentives flowing from the 'live birth per cycle started' calculation? We saw that 'live birth per embryo transferred' may have some advantages in this respect, but it must be admitted that this measure is less easy for patients to understand, and if presented alongside 'live births per cycle started', many patients will understandably believe that the latter measure better captures what matters most to them: namely their chance of having a baby, once they have embarked upon a cycle of IVF.

Rather than simply questioning the best *calculation* by which to measure a clinic's 'success rate', in this section we go further to claim that clinic-specific outcome data are, in fact, *not* useful to patients when making choices about their treatment. There are a number of strands to this claim.

(a) Data are Historical

The data published are always inevitably out of date. The HFEA website is, at the time of writing, displaying outcome rates from 2008. Even if the figures were to give an accurate picture of how the clinic was then performing, the snapshot is necessarily historical, and there may be many reasons why a clinic might be performing differently in 2010.

(b) Patient Numbers in Each Group Are Too Small

In all but the largest clinics, the number of women treated in different age groups is often relatively small, and the data are therefore easily distorted by one or two more or fewer live births. If a clinic treats ten women aged 42–43 in a year, and one of them becomes pregnant, this looks like a success rate of ten per cent. One more pregnancy in this clinic would double this to 20 per cent.

In contrast, if another clinic treats 100 women aged 42–43, and ten become pregnant, again the success rate looks like 10 per cent. One more pregnancy will raise their success rate to 11 per cent. In short, the fewer the cycles performed in the relevant age group, the less reliable the data. The HFEA has recognised this difficulty in recent years, and alongside the clinic's headline 'success rate' for 2008, it also publishes the predicted chance a woman in that age-group has of becoming pregnant at that clinic. The greater the numbers of women treated, the narrower the range. So, for example, a large clinic, let's call it Clinic A, treated 457 women under the age of 35 in 2008, achieving 136 pregnancies. The HFEA then calculate the predicted chance of an average patient in this age-group having a live birth at this clinic as 23.6 – 36.7 per cent. In contrast, in Clinic B, a relatively small clinic, 78 women under the age of 35 were treated in 2008, resulting in 33 pregnancies. As a result, the HFEA's predicted range is much wider: 26.8 – 59.5 per cent. Whether it is useful to know that your chance of success may be somewhere between 27 and 60 per cent is open to question. For smaller groups of patients, the range may be so wide as to be completely meaningless. Clinic C, for example, carried out three donor insemination cycles in women aged 38–39, resulting in no births. The HFEA's predicted range of success for this age group is 0.0 – 76.1 per cent. In the same centre, one woman aged 40–42 had an unsuccessful cycle of donor insemination. The predicted range of success for DI in this centre for women in this age-group is, then, almost laughably as a source of useful pre-treatment information, 0.0 – 90.5 per cent. In short , it is only in the larger centres and for frequently treated age-groups, that the information might have any statistical validity at all. However, this also misses the important point that these predicted ranges apply only to the 'average patient', whoever she may be. Missing from the crude division of female patients according to age is the fact that, while undoubtedly extremely important, age is not the only relevant variable that a potential patient needs to take into account. Ovarian reserve is important too, as are the duration of infertility, whether the patient has had any previous pregnancies, and the number of previous unsuccessful IVF attempts. Each of these factors significantly affects the likelihood of a successful outcome following an IVF cycle (Templeton et al., 1996). A woman aged 33 who has had four previous failed IVF cycles, and whose FSH levels are high would be mistaken if she believed that her chance of a live birth in clinic A is around one in three. It is likely to be much lower than that. In contrast, a woman of 36 undergoing her first treatment cycle, with normal FSH levels, will have a much better chance of success. Moreover, some clinics may even apply patient exclusion policies to rule out from treatment women in these categories, and such exclusions cannot easily be captured in simple statistics.

If the data are not adjusted to take into account these other variables, their validity must be called into question. Templeton et al.'s analysis of all cycles reported to the HFEA over a three year period found that the best chance of success for any patient is in their first cycle of IVF treatment, and that their likelihood of success will reduce with each subsequent unsuccessful attempt

(Templeton et al., 1996). A centre that excludes patients with multiple previous failed cycles from their headline IVF data, either by refusing to treat them at all, or by diverting them to other treatments, will inevitably have higher apparent 'success rates' than a clinic that is willing to treat patients regardless of their previous IVF experiences.

The more variables which are taken into account, the more accurate the prediction of success, and yet this is difficult to do at a clinic-specific level because few have sufficient throughput of patients to generate useful predictive information. On a national basis, this would, however, be possible. While the HFEA does not collect information about every relevant variable – it does not record women's hormone levels, for example – it does know about the number of eggs collected and this statistic is critical. If a woman under the age of 35 has only one egg collected, her chance of a live birth is very low indeed [7.7 per cent, unpublished Lister Hospital data between 2005 – 2008]. In contrast, a 38 year old woman who has more than six eggs collected has a much higher chance of success [33.5 per cent].

(c) Most Clinics Do Not Really Vary Much from Each Other

In practice there is very little variation among the different clinics. In 2006, the HFEA commissioned the National Perinatal and Epidemiology Unit (NPEU) to analyse its data, and the result was that, with the exception of a very small number of outliers, there is no statistically significant difference between the success rates of different clinics in the UK. The NPEU concluded that, 'institutional ranking was statistically extremely unreliable and an imprecise method of summarising clinics' performance' (Kurinczuk et al., 2006).

A prospective patient poring over the HFEA's Choose a Fertility Clinic guide may believe that she can make an effective comparison between her chances of pregnancy in a range of centres, but this is, in fact, an illusion. She has as much chance at Clinic A as she does at Clinic B. It is true that there are a few clinics who appear to be performing better than the vast majority, and some that appear to be worse, and while this may be evidence of more or less effective clinical practice, given the relatively small number of patients involved, it could also be chance, or the result of effective (or ineffective) implementation of strategies designed to maximise one's placing in rankings based upon 'live birth per cycle started', or it could simply reflect the mix of patients treated in that year. Indeed Sharif and Afnan (2003) have argued that the systematic exclusion of poor prognosis patients from some clinics, while other clinics remain committed to the principle of treating patients regardless of their possible negative impact upon outcome data, could lead to a sort of 'double jeopardy', through which the apparent gulf between the 'success rates' of clinics that do and do not operate rigorous patient-selection policies will appear to widen and have a 'domino effect' on the league tables.

(d) Outcome or 'Success' Rate Data May Reduce Patient Choice

The presentation of success rate data, along with other clinic information, as the way to 'find a clinic that is right for you' suggests that the concept of informed choice in relation to healthcare is not limited, as it has been conventionally, to deciding whether or not to consent to a medical procedure, but extends back to the choice of doctor or clinic. Yet it could be argued that choosing between hospitals or clinicians is not autonomy-enhancing, in the same way as being able to choose what treatment one undergoes. Patients want to be treated by suitably qualified doctors, in whom they feel able to place the tremendous trust which goes with submitting to any intrusive medical procedure. They want their clinic to be clean and to be treated with respect by the staff. Provided a clinic meets these basic standards, how can patients exercise a meaningful choice between Clinic A and Clinic B, based upon outcome data which, if properly analysed, indicate no meaningful difference in standards? Indeed, an anonymous editorial in the Lancet in 1999 suggested that league table publication may in fact lead to 'a reduction in 'choice for patients', as clinics rule out the treatment of 'couples with 'difficult' subfertility' and refuse to offer some treatments, such as unstimulated IVF (Anonymous, 1999).

V. MOVING AWAY FROM CLINIC-SPECIFIC 'SUCCESS RATES'?

The HFEA has published clinic-specific outcome data since 1995 with varying levels of detail, qualification and explanation. Patients expect to have access to this information and each year there is considerable media interest in the resulting 'league tables', whether or not these are constructed by the HFEA, as they used to be (via the 'Advanced Search' option), or by the newspapers themselves. What would happen if the HFEA were to refuse to publish clinic-specific data and, following the Australian and New Zealand model, committed itself instead to publishing a detailed and wide-ranging national data-set?

One obvious possibility would be that the press, and patient organisations, would find other ways to obtain data that they continue to believe are useful. Since the HFEA holds the information used to calculate the currently published outcome rates, it could be asked to release this data via an application through the Freedom of Information (FoI) Act (2000), and it is very unlikely to be able to claim one of the statutory exemptions. A decision by the HFEA to refuse to publish clinic-specific outcome data might be interpreted in some quarters as evidence that the HFEA has 'something to hide', and if FoI requests could be used to obtain the information, the only immediate advantage to a refusal to publish would be to eliminate the 'badge' of official approval or respectability that attaches to the HFEA's publication of clinic-specific data (Sharif and Afnan, 2003).

There is not space here to examine in any detail the effect of FoI requests on regulation, broadly conceived, within the UK but it is undoubtedly now the case that a regulator cannot use selective data publication in order to encourage good practice. With very few exceptions, if the HFEA holds a piece of information, it can be forced to disclose it, leading increasingly to the prospective publication of virtually all non-identifying patient information. As a result, there is now an enormous amount of information on the HFEA's website, including all Committee minutes and inspection and incident reports. In our view, the volume of information now available to the public, largely as a result of FoI, increases the need for clear and authoritative guidance on how to make sense of it. The HFEA's role is not just to provide information, but to assist people to interpret it and, crucially for our purposes, understand its limitations. Hence, if the publication of outcome data is inevitable, a blunt 'health warning' is necessary in order to ensure that people are in no doubt about its drawbacks. If clinic-specific data do not provide meaningful information to individual patients, this should be clearly stated.

The HFEA should also lead the way in providing a comprehensive annual analysis of national data as happens in Australia, New Zealand and the US. This publication should cover multiple factors that affect the outcome of IVF, providing trend analysis and much more useful information to women in different age groups. In fact, given the size of the national data set, the HFEA should be able to provide on its website an interactive tool that patients with specific diagnoses or conditions can interrogate in order to obtain much more useful and accurate patient-specific information. Such a webtool could represent an internationally and nationally invaluable source of information providing not only patients and their support groups with detailed and relevant information but which would also be able to provide in-depth analysis for health economists, PCTs and other commissioning organisations. It is this national data set that is of most use and relevance, and which should therefore receive more prominence on the HFEA website than the presentation of clinic-specific outcome rates, under the banner Choose a Fertility Clinic.

In the longer term, what is needed is a cultural shift in attitudes towards data publication. This cannot be done overnight, but if patients and the press could be persuaded that the national data set can, in fact, provide much more accurate patient-specific predictive information, then perhaps it would be possible, as in Australia and New Zealand, to move away from the model of data publication which takes for granted that individual clinics are in competition with each other. Clearly the wider availability of state and/or insurance funding for IVF is part of the picture in ANZ and, in the current economic climate, it is very hard to imagine any expansion in NHS funding of fertility treatment. Money is not the only driver, however, and if patients, clinicians, PCT commissioners and other interested parties could be convinced that the publication of clinic-specific outcome data is a driver for poor clinical practice, and does not facilitate informed choice, perhaps it might be possible to move away from league tables, towards a concerted and collaborative approach to facilitating best practice in the treatment of infertility.

REFERENCES

Anonymous (1999). Information versus Choice in Infertility Treatment *The Lancet* **353**, 1895.

Abdalla, H.I., Bhattacharya, S. and Khalaf, Y. (2010). Is Meaningful Reporting of National IVF Outcome Data Possible? *Human Reprod* **25**, 9–13.

Abdalla, H.I. (2010). Are US Results for Assisted Reproduction Better than the Rest? Is it a Question of Competence or Policies? *Reprod. BioMed. Online* (Reference: RBMO252), **in press.**

Bryan, E. (2003). The Impact of Multiple Preterm Births on the Family. *BJOG* **20**, 24–28.

Elster, N. (2000). Less is More: The Risks of Multiple Births. The Institute for Science, Law, and Technology Working Group on Reproductive Technology. *Fertil. Steril.* **74**, 617–623.

HFEA (2009). *Choose a Fertility Clinic.* http://www.hfea.gov.uk/fertility.html

Kurinczuk J.J., Hockley, C. and Quigley, M.A. (2006). *Report to the Human Fertilisation and Embryology Authority: IVF Success Rates.* National Perinatal Epidemiology Unit, University of Oxford.

Lieberman, B.A., Falconer, D. and Brison, D.R. (2001). Presentation of in-vitro fertilisation results. *The Lancet* **357**, 397.

Min, J.K., Breheny, S.A., MacLachlan, V. and Healy, D.L. (2004). What is the most Relevant Standard of Success in Assisted Reproduction? The Singleton, Rerm Gestation, Live Birth Rate per Cycle Rnitiated: the BESST Endpoint for assisted Reproduction. *Hum Reprod* **19**, 3–7.

Sharif, K. and Afnan, M. (2003). The IVF League Tables: Rime for a Reality Check *Human Reprod* **18**, 483–485.

Strauss, A., Winkler, D., Middendorf, K., Kumper, C., Herber-Jonat, S. and Schultze, A. (2008). Higher Order Multiples – Socioeconomic Impact on Family Life. *Eur. J. Med. Res.* **13**, 147–153.

Templeton, A., Morris, J.K. and Parslow, W. (1996). Factors that affect Outcome of In-vitro Fertilisation Treatment. *The Lancet* **348**, 1402–1406.

Veleva, Z., Karinen, P., Tomas, C., Tapanainen, J. S. and Martikainen, H. (2009). Elective Single Embryo Transfer with Cryopreservation Improves the Outcome and Diminishes the Costs of IVF/ICSI. *Human Reprod.* **24**,1632–1639.

Yueping, A.W., Chambers, G.M., Dieng, M. and Sullivan, E.A. (2009). *Assisted Reproductive Technology in Australia and New Zealand 2007.* Sydney, Australian Institute of Health and Welfare National Perinatal Statistics Unit.

Wolner-Hanssen, P. and Rydhstroem, H. (1998). Cost-effectiveness Analysis of In-vitro Fertilization: Estimated Costs per Successful Pregnancy after Transfer of One or Two Embryos *Human Reprod.* **13**, 88–94.

Index